# The Deepening Darkness

## Patriarchy, Resistance, and Democracy's Future

**Carol Gilligan**

New York University

**David A. J. Richards**

New York University

CAMBRIDGE
UNIVERSITY PRESS

CAMBRIDGE UNIVERSITY PRESS
Cambridge, New York, Melbourne, Madrid, Cape Town, Singapore, São Paulo, Delhi

Cambridge University Press
32 Avenue of the Americas, New York, NY 10013-2473, USA

www.cambridge.org
Information on this title: www.cambridge.org/9780521898980

First published 2009

Printed in the United States of America

*A catalog record for this publication is available from the British Library.*

*Library of Congress Cataloging in Publication data*

Gilligan, Carol, 1936–
The deepening darkness : patriarchy, resistance, and democracy's future /
Carol Gilligan, David A. J. Richards.
    p.   cm.
Includes bibliographical references and index.
ISBN 978-0-521-89898-0 (hardback)
1. Political psychology.   2. Patriarchy.   3. Democracy.   4. Liberalism.
I. Richards, David A. J.   II. Title.
JA74.5.G55 2009
320.801'9–dc22        2008019566

ISBN   978-0-521-89898-0 hardback

For Jim Gilligan and Donald Levy, our lovers, and the most loving of men

When men ceased to be equal, egotism replaced fellow-feeling and decency succumbed to violence. The result was despotism.

Tacitus. *The Annals of Imperial Rome*

It is because [Vergil] discovered and revealed the perennial shape of what truly destroys us – not because he accurately reflects the grandeurs and miseries of a crucial and dynamic age (as he does), not because he croons us gentle lullabies of culture reborn (as he does not) – that we continue to trust him to guide us through the dim mazes of our arrogance and fear.

W. R. Johnson. *Darkness Visible: A Study of Vergil's Aeneid*

Abstract words such as glory, honor, courage, or hallow were obscene beside the concrete names of villages, the numbers of roads, the names of rivers, the numbers of regiments and the dates.

Ernest Hemingway. *A Farewell to Arms*

# Contents

# Acknowledgments

This collaborative work arose from co-teaching a seminar on gender and democracy over the past seven years at the New York University School of Law. When we began teaching together, Carol was working on the book that would be published as *The Birth of Pleasure* (Alfred A. Knopf, 2002) and has been working since then both on a play inspired by *The Scarlet Letter* (performed in different versions in New York City and at the North Carolina School of the Arts) and on a novel, *Kyra*, published last year (Random House, 2008). She has also written a series of papers inspired by questions that came out of our seminar, including "Knowing and Not Knowing: Reflections on Manhood" (*Psychotherapy and Politics*, 2004); "Recovering Psyche: Reflections on Life History and History" (*Annual of Psychoanalysis*, 2004); and "When the Mind Leaves the Body . . . and Returns" (*Daedalus*, 2006). As a direct consequence of ongoing conversations in the seminar, David wrote *Tragic Manhood and Democracy: Verdi's Voice and the Powers of Musical Art* (Sussex Academic Press, 2004); *Disarming Manhood: Roots of Ethical Resistance* (Swallow Press/Ohio University Press, 2005); *The Case for Gay Rights: From Bowers to Lawrence and Beyond* (Kansas University Press, 2005); and (with Nicholas Bamforth) *Patriarchal Religion, Sexuality, and Gender: A Critique of New Natural Law* (Cambridge University Press, 2008). Our collaborative work had been so creative for us singly that we naturally turned to writing a book together that would both clarify our method and show its fertility.

We had been discussing Roman literature and sources in our seminar for some time, but the inspiration for the current collaborative work arose from teaching a term in the fall of 2005 with Eva Cantarella, Professor of Roman Law, Milan University, who visited at the NYU School of Law as part of our Global Program. It was Eva who gave us the idea that Roman history might also support our argument, and, inspired by her insights, we undertook the research and writing that led to the current work. Eva also gave us invaluable bibliographical advice during the period of our revision of the manuscript. We must thank not only Eva but Professor Joseph Weiler, who then headed our Global Program, for facilitating Eva's teaching with us. We are especially in the debt of Simon Goldhill, Eve D'Ambra, and Judith Hallett, the three remarkable readers of our manuscript for Cambridge University Press, who encouraged our project and gave us invaluable suggestions for how to improve it both in general and in detail. We thank as well John Berger, our editor at Cambridge, who supported our project enthusiastically throughout and secured for us the excellent reader's reports that guided our revision of the manuscript. We also wish to express our appreciation to Douglas Mitchell of University of Chicago Press for generously sharing with us a helpful reader's report and acknowledge as well our debt to Phyllis Berk, a brilliant editor, who gave us invaluable advice on matters both organizational and stylistic. David's assistant, Lavinia Barbu, rendered service above and beyond the call of duty in helping us prepare the bibliography, for which we are deeply grateful.

We both learned much from conversations with Normi Noel, Kristin Linklater, and Tina Packer and are in debt to Normi, in particular, for our understanding and use of Shakespeare's *Hamlet* in this work. We thank the students and faculty who discussed our ideas and manuscript with us, as it developed in the seminar we taught in the fall term of 2006, to wit, Russell Ferri, Tiasha Palikovic, Dylan Yaeger, and Professor Cees Maris of Amsterdam University, who was visiting NYU as a Global Fellow; we thank as well the students who discussed the manuscript with us in the fall term of 2007, namely, Kristen Berg, Lauren Burke, Corey Callahan, Isaac Cheng, Edgar Cho, Matthew Dewitz, Rebecca Israel, Tamzin Kinnebrew, Justin Lee, Leah Lotto, Patricia Naftali, Beth Nash, and Yvette Russell. We are indebted to our colleagues Peggy Davis and Moshe Halbertal, to our friends Dana Jack and Wiktor Osiatinsky, and to our former students Maribel Morey and Zvi Triger for their illuminating comments on the manuscript. We are grateful as well for the helpful comments of members of the faculty of law at the National University of Singapore, in particular, Kumuralingam Amirthalingam, Simon Chesterman, and Arun Kumar Thiruvengadam. Finally, our thanks to John Sexton and Jerome Bruner for their wisdom in bringing us together.

The book was researched and written during sabbatical leaves and during summers, supported in part by generous research grants from the New York University School of Law Filomen D'Agostino and Max E. Greenberg Faculty Research Fund. Deans Richard Revesz and Mary Brabeck also facilitated the teaching arrangements and leaves during 2006–07 that made research and writing of this book possible. We are grateful as well for the financial support of the School of Law for the professional editing and indexing of this work.

A work of this sort, so rooted in our personal lives, also arose in conversations with those closest to us, the two remarkable men, James Gilligan and Donald Levy, to whom we have dedicated this work.

Carol Gilligan and David A. J. Richards
March, 2008

# Introduction and Overview

At the end of *Hamlet*, on a stage littered with corpses, Fortinbras enters with drums and colors asking: "Where is this sight?" Horatio responds with a question: "What is it you would see?"

It is the question that inspired us to write this book, a question we asked one another and ourselves in the course of teaching a seminar on gender issues in the psychology and politics of democratic societies, a question that came into sharp focus as we became aware of a darkness, visible but repeatedly obscured. The image comes from Milton, from Book I of *Paradise Lost*: "No light, but rather darkness visible/ Serv'd only to discover sights of woe." It is also the title of W. R. Johnson's remarkable study of Vergil's *Aeneid,* where he traces Vergil's use of "blurred images" and profound uncertainties to reveal the underside of heroism and glory, and of William Styron's haunting memoir of his struggle with depression. In all these works, we find echoes of our theme. Our title conveys our impression that this darkness is now deepening, posing a threat to democracy's future, but we also were inspired by Freud, who writes in a letter to Lou Andreas Salome of his need to deepen the darkness so as to see what has faint light to it. We embarked on our study of loss and patriarchy in this spirit, with an eye to discerning the shoots of ethical resistance.

In the fall of 2005, when we were joined in our teaching by Eva Cantarella, Professor of Roman Law at Milan University, we gained new insights into the sources of the darkness by connecting two strands in the literature on ancient Rome: its public, political, military history and the more recent scholarship on the Roman family. Reflecting on the military history, we asked: What could have sustained the demands imposed on men and women by the imperialistic wars that continued almost without interruption throughout the 400 years of the Roman Republic? How did these demands come to be accepted as in the very nature of things? How did they become part of Augustus's rationalization for the end of

1

the republic and the creation of an autocratic empire, which was to last for another 400 years?

We were intrigued by the evidence that Roman matrons, given men's frequent absences in fighting Rome's continuing wars, played an important role in sustaining the demands of patriarchy. Yet we will argue that their influence as wives, mothers, and sisters – including their wealth and education – led as well to forms of resistance against the constraints imposed upon them, specifically on their intimate relationships and sexual lives. The focus of our Roman sources on sexuality – the severity of its suppression and also the association of sexual freedom or the claim to freedom in intimate life with movements for political liberation – riveted us. When Augustus passed a law criminalizing adultery – the *Lex Julia*, named after his daughter whom he exiled for the crime – he transformed what had previously been a private family matter into a crime against the state. Early Christian emperors extended to adultery the dreaded punishment by the sack (the victim enclosed in a sealed sack with a dog, a cock, a viper, and a monkey, and then thrown into a river), which previously had been reserved for parricide, thus equating adultery with the killing of a father, the ultimate crime within patriarchy (Cod. Theod. 11, 36, 4 [Impp. Constantius and Constans AA. Ad Catullinum]).

Our narrative thus starts in the Rome of Augustus, where we discover a gendered pattern that will deepen through time, bedeviling the subsequent history of constitutional democracies, along with a history of ethical resistance – both extending into the present. Our attention will focus on two writers, Vergil and Apuleius, with the *Aeneid* rendering a darkness visible as an understory shadowing Vergil's epic of patriarchal manhood and the *Metamorphoses* or *The Golden Ass*, Apuleius's second-century comic novel and conversion narrative, laying out a path of resistance and transformation. We will then turn to Augustine for a counternarrative, a conversion from sexuality to celibacy, from tolerance to intolerance within a Christianity now joined with empire, to explore specifically the roots of anti-Semitism, the attack on "carnal Israel" that will shadow the history of Christianity, compromising the legacy of the historical Jesus and erupting most virulently in the twentieth century.

In *The Confessions*, we see once again the darkness foreshadowed in the *Aeneid*, a heroic conception of patriarchal manhood associated with a personal history of loss, of sudden rupture in loving relationships with women, as in Aeneas's relationship with Dido. Thus, we begin to explore the connection between a psychology of trauma accompanied by a loss of voice and memory and a history of militarism and religious persecution that becomes associated with a particular construction of manhood. This will lead us to a consideration of the psychology and politics of ethical resistance within the Christian tradition: the arguments for toleration by radical Protestants such as Bayle and Locke in the late 17th century that laid the foundations for modern liberal constitutionalism; the resistance of the abolitionist feminists in the 19th century, of Martin Luther King in the mid-20th century, and of the former Catholic priest, James Carroll, whose life story moves in the opposite direction from that of Augustine, from celibacy to sexual love, and where resistance against the injustice of the Vietnam War is followed by a questioning of Christian anti-Semitism.

Our interest in the role of sexuality within resistance movements takes us inevitably to Freud, who began by listening to the sexually traumatized voices of women and placed the assault on human sexuality as the *caput Nili*, the head of the Nile, the source of neurotic suffering. As Freud moves away from this position and breaks his alliance with his women patients to adopt a more patriarchal stance, we notice the profusion of quotes from the *Aeneid* in his writing, marking his turn away from women through an identification with Aeneas. With this identification, psychoanalysis, initially aligned with resistance to patriarchy, incorporates an Augustinian misogyny quite foreign to its initial inspiration and moves away from its potential as a method for human liberation.

We note how the conversion narrative of Apuleius and his vision of sexual love based on equality and leading to transformation have come down through the centuries, inspiring artists beginning with Shakespeare, for whom *The Golden Ass* was a prime source. We focus on Nathaniel Hawthorne, writing in the mid-19th century, and specifically his novel *The Scarlet Letter*, which exposes the contradictions between a patriarchal puritanism and the hopes and vision of a democratic society and ends with the prophecy of a time when "the whole relation between man and woman will be established on a surer ground of mutual happiness." We then consider six novels written in the aftermath of the World War I and taking on the image of heroic manhood that sustained its slaughter: Ernest Hemingway's *A Farewell to Arms*, which we read as the anti-*Aeneid*; James Joyce's *Ulysses*, which turns Odysseus into Leopold Bloom and faithful Penelope into the sexual Molly; Edith Wharton's *Age of Innocence*; Virginia Woolf's *Mrs. Dalloway* and *To the Lighthouse*, along with *Three Guineas* where she exposes the roots of fascist violence in patriarchy and explores the possibilities for its resistance; and D. H. Lawrence's *Lady Chatterley's Lover*.

In our final chapters, we turn to the present to consider the implications of our analysis for understanding and resisting the current resurgence of patriarchal demands on both men and women. We ask why gay marriage and abortion have become lightning-rod issues in contemporary American politics. Why these issues? Why now? In doing so, we further explore our argument that patriarchy has remained the strongest force in sexual/social relations and that models of equality are actively countered by its ideology and institutions.

We are aware that our focus on patriarchy is controversial, both because the word itself has lost its root meaning, becoming something of a code word for men's oppression of women, and, we believe, because of a reluctance to confront the effects of patriarchal demands on men and the complicity of women in enforcing such demands on men, on one another, and on the next generation. We are struck by the fact that discussions of gender are often dismissed now as passé – that the darkness associated with gender, the patterns of loss, traumatic rupture of relationships, repression of an ethically resisting voice and also of what might be called sexual voice continue into the present, at times with increasing fervor, despite or perhaps because of the gains toward equality and liberation that women and men have made over the past decades. We address recent discoveries in developmental psychology and neurobiology that have called into question the splitting of reason from emotion, mind from body, and self from relationship, revealing these splits to be falsely gendered and to reflect not only a distortion of human nature but also a manifestation of physical or psychological trauma.

Above all, we have been riveted by the continuation across time and culture of a resistance to patriarchy and an impulse to democracy grounded not in ideology but in what might be called human nature: in our neurobiology and our psychology. The fact that we are inherently relational and responsive beings leads us to resist the gender binary and hierarchy that define patriarchal manhood and womanhood, where being a man means not being a woman and also being on top. While our commitment, at least on certain fronts, to gender equality and our recognition of amatory choice distinguish us sharply from our Roman ancestors, our analysis shows why we need to strengthen both that commitment and that recognition.

Our continuing questions have to do with how and why the repression of a free sexual voice plays such a central role in sustaining patriarchal modes of authority. And similarly, how and why the liberation of sexual voice from the patriarchal "Love Laws" (Arundhati Roy's term for the laws dictating "who should be loved. And how. And how much") is associated with a politics of ethical resistance. In locating the darkness we render visible in patriarchy, we elucidate the demands it makes on women and men, the ways in which it becomes rooted in the inner worlds of people through a psychology of loss and traumatic separation, This psychology plays a key part in sustaining not only patriarchy itself but also the associated ills of racism, anti-Semitism, puritanism, homophobia, and a history littered, as Woolf reminds us in *Three Guineas*, with "dead bodies and ruined houses." In retracing this history along with the evidence of a psychologically grounded ethical resistance, we ask you, the reader, Horatio's question: "What is it you would see?"

# Part One

Roman Patriarchy: Entering the Darkness

# 1  Why Rome? Why Now?

After the fall of the Soviet Union and the Berlin Wall, Fukuyama in a widely cited book claimed that history had come to an end, noting that the values of liberal constitutional democracy were widely embraced. This view now looks antique as we find ourselves, at home and abroad, confronted by violent forms of fundamentalism self-consciously at war with liberal norms and values. History never looked more appealing as a way to understand the challenges we face and why we face them. Among these challenges, which include economic inequality and global warming, two stand out as posing a puzzle that on the face of it strains credulity: the contentiousness over gay rights and abortion within U.S. politics and the focus on the state of Israel within international politics.

Starting from the normative position of political liberalism that requires respect for the basic liberties of conscience, speech, and association, we regard the right to an intimate, sexual life as a basic human right, now constitutionally protected in the United States and elsewhere. Yet in the United States, a reactionary coalition of religious fundamentalists has focused national elections on the sexually tinged issues of gay marriage and abortion. Why such fundamentalist rage at the constitutional recognition of basic rights and their reasonable elaboration?

Similarly, the state of Israel was founded as a consequence of European and American anti-Semitism. Why has anti-Semitism been such a lethal force in twentieth-century European politics? How can we understand its historical place within Christian civilization, and why does it today retain its deadliness in the form of fundamentalist acts of terror directed not only against Israel but also against its allies, including, prominently, Britain and the United States?

Following the terroristic acts of 9/11, the United States responded with a war in Iraq. What warped our judgment about the real threats of terror? How can we understand the readiness to compromise our republican institutions as our leaders justify foreign policies in increasingly imperial terms?

A sense of urgency led us to the collaborative work that expresses itself in this book. What brought us together was our realization that the discipline of the other was necessary to understand our own work more deeply. The public world of constitutional law and development (the field of David Richards) required an understanding of issues in developmental psychology (the field of Carol Gilligan), and conversely, the findings of developmental psychology, in particular evidence of voices of resistance, could not be understood unless and until they were connected to the larger historical and normative world. In this sense, our collaborative and interdisciplinary work made possible insights that neither of us could have come to independently. Carol Gilligan's research in developmental psychology (leading to her book *The Birth of Pleasure*) identified the psychological roots of resistance in adolescent girls and young boys, a resistance grounded in the embodied psyche's immunity to disease and debilitating lies. David Richards had explored the American traditions of resistance to injustice and had come to see (in his book *Women, Gays, and the Constitution: The Grounds for Feminism and Gay Rights in Culture and Law*) the common roots in women and gay men of a resistance to the repression of basic rights for groups of persons, rationalized on the basis of unjust stereotypes they are never permitted fairly to contest. But until we met, discussed, and closely read one another's work, neither of us realized that the psychology Carol had observed might be the basis of the ethical and political resistance David had studied. It was, for us, nothing less than a stunning discovery to see the problem whole, as one of both psychology and politics or law.

This link is at the heart of what we believe we have discovered: the connection between a psychology rooted in the embodied psyche's resistance to disease or debilitating lies and a politics in which such resistance expresses itself in social movements that protest the lies and distortions on which is based the injustice we call moral slavery – the repression that underlies and sustains extreme intolerance.

In a pathbreaking book on relational psychology, *Toward a New Psychology of Women*, Jean Baker Miller observed that women "have been entwined with men in intimate and intense relationships, creating the milieu – the family – in which the human mind as we know it has been formed."[1] What brought us together in collaborative work was the further insight that what unites the crucible of the human mind in the family and public life is patriarchy, which enjoys the power it has had precisely because it has framed the human mind in a psychology at once personal and political. We have, as a woman and man, become creatively entwined, finding in our relationship a new way of understanding why egalitarian relationships are, for women and men, so compelling and so valuable, thus enlarging our democratic vistas.

What is unusual, indeed radical, in our approach is the lens of gender through which we examine these issues. This lens enables us to transcend a feminism that limits its focus to women and to encompass, in one unifying perspective, the impact of patriarchy on men as well as women. Yet we make this argument in an environment quite unfavorable to any serious discussion of gender as it bears on the issues we discuss, an environment in which anything may be discussed but gender. We shall try to expose the defects of this common sense by showing the explanatory and normative power of a gender lens in bringing these issues into sharp focus. By our approach, we also aim to clarify the tensions within ourselves that give rise to all these questions, enabling us for this reason better to answer them responsibly. We argue very much in the critical historical spirit of recent studies of the changing nature of masculinity and war (Leo Braudy, 2003; Joshua Goldstein, 2001), but we focus on one tradition in particular, whose force has been notably important and persistent in the culture and transmission of patriarchy over time, namely, ancient Rome – its republic and empire.

Cullen Murphy has recently explored what he takes to be the contemporary American dilemma – between republic and empire – in a book whose title states its argument: *Are We Rome?: The Fall of an Empire and the Fate of America* (2007). Although his earlier work shows an appreciation of feminist scholarship in biblical studies (Murphy, 1999), Murphy does not explore Roman historical experience or its impact in our terms of patriarchy. What is so alive for us today is less the fall of empire than the tension in Roman life between its republican and patriarchal features, together with the self-conscious strengthening of patriarchy in Augustus's ending of the republic and imposition of autocracy under the empire. We live, more than we think, in this Roman world. Americans inhabit a capital, Washington, D.C., whose columns and pediments are Roman. We live under a written constitution inspired, in part, by the Roman republic. Our loud parades celebrate our military greatness, as Roman parades did. With the fall of the Soviet Union we are the American empire, an imperial position that puts strains on our republican institutions. But we are also a democracy, much more so than the Roman republic ever was. And our convictions about universal human rights have led us to do something Rome never did, namely, to end slavery and to aspire to respect all religions and to treat people of color and women as democratic equals. We have come far but remain deeply flawed in our democracy, as basic rights of intimate life are in political peril, issues of racial and gender inequality persist, and economic inequality worsens.

We turn to Rome then as a way of uncovering the roots of our own tensions between democracy and patriarchy. It was patriarchy, we argue, that led to the collapse of the Roman republic. It was the structure of Roman patriarchy, which Augustine read into Christianity as the established church of the Roman empire, that influenced subsequent polities, many of which modeled their imperialism on Rome (both "czar" in Russian and "Kaiser" in German mean Caesar). When Mussolini and Hitler invented a political religion to sustain fascism, they drew self-consciously on the political psychology and religion of Rome, warring in its name on liberal democracy. The reemergence of this Roman precedent was catastrophic, leading to unprecedented genocide in the heart of civilized Europe and to violence on a scale beyond what even the Romans – the political masters of imperialistic war – could or would have imagined.

Even the otherwise enlightened founders of the American constitutional republic in 1787–88 modeled themselves rather uncritically on the Roman republic, blinding themselves to the degree to which their compromise with slavery and their treatment of women were inconsistent with the democratic values of universal human rights they also espoused. Their blindness also was catastrophic, as the constitutional compromise on slavery ended in civil war. Even today, Americans have interpreted the terrorist attacks of 9/11 in patriarchal terms – as an insult or humiliation to manhood and consequently one that called for violence to undo the shame. Thus the gender dynamic explicated by James Gilligan in *Violence: Reflections on a National Epidemic* (1997) and the gender mythology explored by Susan Faludi in *The Terror Dream: Fear and Fantasy in Post-9/11 America* (2007) can explain the irrationality of the invasion of Iraq.

In our view, democracy remains so much in tension with patriarchy because we lack a critical public understanding of this tension, in part because of the degree to which Roman patriarchy has been absorbed into our religion and political culture. Historical study enables us to unmask the dimensions of the problem, revealing both how our patriarchal assumptions blind us to its existence and how much these assumptions undermine and subvert the liberal democracy we claim to honor and uphold against all enemies, foreign and domestic.

Strikingly, our historical interests in patriarchy were originally neither in Roman political history nor in Roman literature. Initially, we were riveted by the stark role of gender in the tragedies of ancient Greece, in particular, Aeschylus's trilogy, *The Oresteia*. *The Oresteia*, or story of Orestes, is a drama about justice, about civil justice replacing blood vengeance as the foundation for Athenian democracy and the birth of civilization. It witnesses the origin of the trial as a democratic means of resolving disputes. Yet underneath this civic story, a family story roils.

In the *Agamemnon*, the first play of the trilogy, King Agamemnon returns home triumphant after having led the Greek army to victory over Troy. During his long absence, his wife, Clytemnestra had not only entered into an adulterous relationship with Aegisthus, Agamemnon's cousin and deadly enemy, but also had plotted her husband's murder to avenge the death of their daughter, Iphigenia, whom Agamemnon had sacrificed in order to gain the winds that carried the Greek army to Troy. Clytemnestra tricks Agamemnon and then kills him in his bath, like a ritual sacrifice. The play ends with the chorus reminding the usurpers that Orestes, Agamemnon's son, will surely return to avenge his father's murder.

In the second play, *The Libation Bearers*, Orestes, having been sent away in infancy for his safety, returns and is united with Electra, his sister. Together they plan to avenge their father's death by killing their mother, Clytemnestra, and her new husband, Aegisthus. Orestes kills them both, and he in turn, is pursued by the Furies, who hound him for having killed his mother.

The trilogy ends with *The Eumenides*, a contest between the Furies who torment Orestes and Athena who intervenes on his behalf. Athena sets up a trial, bringing in twelve Athenians to judge between Orestes, represented by Apollo, and Clytemnestra, represented by the Furies. Athena herself casts the deciding vote at the trial, acquitting Orestes of the crime of killing his mother and persuading the Furies (the Erinyes) to enter the city of Athens as the Eumenides—the kindly spirits. Blood vengeance yields to civil justice, and the Furies become good women. Thus the tensions between family and state, between loyalty to blood relatives and civic obligations, between the emotions carried by the Furies and reason personified by Apollo and Athena are resolved.

Typically read as dramatizing the founding of the democratic state, the *Oresteia* can also be read as a dramatic rendering of the foundations of patriarchy. The title itself (*Oresteia* or story of Orestes) alerts us to the fact that we are witnessing the initiation of Orestes into what is clearly a patriarchal social order. Athena symbolizes the power that women can wield in patriarchy: She is solely of the father, a girl completely separated from women, a daughter born out of the head of Zeus, who swallowed her mother, turning her into a fly.

For purposes of our initial collaborative study of the links between psychology and politics, this ancient tragedy offered a startlingly apt psychological analysis of the origins of patriarchy. The *Oresteia* focuses our attention on Orestes and his relationship to his father, Agamemnon. Yet the trilogy follows the development of a civilization that both records and turns its back on a traumatic loss. The chorus members' insistent questions – How can we respond to what we know? What can we say? – become our questions. We see Orestes forgiven for killing his mother, Clytemnestra; we hear him spoken of as the good son, loyal to his father, obeying the gods; we hear the grief and anger of the Furies (the women who insist on remembering Iphigenia, the daughter sacrificed by Agamemnon, and who pursue Orestes for killing his mother) spoken of as an impediment to justice; we see the Furies becoming the good women, the kindly spirits, as the price of their admission to the city. We asked ourselves and our students: How shall we respond to knowing this? What can we say?

A history of trauma haunts Aeschylus's trilogy and explains the dissociation that we witness: the separation of both men and women from women, the division of reason from emotion, the sharp line between public and private. Dissociation is a response to trauma: It is a brilliant but costly way of surviving the experience of being overwhelmed. The surviving self dissociates itself from the overwhelmed self by not knowing, not feeling – by acting as if what happened never happened or does not matter. The trauma becomes walled off so that one comes not to know what one knows.

We found astonishing the play's insistence that everyone knows the unspeakable horror: the history of the House of Atreus. After Thyestes went off with his brother Atreus's wife, Atreus murdered Thyestes's sons and then served them to him at a banquet. Agamemnon and Menelaus, the sons of Atreus, repeat this history of child sacrifice. When Paris goes off with Menelaus's wife Helen, Agamemnon sacrifices his daughter Iphigenia and leads the Greek army to Troy to kill the young men. Thus, shame is overcome, honor restored, and manhood established. Aegisthus, a man whose manhood is questioned, is the only surviving son of Thyestes, and Clytemnestra, Agamemnon's wife, has survived his sacrifice of their daughter. The relationship between Clytemnestra and Aegisthus is spoken of in scathing language where the gender of each is questioned. Yet it signifies the coming together of a woman and a man who have survived serious trauma.

David Slavitt, the translator of the *Oresteia* that we studied, asks the reader to observe the gender pattern of the killings and to see it as significant. Agamemnon kills Iphigenia; Clytemnestra, Agamemnon; Orestes, Clytemnestra. The alternation of genders leads to resolution by Athena – a female who is disinterested, Slavitt claims, because she is male-like, virginal, a warrior goddess. Because Athena is patroness of Athens, the dramatist's homage to her expresses both patriotic and matriotic pride.

Slavitt's interpretation, while drawing attention to gender, participates in the movement of the play toward burying the "female." To Slavitt, the fact that Athena has no mother becomes evidence of gender neutrality, rather than evidence of loss. Unwittingly perhaps, he links objectivity and disinterest – the qualities of the ideal judge or juror – with patriarchy, heightening the identification with the father who represents law, order, honor, power, reason, the state, the head of the household, and the only important parent. The parenthetical reference to matriotic pride signifies the collusion of the (absent) mother in this identification.

We noticed that the return of Orestes in the second play eclipses the killing of Iphigenia, just as his acquittal for murder justifies the repudiation of Clytemnestra. In the course of the trilogy Electra explicitly denies that she is like her mother and transfers her love for her mother and her sister, Iphigenia, to her brother. The stories we know (Agamemnon's sacrifice of Iphigenia, the history of the house of Atreus) are retold with new beginnings. The official story now starts with Clytemnestra's murder of Agamemnon; the history of Athenian democracy begins with an act of public treason rather than with the now-unspoken story of family horror and child sacrifice. Thus, the traumatic origins of patriarchy disappear from its public record, and the dissociations between reason and emotion, public and private, men and women come to seem as natural as the separation between day and night, light and darkness.

We noticed also that the trauma at the root of patriarchy involves the loss of a woman: in the stories of Atreus and Menelaus, a man's loss of a woman to another man. Like patriarchy itself, the trauma is gendered. In both stories, children are sacrificed by a man who has found himself helpless in the face of loss and powerless to eradicate shame. The response is horrendous violence, which becomes the proving ground for masculinity and honor.

The tension between the two stories – the psychological drama of trauma and its aftermath and the political drama of establishing civic order – is exquisitely held in a counterpoint of speech and silence. Not knowing gives way to knowing; remembering is followed by forgetting. What can we know, what can we see, what can we say, how shall we respond? – these questions became central to our concerns. What do we know about gender, what can we know, what do we see and hear, what do we feel and think, what histories do each of us carry – personally, in our families, our sexualities, our cultures? What visions of gender do we hold and how do we incorporate our experiences and beliefs about gender into our cultures, our civilization, our cities, our legal system?

Spurred by leading classical scholars – Froma Zeitlin in *Playing the Other: Gender and Society in Classical Greek Literature* (1996) and Simon Goldhill in *Reading Greek Tragedy* (1986) – we were struck by the central role women played as characters in Greek tragedy, written for and by men in a democracy in which women lived in abject isolation from public life. We learned much from the close study of the *Oresteia* and Euripides's *Iphigenia in Aulis* about the psychology of loss that supported the highly patriarchal politics of the Athenian democracy. But it was our turn to the

Roman materials, in particular the close study of Vergil and Apuleius, that opened up for us the question of resistance to patriarchy, as both a psychological and a political question.

We then learned from Eva Cantarella's scholarship on ancient Roman social history that elite Roman women stood in a very different relationship to Roman patriarchy than did Greek women to Greek patriarchy, a difference that gave rise to patterns of resistance to which great artists, Vergil and Apuleius, were acutely sensitive. It was for this reason that we turned, in what was for us a kind of revelation, to the closer study of the Roman materials and what we could learn from them about resistance to patriarchy. What we discovered is something we believe is of value to understanding the tension between patriarchy and democracy, not only in the Roman republic and empire but also in the Western culture so heavily shaped through Augustine in both its religion and politics by Roman patriarchy – a tension that registers pleasure in sexuality suspect.

Others before us, notably Michel Foucault in his late works on the history of sexuality (1978, 1985, 1986), have turned to Greco-Roman sources to understand modern sexuality. Foucault's work, however, takes little interest in women or gender, which has led many classical scholars (Amy Richlin, Lin Foxhall, Simon Goldhill, David Cohen, and Richard Saller) to question both his selection of sources and the interpretation he accords them. We agree with Foucault and with Elaine Pagels (1988) that Augustine played a pivotal role in the radical darkening of the view of human sexuality (beyond anything in Greco-Roman culture) that Christianity was to impart to the modern world, marking a major break by demonizing pleasure per se. But it is precisely what Foucault omits from his account, namely, Roman patriarchy and resistance thereto, that can explain what led Augustine to take the view he did. Even historical work, like that of J. J. Bachofen and Robert Graves, which (in contrast to Foucault) takes an interest in women along lines we find highly suggestive often does so largely through interpretations of myth.

The interpretation of myth in literary texts, notably the *Aeneid* and *The Golden Ass*, certainly plays a role in our argument, but as a way into understanding both the patriarchal psychology and culture that supported Roman imperialism and the evidence of resistance among Roman matrons. It is perhaps the most original feature and consequence of our collaborative approach, intertwining the complementary research and scholarship of a woman and a man, that our argument proceeds through works of *men* (Vergil, Apuleius) who sensitively preserve the voices of resisting Roman *women*. Very few texts written by Roman women have come down to us – a letter arguably by Cornelia to her son Gaius Gracchus (Hallett, 2004), a few poems by Sulpicia (Heath-Stubbs, 2000; Skoie,

1998, 2002; Keith, 1997), and some writings of the Vindolanda military wives (Bowman and Thomas, 1994; Bowman, 1994). We use such texts when we reasonably can, but most of the writing about Roman women comes to us in writings by men in genres that must be read critically because of the ways they reflect men's overall, often patriarchal, political aims (Dixon, 2001). Our argument shows that women's resistance to Roman patriarchy informed the psyches of some of Rome's most sensitive male artists and thinkers, whose work sustains and tries to make sense of the voices of such resisting women. Our method finds in certain Roman artists what we find later in Shakespeare, Hawthorne, Hemingway, and Joyce: a creative voice inspired by relationships to the resisting voices of women. If we are right, this psychology of resistance is as important and creative for men as it is for women, as they join in resistance to patriarchal demands that would otherwise corrupt their relationships.

Another feature of our approach is the way in which it links personal and political psychology, identifying and exploring the tension between democracy and patriarchy in both intimate and political life. As we saw, this tension is posed in the *Oresteia* where the founding of Athenian democracy requires the defeat and the silencing of the Furies, who in entering the city must become good women. We recognize that the Roman republic was never as democratic as Athens nor as open to the forms of theater and philosophy that flourished there. Democratic assemblies of citizen-soldiers played a role in the Roman republic, but very much under the thrall and authority of a small gerontocracy of aristocrats in the Senate who vied for power among themselves, a struggle that eventually collapsed into civil war (Lintott, 2004). Nonetheless, even the limited forms of democracy that the republic had were in tension with Roman patriarchy, and the transition from republic to empire was engineered by Augustus in highly patriarchal terms that legitimated the end of the republic and thus of whatever democracy Rome had had.

What arrests our attention is the tension between democracy and patriarchy in Roman personal and political life. We recognize that ancient notions of public and private were rather different from ours, including the Roman elite view of privacy in domestic space, some of which was for public use (Wallace-Hadrill, 1994). And Roman culture demanded the utmost respect for its institutions, its elders, and its gods. Augustus's policies (including his building programs) were intended to forge a public opinion in support of traditional patriarchal codes of behavior (Zanker, 1990). Both his propaganda against Mark Antony and his Julian laws reflect these dynamics. The blitz campaign that targeted the East and the female as opponents of the empire appealed to Romans of all social levels. The Julian laws express an Augustan obsession with adulterous wives and allocate rewards and punishments to elite males on the basis of who married or remained bachelors. These laws forged a new conception of public and private with consequences for state action and can thus be seen as part of Augustus's campaign for moral reform, including a religious revival (Milnor, 2005). The state's attempt to program intimate behavior through the Julian laws was extraordinary, provoking elite Roman women to protest. In this light, we believe that it was Augustus's appeal to Roman patriarchal psychology that made his politics both attractive and abrasive.

We observe that the tensions between democracy and patriarchy remain very much with us today, carried forward by a Christian religion and related politics in thrall to the traditions of Roman patriarchy and in many ways inconsistent with the Christianity of the Gospels. But the greatest threat to democracy in recent times was totalitarianism: the rise of fascism in Italy and Germany, culminating in World War II, and the rise of Stalinism. We find that the Roman patriarchal psychology we discuss in this book adds a causal stream to the understanding of why fascism first arose and flourished in Europe. The appeal that a movement so mindless exerted in countries noted for their intellectual and cultural achievements can be explained in terms of a political psychology rooted in the very soil of that civilization. If we are right about its power and its persistence, our exploration of Roman patriarchal psychology may illuminate and help us to resist some of the threats to democracy we continue to face.

Our argument thus is exploratory and inductive, raising new kinds of questions about a range of materials, developing hypotheses, and seeing where they lead. In the course of this collaborative work, we have come to see the role of patriarchy in the formation and transmission of irrational prejudices that subvert democratic values. In mapping these terrains, we were surprised by the explanatory and normative fertility of the patterns we encountered. Our mapping is not the last word on these matters. In a field of human experience so historically complex, morally and politically important, and psychologically profound, how could it be? We hope, however, that our efforts will excite and absorb others, leading to further discoveries and a sense of new alternatives in our ways of thinking and living – in religion, psychology, politics, and personal life.

Our topic in this work is thus at once cultural and psychological: the roots of powerful patterns of patriarchal manhood and of resistance to such patterns in republican and imperial Roman culture, including the period when Christianity is first adopted as the established church of Rome (Constantine) and then coercively imposed, repressing all pagan religious practice to the contrary (Theodosius). The origins of Christian intolerance in general and anti-Semitism in particular lie in this period, notably legitimated by Augustine of Hippo, who uncritically assumes (so we argue) Roman conceptions of patriarchal manhood. We are interested in how such conceptions of manhood were established and transmitted and in how resistance to them arose and was carried forward. Our focus then is both on the cultural and psychological power of the dominant pattern and on the persistent and growing power of a resisting voice, one we see as critical to democracy's future.

We use an interdisciplinary methodology to study how patterns of injustice and moral slavery are supported by the repression of resisting voice and to show how such resisting voice is rooted in the human psyche and preserved in cultural forms that develop and sustain it. Our working hypothesis is that gender stereotypes play a pivotal role in supporting not only sexual inequality and homophobia but also extreme religious intolerance and racial discrimination. In particular, we focus analytically on both the culture and psychology we call patriarchy as the nerve of the problem, an arrangement of authority that accords ultimate authority to the voices of fathers as the model for legitimate authority. We offer a developmental psychology that explains how such patriarchal authority arises and is sustained, namely, by traumatic breaks in personal relationships (including of sons to mothers), leaving a devastating sense of loss and a disjuncture between relationship and identification. The patriarchal voice becomes internalized, along with its gender stereotypes, accepted as in the nature of things or as the price of civilization. Thus the link between trauma and tragedy.

In the spirit of Sandor Ferenczi's "The Confusion of Tongues between Adult and Child" ([1932] 1949) and Ian D. Suttie's *The Origins of Love and Hate* ([1935] 1999), we offer a psychology of trauma as an explanatory hypothesis for the power and appeal of the various forms of patriarchal institutions and practices in diverse periods and cultures. We also use this psychology to explain how resistance to unjust authority arises and is sustained and transmitted, namely, by voices that contest such losses and thus reveal patriarchy's unnaturalness. What patriarchy precludes is love between equals, and thus it also precludes democracy, founded on such love and the freedom of voice it encourages. Political resistance is in its roots the same resistance against patriarchy that individuals and couples summon in loving; similarly, artistic resistance is at once an expression of desire and a political statement.

One of our recurring questions in this book is how and why the repression of free sexual voice plays such a central role in sustaining patriarchal modes of authority, and similarly, how and why the recovery and expression of such voice appears to play an important role in resistance. By free sexual voice, we mean a voice not constrained by the Love Laws of patriarchy, and our questions follow from the observation that the reassertion of patriarchy is typically accompanied by the strengthening or more rigorous enforcement of its Love Laws, the laws that constrain whom and how and how much we may love (Roy, 1998). Sexuality and sexual voice are integral to the human psyche, expressing desires that not only give us the greatest pleasures in loving association and living but also contribute to a healthy sense of our bodies and appetites, our creativity, indeed our intelligence, including our ethical intelligence. This perspective casts a flood of light on how and why patriarchal patterns, in rationalizing forms of moral slavery, war on free sexual voice and, in particular, on the role such voice plays in the lives of the women and men who would reasonably contest such patterns.

The repression of sexual voice makes psychologically possible the dissociation that impedes ethical intelligence as well as the various forms of resistance to which such intelligence leads. Patriarchal values and assumptions introduce shame into any sexuality that resists their premises, and such shame extends to what we desire and what our bodies tell us (Damasio, 1999; Gilligan, 2002). We can see the consequences of such demands on girls in adolescence, compromising their honest sense of relationship and thus their resistance to abuse (Brown and Gilligan, 1992). Conversely, the empowerment of sexual voice often sustains resistance to moral slavery and explains the deep roots of such resistance in the human psyche.

The oldest literature that has come down to us, *Gilgamesh*, illustrates our thesis. *Gilgamesh* shows us a powerful, terrifying ruler, whose exercise of power included sexual violence against women: "nor the wife of the noble; neither the mother's daughter/nor the warrior's bride was safe." To secure "the wise shepherd, protector of the people" (p. 4), the gods create an equal for Gilgamesh, "the double,/the stormy-hearted other, Enkidu," a wild, feral creature (p. 5). Gilgamesh sends a temple prostitute to have sex with Enkidu, who is longing for a companion, but Enkidu can only find the intimate relationship he seeks with his equal, Gilgamesh. Gilgamesh and Enkidu wrestle, after which they "embraced,/ and kissed, and took each other by the hand" (p. 15). When told by his mother that Enkidu would not forsake him, Gilgamesh "listened, and wept, and felt his weakness./ Then Enkidu and Gilgamesh embraced" (p. 16). Thus, Gilgamesh becomes the good ruler the gods want him to be.[2]

In this astonishing and most ancient of narratives, an intimate relationship between equals releases men from their wildness and makes possible a strength in resisting and overcoming enemies not otherwise possible: "the strong companion, powerful as a star,/ the meteorite of the heavens, a gift of the gods ... [t]wo people/ companions,/ they can prevail together against the terror."[3] Such men have sex with women. However, heterosexual sex, whether with a prostitute (Enkidu) or with a goddess

(Gilgamesh rejects the goddess Ishtar's sexual overtures later on), does not ultimately satisfy human needs for loving connection, person with person, since under patriarchy, such sex is either degraded (the prostitute) or idealized (the goddess). Sexual intimacy with a woman could only satisfy this need if women were equals of men, a thought the ancient epic does not entertain. The intensely homoerotic relationship of Enkidu and Gilgamesh can meet this need because they are, as men, equals. They become human, released from terrifying propensities to violence, through an intimate relationship that enables them to listen, to weep, and to feel not only their strength but also their weakness – an insight that can readily be extended in the present context to all persons, independent of religion or ethnicity or gender or sexual orientation.

We come, then, to a fuller understanding of the place of literature in this book. Great artists are uniquely sensitive to the issues of voice that interest us, including the cultural and psychological forces that can lead men into patriarchal manhood: into accepting its desolating losses as in the nature of things and adopting a way of life that rationalizes a violence that knows no reasonable limits. And as artists, they are also attuned to the voices of resistance.

In the work of Vergil, Apuleius, and Augustine himself, the abstractions of gender theory become voiced in narratives depicting the adoption and/or rejection of a way of life that deforms love and rationalizes violence. Embedded in a narrative form, they take on a developmental trajectory (a movement through time) and a relational structure that is akin to the argument we have set out to explore and explain. As Vergil's *Aeneid* and Augustine's *Confessions* will take us into the heart of Roman patriarchal manhood, making the darkness visible, so Apuleius's *Metamorphoses* will show us a way out, its light reflecting perhaps the place and time in which it was written: North Africa, in the midst of the longest period of peace and prosperity the Roman Empire was ever to know.

In summary, then, our claim is that patriarchy calls for and legitimates the traumatic disruption of intimate relationships and that the effect of such trauma on the human psyche is precisely to suppress personal voice and relationships in an identification with the patriarchal voice that imposed the disruption. This disruption of intimate voice has concomitant commitments to honor, to institutions that rigidly control sexual interactions according to closely defined social boundaries (the Love Laws), and to violence as a means of enforcing such control. The historical and conceptual roots of all this are to be found in ancient Roman society and the adoption and propagation of such values through normative, Augustinian Christianity in its most Pauline guise. Against such a system, we sound out the voices of resistance both in literature and in peaceful resistance movements, which need cherishing.

# 2  *Roman Patriarchy and Violence*

There are two important strands in the historical literature on ancient Rome. First is the literature on the public political and military life of Rome,[1] which started as a small city-state under the rule of elected kings and turned upon their expulsion into a form of aristocratic republic that aggressively expanded over the next four centuries to rule the entire Mediterranean basin and much more. Its success led to civil wars that discredited republican government, making possible the transition under Augustus to what Roman republicans traditionally despised, the rule of kings, to wit, autocratic imperial rule that was to endure for yet another 400 years. Its decline was given a still classical statement in Gibbon's masterpiece, *The Decline and Fall of the Roman Empire*.[2] Second is the more recent literature on the Roman family.[3] These two literatures, with a few notable exceptions,[4] exist largely in isolation from one another: that on public life written largely by men, that on family life largely by women. We find a link between these two literatures in the concept central to our inquiry, patriarchy.

Patriarchy is an anthropological term denoting families or societies ruled by fathers. It sets up a hierarchy – a rule of priests – in which the priest, the *hieros*, is a father, *pater*. As an order of living, it elevates some men over other men and all men over women; within the family, it separates fathers from sons (the men from the boys) and places both women and children under a father's authority.[5]

The Roman conception of authority was highly patriarchal in both the public and private domains, and at the core of both, as our interpretation of patriarchy suggests, lay Roman religion. Roman politics, personal life, and religion were tightly integrated, a fact that has led astute students of ancient Rome from Polybius[6] to Niccolo Machiavelli[7] to think of Roman religion as easily manipulable by its leading politicians to serve their ends, including their aggressive imperialistic adventures. Except for the Vestal Virgins, the various orders of Roman priests, including the augurs required to signify that the gods were propitious to some proposed undertaking, were occupied by leading politicians (Julius Caesar, for example, was elected *pontifex maximus*).[8] Although the various priesthoods under the republic look to our eyes highly decentralized, the interpretation of all religious questions was in the hands of the Senate, as final arbiter, and the Senate was also the main body that conducted foreign policy, including Rome's wars.[9] The Senators, called the Fathers, thus exercised a patriarchal authority over the meaning of Roman religion.[10]

The transition from an elected monarchy to a republic in 5th-century B.C.E. Rome led to the apparent increase in positions of political leadership (for both patrician and plebeian males), because under Rome's republican form of government, political responsibilities were much more broadly shared than under the monarchy. It was the duty of all male citizens who satisfied property requirements to leave their farms and serve in Rome's armies.[11] Correspondingly, it is under the republic that we see the beginning of Rome's expansion of military operations.[12] What is historically remarkable is the extraordinary belligerence:

> The Roman's state bellicosity is indicated not only by the frequency with which it went to war, but also by the high proportion of its citizen manpower that was regularly committed to military service. . . . These figures [of military service] . . . represent a very high level of military involvement as Roman citizens, which as far as we know cannot be matched by any other pre-industrial state.[13]

The Roman view was that Rome fought just wars only,[14] but on close examination there is good reason to believe that their wars often cannot thus be justified,[15] resting, rather, on a militaristic ethos that led the leaders and people of the Roman republic to regard imperialistic conquest as their mission. The Roman style of war, exemplified by two of its greatest generals, Julius Caesar and Pompey, was always highly aggressive,[16] and political power under the republic was tied to military leadership and success. Cicero, an orator, lawyer, and writer but not a military leader, remained largely on the periphery of political power during the civil war and ultimately was murdered when it served the interests of Antony and Octavian.[17] Violence became a way of life for Romans, directed not only against its enemies but increasingly against one another.[18]

Roman patriarchy legitimated this militaristic ethos, imposing its hierarchical religious demands not only in public life but in private life as well. In the Roman home, fathers were the priests, having authority over domestic rituals and lives. The remarkable powers of the Roman father, the *patria potestas*, gave him

> unlimited authority over all his legitimate children, irrespective of whether or not they were married, and of their offspring as long as he lived. Thus, for example, the *pater familias* has the right to expose his child, to scourge him, to sell him, to pawn him, to imprison him, and, *in extremis*, even to kill him.[19]

While exercising such patriarchal authority in their families, Roman fathers were in turn subject to the patriarchal authority exercised by the Fathers in the Senate.

These interacting and reinforcing patterns of patriarchy both rest on and explain evidence of an underlying personal and political psychology in both the men and women who sustained the belligerent militarism of the Roman republic and empire. We are struck, in this connection, by the way Josephus, a close and respectful observer of the Roman army in action (in the imperial period), describes Roman men:

> [T]heir nation does not wait for the outbreak of war to give men their first lesson in arms; they do not sit with folded hands in peace time only to put them in motion in the hour of need. On the contrary, as though they had been born with weapons in their hand, they never have a truce from training, never wait for emergencies to arise. Moreover, their peace manoeuvres are not less strenuous than veritable warfare; each soldier daily throws all his energy into his drill, as though he were in action. Hence that perfect ease with which they sustain the shock of battle: no confusion breaks their customary formation, no panic paralyzes, no fatigue exhausts them; and as their opponents cannot match these qualities, victory is the invariable and certain consequence. Indeed, it would not be wrong to describe their manoeuvres as bloodless combats and their combats as sanguinary manoeuvres.[20]

According to Josephus, Roman men are so steeped in militarism that they appear "as though ... born with weapons in their hand."

Of course, no baby is born this way. Quite the opposite; human babies are remarkable for their relationality, their desire for and responsiveness to human connection. Since Josephus's Romans are neither relational nor emotionally sensitive, these human capacities have been blunted or stamped out of them. Our question, then, is how could Roman patriarchal culture so structure both private and public life so as to render this outcome seemingly natural or inevitable?

We turn in this regard to the contemporary literature on trauma and its effects on human neurophysiology and psychology.[21] The now-well-documented consequence of trauma is a loss of voice and of memory, in particular, loss of the voice of intimate relationship. This loss or suppression of voice, however, is often covered by an identification with the voice of the person who imposed the trauma and an internalization of the demands that this more powerful person imposes on one's life. The crucial mechanism here is dissociation: the psychological process through which the surviving self separates itself from the self that was overwhelmed. A voice that speaks from experience is silenced in favor of a voice that carries more authority, leading to a replacement of one's personal sense of emotional presence and truth with what Sandor Ferenczi, the Hungarian psychoanalyst, describes as an "identification with the aggressor,"[22] the taking on as one's own the voice and demands of the oppressor. This process, leading to what Ferenczi observed as false compliance, is in itself largely unconscious, due in part to the loss of memory that follows the traumatic rupture of relationships.[23]

Josephus's observations suggest a personal and political psychology in which such traumatic breaks in intimate relationships are both normal and normative, justified by the demands of patriarchy: in effect, an institutionalized trauma that supports and sustains the required militaristic ethos. In the case of Roman patriarchy, these demands took the form of a highly gendered code of honor, coupled with institutionalized practices of shaming. The honor of a Roman citizen rested on his being willing and able, with the complicity of women, to engage in both Roman politics and their expression in continual imperialistic wars. This involved not only military service with its risks of injury and loss of life but also a willingness to disrupt personal relationships.

A family living under the rule of the Roman *patria potestas* experienced a form of oppression at the center of intimate life, including control not only over inheritance and genealogy but also over the use of force to hold people in line.[24] Even if many Roman fathers declined to exercise these powers oppressively, the very legitimation of such power, as a model for what legitimate power is, makes the traumatic disruption of any intimate relationship, including that between fathers and sons, acceptable. Polybius, a Greek whose home town had been damaged by Romans, noted in mixed horror and admiration that "there have been instances of [Roman] men in office who have put their own sons to death, contrary to every law or custom, because they valued the interest of their country more dearly than their natural ties to their own flesh and blood."[25] In place of intimate relationship, the son identifies with the honor of his father, and of his father before him, honor descending through a line of fathers.

The mechanism of such honor codes is again beautifully illustrated by Polybius, who portrays the ritual he describes as very much at the heart of the psychology of Roman imperialism:

> Whenever one of their celebrated men dies, in the course of the funeral procession his body is carried with every kind of honour into the Forum to the so-called Rostra.... The whole mass of the people stand round to watch, and his son, if he has left one of adult age who can be present, or if not some other relative, then mounts the Rostra and delivers an address which recounts the virtues and successes achieved by the dead man during his lifetime. By these means the whole populace ... are so deeply engaged that the loss seems not to be confined to the mourners but to be a public one which affects the whole people. Then after the burial of the body ... they place the image of the dead man in the most conspicuous position in the house.... This image consists of a mask, which is fashioned with extraordinary fidelity both in the modeling and its complexion to represents the features of the dead man.... And when any distinguished member of the family dies, the masks are taken to the funeral, and are there worn by men who are considered to bear the closest resemblance to the original....
>
>   They all ride in chariots ... and when they arrive at the Rostra they all seat themselves in a row upon chairs of ivory. It would be hard to imagine a more impressive scene for a young man who aspires to win fame and practice virtue....
>
>   [T]he most important consequence of the ceremony is that it inspires young men to endure the extremes of suffering for the common good in the hope of winning the glory that awaits upon the brave.[26]

Such rituals enacted the patriarchal relationship of fathers to sons, leading sons to identify with a sense of family honor stretching into the past. Since fathers were often absent from family life (either through absence in war or death in war or, given the significant age differences from their wives, through natural death), Roman matrons, as wives and mothers, became crucial players in the patriarchal system.

Women, in the terms of this gender ideology, did not exist as persons with a mind and sexuality of their own, for the terms of Roman arranged marriage respected neither. Such powers of fathers or even of brothers over their sisters (Augustus married his beloved sister, Octavia, to Antony) were, under the republic, important means to social solidarity. This was particularly true among otherwise highly competitive Roman republican men, struggling for leadership and honor in politics and war. Such men often sought, by enlisting the power of fathers or brothers, to elevate their status and political appeal through marriage to a higher status woman, as Octavian did through his marriage to Livia.[27] Thus are new alliances formed. Pompey and Julius Caesar manage, for example, to cooperate politically as long as Pompey is married to Caesar's sister; when she dies and Pompey refuses Caesar's request that a comparable marriage be arranged,[28] the cooperation collapses and civil war follows.

This function of arranged marriage under Roman patriarchy led to the particular weight that Romans traditionally placed on the chastity and fidelity of women, for only such limitations on women's sexuality could assure their husbands that the women's children were his. An honor code of this sort invests men's sense of honor in a control over women's sexuality that disrupts any relationships women might otherwise form or want to form. Indeed, such control is a perquisite of male honor in such a patriarchal system, and any attack upon it constitutes an insult that elicits and justifies violence. The link between traumatic disruption of intimate relationships and violence is thus reinforced.

Marriages in Rome were arranged by fathers, crucially to advance dynastic ends. Consequently, the relationships of Roman wives to their husbands could be emotionally quite shallow.[29] For example, Augustus married his daughter, Julia, successively to Marcellus, Agrippa, and Tiberius, the last of whom she apparently deeply disliked. And at the order of Augustus, Tiberius divorced a beloved wife to marry Julia.[30] The political career of Augustus himself (then called Octavian) evidently took off only when he married Livia, whose father and then husband had both fought against Octavian and Antony at Philippi. Livia's father, upon defeat by Octavian and Antony, had committed suicide. Nonetheless, with the support of her husband (by whom she was then pregnant), she divorced him to marry Octavian.

Although Augustus apparently loved Livia and their marriage had unusually egalitarian features (including consultations with his highly intelligent, astute wife on all matters public and private), Livia came to marry Augustus very much in the context of Roman patriarchal marriage. Not only was she, a higher status woman, chosen at least in part by Augustus to advance his status and career, but she also married him under the shadow of traumatic loss (her father's suicide) and, given the military and political failures of her husband, in order to preserve her own life and his, as well as the life of her son by her first husband, Tiberius. Livia's living out the idealized conception of a good Roman wife makes sense against this background; her profound influence on her husband is, consistent with Roman patriarchy, never a public matter, always staying within the strict bounds of propriety.[31] With Livia, his mother, very much in his corner, Tiberius was to succeed Augustus as emperor even though he was not Augustus's child.

Livia's strategic moves following traumatic loss exemplify the psychology of Roman patriarchal womanhood.[32] The power of fathers and even husbands to inflict such losses on both men and women gives rise to an armored psychology in both that is consistent with the gender roles required of them, including the violence triggered by any violations of women's chastity. These patriarchal values are discernible in Livy's history of Rome, where he gives us two notable examples of such violence. Both associate the founding or refounding of republican government with revulsion against violence spurred by threats to the chastity of wives or daughters.

First is the expulsion of the last king of Rome, Tarquinius Superbus, explained by Livy in terms of the lust of his son, Sextus Tarquinius, for Lucretia, the beautiful wife of a friend, Collatinus. Sextus entered the bedroom of Lucretia armed with his sword and threatening her life, but "the fear of death could not bend her will." Failing that, Sextus put the threat as one to her posthumous honor: He would kill her and then her slave and lay the naked body of the slave next to hers, a situation that, when discovered, would lead to the general belief "that you have been caught in adultery with a servant" (meaning a slave). Lucretia yielded on these terms, and when she explained to her father and husband what had happened, they insisted she was morally innocent. Livy narrates her reply:

> "What is due to *him*," Lucretia said, "is for you to decide. As for me, I am innocent of fault, but I will take my punishment. Never shall Lucretia provide a precedent for unchaste women to escape what they deserve." With these words she drew a knife from under her robe, drove it into her heart, and fell forward, dead.[33]

It was the righteous indignation of Lucius Junius Brutus, son of the king's sister Tarquinia, at this outrage that led to the violent expulsion from Rome of its last king and his family and the establishment of the republic around 509 B.C.E.

In what Livy calls "the second crime in Rome," the dictatorial powers of the *decemvirs* were ended in 449 B.C.E.: "Its origin was lust, and in its consequences it was no less dreadful than the rape and suicide of Lucretia which led to the expulsion of the Tarquins." Appius, one of the decemvirs, lusted after a beautiful girl, Verginia, the daughter of Verginius, a centurion then serving in the Roman army. Verginius had already betrothed his daughter to an ex-tribune, Icilius. To achieve his ends, Appius ordered a dependent of his own to claim against all comers in court that Verginia was his slave and thus available for sexual relations, as slaves were in Rome. The claim and the trial, though completely fraudulent, were sustained by Appius even against the protests of Verginius and Icilius. To protect the reputation of his daughter from the sexual relations that seemed imminent, Verginius killed her, an act that aroused Romans violently to overthrow the decemvirs and reestablish the republic.[34]

What interests us about both cases is the violent response to the alleged unchastity of wives or daughters, not only against the men who threaten rape but also the suicide or murder of women (Lucretia and Verginia). In each narrative, the insult to the honor of husbands or brothers elicits violence against both perpetrators and victims. Lucretia, as Livy portrays her, is what patriarchy requires her to be: dissociated through trauma from her experience and identifying with her patriarchal role.[35]

Within these structures of Roman patriarchy lay the relationship of mothers to their sons. Such relationships were rigidly controlled by the duty of mothers to educate their sons into assuming their patriarchal roles. At least two of Rome's most remarkable leaders (Julius Caesar and Octavian, later Augustus) were unusually close to their mothers, both actively involved in advancing their son's careers.[36] Tacitus, writing in the late first or early second century C.E., discussed the mother's role in raising children in a passage that presented Caesar's mother, Aurelia, as an ideal:

> In the good old days, every man's son, born in wedlock, was brought up not in the chamber of some hireling nurse, but in his mother's lap, and at her knee. And that mother could have no higher praise than that she managed the house and gave herself to her children. . . . In the presence of such a one no base word could be uttered without grave offence, and no wrong deed done. Religiously and with the utmost diligence she regulated not only the serious tasks of her youthful charges, but the recreations also and their games. It was in this spirit, we are told, that Cornelia, the mother of the Gracchi, directed their upbringing, Aurelia that of Caesar, Atia of Augustus: thus it was that these mothers trained their princely children.[37]

Yet Roman mothers of the elite often had little to do with babies, who were cared for by nurses, often slaves, endearingly addressed by their young charges as "tatae."[38] Indeed, sometimes a Roman mother like Agrippina the Younger, mother of Nero, was through the vagaries of Roman politics absent entirely from her son's life in some of his earliest years.[39] At later stages, however, as Tacitus observes, the patriarchal system enlisted Roman matrons, often in collaboration with their brothers, into playing important roles in the inculcation in their sons of the required sense of patriarchally defined responsibilities, roles characterized by "disciplinarian skills rather than indulgence or over-protectiveness, even towards small children."[40]

The model here was Coriolanus's mother (Venturia, in Livy's history), who persuaded her son, who had been unjustly exiled from Rome, not to fight against the city of his birth, thus saving Rome at his expense.[41] The consequence was an anger directed toward mothers, so that even when a woman like Livia played a supportive and evidently very important role in her husband's political life and success, she was, as mother to Tiberius, "that feminine bully, his mother."[42] Livia, ambitious for her son to become emperor, supported Augustus's order that Tiberius divorce his wife to marry Julia (Augustus's daughter), a separation that was for Tiberius traumatic. And against this backdrop, we can make sense of Tiberius's rather rigid identification with Roman gender ideology, in terms of which he would later criticize his mother whenever she exercised political responsibilities inconsistent with his view of the proper role and station of women.[43] Similarly, and more drastically, Nero, who would never have become emperor without his mother's strenuous efforts on his behalf, when challenged by his imperious mother to disrupt both his intimate sexual liaisons and his artistic interests, turned to homicidal violence against her.[44]

The pivotal role of honor in Roman politics and culture has been observed by a number of historians. A kind of emulative competition by men and women in the terms of the honor code was as important to Roman personal and political psychology as the more material consequences of their imperial wars, including the wealth that poured into Rome as booty and tribute from their wars and the huge numbers of slaves thus secured who played a key role in Roman economy and culture (defeated enemies were often enslaved).[45] Roman public and private life both rested on and supported the gender ideology that the Roman honor code sustained: one in which almost any insult to manhood elicited violence.[46] As traumatic loss in intimate relationships deadens the psyche's inborn responsiveness and suppresses personal voice, it gives rise to the armored terms of gender identity that the honor code enforces. Indeed, the stability of patriarchy requires the suppression of any voice in women or men that might, on reasonable grounds, contest its terms, a suppression which itself relies on the power of gender by deeming the resisting voice in men unmanly or effeminate and in women unwomanly.

Until the late republican period, the Roman patriarchal system had organized and mobilized these psychological propensities to violence into forms of politics and war that maintained a remarkable level of national solidarity. There were, of course, deep internal constitutional conflicts between patricians and plebeians, and Rome sometimes experienced devastating defeats, for example, early in its history by the Gauls (who sacked Rome)[47] and at the hands of Hannibal in 216 B.C.E. at Cannae in the Second Punic War, a war nonetheless ultimately won by Rome.[48] But the presence of powerful enemies secured a remarkable solidarity among Roman citizens, directing outward the violence motivated by insult. It was only when Rome decisively defeated its most powerful antagonists (in particular, Carthage in the Third Punic War) that Roman violence turned internecine in the civil wars, which started with something Roman politics had not seen before: the murder by patricians of the Gracchi brothers, tribunes of the people, with whom patricians deeply disagreed. As Montesquieu trenchantly observed, "[t]here had to be dissensions in Rome, for warriors, who were so proud, so audacious, so terrible abroad could not be very moderate at home"; thus, when secure at home without powerful enemies, "[t]heir fierce humor remained; the citizens were treated as they themselves had treated conquered enemies, and were governed according to the same plan." Montesquieu notes the power over Romans of the extreme form of patriarchy that governed both their public and private lives, so that under the republic its laws "are observed not through fear, nor through reason, but through passion."[49] Once this passion for patriarchal order and status could no longer be satisfied by a common enemy, it turned into conflict among Romans themselves, for example, the conflict between Julius Caesar and Pompey.

One of the marks of how unusual a personality Julius Caesar had as a Roman man was his resistance to the dictator Sulla's demand that he divorce his wife (Caesar very nearly was executed over this matter), when, in contrast, Pompey supinely obeyed Sulla's similar command.[50] Of course, Caesar was as aggressively successful a military leader as Pompey, willing, like Pompey, to inflict appalling costs on Rome's enemies.[51] But Caesar's remarkable gifts as a Roman leader, including the devotion of his troops to him – "a love affair"[52] – and his vaunted clemency to his political enemies, show that resistance to patriarchal demands was sometimes possible even for Roman men.[53] Yet Caesar's assassination suggests how dangerous such resistance could be.

When Julius Caesar comes to explain his reasons for taking up arms against Pompey, he pinpoints the problem in Pompey's "desire that no one should match his own status"[54] and gives his reasons for undertaking civil war in terms of an unjust threat to his dignity. Caesar, describing himself (as he usually does in his writings)[55] in the third person, observes that "his standing had always been his first consideration, more important than his life."[56]

There is inherently a tension between democracy and patriarchy. Democracy defines legitimate politics in terms of the equal voice of those subject to political power. Patriarchy, imposing the hierarchical rule of fathers, denies the equal voice of those subject to its rule (lesser men, women, and children). The patriarchal structures of ancient Greece were, certainly in their treatment of women in ancient Athens, as bad, indeed worse than those of Rome.[57] But the Athenian democracy protected a right of free speech in the democratic assembly, which allowed for questioning of its institutions. It also encouraged forms of philosophy and theater that exposed its mistakes and the tragic costs of its policies, including those inflicted on women. The Athenian democracy, with rights of free speech and participation much broader than those of Rome, lived nonetheless in very real tension with its patriarchal treatment of women.

In contrast, Roman entertainment both expressed and reinforced the prevailing militaristic ethos, taking the form of gladiatorial contests, a custom that apparently replaced human sacrifice as an offering to the dead.[58] And this ethos also explains the contempt of Romans for the critical power of a theater like that of the Athenian democracy[59] or for any philosophy that would fundamentally question their institutions and practices (the Greek skeptical philosopher Carneades, who questioned Romans' beliefs in their just wars, was for this reason promptly exiled).[60] The Roman prejudice against philosophy was only overcome when it was adapted to serve their practices, for example, Roman stoicism.[61] Roman elites studied the philosophy they found congenial (including, as we shall later see, Epicureanism as well as stoicism); most spoke Greek and some wrote in Greek (for example, Marcus Aurelius).[62] Roman prejudices against the theater in general and actors in particular ran so deep that horror at Nero's love of acting publicly in plays may have been as much responsible for his downfall as his other excesses (even the judicious Tacitus refers to Nero's acting as "the national disgrace").[63]

In contrast to Athens, under the republic the Roman democratic assemblies, which both made laws and elected the leading officials of the state, were open to all male citizens, but the agenda was set by officials and no right of free speech inhered in the citizenry; only in the aristocratic Senate was there anything like free and open debate, and even there the terms were set by officials and dominant politicians.[64] The terms of the Roman honor code were thus effectively sacrosanct, enforcing a highly gendered sense of identity that, if insulted, expressed itself in violence.

The Roman republic was, therefore, much less democratic than Athens, and even more compromised by the extreme form of patriarchy that governed both its public and private life. Nonetheless, it certainly had democratic features, including not only the democratic assemblies but the tribunes of the people, who could veto the actions of the Senate and interpose their authority to stop hostile state action against a plebeian. In addition, over its long constitutional history, the republic eventually opened even membership of the Senate to nonpatricians and Roman citizenship well beyond the ethnic limitations of democratic Athens.[65] Its patriarchy, however, ran so deep in the Roman psyche that if democracy or patriarchy had to go, it was clear which option Romans would embrace. Thus, in the wake of the civil wars, Romans under the leadership of Augustus sacrificed their republic and embraced an autocratic monarchy more congenial to their patriarchal religion.

The period of the civil wars becomes a kind of laboratory for us in showing how republican institutions could function in the circumstances of Rome's remarkable imperialistic success, a success which those institutions had undoubtedly made possible. This experiment reveals both the competitive struggles for honor among such highly individualistic, talented politicians and military leaders as a Marius and a Sulla, Pompey and Caesar, Octavian and Antony and a generation of Roman elite women who bridle in relationship to these driven, competitive men against the traditional, patriarchal view of women's roles. The civil wars destabilized both the republic and Roman patriarchy, as the lives of women in this period show. When Augustus establishes the imperial system, he effectively buries the republic and seeks to reestablish, on sounder institutional grounds, the patriarchy he believes more central to Roman identity than its long-standing republican institutions. The responses of Roman women to this demonstrates both the power of resistance and the rage patriarchal fathers unleashed on their defiant daughters.[66]

We see the challenge to the patriarchal order both in political women – Hortensia, Fulvia, Sempronia, and later in Agrippina the Elder and Agrippina the Younger – and in the freer sexual lives of these new Roman women, including Augustus's daughter and granddaughter, whose erotic lives became the subject of Roman poets such as Catullus, Propertius, Tibullus, Ovid, and even one woman poet, Sulpicia.[67] We begin with the political actions of women before turning to the expression of sexuality and its repression.

Hortensia and Fulvia became political actors during the last period of the civil wars when Octavian and Antony join with Lepidus in the triumvirate to defeat the assassins of Caesar. They then war on one another, leading to Octavian's triumph at Actium and the deaths by suicide of both Antony and Cleopatra. Hortensia, the daughter of the great orator who rivaled Cicero in the courts, appears once in the historical record of Appian as she leads a group of wealthy Roman women who challenge a tax the triumvirs imposed on their property, first by protesting to the triumvirs' womenfolk. Both Octavian's sister Octavia and Antony's mother Julia received them with sympathy, but Antony's then-wife Fulvia brusquely rebuffed them. In response, Hortensia led these women to make a public demonstration, forcing their way to the triumvirs' tribunal in their forum.

Speaking for these women (many of whose husbands and fathers had been proscribed by the triumvirs, legitimating their murders and seizure of their property.) Hortensia made a powerful appeal in the following terms:

> Do you allege that we, like our menfolk, have wronged you? If so, proscribe us too, as you proscribed them. But if we women have voted none of you an enemy of the state, nor torn down your houses, nor destroyed your army or put another in the field against you, nor prevented you enjoying command or honours, why do we share the punishment when we have not collaborated in the crime? Why should we pay tax, when we have no share in magistracies, or honours, or military commands, or in public affairs at all, where your conflicts have brought us to this terrible state?[68]

The triumvirs, disturbed by this unseemly display, instructed their attendants to clear the women, but the response of the Roman crowd was so hostile that the attendants were stopped and the matter postponed to the next day. At that time, the triumvirs narrowed the group of women to whom the tax would apply and included as well those men whose property was of a certain amount.[69]

Fulvia had her most famous involvement in public affairs in a relatively brief period, from 44 B.C.E., after Caesar's murder, to 40, when she herself died. This was a period when Octavian and Antony were at odds. Octavian was ready to take revenge on the murderers of Caesar, whom, after adoption by Caesar, he called his father; Antony was not ready, or not yet. After Antony's defeat by forces of the Roman Senate at Mutina in 43, Fulvia – with Antony's mother and others – acted aggressively as her husband's political agent in Rome. She visited the houses of senators to make sure that her husband was not declared, as Cicero had urged, a public enemy. Later, with both Antony and Octavian absent from Rome, Fulvia exercised more power over the Senate than Antony's brother, who was one of the consuls, the supreme Roman political status, for that year.[70] Subsequently, when Octavian returned to Rome, Antony was in the East beginning his affair with Cleopatra. Fulvia, in alliance with Antony's brother, decided to resist Octavian by force in ways unprecedented for Roman women: girding on a sword, leading assaults, holding councils of war with senators and knights.[71] Both her military efforts and those of Antony's brother at Perusia failed.[72]

Octavian's bloodthirstiness in this period included his brutal role in the proscriptions and his cruelties at Philippi,[73] where his own military performance was undistinguished and, by Roman standards, cowardly. All this stands in sharp contrast to Julius Caesar and his famous clemency for his former enemies, a clemency that did not stop them from murdering him, a fact Octavian never forgot. Fulvia escaped to Athens where she died, freeing Antony to make a new alliance with Octavian by marrying his sister Octavia.

The question of women as sexual actors was, however, even more incendiary. We see in these women something experienced earlier in Roman history during the Bacchanalian scandals of the second century B.C.E., namely, forms of resistance to Roman patriarchy that support our suggestion that such resistance is rooted in the psyche. The Romans had established a patriarchal religion that legitimated its gender ideology, and for this reason, under the republic the Senate, as final arbiter of religion, was at times hostile to non-Roman Eastern religions, especially when those religions were interpreted as threatening the gendered honor code at the core of Roman patriarchy. (At other times, Romans, though ideologically hostile to the East, were syncretic in their religious tastes, including the Far Eastern religions of Magna Mater/Cybele/Isis, etc.)[74]

In the second century B.C.E., the Greek cult of Bacchus, with its nocturnal rites in which women and men might pursue their interests in sexual relations, religiously legitimated free sexual associations of both sexes on terms of female leadership that flouted the control on women's sexuality imposed by Roman patriarchy. The response was one of hysteria and panic at the alleged Bacchanalian conspiracy.[75] When the Senate in 186 B.C.E. forbade such rites, Livy recorded a long speech to the Roman people in justification of the Senate's action. What threatened the Senate and its patriarchal religion was the impact of such free associations on the propensity to violence of Roman men, overriding their crucial role in protecting women's chastity as the rationale for such violence:

> What kind of gatherings do you suppose these to be, gatherings, in the first place, held at night, and, secondly, gatherings where men and women meet promiscuously? If you knew at what age male persons are initiated you would feel pity for them – yes, and shame. Citizens of Rome, do you feel that young men, initiated by this oath of allegiance, should be made soldiers? That arms should be entrusted to men called up from this obscene shrine? These men are steeped in their own debauchery and the debauchery of others; will they take the sword to right to the end in defence of the chastity of your wives and your children?[76]

Without the patriarchally imposed duty to defend the chastity of their women, the consul argues, how can Romans be the violent men that Roman patriarchy requires?

Writing about the conspiracy of Catiline during the period of the civil wars, Sallust identifies, among Catiline's adherents,

> a number of women who in their earlier days have lived extravagantly on money that they obtained by prostituting themselves, and then, when advancing age reduced their incomes without changing their luxurious tastes, had run headlong into debt. These women he thought, would do good service by acting as agitators among the city slaves and organizing acts of incendiarism; their husbands, too, could be either induced to join his cause, or murdered.[77]

Only one such woman is named: Sempronia, who was the mother of Decimus Brutus, one of the assassins of Caesar. She was, Sallust tells us,

> favoured . . . not only with birth and beauty, but with a good husband and children. Well educated in Greek and Latin literature, she had greater skill in lyre-playing and dancing than there is any need for a respectable woman to acquire, besides many other accomplishments such as minister to dissipation. There was nothing that she set a smaller value on than seemliness and chastity, and she was as careless of her reputation as she was of money. Her passions were so ardent that she more often made advances to men than they did to her.[78]

Sallust may be coloring his history in the terms of patriarchy, recirculating stereotypes of female transgression. Nonetheless, what speaks through his narrative is an elite woman's resistance to precisely those patriarchal controls on her sexuality, a resistance that Roman patriarchy must and did condemn.

To put this matter in context, we need to see Octavian in perspective. In securing political power against enormous odds, he was coldly ruthless, perpetrating not only sadistic cruelties on enemies at Philippi but very possibly the human sacrifice of 100 enemies at Perusia. Once the alliance of Octavian and Antony defeated Caesar's murderers at Philippi, Octavian's only real competitor for power was Antony, clearly the much better soldier and thus, in the traditional Roman patriarchal scheme of things, the better man. Although Octavian was capable of great personal courage, his military record was poor, marred by incapacitating illness, for example, at Philippi and elsewhere. However, Octavian was much more calculating than Antony, often betraying his promises to him.[79] He wisely secured the indispensable support and help of two lifetime friends, Agrippa, a brilliant general and administrator, and Maecenas, an excellent diplomat and lover of the arts, who would gather around himself, and thus later around Augustus, poets of the stature of Propertius, Horace, and Vergil.

Octavian always held before his eyes the example of Julius Caesar: a man of military and political genius, courageous, an individualist, improvisatory, famously quick in his responses, one of Rome's best writers and orators, a passionate lover of women in and outside marriage including Cleopatra, Queen of Egypt – perhaps the only woman among his sexual partners who was his equal[80] – and a lover of men. Octavian, in contrast, "constantly quoted such Greek proverbs as 'More haste, less speed,' and 'Give me a safe commander, not a rash one.'"[81] As we earlier observed, there was every reason to think that at the time of Julius Caesar's murder, Antony (the older, more courageous and able military man as well as experienced politician) would have the decisive competitive edge over Octavian, if a competition to the death between them should prove necessary. Consequently, Octavian may have hoped that such a competition would not be necessary. Antony had served under Caesar in his wars, was allied with him politically, and was not involved in his murder, which apparently shocked him as much as it did Octavian. Indeed, it was Antony's speech at Caesar's funeral that may have decisively turned the tide of the army and the people against the small group of senators (the Liberators, as they called themselves) who had killed Caesar.[82]

At first, Antony apparently found it difficult to take the 19-year-old Octavian seriously. Octavian himself sought alliances against Antony even with senators such as Cicero, who were sympathetic to the Liberators. But the alliances did not last long, as Octavian under the triumvirate joined with Antony and thus agreed to the savage murders of the proscriptions, including Cicero. Cicero's head and the hands he used in his oratory were cut off and prominently displayed on the Speakers' Platform in the Forum, and "it is said that Fulvia took the head in her hands, spat on it and then set it on her knees, opened its mouth, pulled out the tongue and pierced it with hairpins."[83]

Octavian's willingness to work with Antony was cemented by the marriage of Antony to Octavia, who made notable efforts to maintain the alliance when it came under strain because of Antony's affair with Cleopatra. If Antony had been a more conventional Roman patriarchal man, all might have gone well. Certainly, Octavian was, as earlier suggested, a highly corporate leader and could have found a way to work with

Antony. But Antony had something that Augustus would never achieve: the common touch, which was part of

> the man's popularity. His troops worshipped him not just for his swagger and profanity, but for the delight he took in public carousing and his pleasure in eating with his men. Many found even his sexual appetites attractive, tempered as they were by a fondness for helping others in their love affairs and a willingness to laugh with others at his own. Again, his lavish generosity won him fervent supporters on his road to power. Another man with such traits might be called a braggart, a libertine, and a spendthrift. Antony was forgiven much because he was well-liked.[84]

In *The Second Philippic*, written in the short-lived period of his alliance with Octavian, Cicero had savagely attacked Antony for many of his excesses in eating and drinking and in sex, including his youthful homosexual affair with Curio, the second husband of Antony's then-wife Fulvia, about which Cicero obsessively rants.[85] These were appetitive excesses that Romans were prepared to forgive. But there was another aspect of Antony's personality that more deeply disturbed patriarchal Romans: showing affection in public to his wife, "a mockery of Roman decorum and decency."[86] It was quite bad enough to show such affection for a Roman wife (Fulvia), but what Roman patriarchal men evidently could not stomach, including some of the soldiers who most loved Antony and had followed him for years, was his passionately demonstrative sexual love for a foreign woman, Cleopatra VII of Egypt.

Absolute ruler of a wealthy and ancient nation, Cleopatra was highly intelligent, politically ambitious, multilingual, and well educated, someone whom Antony took seriously not only as a sex partner, intimate friend, and fun-loving roisterer but, increasingly, as a political and even military leader. Antony never gave Cleopatra all she wanted or demanded; he rejected, for example, her desire to annex the lands ruled by Herod.[87] But this remarkable woman clearly opened the hearts and minds of two leading Roman men (Caesar and Antony) in ways no Roman woman had. With Caesar, for example,

> [i]t may be that the twenty-two-year-old queen was the first and only person, since the death of his daughter Julia, who had understood Caesar, that she not only amused him and allowed him to conquer her, but knew how to pierce the shell of isolation that increasingly surrounded this man of fifty-two, to tempt him out of it and release him from it – with such insight and affection, such subtlety and grace, that he could perhaps even learn from her and allow himself, in some measure, to be conquered by her, as by no other.[88]

Cleopatra ruled in Egypt both as absolute monarch and as a god (the new Isis) in the tradition of pharaonic rule. She neither understood nor sympathized with republican rule, and her influence on Caesar (and later Antony) may have spurred the increasingly monarchical quality of their ambitions. Caesar had brought Cleopatra to Rome with her young son by him. Claiming descent from Venus, Caesar set up in the Temple of Venus Genetrix, the mother of Aeneas, a golden statue of Cleopatra opposite that of the goddess. Cleopatra was in Rome at the time of Caesar's murder; thinking of herself as the new Isis, she may have experienced this event as the traumatic murder of Osiris. From this perspective, her passion for Antony may have had a deeply personal, religious significance: In sexually loving him, she brought back to life, as Isis did for Osiris (and all pharaohs over time), the man she loved.

Cleopatra's love for Antony had, if anything, a more profound impact on him both as a man and a military and political leader in ways that scandalized even the Romans who loved him, let alone his enemies, notably Octavian, who came to seek a way to defeat him decisively.[89] Perhaps the closest historical text to the events in question is Plutarch's *Antony* (the central influence on Shakespeare's play), where he describes Antony's love thus:

> Antony showed to all the world that he was no longer motivated by the thoughts and motives of a commander or a man, or indeed by his own judgment at all, but what was once said as a jest, that the soul of a lover lives in some one else's body, he proved to be a serious truth.[90]

The turning point for Octavian was Antony's divorce of Octavia, which not only broke the bonds that had united Octavian and Antony but, from the perspective of Octavian's highly patriarchal conception of honor, also dishonored him as Octavia's brother, an insult that would elicit and legitimate violence. With the indispensable assistance in war of Agrippa and in diplomacy of Maecenas, Octavian had defeated Pompey's son, who had threatened Rome's food supply; Antony, in contrast, had had to abandon his war on the Parthians.

The decisive act, however, was Antony's marriage to Cleopatra in circumstances that included public ceremonies of their reigning as co-rulers of the Eastern Empire with Alexandria as their capital. A bitter propaganda war followed between Octavian and Antony in which the highly gendered terms of Roman patriarchy were prominently invoked on both sides.[91] Octavian could draw not only on the patriarchally defined invective of Cicero's *Second Philippic* but also on Roman patriarchy's common sense that a woman ruler in the domain of politics and war was unnatural and that a Roman political and military leader sharing rule with her was unnatural as well. When Rome declares war, it will do so on Cleopatra, the foreigner queen, not on Antony, the beloved and generous general who had, from the Roman point of view, lost his mind to a woman. In this propaganda war Antony never stood a chance, in particular once he refused the plea of his advisers that Cleopatra not be present at the final military confrontation with the forces of Octavian and Agrippa at Actium.

It is at this point that some of Antony's closest friends defected to Octavian, taking with them confidential information about Antony's will that Octavian would ruthlessly make public, including the provision, against all law and custom, that Cleopatra was to be his heir and that he and Cleopatra were both to be buried in Alexandria, not Rome. It is doubtful that there was ever much of a battle at Actium, but what took place there was abortive for Antony who left in the midst of the sea battle to follow Cleopatra's ship back home to Egypt. The soldiers who had loved Antony found this incomprehensible. They defected to Octavian, leaving Antony and Cleopatra to commit suicide and be buried in Alexandria in a common tomb.[92]

Octavian won the conflict with Antony because, on balance, he was the more astute political and military leader of Roman men. Octavian identified himself with Apollo, Antony with Bacchus and Hercules. Octavian loved a Roman woman, Livia, who helped advance his political ambitions, but always within the closeted terms that patriarchal women traditionally observed; Antony loved a foreign women and queen, publicly sharing both political and military power with her in ways that scandalized Roman patriarchal values. Octavian identified his life and his rule, as Augustus, with traditional Roman patriarchal religion. Antony, in contrast, gravitated to the religions of Greece and Egypt, including the religion of Isis, which Augustus and Tiberius would forbid in Rome.[93] These differences clarify Octavian's victory and Antony's defeat.

It is a different question of whether, as men in their relationships to the women they loved, they lived as differently as the propaganda war between them might suggest. A letter we have from Antony to Octavian, before their decisive break, suggests an underlying common way of life:

> What has come over you? Do you object to my sleeping with Cleopatra? But we are married; and it is not even as though this were anything new – the affair started nine years ago. And what about you? Are you faithful to Livia Drusilla? My congratulations if, when this letter arrives, you have not been in bed with Tertullia, or Terentilla, or Rufilla, or Salvia Titisenia – or all of them. Does it really matter so much where, or with whom, you perform the sexual act?[94]

What came between them was their different relationships to Roman patriarchy, Octavian identifying himself with its traditional values and way of life, Antony coming through passionate sexual love to a stance of resistance.

After the defeat of Antony, Octavian, now Augustus, undertook to intensify the hold of patriarchy on Roman public and private life, as if patriarchy, not republican self-government, was essential to Roman political and military successes. This included the revival of ancient Roman religious rituals and a massive building program that would give them an architectural expression.[95] His wife Livia's restoration of a temple of Fortuna Muliebris revived the cult established early in the fifth century B.C.E. connected to the legend surrounding Coriolanus, honoring the patriarchal role exemplified by Coriolanus's mother in saving Rome at the expense of her son.[96] Augustus's program of restoration included legislation sponsored by him that sought to return Roman family life to its traditional forms, in particular, putting the patriarchal lid back on the men and women who had enjoyed greater sexual liberties in the late republic.

In contrast to Caesar's rule, Augustus's was a corporate undertaking that retained the forms of the republic but consolidated ultimate power in himself and his ruling circle (including, crucially, Agrippa, Maecenas, and, behind the scenes, Livia). He established an imperial autocracy and bequeathed it to his successors, who would render it even more autocratic and absolutist because much less intelligently corporate than Augustus's rule. This shift in political power achieved covertly what Caesar could not achieve overtly, the end of the republic, thus stripping the Roman Senate and people of the powers of self-government that they had enjoyed under the long history of republican government.

To understand the depth of this conflict, we need to be clear that Octavian's success, as Augustus, turned at crucial points not only on the way he rather conspicuously lived his life as a patriarchal Roman man but also on the way, early in his political career, that he aggressively used the gender ideology of Roman patriarchy against his enemies, in particular, Antony.

At the heart of this reactionary legislative program was the *Lex Julia de adulteriis coercendis*, which punished the nonmarital sexual relations of adultery and criminal fornication (any sexual relations of or with a virgin or a widow), adultery incontestably being the main offense condemned. Through this legislation, Augustus drastically curtailed the range of possible sexual partners for Roman men outside marriage, at least insofar as this range was defined at law. Exempt women included prostitutes, procuresses, slaves, convicted adulteresses, and foreigners not wed to Roman citizens. Other laws included the *Lex Julia et Papia,* which imposed restrictions on marriage (members of the senatorial order, for example, could not marry freedmen or freedwomen) and limited the rules of succession (for example, the unmarried could not inherit under a will). Further measures related to public life gave precedence to men with children in political life and prohibited the unmarried from attending public spectacles and entertainments. None of these measures was popular, as they limited the freedoms that Roman men and women had traditionally assumed. They were, however, required, Augustus argued, for the revival of Roman virtue, by which he meant patriarchal virtue.[97]

Before the passage of the *Lex Julia de adulteriis coercendis,* the repression of sexual misbehavior had been a private matter. If the husband caught an adulterous pair in the act, he might kill both parties on the spot. Other cases dealt with punishment by the father of the offending woman. Under the *Lex Julia,* such acts were punished for the first time by a trial in a standing criminal court, the *quaestio perpetua de adulteriis.* Criminal penalties were ordained for the adulterous female spouse and her lover. These included exile to separate islands for both parties, as well as confiscation of one-half of the lover's property and one-third of the adulteress's, as well as one-half of her dowry. A woman convicted under the Augustan adultery statute was forbidden to remarry.[98] The movement over time to increasingly severe penalties culminated in the provisions of Constantius and Constans in 339, which called for strict enforcement of the law against adultery and also decreed that adulterers be punished "as though they were manifest parricides," by being sewn up in a leather sack with a dog, a cock, a viper, and a monkey, and cast into a river or the sea.[99]

The *Lex Julia de adulteriis coercendis,* like most criminal statutes, allowed anyone to launch an accusation. Yet unlike other criminal statutes, this statute created a special right of accusation of the husband and father of the woman accused of adultery. The right of the father was as accessory to that of the husband, in the sense that it turned on the act of the latter (divorce) to be legitimized and stipulated that where both raised an accusation, the husband was to be preferred.

Another feature of the law was the *ius occidendi.* This granted the husband and father the right to kill the guilty party or parties on the spot. Here, the respective positions of husband and father were the reverse of the *ius accusandi:* The father was given pride of place. He might kill both daughter and lover (presumably, as an expression of legitimate patriarchal rage), but under no circumstances might the husband kill his wife.

The *Lex Julia* lowered the status of the wife found guilty of adultery to that of a prostitute and correspondingly defined the actions of a complaisant husband as *lenocinium*, an accessory as fully liable as the principals. At the same time, it exempted true prostitutes and procuresses from its sanctions. They were able to practice their professions without fear of prosecution for adultery, fornication, or *lenocinium*. In short, the law created certain defined statuses for women, statuses that reflected a traditional complex of patriarchal values in establishing a firm connection between social rank and acceptable sexual behavior – good married women had sex only with their husbands, whereas bad married women had sex extramaritally and in doing so were the equivalent of prostitutes.

Roman men and women were not enthusiastic about this legislation, and two striking examples of resistance by Roman women have come down to us. In the first, some Roman women sought to evade the punishment meted out to a woman under the *Lex Julia*, as well as an outright ban placed on the practice of prostitution by women of the equestrian and senatorial orders. For example, Vistilia, of upper-class lineage, attempted to escape prosecution for adultery by claiming the exempt status of a prostitute. The Senate passed judgment on Vistilia, exiling her to an island, and decided that henceforth no woman whose grandfather, father, or husband had been a Roman *eques* would be permitted to prostitute herself, thus closing the loophole in the adultery law that Vistilia had tried to exploit.[100] The second and more striking example was of resistance within the imperial family itself, first by Julia the Elder, daughter of Augustus, and later by Julia the Younger, Julia's daughter.

Julia was Augustus's only surviving child, the daughter of his marriage to Scribonia, whom he divorced to marry Livia. Consistent with the role played by patriarchal values in his public and private life, Augustus carefully supervised the education of his daughter and granddaughters, making sure it

> included even spinning and weaving; they were forbidden to say or do anything, either publicly or in private, that could not decently figure in the imperial day-book. He took severe measures to prevent them forming friendships without his consent, and once wrote to Lucius Vinicius, a young man of good family and conduct: "You were very ill-mannered to visit my daughter at Baiae."[101]

Like other patriarchal Roman men, Augustus arranged marriages for Julia that were designed to advance his dynastic purposes. She was married to Marcellus, the son of his sister Octavia, and after his untimely death to Agrippa, who had been so important in Augustus's rise to power and success. With Agrippa she had five children: Agrippina the Elder, Gaius, Lucius, Julia the Younger, and Agrippa Postumus, two of whom, Gaius and Lucius, were groomed by Augustus to succeed him (although both, to Augustus's grief, died as young men). After Agrippa's death, Augustus married Julia to Livia's son Tiberius, another possible successor to the Principate, who in fact did succeed Augustus. Neither Julia nor Tiberius wanted the marriage: Julia was "defiant and unfriendly to her new husband,"[102] and Tiberius had been forced to divorce a woman he loved, Vipsania, who had already borne him one son and was pregnant with another. Suetonius tells us:

> Tiberius continued to regret the divorce so heartily that when, one day, he accidentally caught sight of Vipsania and followed her with tears in his eyes and intense unhappiness written on his face, precautions were taken against his ever seeing her again.[103]

Julia had evidently been having affairs with various men for years (as Augustus had with various women,[104] including the wife of his friend Maecenas),[105] even during her marriage to Agrippa. When asked about how, in light of this, she had always managed to have children that resembled Agrippa, she replied: "Passengers are never allowed on board until the hold is full."[106] Augustus had, of course, earlier passed the *Lex Julia*, which subjected such adulteries to criminal prosecution.

The crisis year for Julia and her father over this matter came, strikingly, in precisely the year 2 B.C.E., when Augustus, in light of his achievements, accepted the title *"Pater Patriae,"* Father of the Fatherland.[107] Augustus had by this time deeply invested his sense of self not only in traditional Roman patriarchal values but also in an attempt to legitimate his rule and end republican self-government by reviving ancient patriarchal religious practices, neglect of which he believed and wanted others to believe had been responsible for the civil wars. The *Lex Julia* was clearly a cornerstone of what he regarded as his life's work, a work that Romans now rather sycophantically applauded. Julia's adulteries at this point took a conspicuously public form, including "revels and drinking parties by night in the Forum and even upon the Rostra"[108] (the platforms from which speakers spoke). Seneca gives us the fullest description:

> The deified Augustus relegated his own daughter, who was so promiscuous as to be beyond reproach of promiscuity, and made public the scandals of the imperial household: to wit, the lovers were admitted in droves, that the city was traversed with nightly revels, that the very Forum and speakers' platform, from which her father had proposed his legislation on adultery, received her vote as a venue for fornication, that there was a daily gathering about the statue of Marsyas, when, having turned from an adulteress into a prostitute, she sought the right to every sexual indulgence under a lover who was an utter stranger to her.[109]

Seneca, with typical rhetorical overkill, calls Julia a prostitute, as the *Lex Julia* would require. But both the publicity and the place of her sexual revels suggest public protest, specifically of her father's legislation. The statue of Marsyas may have been a place where prostitutes gathered, but Marsyas was also, symbolically, a satyr who challenged Apollo, the god with whom Augustus most closely identified. There is another point that Seneca underscores elsewhere: the sex was freighted with a larger meaning both for Julia and her lovers, and the meaning clearly invokes, almost ritually, the love of Cleopatra and Antony (one of Julia's most prominent lovers was Iullus Antonius, the son of Octavia and Antony): "[A]ll the noble youths bound to her by adultery as though by an oath kept alarming his [Augustus's] feeble old age, as did Iullus and a second formidable woman linked to an Antony."[110]

Roman historians such as Velleius Paterculus tend to sexualize Julia, "setting up her own caprice as a law unto itself."[111] Seneca does so as well, but the sexual bond between Julia and her lovers, "adultery as though by an oath," suggests to us that there may have been a moral, even religious, point to the public form her actions took, a self-conscious enactment precisely of a Bacchanalian rite of the sort the Senate under the republic had (as we earlier saw) forbidden – and Bacchus had been, of course, the god with whom Antony most closely identified. It seems reasonable to think that we may have here a public religious rite that, by its timing, place, and the identity of its participants (the daughter of Augustus and the son of Antony) protested Augustus's legislation against adultery in an act of public resistance. This protest invoked the memory of the lovers Cleopatra and Antony along with an alternative religious tradition, that of Bacchus or the cult of Isis, in which the sexuality of free women like Cleopatra was celebrated and valued. Julia would certainly have known of her father's many adulteries and, by identifying herself as an adulteress in this way, would also be raising the age-old question of the hypocrisy of the double standard, except that she was willing to admit in public to what Roman men like Augustus did in private.

Augustus's anger was extreme: "[H]e was filled with rage,"[112] and his actions were brutal:

> He wrote a letter about her case to the Senate, staying at home while a quaestor read it to them. He even considered her execution; at any rate, hearing that one Phoebe, a freedwoman in Julia's confidence, had hanged herself, he cried: "I should have preferred to be Phoebe's father!" Julia was forbidden to drink wine or enjoy any other luxury during her exile; and denied all male company, whether free or servile, except by Augustus' special permission and after he had been given full particulars of the applicant's age, height, complexion, and

of any distinguishing marks on his body – such as moles or scars. He kept Julia for five years on a prison island before moving her to the mainland, where she received somewhat milder treatment.[113]

Most of Julia's lovers were exiled, but Iullus Antonius (brought up in the imperial household with Julia, himself a noted poet, married to one of the daughters of Octavia, and having served in various posts of distinction under the Augustan regime, including a priesthood, and as praetor, consul, and governor of a province) was compelled to commit suicide.[114] When it came to the son of Antony, Augustus's rage became homicidal.

Even to contemporaries who otherwise rarely challenged him, Augustus's actions (and the underlying rage) seemed disproportionate:

> [N]othing would persuade him to forgive his daughter; and when the Roman people interceded several times on her behalf, earnestly pleading for her recall, he stormed at a popular assembly: "If you ever bring up this matter again, may the gods curse you with daughters and wives like mine!"[115]

Seneca tells us that Augustus himself came to regret what he had done:

> Afterwards, when by lapse of time shame took the place of anger in his mind, he lamented that he had not kept silence about matters which he had not learned until it was disgraceful to speak of them, and often used to exclaim, "None of these things would have happened to me, if either Agrippa or Maecenas had lived."[116]

The later historian Tacitus makes clear how intemperately Augustus viewed what Julia had done and that his autocratic treatment of her did not conform either to Roman custom or to the due process required by his own legislation: "he used the solemn names of sacrilege and treason for the common offence of misconduct between the sexes. This was inconsistent with traditional tolerance and even with his own legislation."[117]

It was Augustus's own frenzied interpretation of his daughter's resistance (as "sacrilege and treason") that may have led to Pliny's interpretation of it in terms of "her plots against her father's life,"[118] an interpretation considered baseless.[119] What we believe the record shows is a daughter's increasingly public, conscientious resistance to her father's legislation that targeted women's sexuality.

We know that Julia was the only child of Augustus, trained, as we have seen, in Augustus's own highly gendered conception of women's roles and one who, for much of her life, did her duty as those roles demanded: Her marriages were arranged by Augustus to advance his dynastic ends, and at least two of the children produced in those marriages were intended by Augustus to succeed him and would have, had circumstances permitted. Macrobius preserves more intimate details of Julia's relationship to her father ("she habitually misused the kindness of her own good fortune and her father's indulgence"),[120] including three incidents of her good-humored, witty responses to Augustus's attempts to hold her in line.[121] First, there was Augustus's shock at her wearing an immodest dress, but he kept silent, and upon seeing her in a more modest dress, praised her as wearing something "more becoming in the daughter of Augustus," to which Julia replied: "Yes, for today I am dressed to meet my father's eyes; yesterday it was for my husband's." Second, at a display of gladiators, Augustus critically noted that the suite of his wife Livia contained older men of distinction whereas Julia was surrounded by "young people of the fast set." Her father sent his daughter a letter of advice, "bidding her mark the difference between the behavior of the two chief ladies of Rome," to which she replied, "These friends of mine will be old men too, when I am old." Third, when a friend urged Julia to conform more closely with Augustus's simple tastes she replied: "He forgets that he is Caesar, but I remember that I am Caesar's daughter."[122]

Macrobius also preserves deeper divergences both of ethics and temperament between Julia and her father. Julia's views of sexuality may have been those of the Roman daughter who, to someone asking in surprise why it was that among the lower animals the female sought to mate with the male only when she wished to conceive, replied: "Because they *are* the lower animals."[123] In addition, Macrobius writes of "her high spirits," noting that she

> had a love of letters and a considerable store of learning – not hard to come by in her home – and to those qualities were added a gentle humanity and a kindly disposition, all of which won for her a high regard; although those who were aware of her faults were astonished at the contradiction which her qualities implied.[124]

We are struck by the Roman patriarchal sense of a contradiction between Julia's free sexuality and her intelligence and goodness, "a gentle humanity and a kindly disposition," similar to what we observed earlier in Sallust's description of Sempronia. In our view, there is no such contradiction. To the contrary, it is precisely the kind of free sexuality we find in Julia and Sempronia that clarifies the psychological basis of their resistance to Roman patriarchal claims, in Julia's case, to her father's own legislation and the underlying hypocrisy she believed it reflected.

The wider significance of such resistance is suggested by the republican Roman historian Tacitus, who, in contrast to Lucan and Seneca, does not even attempt to justify the imperial autocracy,[125] but anatomizes its moral and political enormities. Strikingly, he prefaces his own unusually powerful attack on Augustus's legislation dealing with the family, including the *Lex Julia* and other statutes, with the history of the treatment of Julia by her father. For Tacitus, Julia was critically questioning legislation that attacked essential freedoms of Roman republican liberty, making possible the supine and sycophantic citizenry that would accept "peace and the Principate."[126] Tacitus was in no sense what we would today call a feminist, but we are struck by the feminist edge in the way such an acute critic of the imperial system makes Augustus's legislation central to his criticism. As Tacitus saw it, Augustus's aim was to end the political equality central to the rule of law of the Roman republic, noting that "when men ceased to be equal, egotism replaced fellow-feeling and decency succumbed to violence. The result was despotism."[127] Augustus's legislation was to quash the equal liberties of intimate sexual life so that men, losing any sense of a dignity rooted in personal freedom, would accept the loss of the republic. For this purpose,

> restraints [of essential liberties] were stricter. There were spies, encouraged by inducements from the Papian-Poppaean law, under which failure to earn the advantages of parenthood meant loss of property to the State as universal parent. The spreading encroachments of these informers grievously affected all citizens, whether in Rome, Italy, or elsewhere, and caused widespread ruin and universal panic.[128]

Tacitus describes the impact of such legislation on Roman male citizens, whose political competences required a psychological basis, both personally and politically, in "freedom and wholeheartedness,"[129] arising from the right to make decisions regarding intimate matters of sexual love rooted in respect for the freedoms of mind and body. What Augustus's legislation aimed to achieve was a legal and political war on precisely such freedoms, a traumatic disruption of intimate life that would give rise to a dissociation from one's mind and body and foster the acceptance of political autocracy – what Tacitus called the tyranny of imperial rule.[130]

Tacitus makes his critical point in terms of the impact of such legislation on Roman male citizens, but the very fact of Julia's resistance, as we understand it, shows that the same psychological process would apply to women as well. The very fact that Julia drew to her so many important Roman men supports our sense that we are dealing here with a significant historical example, perhaps one of the first such examples,

of men joining with women to protect and sustain one of the freedoms at
the heart of a democratic republic.

Thus understood, Augustus's rage makes sense to us as he faces, as
an older man, a daughter's resistance, which must have struck him to the
heart as the return of the repressed, his old enemies Antony and Cleopatra, on whose defeat his own success depended. As Augustus breaks relationship with the daughter he clearly had loved, or thought he had loved,
we glimpse the loneliness of a patriarchal man who had carried Roman
patriarchy to its logical conclusion, ending the democratic republic Rome
had historically enjoyed and under which it had prospered. In the midst
of such division between Augustus and his daughter, we note that one
person who reenters history at this point is Scribonia, the mother of
Julia, with whom Julia had not lived for most of her life: "[H]er mother
Scribonia accompanied her [Julia] and remained with her as a voluntary
companion of her exile."[131]

That Julia's resistance reflects something psychologically deep in
Roman women of her period and background is shown by its recur-
rence in her daughter, Julia the Younger, in C.E. 8. A new public scandal
gripped Rome: Julia, it was alleged, had slipped into the adulterous ways
of her mother. She was therefore relegated to a barren island where she
would remain for twenty years.[132] This time, however, Augustus's anger
extended not only to his granddaughter but to one of Rome's greatest
poets, Ovid. Ovid was not actively complicitous with the scandal, yet
Augustus was vindictive toward a poet who had not served the state but,
rather, had addressed himself to celebrating the erotic lives of Roman
men and women. He used the occasion of Julia's disgrace "to make a
demonstration – perhaps to find a scapegoat whose very harmlessness
would divert attention from the real offences of Julia."[133] Ovid was exiled
to Tomi, a Greek city on the coast of the Black Sea, where he would spend
the rest of his life.

We are struck by the vindictiveness of Augustus's rage at the sexual
voices and lives of his daughter and granddaughter and at a great Roman
poet who took such voices seriously. Augustus had made a choice between
democracy and patriarchy, clearly opting for patriarchy, a reactionary
form of which he used to justify not only his victory over Antony but also
his success in becoming Rome's first absolute ruler since the expulsion
of the Tarquins.

At the end of his life, Augustus made two remarks, the one directed at
his public, the other for Livia alone: to his friends, "Have I played my part
in the farce of life creditably enough?"; to Livia, "Goodbye, Livia: never
forget our marriage."[134] Augustus, self-consciously as actor, was the man

who not only acted as though traditional Roman institutions still existed but also claimed to have restored many such institutions. Something had gone terribly wrong, leading to the civil wars, and Augustus's task had been to restore Roman institutions so that this internecine bloodshed would never occur again. In fact, Augustus ended what had made Rome the leading imperial power of the world, its republican government. In the acid terms of Tacitus, "there was nothing left of the fine old Roman character. Political equality was a thing of the past; all eyes watched for imperial commands. . . . [A]t Rome, consuls, senate, knights, precipitately became servile."[135]

Augustus was able to succeed in this charade, persuading others as well as himself, because he had embraced patriarchy as the supreme value of Roman life, eliminating its tension with republican institutions and values. Thus his appeal, at the moment of his death, surely as sincere as anything Augustus had said or done, to his highly patriarchal marriage as the one value never to be forgotten. Livia had played the role of good Roman wife as no other woman of her generation did or could, which explains the honors Augustus heaped on her both during his life and after his death.[136] His daughter Julia, however, came to resist such roles, and her conflict with her father became catastrophic for them both.

Augustus drew his power and appeal from the internecine violence of the civil wars, which he claimed to have ended. But the problem of Roman violence, rooted in the honor codes of patriarchy, did not end with Augustus. If anything, the violence, in an absolutist state form, had fewer limitations than had existed even in the worst days of the republic. No one more acutely studied how and why Augustus's concentration of power in the emperors corrupted them than did Tacitus, who shows how a good man and leader like Tiberius, once he acquiesced in the destruction of his personal happiness by divorcing the woman he loved, had "been transformed and deranged by absolute power."[137] If this could happen to Tiberius, it could happen to lesser men, and it often did, as the subsequent history of the Roman emperors clearly shows (think of Caligula, Nero, and Domitian, in the first century alone). It is also under Augustus that the Roman army was put on an increasingly well-paid professional footing, no longer bound, as it had been under the republic, to the regular military service of citizens and owning allegiance to the emperor alone, who paid them. Roman soldiers thus increasingly lived in isolation from the rest of Roman culture, subject to Augustus's command, for example, that they not marry, an unthinkable requirement under the republic.[138] Over time, it was Roman armies, not Roman citizens, who determined who should rule in Rome, and the wars among these armies under the empire became as bad, if not worse, than the civil wars. So Augustus, who thought he was solving the problem of Roman violence, in fact exacerbated it. And the power of Roman elite women, if anything, increased.

Both Agrippina the Elder and her daughter, Agrippina the Younger (wife of the Emperor Claudius and mother of Nero) were Roman political women very much on the model of Fulvia. As we have indicated, Roman elite women had always played important, indeed crucial, roles in Rome's patriarchal system, but mostly behind the scenes. Livia, Augustus's wife, was in this mode; her advice was taken seriously by her husband and often followed, as shown by Augustus's remarkable practice of always writing down his questions for Livia before he raised them.[139] Her political shrewdness is attested by no less than Caligula, who referred to his great-grandmother as "Ulysses in petticoats."[140] Agrippina, mother and daughter, exercised their political power openly. Agrippina the Elder joined her husband Germanicus when he led Roman troops in Germany. When the troops, after the death of Augustus, mutinied and refused to obey Germanicus, Agrippina, then pregnant and with her young son Caligula, shamed Roman troops into obedience to her husband. She later stepped in to rescue her husband from his mistakes, assuming the role of a commander by helping soldiers and, at a crucial point, blocking the demolition by terrified Roman soldiers of a bridge over the Rhine, thus saving her husband's armies across the river in Germany.[141] Tiberius, the new emperor, was enraged by the public role Agrippina took and, after the death of Germanicus, exiled Agrippina – who so furiously resisted the soldiers that she lost an eye. Tiberius was later responsible for her death, as well as the deaths of her sons Nero and Drusus.

Agrippina the Younger displayed the same qualities as her mother both as the wife of Emperor Claudius and as the mother of Nero, who, largely due to her efforts (which may have included the poisoning of Claudius), succeeded Claudius. Her assistance to her husband may have been as significant as Livia's to Augustus, but when her son became emperor, her insistence on playing a more public role in politics may have been one of the reasons he turned on her with homicidal rage.[142] Men like Tiberius and Nero were threatened in their honor by women like Agrippina, mother and daughter, and, as with patriarchal men everywhere, an insult to honor elicits violence.

In sum, the root of the problem, in our analysis, lay in Augustus's uncritical acceptance of Roman patriarchy, which, if anything, took a more rigid and absolutist form under his rule. Roman religion had always been highly patriarchal and political, but previously it was subject to final political control by a collegial body, the republican Senate. Under

Augustus, the emperor as *pontifex maximus* centralized such control in himself, self-consciously reviving ancient rituals played out on the stage of a massive program of building new temples and the like and imposing on Romans of his generation the more rigid forms of patriarchy that his laws on the family both reflected and enforced. It was this patriarchal legacy that the Christian Church was to absorb uncritically when, under Constantine and his successors, it became the established church of the Roman empire.

Our study thus begins with the powerful role patriarchy played in Augustus's success. Its legacy was the patriarchal construction of manhood that he enlisted to rationalize what he achieved, including the legislative force he brought to bear on restricting women's sexuality. The loss of republican freedoms coincided with a loss of sexual freedom – a coincidence we will continue to explore and seek to explain. In the next chapter we present a close study of Vergil's *Aeneid*, which clarifies the personal and political psychology that sustained the appeal of Augustus. We then turn to two conversion narratives that bear directly on our question: Apuleius's *Metamorphoses*, which plots a way out of patriarchy, very much in the spirit of resisting Roman women we have studied in this chapter, and Augustine's *Confessions*, which shows how a patriarchal construction of Roman manhood framed Christianity's understanding of its role and mission. It is of particular interest, in light of our observations thus far, that the conversion narrative of the *Metamorphoses* involves the achievement of equality in an intimate and healing sexual relationship between a man and a woman, Cupid and Psyche, leading to the birth of their daughter named Pleasure and reflected as well in the religion of Isis, whereas Augustine's *Confessions* tracks a conversion from sexuality to celibacy and from an intimate, loving relationship with a woman to misogyny and intolerance, including Christian anti-Semitism.

# 3  *Vergil on the Darkness Visible*

Vergil's *Aeneid* is often taken to be a self-consciously written apology for the form of Roman imperial power established by Augustus Caesar. As we observed, Octavian Caesar had defeated the forces of his erstwhile ally Mark Antony, allied with his lover and now wife, Cleopatra VII, ruler of Egypt. The very idea of a woman ruler was odious in patriarchal Rome, let alone a woman ruler known for her sexual powers not only over Antony but also over Julius Caesar himself, through whom Octavian claimed authority under Caesar's will. From this patriarchal Roman perspective, once Octavian triumphed over Antony and Cleopatra (adopting the name Augustus in 27 B.C.E.), Vergil's portrait of Dido, the ruler of Carthage, would have been reasonably construed as a portrait of Cleopatra.

Like Cleopatra, Dido rules a nation, Carthage, indeed a nation that was once Rome's greatest rival for supremacy over the Mediterranean and that came very close to defeating Rome in the three wars they fought. Dido, a widow, is also in Vergil's poem a sexual foreign woman who desires Aeneas, but one who struggles with her vow to her dead husband not to marry again or become involved sexually with a man.[1] Despite her compunctions, Dido acts on her sexual desires and has an affair with Aeneas.

On both these scores – ruling as a woman and acting on sexual desire – Dido would, in the Roman mind, have counted as a bad woman, deviating from her natural place in the patriarchal order of things by acting on the authority of her own political and sexual voice, rather than the voice of her father or husband. Aeneas, in contrast, would exemplify Roman manhood, certainly highly sexual (he clearly loves Dido sexually and initially embraces her power, joining with her to build a new city), but ultimately a patriarchal man, bound to the will of his father that he establish a new Troy in Latium (Rome). Thus, he abruptly breaks his relationship with Dido when reminded by the gods of his duty and conforms to the demands placed on him by patriarchy. From the patriarchal Roman point of view, the very idea that Aeneas would remain in Carthage (a commercial state where military service was not even a duty of its citizens) and join Dido in realizing her political vision would be an unthinkable, unnatural inversion of the order of things. It is this patriarchal order that in Latin etymologically links bravery and virtue – the word *virtus* is inherently about military men.[2]

From this perspective, Vergil's narrative conforms to and works within the Roman order of things, confirming the heroic stature of patriarchal manhood. Aeneas's repudiation of passionate sexual love for an anti-patriarchal woman confirms Augustus's heroic stature in defeating an Antony degraded by his political and sexual relationship to an anti-patriarchal woman (and foreigner, to boot). Aeneas's later political marriage to Lavinia, a woman he does not love and who does not love him, is wholly consistent with the order of things, which relies on men and women willing and able to break any personal ties that conflict with their patriarchally defined duties. And as if to dispel any doubt as to his patriarchal lineage, Aeneas is depicted at the beginning of the epic as carrying his aged father and leading his young son, thus earning the epithet "pious Aeneas."

The *Aeneid* must be placed in the context of the transition from the republic to the empire, as Romans who had been living under republican government for four centuries struggled to understand what roles they could and should play under the empire. The poets of Augustan Rome, including Vergil, had a complex relationship to the political developments around them that cannot be reduced to any simple modern conception of propaganda, though there were undoubtedly strands of Augustan propaganda in their work. The generous patronage of Maecenas, an important friend and ally of Augustus, brought them into a close relationship to the political events around them and even to Augustus himself. For this reason, in 37 B.C.E. Maecenas brought Vergil and other poets to Brundisium.[3] Maecenas also gave the poets the kind of support and freedom that enabled the best of them, including Vergil, to bring their artistic gifts to bear not only on making sense of a period of remarkable change in Roman institutions and sensibility,[4] but also in truthfully exploring the demands and strains that the Augustan form of patriarchy imposed on the Roman psyche.

Vergil had himself lived through the terrors and hopes of the final civil wars unleashed by the assassination of Julius Caesar, experiences which left their marks on his earliest published poetry, the *Eclogues*.[5] In Vergil's *First Eclogue*, for example, shepherds converse in dialogue about the impact of the civil wars on their farms, which during this period had

been summarily seized and then used as payment to the soldiers serving
in the wars. Suetonius tells us that Vergil was grateful to three patrons
at the time of the *Eclogues,* "because at the time of the assignment of
the lands beyond the Po, which were divided among the veterans by
order of the triumvirs after the victory at Philippi, these men had saved
him from ruin." And later, he was grateful to his patron Maecenas, who
"had rendered him aid when the poet was still but little known, against
the violence of one of the veterans, from whom Vergil narrowly escaped
death in a quarrel about his farm."[6]

Thus, in the *First Eclogue*, in passages that may well be autobiographical, one of the shepherds, Tityrus, praises the intervention of the godlike
youth in Rome (who may have been Octavian) who intervened to confirm
him in possession of his little holding, which was at threat of seizure.
His interlocutor, Meliboeus, has been expelled from his property and is
setting out on a trek that will take him far from what was once his home.
At the close of the conversation, Tityrus says he will never forget his
benefactor:

> "Stags will browse in the pastures of the air
> And the sea will cast up its fish on the naked shore,
> The exiled Parthian drink from the river Saone
> And the German drink from the Tigris, before that face
> That way he looked at me, will fade from my heart.
> But *we* have to leave our homes and go far away,
> Some to the thirsty deserts of Africa,
> Some to Scythia, some to the region where
> Oaxes rushes over its chalky bed,
> Some as far away as among the Britons,
> Utterly cut off from all the world. . . .
> Have we done all this work
> Upon our planted and fallow fields so that
> Some godless barbarous soldier will enjoy it?
> This is what civil war has brought down upon us.
> So, Meliboeus, carefully set out
> Your plans and pear trees, all in rows – for whom?
> For strangers, for others, we have farmed our land."
>                       (David Ferry translation, *First Eclogue*, pp. 7–9)

On the one hand, the impossibility of the cross-migration of Germans
and Parthians would signal to the Roman reader that it is the empire that
would stop such an incursion. On the other, Meliboeus's desolate reply is
more political: Without challenging Tityrus's confidence about the immo-
bility of Germans and Parthians, he observes that such a displacement
is, because of the civil war, already in process, not on the borders but at

the heart of the empire. How can anyone feel secure in the midst of such dislocation?[7]

Tityrus's benefactor is not the only example of a god-man in the *Eclogues*. The *Ninth Eclogue* offers the snatch of a song in praise of the comet that had been popularly interpreted in this period as the soul of the deified Caesar:

> "Look, Venus's grandson Caesar's star is rising ...
> The start that brings such joy to the ripening grain."
> (*Ninth Eclogue*, p. 75)

The *Fifth Eclogue* presents the death and apotheosis of Daphnis, paragon of shepherds: Nature is stricken when he dies, only to flourish when he takes his place on Olympus. (pp. 35–43), and the *Fourth Eclogue* speaks of a mystical child who

> ... will share in the life of the gods and he
> Will see and be seen in the company of heroes,
> And he will be the ruler of a world
> Made peaceful by the merits of his father.
> (*Fourth Eclogue*, p. 29)

The child is almost certainly the anticipated issue of the marriage of Octavia and Antony, which Romans hoped would mark the end of the civil wars. Such apocalyptic hopes bespeak the fear and despair from which they arose.

Vergil's next work, the four books of the *Georgics*,[8] are said by Suetonius to have been read by Vergil to Augustus in 29 B.C.E., as he rested on the way back from Actium (recovering from a throat ailment), where his forces had defeated those of Antony and Cleopatra.[9] The poem, whose subject matter is farming, is Vergil's most personal and exquisitely beautiful statement of the Epicurean philosophy in which he believed. Both its content and poetry are profoundly influenced by the remarkable Roman Epicurean philosopher and poet Lucretius, who had lived and written during the period of the final civil wars (dying, Suetonius pregnantly observes, on the same day Vergil is born). Epicureanism was a scientific, naturalistic philosophy, based on the atomism of the Greek philosophers Democritus and Leucippus, which Epicurus developed into an ethical teaching. The task of a well-lived life was to come to understand the causes of things and, in the light of that study, to strip one's life of all illusions.

Farming plays the role it does in the *Georgics* because its intelligent study and practice require people closely to observe and study nature – the change in seasons as they affect crops, the quality of soils, the growth and fertility of animals and plants and their appropriate care, and the like. The close study of some creatures, for example, the integrated and industriously cooperative work of the bees,[10] yields, for Vergil, an illuminating model for the criticism of human communities in which people are distracted from productive work by illusions, including, prominently, wars:

> O greatly fortunate farmers, if only they know
> How lucky they are! Far from the battlefield
> Earth brings forth from herself in ample justice
> The simple means of life, simply enjoyed.
>> (David Ferry translation, *Georgics*, p. 83)

Farming is, for Vergil, properly understood as the practice of which Lucretian Epicureanism is the only good theory, since it disciplines the mind and body to the rigorous terms of the causes of things, freeing us from illusions:

> That man is blessed who has learned the causes of things
> And therefore under his feet subjugates fear
> And the decrees of unrelenting fate ...
> Nor does he have experience of the iron
> Hard-heartedness of the law, the Forum's madness,
> Insolence of bureaucratic office.
>> (*Georgics*, pp. 85–7)

In the wake of the civil wars, Vergil offers farming as an alternative discipline in the virtues of a well-ordered life, an alternative which he opposes quite clearly to the traditional pattern of Roman rule:

> The loud blare of a military trumpet
> Or the clanging of a sword on the hard anvil.
>> (*Georgics*, p. 89)

There is obviously a critical edge to Vergil's way of stating the problem, farming versus Roman politics and its wars, as if Romans faced a stark alternative. The appeal to farming may have been anachronistic even when Vergil wrote. Old patterns of small farms were in decline, replaced by plantations owned by absentee landlords and in which farm labor was largely done by slaves. The Roman economy increasingly depended not on farmer-soldiers but on the wealth that poured into Rome as a consequence of its imperialistic triumphs (including farm products from Egypt) and on the more immediate gains from conquest: booty and slaves.[11] But, Vergil's insistence on structuring Roman experience in terms of stark alternatives suggests a deep distaste for the traditional republican terms of Roman politics, discredited for many by the civil wars.

Vergil is quite clear about his own views on recent events like the murder of Caesar: a time of "[t]reachery," "Caesar's light was quenched," "the sun, in pity for Rome . . . covered with darkness," leaving an "impious generation . . . in fear [of] eternal nights" (*Georgics*, p. 39). And about the horrors of civil wars, including the battle of Philippi at which the forces of Antony and Octavian defeated the Liberators (led by Brutus and Cassius): "brother Romans" clashing "in war with one another," leaving fields of the dead and their weapons that "a farmer laboring there" will one day plough up and "wonder at" (*Georgics*, p. 41).

He is explicit about his hopes for Augustus (lines Augustus would have heard when Vergil read the poem to him):

> O Caesar, the gods begrudge your care for us;
> Right and wrong are turned into one another;
> War everywhere in the world; crimes everywhere,
> In every way and every shape and form;
> No honor at all is given to the plow;
> The fields are barren and empty, the farmers gone;
> The crooked sickles are beaten into swords;
> There's war on the Euphrates; on the Rhine;
> Neighboring cities break their mutual oaths,
> Sword against sword; Mars rages everywhere.
>                                    (*Georgics*, p. 41)

The role of Augustus in bringing an end to the civil wars is interpreted in the *Georgics* in terms of divinity. In the proem of the *First Georgic*, Vergil begs the favor of divinities of the land and then addresses Augustus who is ultimately to join their godly ranks.[12] The *Third Georgic* presents this divine mortal from a quite different perspective, namely, Vergil's passion to create a poetry that will, as it were, crown and consecrate Augustus:

> . . . I too must find
> The way to rise in flight above the earth,
> Triumphant on the speech of men, for I
> Will be the first, if life be granted me,
> To bring the Muses home from Helicon
> To my own native country, Mantua,
> I'll bring the Idumaean palms to you,
> And on the green fields there beside your river . . .
> I'll build a temple made of Parian marble,
> And Caesar will be seated in the center.
>                                    (*Georgics*, p. 93)

Vergil acknowledges Maecenas as the inspiration for the *Georgics*, leading the poet to sing of Augustus himself:

> And soon I'll gird myself to tell the tales
> of Caesar's brilliant battles, and carry his name
> In story across as many future years
> As the years that have gone by, from the long-ago
> Birth of Tithonus to that of Caesar himself.
>
> (*Georgics*, p. 97)

The form this song took was Vergil's epic of the founding of Rome, the *Aeneid*, begun shortly after 29 B.C.E. and almost completed when, attempting to return to Rome in the company of Augustus, he fell ill, and died at Brundisium in September, 19 B.C.E. (He was buried near Naples, where he owned a villa.) Vergil had left orders that his unfinished *Aeneid* should be burned, but Augustus overrode Vergil's commands, ordering his literary executors Varius Rufus and Plotius Tucca to preserve it and to publish it. It was issued two years later.

Suetonius reports Augustus's continuing interest in Vergil's work on this poem:

> Augustus indeed (for it chanced that he was away on his Cantabrian campaign) demands in entreating and even jocosely threatening letters that Vergil send him "something from the 'Aeneid'"; to use his own words, "either the first draft of the poem or any section of it that he pleased." But it was not until long afterwards, when the material was at last in shape, that Vergil read to him three books in all, the first, fourth, and sixth. The last of these [which expresses grief at the loss of Marcellus, the son of Octavia, Augustus's sister, who had died] produced a remarkable effect on Octavia, who was present at the reading; for it is said that when he reached the verses about her son, "Thou shalt be Marcellus," she fainted and was with difficulty revived."[13]

The poem is not, as the *Georgics* had suggested it would be, explicitly about Augustus, although his triumphs are mentioned at least twice: in Book VI, the underworld scene, where the ghost of his father Anchises tells Aeneas about the future of his line, including Augustus, and Book VIII, when Aeneas scans the shield his mother Venus had Vulcan make for her son and sees a depiction of Augustus's triumph over Antony and Cleopatra at Actium. Why, then, Augustus's absorbing interest?

Although not biographical, the poem is about a man and also about the project of manhood. Augustus started his career in vengeance for the death of Caesar, the man he regarded as his father, and attempted to effect the form of autocratic absolutism he believed his father sought. It was always Augustus's project, once he defeated Antony and Cleopatra, to rationalize the ending of the republic and the beginning of the imperial autocracy. Vergil conceived the *Aeneid* very much in these terms, and he traces the kind of man who had now saved Rome from itself (Augustus) back to Aeneas. Julius Caesar, "father" of Augustus, had explicitly claimed in public speeches his direct descent from Venus and her son Aeneas. Thus, Augustus found in the *Aeneid* the kind of narrative he was seeking, focusing not on the history of republican government in Rome but on the pre-republican founding of Rome – a continuation of the Homeric epics, the *Iliad* and the *Odyssey*. Not only does Vergil extend their narrative, as Aeneas is a character in the *Iliad*, one of the very few Trojan men to survive defeat in the Trojan War; but he portrays him in terms of various Homeric heroes. Books I–VI of the *Aeneid* track the *Odyssey*, Books VII– XII, the *Iliad*.

At a deeper level, the *Aeneid* also appeals to the personal and political psychology of insulted patriarchal manhood in the Greek epics, insults that give rise to violence in the *Aeneid* as they earlier did in the *Iliad*. The patriarchal cross-reference is, in Vergil, quite self-conscious. For example, Turnus, Aeneas's main antagonist in Books VII–XII, refuses to go along with his monarch's plan of marrying his daughter, Lavinia, to Aeneas and explodes into the violence that is the main subject of these books because Lavinia had been engaged to marry him. The psychological source of Turnus's violence is this insult to his manhood. Vergil puts into the mouth of Turnus a reference to the Trojan War, as he compares his fate with that of Menelaus whose wife, Helen, was stolen by Paris:

> I have my fate as well, to combat theirs,
> To cut this criminal people down, my bride
> Being stolen. Pain over such a loss is not
> For the Atridae only, nor may only
> Mycenae justly have recourse to arms.
>                         (Book IX, ll. 190–5)

Vergil, however, reads back into Aeneas a conception of patriarchal manhood much more demanding than that of the Homeric epics. In the *Iliad*, for example, Homer offers two richly characterized, absorbing heroes, both of whom instantiate heroic virtues, but of quite contrasting kinds – Achilles and Hector. Achilles is a passionate individualist and acutely sensitive to insults to his honor, a sense of honor that for his lover Patroclus is "[c]ursed courage," an oxymoron that makes him terrible to behold in and because of his excellence.[14] Achilles thus revolts against the authority of Agamemnon. When his booty in war (Briseis) is brusquely taken from him by Agamemnon, Achilles sulks in his tent, depriving

the Greeks of their best fighter, until his beloved Patroclus is killed by
Hector, provoking Achilles to return to the battle. Hector, in contrast,
is a highly responsible family man, critical of Paris's affair with Helen,
but nonetheless willing to undertake his duties of defending Troy as his
father, Priam, and other leaders of Troy collectively decide. Both men are
portrayed as remarkable heroes, courageous and brilliant in war.

That Achilles kills Hector in battle does not, in the Homeric scheme
of things, make Achilles the better man. Each man has his heroic virtues,
and the fortunes of war are such that each man will die in battle. In
the moving scene at the end of the epic, where Priam persuades Achilles
to return the body of his son for appropriate burial, Priam and Achilles
acknowledge a common sense of the tragic losses they share – Achilles,
the loss of his lover Patroclus, and Priam of his son Hector, reminding
Achilles of the loss his own father will experience when he learns of the
death of his son, when it occurs, as it shortly will.[15] What makes this scene
so deeply moving is its poignant sense of the human need of the war hero,
Achilles, for the tender care of a good father, represented by Priam, who
is more of a father to Achilles than the patriarchally narcissistic leader of
the Greeks, Agamemnon, ever was.[16]

Vergil does not embrace the Homeric conception of a range of heroic
alternatives because that would make room for the more individualistic
virtues of the Roman leaders of the republic, whose competition for power
was essential to the imperialistic successes of Rome. Whereas under the
republic, such Roman leaders could in the Senate collegially define the
terms of Roman religion, Augustus had now concentrated such power
in himself as emperor. Rome no longer afforded space for competing
conceptions of authority and leadership. For this reason, there is only one
conception of manhood in the *Aeneid*, namely, that of Aeneas, expressed
in the patriarchal image of Aeneas leading his family from the burning
shell of defeated Troy, bearing the weight of his father on his shoulders,
holding his son by the hand, his wife walking behind:

> "When I had said this, over my breadth of shoulder
> And bent neck, I spread out a lion skin
> For tawny cloak and stopped to take his weight.
> Then little Iulus put his hand in mine
> And came with shorter steps beside his father.
> My wife fell in behind."
>                         (Book II, ll. 936–42)

The piety of Aeneas, his salient virtue, is his sense of duty to his
father and ancestors, as well as his duty to the men who will follow
him, including Augustus. We described in Chapter 2 the Roman ritual

of death whereby mourners wore masks of the dead man's ancestors. Aeneas's piety gives expression to the psychology such rituals forged and sustained. Vergil, in effect, reads into Aeneas the patriarchal psychology Augustus was now requiring of the Roman people, namely, obedience to him as the semidivine representative of the gods on earth.

In Books VII–XII, Aeneas is contrasted with Turnus in ways that may have been modeled by Vergil on Hector and Achilles in the *Iliad*. But Aeneas is the only person of heroic virtue. Turnus, who refuses to obey what his king requires, is portrayed not only as a man of no virtue but also as mad, his consciousness distorted by a rage traced in the epic to Juno. Vergil's support for the new kind of religion and politics that Augustus forged leads him thus to make only Aeneas (who represents Augustus) the person of virtue, and to dismiss, in the form of Turnus, the more individualistic men who had flourished under the republic.

It is clear, then, why Augustus would have been absorbed by the *Aeneid*. Vergil's epic explained and justified what Augustus had done and was doing in politics by tracing his more rigid patriarchy to earlier Roman history. The new Roman man – no longer a republican citizen – was a subject of the emperor, who enjoyed absolute power over religion and politics.

There was, however, another strand to the narrative and poetry that Vergil invented in the *Aeneid,* also appreciative of Augustus's achievement but sensitive to its psychological costs. In *Darkness Visible*,[17] W. R. Johnson points out the artistic innovations of Vergil's poetry, and we have learned from his analysis, as well as from Marilyn Skinner's exegesis of the love story in "The Last Encounter of Dido and Aeneas."[18]

Books 1, IV, and VI, the parts of the *Aeneid* Vergil read to Augustus, tell of the tragic love of Dido and Aeneas. As I and IV take us into Dido's passion, we feel with her the shock of Aeneas's abrupt departure from Carthage. It is in Book VI, the underworld scene, that Aeneas reveals his love and feels his grief at the consequences of his leaving, thus overcoming, momentarily, his dissociation from his own feelings. In Books VII–XII, we see the consequences of the armored manhood that has turned a pious man and sensitive lover into one subject to homicidal furies against those who threaten his honor. The love story, which may have moved Augustus as it does us, is crucial to understanding the violence that follows. To see this trajectory and the magnitude of Vergil's accomplishment, we follow the unfolding of the love and the violence.

Vergil places Aeneas's meeting with Dido very near the beginning of the *Aeneid*. Their introduction is prefaced by three narratives about the gods. First, there is the intervention of "[b]aleful Juno in her sleepless rage" (Book I, l. 8), who is responsible for the storm that drives Aeneas

off course to Carthage. Second, there is a colloquy between Jupiter and
Venus, the mother of Aeneas, in which Jupiter assures Venus of her son's
destiny as the founder of Rome and its future glories:

> "For these I set no limits, world or time,
> But make the gift of empire without end."
> (Book I, ll. 374–5)

And finally, Venus, appearing to her son as a girl, tells him where he is
and relates the past history of Dido, urging him to meet her.

Dido had fled from Tyre after her brother killed her husband
Sychaeus. Having taken a vow to remain a widow, she founds and builds
Carthage, which she rules as its queen. As Venus departs, Aeneas recog-
nizes her as his mother and laments her emotional distance from him:

> "... You! Cruel, too!
> Why tease your son so often with disguises?
> Why may we not join hands and speak and hear
> The simple truth."
> (Book I, ll. 558–61)

Swathed in a cloud that conceals him, Aeneas inspects the great buildings in Dido's recently constructed city, including "a great temple planned
in Juno's honor" (Book I, l. 606). He is moved by depictions of the Trojan
War. Still covered, he watches as his followers introduce the Trojans to
Dido and she welcomes them, offering shelter and support and extending
an invitation "[t]o join us in this realm on equal terms" (Book I, l. 777).
When Aeneas reveals himself, Dido

> Stood in astonishment, first at the sight
> Of such a captain, then at his misfortune....
> (Book I, ll. 837–8)

She identifies his suffering with her own. saying:

> "... My life
> Was one of hardship and forced wandering
> Like your own, till in this land at length
> Fortune would have me rest. Through pain I've learned
> To comfort suffering men."
> (Book I, ll. 857–61)

Vergil's poetry, through the vehicle of the gods, now takes us into
Dido's subjectivity, her experience of a growing love for Aeneas. Her
sexual passion is portrayed in terms of Venus's strategy to keep Dido on
her side "by profound {l}ove of Aeneas" (Book I, ll. 924–5), thus saving
her son from the "Tyrians' double dealing" (Book I, l. 903). The vehicle

is her son Cupid, "Amor, god of caressing wings" (Book I, l. 906), who, having taken on the form of Ascanius, Aeneas's young son, is instructed by his mother:

> "So that when Dido takes you on her lap
> Amid the banqueting and wine, in joy,
> When she embraces you and kisses you,
> You'll breathe invisible fire into her
> And dupe her with your sorcery."
>                                        (Book I, ll. 936–40)

For her part,

> . . . the Phoenician queen,
> Luckless, already given over to ruin,
> Marveled and could not have enough [of Cupid, as Ascanius]. . .
> And she with all her eyes and heart embraced him,
> Fondling him at times upon her breast.
> He had begun to make Sychaeus fade
> From Dido's memory bit by bit, and tried
> To waken with new love, a living love,
> Her long settled mind and dormant heart.
>                                        (Book I, ll. 971–85)

After Aeneas tells Dido at length about the sad story of his life until now (Books II–III), Vergil again shifts the scene to Dido's psyche:

> The queen, for her part, all that evening ached
> With longing that her heart's blood fed, a wound
> Or inward fire eating her away.
> The manhood of the man, his pride of birth,
> Came home to her time and again; his looks,
> His words remained with her to haunt her mind,
> And desire for him gave her no rest.
>                                        (Book IV, ll. 1–7)

Troubled by her desires, Dido turns for advice to her sister Anna, who urges her to act upon them, not only for her own good as a woman but also to ensure an alliance with Aeneas, which could only make the city more powerful:

> "What a great city you'll see rising here
> And what a kingdom, from this royal match!"
>                                        (Book IV, ll. 67–8)

Overcoming her scruples, Dido now sacrifices to Juno, "[w]ho has the bonds of marriage in her keeping" (Book IV, l. 83), but Vergil queries,

> What good are shrines and vows to maddened lovers?
> The inward fire eats the soft marrow away,
> And the internal wound bleeds on in silence.

Then,

> Unlucky Dido, burning in her madness
> Roamed through all the city, like a doe
> Hit by an arrow, shot from far away
> By a shepherd hunting in the Cretan woods –
> Hit by surprise, nor could the hunter see
> His flying steel had fixed itself in her;
> But though she runs for life through copse and glade
> The fatal shaft clings to her side.
> (Book IV, ll. 92–102)

At this point, Vergil introduces Juno herself into the narrative. She tells Venus that there is no reason now for continuing contention between them. Venus had been the supporter of the Trojans, Juno of the Greeks, after the Trojan prince Paris had chosen Venus over her. Juno proposes:

> "...Why do we not
> Arrange eternal peace and formal marriage?
> You have your heart's desire: Dido in love,
> Dido consumed with passion to her core.
> Why not, then, rule this people side by side
> With equal authority!"
> (Book IV, ll. 141–6)

To cement this alliance, Juno arranges a storm, causing Aeneas and Dido to seek shelter in a cave where they become lovers. Their relationship now, Venus and Juno agree, is a marriage. Two voices enter the narrative at this point: the combined voice of Juno and Dido, who "thought no longer of a secret love/But called it marriage" (Book IV, ll. 236–7), and a patriarchal voice characterizing Dido's conduct as her "fault" (Book IV, l. 238).

Venus's agreement is an insincere strategy because as patriarchal mother, she is invested only in her son and his mission, not in his co-ruling Carthage with a woman. At this point, the honor codes of patriarchal manhood enter the poem with a vengeance, as Iarbus, Dido's rejected suitor and enemy, appeals to Jupiter in terms reminiscent of the gendered insults directed by Octavian against Antony:

> "After refusing to marry me [Dido] has taken
> Aeneas to be master in her realm.
> And now Sir Paris with his men, half-men,
> His chin and perfumed hair tied up
> In a Maeonian bonnet, take possession."
>                              (Book IV, ll. 286-2–93)

Jupiter's response is to send Mercury to remind Aeneas of his duty, and the point is put to Aeneas in terms of the insult to his manhood he would suffer should he remain with Dido in Carthage, dishonoring not only himself but his son:

> "... Is it for you
> To lay the stones for Carthage's high walls
> Tame husband that you are, and build their city?
> Oblivious of your own world, your own kingdom....
> If future history's glories
> Do not affect you, if you will not strive
> For your own honor, think of Ascanius
> Think of the expectations of your heir,
> Iulus, to whom the Italian realm, the land
> Of Rome, are due."
>                              (Book IV, ll. 361–76)

Aeneas is traumatized, and we witness his dissociation:

> Amazed, and shocked to the bottom of his soul
> By what his eyes had seen, Aeneas felt
> His hackles rise, his voice choke in his throat.
> As the sharp admonition and command
> From heaven had shaken him awake, he now
> Burned only to be gone, to leave that land
> Of the sweet life behind.
>                              (Book IV, ll. 379–85)

The impact of trauma shows itself in Aeneas, as it usually does, in a loss of voice (struck by a kind of terror, he prepares to flee Carthage without telling Dido) and a loss of memory (of Dido and what she had meant to him).

The effect on Dido is devastating. Learning of Aeneas's plans, she is

> ... Furious, at her wits' end,
> She traversed the whole city, all aflame
> With rage, like a Bacchante driven wild

By emblems shaken, when the mountain revels
Of the odd year possess her, then the cry
Of Bacchus rises and Cithaeron calls
All through the shouting night.
(Book IV, ll. 409–15)

She confronts Aeneas, charging him:

"You even hoped to keep me in the dark
As to this outrage, did you, two-faced man,
And slip away in silence? Can our love
Not hold, can the pledge we gave not hold you,
Can Dido not, now sure to die in pain. . . . Oh heartless! . . .
. . . I beg you,
By these tears . . .
Yes, by the marriage that we entered on,
If ever I did well and you were grateful
Or found some sweetness in a gift from me,
Have pity now on a declining house! . . . To whom
Do you abandon me, a dying woman,
Guest that you are. . . . If at least
There were a child by you for me to care for,
A little one to play in courtyard
And give me back Aeneas, in spite of all,
I should not feel so utterly defeated,
Utterly bereft."
(Book IV, ll. 417–54)

Yet he steels himself against her pleas, defending himself as the agent
of the gods and denying that he had ever entered into a marriage. Thus
Aeneas,

. . . by Jove's command held fast his eyes
And fought down the emotion in his heart.
At length he answered:
"As for myself, be sure
I never shall deny all you can say,
Your majesty, of what you meant to me.
Never will the memory of Elissa
Stale for me, while I can still remember
My own life, and the spirit rules my body.
As to the event, a few words. Do not think
I meant to be deceitful and slip away.
I never held the torches of a bridegroom,
Never entered upon the pact of marriage.
If Fate permitted me to spend my days

By my own lights, and make the best of things
According to my wishes, first of all
I should look after Troy and the loved relics
Left me of my people . . .
But now it is the rich Italian land
Apollo tells me I must make for, Italy,
Named by the oracles. There is my love;
There is my country. If, as a Phoenician,
You are so given to the charms of Carthage,
Libyan city that it is, then tell me,
Why begrudge Teucrians new lands. . . . Are we not
Entitled, too, to look for realms abroad? . . . So please no more
Of these appeals that set us both afire.
I sail for Italy not of my own free will."

(Book IV, ll. 456–499)

Dido questions the justice of the gods who require such things of a lover
and furiously promises vengeance:

"The time is past when either supreme Juno
Or the Saturnian father viewed these things
With justice. Faith can never be secure.
I took this man in, and in my madness then
Contrived a place for him in my domain,
Rescued his lost fleet, saved his shipmates' lives.
Oh, I am swept away burning by furies! . . .
If divine justice counts for anything,
I hope and pray you on some grinding reef
Midway at sea you'll drink your punishment
And call and call on Dido's name!
From far away I shall come after you
With my black fires, and when cold death has parted
Body from soul I shall be everywhere
A shade to haunt you! You will pay for this
Unconscionable! I shall hear! The news will reach me
Even among the lowest of the dead!"

(Book IV, ll. 512–38)

But her threats are to no avail.

When Aeneas leaves, Vergil takes us into Dido's despair, her desolation
and finally her madness, leading her to kill herself:

On Dido in her desolation now
Terror grew at her fate. She prayed for death.
Being heartsick at the mere sight of heaven. . . .
In nightmare, fevered, she was hunted down

By pitiless Aeneas, and she seemed
Deserted always, uncompanioned always,
On a long journey, looking for her Tyrians
In desolate landscapes –
As Pentheus gone mad
Sees the oncoming Eumenides, and sees
A double sun and double Thebes appear,
Or as when, hounded on the stage, Orestes
Runs from a mother armed with burning brands,
With serpents hellish black,
And in the doorway squat the Avenging Ones.
                    (Book IV, ll. 622–55)

That Dido turns to violence against herself shows the hold over her psyche
of the insult to her honor as a woman. But her descent into madness also
reflects the disruption in her sense of reality when she can make no sense
of Aeneas's actions, seeing him now as a "pitiless" man, as if the love
affair itself had been a hallucination.

Vergil does not at this point in the narrative take us into the psyche of
Aeneas. We witness his loss of voice and memory. We know that Jupiter
himself (the highest patriarchal god) had commanded his suppression
of emotion. We hear Aeneas's speech to Dido denying that they were
married, as Juno, the goddess of marriage, herself had claimed. We hear
him speak of what Dido meant to him, but in light of his actions, his
words have no emotional resonance.

It is, therefore, a revelation when in Book VI, descending into the
underworld to speak with his father, Aeneas comes upon the ghost of
Dido, at first wondering if he is hallucinating but then weeping and speaking tenderly to her:

"Dido, so forlorn,
The story then that came to me was true,
That you were out of life, had met your end
By your own hand. Was I, was I the cause?
I swear by heaven's stars, by the high gods,
By any certainty below the earth,
I left your land against my will, my queen.
The gods' commands drove me to do their will,

As now they drive me through this world of shades,
These mouldy waste lands and then depths of night.
And I could not believe that I would hurt you
So terribly by going. Wait a little.
Do not leave my sight.
Am I someone to flee from? The last word

Destiny let me say to you is this."
Aeneas with such pleas tried to placate
The burning soul, savagely glaring back,
And tears came to his eyes. But she had turned
With gaze fixed on the ground as he spoke on,
Her face no more affected than if she were
Immobile granite or Marpesian stone.
At length she flung away from him and fled,
His enemy still, into the shadowy grove
Where he whose bride she once had been, Sychaeus,
Joined in her sorrows and returned her love.
Aeneas still gazed after her in tears,
Shaken by her ill fate and pitying her.
                                    (Book VI, ll. 575–639)

What we see, as if in dim moonlight (Vergil's image), is Aeneas's tender love for Dido, precisely what we have never seen before in the poem, certainly not in Book IV.

In her brilliant study of this scene, Marilyn Skinner[19] shows how its poetry symmetrically reverses the roles of Dido and Aeneas in Book IV: Whereas in Book IV we see and feel Dido's love and Aeneas's loss of voice and memory, in the underworld scene of Book VI, we see and feel Aeneas's love and Dido's loss of voice and memory. For Romans of Vergil's time and after, Dido's implicit rage would offer a way of understanding the enmity of Carthage for Rome, an enmity manifest in the three Punic Wars, in one of which Carthage came very close to defeating Rome. But the adverb "savagely," used here to describe Dido's glaring, will be applied at the end of the epic to Aeneas. Love has turned to savagery, as Dido is forsaken and Aeneas's "once kindly ears" have been "blocked by God's will" (Book IV, l. 609).

The pathos of Aeneas's devotion to his patriarchal duty is starkly evident when the ghost of his father eludes him. Anchises, whose ambitions for his son so weighted him down, remains untouched by his son:

. . . tears brimmed over
And down his cheeks. And here he tried three times
To throw his arms around his father's neck,
Three times the shade untouched slipped through his hands,
Weightless as wind and fugitive as a dream.
                                    (Book VI, ll. 938–42)[20]

The impact of patriarchy on men has already been powerfully displayed in the poem, as Mercury, carrying the patriarchal injunction of Jupiter, separates Aeneas from Dido by insulting his manhood. In response,

Aeneas literally closes down and silently ruptures his relationship with
Dido. Yet now, after showing us Aeneas's love for Dido, Vergil renders the patriarch, the father, as "[w]eightless as wind and fugitive as a
dream."

We know that relationships of fathers and sons under Roman patriarchy were tense and often hostile. Vergil's poetry underscores how far
the psychology of dominance and submission is from loving relationship
based on mutual touch. As Aeneas reaches for such love, it slips through
his hands.

Books I, IV, and VI thus give us an acutely observed and articulated account of the way in which patriarchy disrupts intimate relationships when they threaten its demands and how such disruption trauma-
tizes not only love but the capacities for reading and responding to the
human world, central to our ethical intelligence. What renders the relationship of Dido and Aeneas so threatening to the patriarchal order of
things is precisely what threatened Romans in the egalitarian relationship of Antony and Cleopatra: equality between a man and a woman in
love, which Vergil's portrayal of Dido (the African Semitic queen) and
Aeneas (a Trojan military leader, soon to be founder of Rome) clearly
echoes.

Vergil, of course, carefully follows the patriarchal party line on Antony
and Cleopatra (whose name he cannot bring himself even to mention)
when, in Book VIII, he describes the depiction on the shield that Venus
had secured from Vulcan for her son of the events at Actium:

> Then came Antonius with barbaric wealth
> And a diversity of arms, victorious
> From races of the Dawnlands and Red Sea,
> Leading the power of the East, of Egypt, . . .
> And in his wake the Egyptian consort came
> So shamefully. . . . The queen
> Amidst the battle called her flotilla on
> With a sistrum's beat, a frenzy out of Egypt,
> Never turning her head as yet to see
> Twin snakes of death behind, while monster forms
> Of gods of every race, and the dog-god
> Anubis barking, held their weapons up
> Against our Neptune, Venus, and Minerva.
> Mars, engraved in steel, raged in the fight
> As from high air the dire Furies came
> With Discord, taking joy in a torn robe,
> And on her heels, with bloody scourge, Bellona.
> (Book VIII, ll. 926–52)

The portrait of Dido and Aeneas lies alongside such bromides and pieties, revealing the darker side of patriarchy. There was, Vergil suggests, an alternative to a Roman rule based on imperialistic war, namely, an egalitarian relationship between men and women in a commercial state like Carthage. But threatened by such an alternative, patriarchy must destroy it, first in love and later in war.

Vergil thus gives us a powerful rendering of the underpinnings of Roman violence. Patriarchy, as we suggested in Chapter 1, traumatically breaks personal relationships, and the Dido-Aeneas episode illustrates how it works, in this case, in the consciousness and actions of a Roman hero. But the trauma that deadens ethical intelligence in personal life does so in public life as well, making psychologically possible the construction or projection of an imagined enemy, a threat to one's honor, an insult that mandates violence.

Carthage was, for the Romans, such an enemy, and it is significant that Vergil associates the Roman need for an enemy with a woman, Dido, who seeks equality in love and rule and who questions the moral authority of the patriarchal gods. Once the love between Aeneas and Dido is construed as an insult to his honor and a forfeiture of his mission, he abruptly leaves her and sets out, through war, to prove his manhood. With the carefully trained eye of the naturalistic observer, Vergil shows us the loss of voice that follows trauma and more specifically, the covering over of resisting voice that otherwise might challenge the patriarchal authority.

The psychological brilliance of the Dido-Aeneas episode lies in the way it portrays the effects of trauma on the consciousness of an otherwise good man: namely, his loss of voice and memory. The insult to Aeneas's manhood elicits a violence that will ultimately render this loving and pious man savage. In Dido, the corresponding insult to her womanhood elicits violence against herself and a call for continuing hatred of her people against the Romans – for a leader (Hannibal) who would wreak vengeance on them: "rise up from my bones, avenging spirit!" (Book IV, l. 869). Vergil also depicts the psychology underlying what we have called "moral slavery," the abjection of people deprived of any voice to challenge their subjection. Aeneas's loss of voice makes the point. A man thus unable to feel, let alone act on his love is capable of anything. It is the power of a personal and political psychology that, in service to patriarchal ambitions, can suppress ethical voice and intelligence when honor is at stake.

Books VII–XII then show us this psychology at work in public life, not only in Aeneas but in his enemies, notably Turnus. We have already described how Turnus, in contrast to Aeneas, refuses the patriarchal demands of his king that he break his engagement to the king's daughter,

Lavinia, so that she can marry Aeneas. For Turnus, this is an insult to his manhood, and Aeneas's marrying Lavinia is an equivalent basis for war. Vergil conveys the power of this psychology through Juno's rage as she aroused one of the Furies, "Allecto/Grief's drear mistress, with her lust for war" (Book VII, ll. 444–5), who entered first the psyche of Amata, wife of King Latinus, "and breathed/Viper's breath in her" (Book VII, ll. 483–4), and then the soul of Turnus:

> Enormous terror woke him, a cold sweat
> Broke out all over him and soaked his body.
> Then driven wild, shouting for arms, for arms
> He ransacked house and chamber. Lust of steel
> Raged in him, brute insanity of war,
> And wrath above all....
>                         (Book VII, ll. 631–636)

All the succeeding events, in which Turnus incites others to violence against Aeneas and leads them against him, are rooted in this psychology:

> ...high rage and mindless
> Lust for slaughter drove the passionate man
> Against his enemies.
>                         (Book IX, ll. 1054–6)

Meanwhile, Lavinia – the object of contestation between Turnus and Aeneas – remains just that, an object. She says not a word through the poem, appearing beside her mother, "the cause/Of so much suffering, lovely eyes downcast" (Book XI, ll. 652–3). Later, after listening to her mother, Amata, railing to Turnus that Lavinia must never marry Aeneas, she

> ...streamed
> With tears on burning cheeks; a deepening blush
> Brought out a fiery glow on her hot face...
> Desire stung the young man as he gazed,
> Rapt, at the girl. He burned yet more for battle.
>                         (Book XII, ll. 92–100)

Violence here turns on the honor of women, whose desire is beside the point.

Vergil, however, makes his point about the insensate character of violence not only in terms of Turnus, who challenges, after all, the kind of patriarchal obedience that Aeneas exemplifies, but in terms of Aeneas himself. Upon hearing of the death of Pallas, the son of his ally Evander, at the hands of Turnus, Aeneas makes his way to Turnus and takes no prisoners en route. Some of his victims plead with him:

> "I pray you by your father's ghost and by
> Your hope of Iulus' rising power, preserve
> A life here, for a father and a son."
> (Book X, ll. 735–7)

This person even offers Aeneas money in return for sparing him, but Aeneas wants blood and slays him along with others, even tormenting one after killing him:

> Speaking above him from his pitiless heart:
> "Lie there now, fearsome as you are. No gentle
> Will ever hide you in the earth
> Or weight your body with a family tomb.
> Either you stay here for the carrion birds
> Or the sea takes you under, hungry fishes
> Nibble your wounds."
> (Book X, ll. 782–8)

In the battle with Lausus, who is trying to save his father Mezentius from Aeneas's onslaught, Aeneas's anger "boiled up higher" (Book X, l. 1140), but upon killing him,

> . . . seeing the look
> On the young man's face in death, a face so pale
> As to be awesome, then Anchises' son
> Groaned in profound pity. He held out
> His hand as filial piety, mirrored here,
> Wrung his own heart, and said:
> "O poor young soldier,
> How will Aeneas reward your splendid fight?
> How honor you, in keeping with your nature?
> Keep the arms you loved to use, for I
> Return you to your forebears, ash and shades,
> If this concerns you now. Unlucky boy,
> One consolation for said death is this:
> You die by the sword-thrust of Aeneas."
> (Book X, ll. 1148–61)

Even in his state of pitiless rage, Aeneas can still appreciate the honor of Lausus, a son defending his father, not backing down from a challenge and unafraid of confronting someone he knows to be a great warrior. Yet in the very last scene of Book XII, we see Aeneas again out of control. For all his faults, Turnus is a brave man who does not shy away from battle. He has been defeated and is at Aeneas's mercy, but when Aeneas sees Turnus wearing the strap Pallas wore when Turnus killed him, he "blaz[es] up,"

> And terrible in his anger, he called out:
> "You in your plunder, torn from one of mine,
> Shall I be robbed of you? This wound will come
> From Pallas: Pallas makes this offering
> And from your criminal blood exacts his due."
> He sank his blade in fury in Turnus' chest.
> Then all the body slackened in death's chill,
> And with a groan for that indignity
> His spirit fled into the gloom below.
>                     (Book XII, ll. 1290–8)

In the final lines of his unfinished epic, Vergil thus shows us Aeneas, the best of patriarchal men, so in the grip of fury that he acts not like an honorable soldier but like a savage: "pius Aeneas" has become "saevus Aeneas."[21] To this extent, even in terms of the Roman ideal of a good soldier (able to control his impulses when they prove inappropriate), Aeneas is a less-good soldier, subject to a psychology that blocks his humanity.

How and why was Vergil able to go so deeply into the personal and political psychology of patriarchy? Why did he forge a new kind of narrative and poetry to convey what he saw? Clearly, he was a sensitive observer of men and women, including Augustus himself. We suggest that his insights may have been sharpened by two features of his life and thought that placed him quite outside the normal demands of patriarchy: first, the nature of his own sexuality and life, and second, his philosophical commitment to Epicureanism.

Suetonius tells us that Vergil

> was especially given to passion for boys, and his special favourites were Cebes and Alexander, whom he calls Alexis in the second poem of his 'Bucolics.' This boy was given him by Asinius Pollio, and both his favourites had some education.... Certain it is that for the rest of his life he was so modest in speech and thought, that at Naples he was commonly called 'Parthenias' ['The Maiden'].[22]

Scholars have come to regard Vergil as what we would now call a gay man.[23] He appears to have been exclusively pederastic/homoerotic in his practices. Many, perhaps most, Roman elite men both married women and penetrated boys. Vergil resisted the patriarchal demands to marry and have children and does not appear to have had sex with women. If we take Suetonius's word about the *Second Eclogue*, namely, that its depiction of Corydon's passion for Alexis is autobiographical, it suggests some unhappiness in Vergil's love life (Alexis rejects Corydon). One of the benefits of owning slaves was their availability for sex, and homoeroticism flourished in classical Rome, but "real men" played only the active role and did so with slave boys.

Further, Vergil, as an Epicurean, would philosophically not have expected much from sex, which the philosophy regarded as a distraction from the deeper pleasures of friendship and conversation in the garden. For this reason, Vergil may have been particularly sensitive to the problem of love under Roman patriarchy, both because he was a Roman man – albeit an unusual one – and thus experienced the difficulties all Roman men did in this domain and because as a man who loved men, he was sensitive to the problem of loving men under patriarchy, a problem and perspective he shared with Roman women.

This can explain what is most astonishing about the *Aeneid:* Vergil's empathy for Dido, her love and her plight. We suspect that Vergil may have originally intended to write about Dido, consistent with her stance of resistance to patriarchal demands on women, in the same way he treats Cleopatra later on, namely, as an unnatural monster. But like Leo Tolstoy as he wrote *Anna Karenina*,[24] Vergil seems to have fallen in love with Dido and perhaps saw her as himself, often in love with men whom patriarchy has rendered incapable of sustaining love. Vergil stands, in this respect, in the tradition of subsequent gay writers such as Tennessee Williams who create sexually complex, passionate, highly intelligent, and powerful women (like Blanche DuBois in *A Streetcar Named Desire*), finding perhaps in the plight of such women under patriarchy their own plight as gay men. Vergil's status as a Roman man but an outsider to Roman patriarchal manhood may have rendered him acutely sensitive to the subjectivity of a woman like Dido and given him insight into the dissociated psychology of violent men who live out the patriarchal demands of their culture: good men, like Aeneas, turned, through trauma, into savages.

Vergil's friends in Naples, where he largely lived, included the Epicurean philosopher Siro, with whom the poet studied.[25] The impact of the Epicurean philosopher Lucretius is obvious in his most personal work, the *Georgics*. After finishing the *Aeneid*, he intended "to give up the rest of his life wholly to philosophy."[26] But there is a puzzle about why a serious devotee of Epicureanism would be interested in or absorbed by a project such as the *Aeneid*, an epic poem about Roman politics in which Epicurean philosophy, which called for stripping oneself of the illusions of public life and withdrawing into the garden, took little interest. Vergil's treatment of love as dangerous and distracting is certainly the position Epicurean philosophy would take, but why the interest in a public man like Aeneas and, in the background, Augustus?

We find an integral connection between Vergil's philosophy and what absorbed him in the *Aeneid*, a connection that clarifies the role the gods play in his epic narrative. There is nothing in the *Aeneid* really comparable to the minute-by-minute intervention of the gods in human affairs in the *Iliad* and *Odyssey*, where human actors often appear as chess pieces moved by them. Why the difference?

Epicurean philosophy was attractive in the ancient world precisely because it did not skeptically challenge the existence of the gods. Democritus, an early Epicurean (born about 460 B.C.E.), questioned the common assumption of philosophical deism and atheism that ordinary religious beliefs are nonsensical. The most important piece of evidence about his views, brought to our attention and analyzed for us by Donald Levy (a philosopher of psychoanalysis and its history),[27] is the following ambiguous passage, in which much depends upon the meaning given to its key term *eidola*, which can be translated as *shapes, images, specters, phantoms*:

> Democritus says that certain *eidola* approach men, and that of these some are beneficent, some maleficent – that is why he even prayed (*eucheto*) to attain felicitous *eidola*. These are great, indeed enormous, and hard to destroy though not indestructible; and they signify the future to men, being seen and uttering sounds. Hence the ancients, getting a presentation of these very things, supposed that there was a god, there being no other god apart from these having an indestructible nature.[28]

Is this an atheistic reductive analysis of the gods as figments, or is it an attempt to rationalize some version of religious belief? Are the eidola merely dream images, genuine divinities, or something else? Some philosophers opt for a view of Democritus as an atheist, assuming the eidola to be dream images.[29] But nothing indicates that we are always asleep when the eidola "approach"; indeed, the Roman poet Lucretius (99–55 B.C.E.), drawing upon Democritus, asserts that "men had visions when their minds were awake" as well as "more clearly in sleep."[30]

It would only make sense for Democritus to pray to these visions if they do not just happen to be true about the future but have some causal relation to the future as well. We can certainly imagine indestructible things in dreams, but Democritus refuses to say that any eidola are completely indestructible. It seems likely that Democritus meant to say that although the eidola may never cease to exist, their power can be reduced, even if only for a time; the eidola constantly approach humans and can be prevented, if at all, only briefly and with great effort. This might reasonably be compared with psychoanalytic complexes, or even

Jungian archetypes. These, too, are very powerful and can be deprived of their power only with great difficulty. On this view, Democritus denied that the admittedly projective character of ordinary belief in the gods makes them irrational. Ordinary ideas of the gods may not be accurate, but they are not irrational and never were: they have always originated in the approach to humans of eidola, which they represent, however inaccurately. Although humans may err in various ways in their ordinary beliefs about the gods – for example, in thinking them indestructible when they are really only hard to destroy – there is nothing irrational in this, since the eidola really exist, are hard to destroy (in Freud's sense), and are the closest things to gods as ordinarily conceived.

This reading of Epicurean philosophy on the gods casts light on the role that the gods play in the *Aeneid*. Vergil, as an Epicurean, was interested in the causes of things, as the *Georgics* makes clear. But the *Georgics*, ostensibly about farming, is in fact about the disruption of farming by Roman politics and its wars, including civil wars. The subject matter of the *Aeneid* is, as we have now seen, the actions and motivations of men and women under patriarchy, focusing on the interconnected problems of love and violence. Vergil brings the eye and ear of a perceptive and sensitive naturalistic psychologist to this subject matter and, as a creative artist, invents a narrative method that renders visible a psychological darkness.

The gods in the *Aeneid*, in contrast to the *Iliad* and *Odyssey*, do not play an active role themselves and are as much subject to fate as the human beings they observe. There is, however, one notable exception, namely, Juno, whose rage begins the poem and pervades the narrative to its violent end. Our reading of Democritus suggests that Juno plays the role she does as an image, an *eidolon*, of a deep psychological pattern, enormously powerful and resistant to change. In displaying the psychological phenomena of trauma and dissociation that have only relatively recently been identified and studied by psychologists, Vergil takes the approach of a naturalist, describing what he observes. He invented a poetry and a narrative art to convey the loss of voice and memory, and Juno plays the role she does in the poem as a way of revealing the persistence of a psychology, keyed to gender, that Vergil locates at the foundation of Rome.

Whereas the gods in the *Iliad* and *Odyssey* are closely matched with the opposing sides in the Trojan War, Juno in the *Aeneid* is a force on both sides and sometimes moves, surprisingly, between them. This is particularly striking in the Dido-Aeneas episode. Venus, as we have seen, is always closely allied with her son and only strategically commands Cupid to elicit Dido's sexual passion for Aeneas. Juno, the goddess of marriage, allies herself with Venus at this point because she comes to see the marriage of Dido and Aeneas as a way of bringing the tragedy of Troy to a fitting resolution: a marriage between equals as co-rulers of Carthage, a commercial state. Venus shows no interest in what happens to Dido; as a patriarchal mother, she is only invested in her son and his patriarchal destiny. Juno, on the other hand, stands in a more critical relationship to patriarchy *and* in particular to the way it destroys the only genuine love between a man and woman in the epic, imposing instead an arranged marriage between Aeneas and Lavinia, who barely know one another.

Vergil's interest in Juno's rage, as both an artistic symbol and a psychological explanation, was prefigured by the place of angry women in Greek tragedy, most notably, the Furies in Aeschylus's *Oresteia*. The Furies emerge after Orestes kills his mother Clytemnestra, after she killed her husband Agamemnon, who had earlier sacrificed their daughter Iphigenia in order to secure favorable winds for the Greek troops to be carried to Troy. After the trial of Orestes in Athens at the end of the trilogy, Orestes is acquitted by the deciding vote of the goddess Athena, on the basis of the explicitly patriarchal view that the killing of a father and a king is much worse than the killing of a mother. The Furies are persuaded to become the Eumenides (the Kindly Ones). The *Oresteia* thus justifies the founding of Athenian democracy in terms of the suppression of the resisting voices of its women, who were to live in subjection to men.

Vergil's treatment of Juno is quite different. She is portrayed as the sponsor of the egalitarian love of Dido and Aeneas, a love Juno calls a marriage. Her anger arises from the traumatic disruption of such sexual love, and it is she in Books VII–XII who commands various subdivinities (Allecto, Iris, Jugurtha) to fill the psyches of Turnus, Amata, and others with aggressive violence against the Trojans. The rage she expresses also consumes Aeneas as he turns to savage violence at the end of the *Aeneid*. Vergil conveys her stance in a passage Sigmund Freud will use (in a variant translation) as his epigraph to *The Interpretations of Dreams*:

> "... If I can sway
> No heavenly hearts I'll rouse the world below."
> (Book VII, ll. 425–6)

Patriarchal religion rules all the gods of the *Aeneid*, except for Juno, who is the one resisting voice. The suppression of her voice is necessary for the powerful role played by patriarchy in Roman personal and political psychology, and it is the trauma of such suppression that marks the Roman propensity to illimitable violence. Accordingly, Juno dominates the entire narrative of the *Aeneid* because, consistent with its author's Epicurean naturalism, she expresses what Vergil came to see as the psychology underlying Roman patriarchy. It is to Juno that Dido appeals in her final call for vengeance, predicting her avenger, Hannibal. The classics scholar Judith Hallett sees the anger of noble women in the *Aeneid* (Juno, Dido, and others) as capturing a voice that Vergil picked up from Roman women, both in his period and the past, including possibly Cornelia's furious letter to her son Gaius Gracchus pleading with him not to run for tribune (Gaius becomes tribune and is, like his brother, Tiberius, assassinated in that role).[31]

On close examination, the *Aeneid* offers not only a celebration of Augustus's triumph but also a piercing revelation of the psychological costs Romans endured to make this triumph possible. Why were Augustus and others so absorbed by it? We offer two speculations. First, the very truth of what Vergil tells us may have moved Romans, including Augustus, as great tragic art does. And second, the *Aeneid* is a narrative about a hero, in particular a Roman hero, who is quite different from the Greek heroes of the *Iliad* and *Odyssey*, and even different from the individualistic Roman heroes of the late republic. It is very much part of the heroic story Vergil tells that men, heroic men like Aeneas, pay a terrible psychological price for the good they do others. From this perspective (the perspective, surely, of Augustus himself), the truthful story Vergil tells would only advance the overall power of the heroic depiction by making clear the kinds of burdens and sacrifices embraced by Augustan Roman heroes.

Augustus was, in fact, quite different from Aeneas in two respects: He was not a military man of any stature,[32] and in his marriage to Livia, whom he loved, he took her advice both on private and public matters very seriously.[33] So Augustus may have been much more absorbed by the public triumphalism of the *Aeneid*, in which he is depicted as its culmination, than by its private horrors, which may not have touched his personal experience as they may have touched the lives of many others.

It does not follow, however, that Vergil himself took this view. We know he wanted the manuscript destroyed, and we doubt that this was just because some parts of it had not been subject to final revision. Our interpretation is that as Vergil struggled more deeply with the creative problem he set himself, he found himself in crisis over what he had discovered, namely, that the problem of love and violence under patriarchy had no end and that Augustus, in particular, had, if anything, exacerbated the problem. Certainly, Juno's willingness at the end of the *Aeneid* to allow Aeneas to triumph over Turnus is less than full-hearted, which suggests that the psychology she exposes remains powerful and active. We note the psychological crises that other creative artists have endured after entering the heart of patriarchal darkness in their work – Tolstoy after writing

*Anna Karenina*,[34] Woolf after *Mrs. Dalloway* and *To the Lighthouse*,[35] and Joseph Conrad after *Heart of Darkness* and *Under Western Eyes*.[36] Vergil was the first artist we know of to map this dark, unspeakable terrain, and he may have regarded what he discovered as an insoluble problem and the poem therefore a failure – its triumphalist ambitions nugatory and self-destructive.

We are told by Suetonius that near his end, "in his mortal illness Vergil constantly called for his book-boxes, intending to burn the poem himself."[37] Was Vergil, who identified with Dido, now reenacting her despair, burning what he must have regarded as most intimately himself, his masterpiece?

# 4  *Apuleius on Conversion*

Gibbon classically observed of the second-century Roman empire:

> If a man were called to fix the period in the history of the world, during which the condition of the human race was most happy and prosperous, he would, without hesitation, name that which elapsed from the death of Domitian to the accession of Commodus. The vast extent of the Roman empire was governed by absolute power, under the guidance of virtue and wisdom. The armies were restrained by the firm but gentle hand of four successive emperors, whose characters and authority commanded involuntary respect. The forms of the civil administration were carefully preserved by Nerva, Trajan, Hadrian, and the Antonines, who delighted in the image of liberty, and were pleased with considering themselves as the accountable ministers of the laws. Such princes deserve the honour of restoring the republic had the Romans of their days been capable of enjoying a rational freedom.[1]

Certainly, not all peoples benefited from the remarkable period of peace Gibbon describes under which "the policy of persecuting Christians first became widespread" and "the Roman provinces were racked with the revolt of the Jews under Trajan and Hadrian."[2] But in contrast to the centuries of imperial misrule and recurrent civil wars over the imperial succession, the period in question was marked by much more responsible government and general peace. The emperors Hadrian and Marcus Aurelius were famously devoted to Greek art and culture, including philosophy, and Marcus Aurelius wrote his Stoic *Meditations* in Greek, not Latin.[3]

Two novels, both deeply learned and sensitive to historical context, deal with this period, Marguerite Yourcenar's *Memoirs of Hadrian*[4] and Walter Pater's *Marius the Epicurean*.[5] Yourcenar frames her story through the eyes of Hadrian himself, a man of passionate curiosity, not only in philosophy and art but in the mystery religions of Greece, Asia, and Egypt.

One of the most traveled of Rome's leaders, Hadrian was a great builder and restorer, anticipating – in Yourcenar's reading of him – a common market and political structure of diverse peoples:

> that the might and majesty of the Roman Peace should extend to all, insensibly present like the music of the revolving skies; that the most humble traveler might wander from one country, and without danger, assured everywhere of a minimum of legal protection and culture; that our soldiers should continue their eternal pyrrhic dance on the frontiers; that everything should go smoothly, whether workshops or temples; that the sea should be furrowed by brave ships, and the roads resounding to frequent carriages; that, in a world well ordered, the philosophers should have their place, and the dancers also.[6]

Yourcenar's Hadrian aspires to a liberal union of peoples:

> "Over separate nations and races, with their accidents of geography and history and the disparate demands of their ancestors or their gods, we should have superposed for ever a unity of human conduct and the empiricism of sober experience, but should have done so without destruction of what had preceded us."

Its guiding norm was: *"Trahit sua quemque voluptas.* Each to his own bent; likewise each to his aim or his ambition, if you will, or his most secret desire and his highest ideal."[7]

The seriousness and sensitivity with which Yourcenar, a lesbian, takes the historical Hadrian's consuming erotic passion for a young man, Antinous, makes her narrative riveting.[8] Hadrian has cultivated an armored Roman self-sufficiency based on detachment and has come even to believe Roman propaganda about the divinity of the emperor and thus his own. Trapped in an idealization of himself and of the beauty of Antinous, he turns abusive toward him, and the desperately alone, contemptuously treated Antinous commits suicide. Hadrian's remorse takes the form of yet another idealization, making Antinous a god and building a city and temples to honor his divinity. Hadrian's love for Antinous, like Aeneas's for Dido who also commits suicide, is a tragic love.

Pater's *Marius the Epicurean* situates itself in a later period of the second century, the rule of Marcus Aurelius, and is written from the point of view not of the emperor but of Marius, a highly educated Roman who serves the emperor, editing his writings for eventual publication. Apuleius is a character in this novel, which also includes a translation of the Cupid and Psyche story. Pater portrays the remarkable range both of philosophies and religions that were available to Romans and others of this period, with Roman tolerance extending to all philosophies and even religions so long as they conformed to the minimum civic obligation of sacrificing to Rome's gods. Only the Jews, on historical grounds, were exempt from this obligation. Christianity, as a new religion, was not, which explains Roman persecution when it occurred even under Marcus Aurelius. His reign witnessed the trial and execution of Justin, whose highly philosophical apologetic writings – Socrates and Jesus are favorably compared – have come down to us.[9]

Certainly, as Gibbon notes,[10] the Romans of this period would have found unthinkable the terms of Theodosian intolerance at the end of the fourth century – forbidding coercively all religious practices except those of orthodox Christianity – let alone state persecution of heretics, which Augustine was to justify.[11] Pater tells a conversion narrative as Marius moves from his philosophical interests to Christianity, but the narrative is told by Pater as one of traumatic loss. The one passion of Marius was clearly for another man, a man who dies. It is this loss that renders him open to a personal love without loss, a love he finds, as Augustine also would, in the God of Christianity. Pater's sense of Christianity is certainly not orthodox and is expressly distinguished from the Christianity of Constantine. In fact, his interest in the second century is precisely to identify a form of Christianity more attractive and reasonable than its later persecutory forms. Second-century Christianity is thus depicted as a religion of women and children, and the one Christian leader discussed is a woman, Cecilia, a person of responsive maternal affection and conscience. The experience of God is, for Marius, "[t]he sentiment of maternity."[12]

Both these novels take us into the openness to new philosophies and religions in a period when relative peace and prosperity relieved the Roman mind from the relentless demands of military power. They take us as well into the sense of love as problematic and worthy of reexamination, a problem explored in the novel of Apuleius that we study in depth here, namely, his *Metamorphoses*, also known as *The Golden Ass*.[13]

Apuleius was, like Augustine two centuries later, North African – indeed, from a city, Madauros, where Augustine would later study (both also studied in Carthage). Augustine's education was, however, in Latin (his Greek was meager) and limited to Madauros and Carthage, where he trained to become a rhetorician, a career he was to pursue in Rome and Milan, the city of his conversion. Apuleius's education, in contrast, prominently included both Latin and Greek, and he studied in Athens, the center of Greek intellectual culture, the city beloved of Hadrian. The greatest philosophical and literary influence on him was Plato, in particular the *Symposium*, *Phaedrus*, and *Timaeus*.

Apuleius is an important figure in the form of second-century Platonism called middle Platonism, or sometimes the second sophistic. An example of the syncretic style of philosophical/religious argument of this period was Plutarch's *De Iside Et Osiride*,[14] a work certainly known to Apuleius.[15] Plutarch argues that the Hellenistic religion of Isis and Sarapis, which in turn derived from the ancient Egyptian religion of Isis and Osiris, could be reasonably interpreted to reflect philosophically defensible Platonic principles and doctrines, specifically, Plato's view, in the *Timaeus*, of intervening agencies between human beings and the otherwise remote and inaccessible God of Platonic theology. Apuleius's theory of daimons is an elaboration of Plutarch's philosophical/religious hermeneutics, and his own interest in the religion of Isis, shown, as we shall see, in *Metamorphoses*, is philosophically consistent, as Plutarch notes, with the syncretic style of second-century Platonism. But there is a wholly original feature of Apuleius's interest in the Isis cult, not anticipated by Plutarch: namely, the role that conversion to the Isis cult may have played in Apuleius's life and the creative sense he made of it in *Metamorphoses*.

Apuleius was, like Augustine later, trained in rhetoric, and we have examples of his rhetorical performances that show remarkable ability.[16] The most important and suggestive of these examples is Apuleius's *Apology*,[17] his quite long defense, almost certainly successful, against charges that he had used magic to win the love of a wealthy North African widow, Pudentilla. In a letter, Augustine tells us that in his time, Apuleius was considered a magician and coupled with the famous sorcerer Apollonius of Tyana; as wonder-makers, they were equal or preferred to Christ.[18] Apuleius met Pudentilla through one of her sons, a friend from his student days in Athens, and he tells a story of estrangement from his friend after visiting him at his mother's home, where he falls ill and is nursed back to health by Pudentilla, in the course of which they fall in love and marry. What Pudentilla's relatives could not credit is that she might have fallen in love with a significantly younger and much less wealthy but very handsome man and that he might have fallen in love with her. The marriage of Pudentilla and Apuleius certainly violated the patriarchal terms of Roman marriage: It was not arranged to advance dynastic ends but was a love match, and one remarkably egalitarian for the period, both of which features may explain why it was challenged as somehow illegitimate.

Apuleius defends himself against the charges of illegal magic. He points not only to his own considerable attractions both of body and mind but also to Pudentilla's intelligence and learning and, very strikingly, to her sexual needs as a woman, suggesting an unhealthy, perhaps depressive, deprivation that his sexual love nourished back into health and vitality. He also points out the steps he took to make sure that his marriage to the wealthy Pudentilla did not compromise the inheritance of her sons. Finally, Apuleius's defense of Pudentilla includes a remarkable assertion of her right to sexual happiness:

> "So you, basest of men, are probing your mother's feelings in such matters, you check on her eyes, count her sighs, explore her emotions, intercept her letters, convict her of love? So you are trying to find out what she does in her bedroom, preventing her being not just a woman in love, but even a woman in general? Do you think she has no other feelings than those of a mother?"[19]

Augustine wrote of Apuleius's *Metamorphoses* or *The Golden Ass* in the course of discussing the transformation of humans into animals:

> Afterwards, when they had finished their jobs, they were restored to their original selves. And yet their minds did not become animal, but were kept rational and human. This is what Apuleius, in the work bearing the title *The Golden Ass*, describes as his experience, that after taking a magic potion he became an ass, while retaining his human mind. But this may be either fact or fiction.[20]

*Metamorphoses* is ostensibly written by one Lucius, a Greek, about his travels in Thessaly, but abruptly, late in the narrative, he becomes Apuleius of Madauros ("a man from Madaura").[21] Augustine's remark "this may be either fact or fiction" suggests that the narrative is both, which is to say a fictionalized autobiography of conversion, one that anticipates Augustine's *Confessions*, his own autobiography of conversion, written some two centuries later.

We can, of course, never know the degree to which *Metamorphoses* is fictionalized autobiography, and certainly, as John Winkler has been at pains to argue in *Auctor & Actor* (1985), the narrative has startling shifts of perspective that suggest to him, a postmodernist, an ironic sense of play, including about the religious conversion to Isis that ends the novel. Winkler's reading, however, makes little or no sense of what may be most original in the narrative, the Cupid and Psyche story at its center. The startling shifts of point of view in the narrative may be better explained, as Nancy Shumate has more recently argued in *Crisis and Conversion in Apuleius's Metamorphoses* (1996), as reflecting the sense of despairing, traumatizing crisis in human life as it was lived under Roman patriarchy that prepared the way for what is quite genuine in the narrative: conversion to the religion of Isis. We are impressed by Shumate's interpretation, not least because it draws such striking comparisons between Apuleius and Augustine as narrators of their own sense of despair at the conditions of human life, a despair resolved by conversion.

The autobiographical character of the novel is supported both by its express identification of Lucius with Apuleius near the end and by the little we know of Apuleius's personal life. The Apuleius of the *Apology* is a man of restless curiosity, one accused of illegal magic – features of personality and situation that mesh with the Lucius of *Metamorphoses*, who is driven by a curiosity that leads him to dabble disastrously in the magic powers of witches, thus turning himself into an ass. His redemption through Isis meshes as well with Apuleius's love and marriage to Pudentilla, who restores Apuleius to a human state, as Isis restores the fragmented Osiris to wholeness. And, a woman's sexual love, in both cases, is at the heart of the transformation.

That he writes a Latin novel, expressly drawing on the genre of Greek novels that flourished in the Hellenistic and Roman periods, illuminates Apuleius's aims as an artist. The influence of Ovid's long poem, *Metamorphoses*, prominently featuring change and transformation – divine and human – but all within a framework of the pagan Roman gods, is also quite clear.[22] Apuleius's *Metamorphoses* is based on a now-lost Greek novel, a shorter form of which has come down to us, notably without the narrative complexity of Apuleius and without either Cupid and Psyche or the Isis conversion.[23]

In all the Greek novels now preserved and translated in B. P. Reardon's *Collected Ancient Greek Novels*,[24] the standard narrative tells of a man and woman, sometimes so beautiful that they are taken to be gods, who fall in love but must then endure long periods of separation, which test the mettle of their loves until they are restored to one another as, finally, a happily married couple. Two of these works – Achilles Tatius's *Leucippe and Clitophon*[25] and Longus's *Daphnis and Chloe*[26] – are remarkable not only for their literary quality but also for their treatment of the powerful, expressly religious sexuality of women: "let us enter Aphrodite's inner sanctum and initiate ourselves into her mystic liturgy."[27] The worship of Isis (one of whose manifestations is Aphrodite) as the goddess who brings the lovers back into relationship is prominently featured. Two scholars, Karl Kerenyi and Reinhold Merkelbach, have argued that these Greek novels are allegorical expressions of the religious mystery cults, including the religion of Isis.[28]

Apuleius's choice to write in Latin a novel based on this genre of Greek novels clarifies his artistic and religious purposes in writing *Metamorphoses*. While his other works are highly derivative, this original literary work may reflect his finding, in the genre of the Greek novel, a form adequate to what he had come to see as the problematic character of sexual love in the second-century Roman world, a love that, as in *Memoirs of Hadrian* and *Marius the Epicurean*, often took a tragic turn.

We read *Metamorphoses* in line with its interpretation in *The Birth of Pleasure*. A world of patriarchal authority is portrayed, one in which women barely exist as persons, an order rationalized by gender stereotypes that either idealize women as asexual or denigrate them, if sexual, as monstrous witches.[29] With the exception of the Cupid and Psyche story and the Isis chapter, the novel displays an unredeemed patriarchal world. Apuleius piles narrative on narrative (sometimes, narratives within narratives) in which the dominant theme is the adulterous interests of highly sexual women, trapped in loveless arranged marriages with older men and seeking out younger men, often ruthlessly turning to deceit and murder to achieve their ends. Men in this unredeemed world are no better, whether straight or gay – Thrasyllus who kills his friend to possess his wife, or the Syrian priests who pressed their sexual demands on "a robust young peasant, finely equipped in loin and groin."[30] The one Roman soldier depicted explodes in violence, triggered by the imagined insult of an innocent gardener. The only rather idealized couple, Charite and Tlepolemus, suffer ordeals, but their escape and marriage are not, as in comparable Greek novels of this type, the end of the story, as Tlepolemus is shortly killed and Charite commits suicide. In this violent, patriarchal landscape, love either cannot exist or ends in loss.

More than in any comparable Greek novel, *The Golden Ass* insists that we see this frightening, claustrophobic terrain. Although the novel's forms are highly artificial, what it tells us about the people of this period, including the problem of love and violence under patriarchy, is grimly realistic, making it one of the more informative sources for what life was like outside the great cities of the second-century Roman Empire, in areas like Thessaly with few Roman soldiers and many bandits.[31]

It confirms the realism of the novel that Lucius's one sexual relationship, before his transformation into an ass, is with a slave girl, Photis. The relationship is portrayed by Apuleius as quite sensual, robust, and active on both sides:

> By now her passion was beginning to match and rival my own; her mouth opened wide, and her perfumed breath and the ambrosial thrust of her tongue as it met mine revealed her answering desire. "This is killing me," I said. "I'm really done for unless you're going to be kind to me." Kissing me again, "Keep calm," she said, "I feel just the same, and I'm all yours, body and soul, Our pleasure shan't be put off any longer; I'll come to your room at dusk. Now that's enough; go and prepare yourself, for it's going to be a non-stop battle all night long, with no holds barred." (p. 27)[32]

The sensuality, however, is trapped within a system of slavery that required slaves like Photis to be thus sexually available to young men like

Lucius: Apuleius wants us to see all this, including its sensuality not only for masters but sometimes for slaves. Lucius is portrayed very much as a privileged, wealthy, young, handsome, arrogant, rather shallow Roman Don Juan – as Apuleius may have been before his marriage and trial, a man who has never seriously questioned the system from which he benefits, though he is otherwise immensely curious about how women, as witches, operate within this system, which is, of course, his undoing.

Lucius's transformation into an ass enables him to see and experience many things, including what it is like to be on the losing end of a patriarchal system of privilege he would not otherwise, as a privileged Roman man, have seen. The ethical power of the narrative, as both an investigation and critique of the impact of patriarchy on women and men, is precisely that it places so privileged a Roman man in the most abject possible position, as bad or even worse than a slave, man as beast, a servile laborer and a sexual object.[33] His journey becomes, if anything, more nightmarish as the narrative proceeds, with Lucius the ass descending into a kind of Dantesque Inferno as the pattern and pace of violence become more intense and horrific.

His final degradation is sexual humiliation – a sexual woman taking pleasure in his asinine endowments, to be followed by the spectacle of a female criminal who is to take similar pleasure in public. Again, as in the Photis episode, Apuleius insists that we see the pleasure of a woman and man even in abject sex:

> Next she kissed me lovingly, not the sort of kisses that pass current in the brothel...; hers were the real thing and heartfelt, as were her endearments – "I love you," "I want you"...and all the other things women say to excite men and prove how much they care for them.... Meanwhile she went on murmuring endearments and kissing me repeatedly and moaning tenderly and fluttering her eyelids seductively, and then finally, "I have you," she cried, "I have you my dove, my sparrow," and with that she showed how empty and foolish my worries and fears had been [about the size of his sex organ]. For holding me tightly embraced she welcomed me in – all of me, and I mean all. (p. 185)

The role reversals central to *Metamorphoses* take their last ironic turn, as Lucius must endure what both women and slaves under patriarchy standardly suffer. It is this last bitter turn of the patriarchal screw on a patriarchal man that leads to Lucius's vision of Isis, as if he awakes or is finally able to awaken from the nightmare that has held him so powerfully, so tenaciously, for so long.

Apuleius offers us an alternative to this nightmare at two points in the novel: the Cupid and Psyche story, in Books 4–6, and the Isis narrative, in Book 11. If we are to resist the extraordinary power of patriarchy over our lives and loves, we must find a ground for resistance that has both a psychological and ethical/religious appeal greater than that of patriarchy. The Cupid and Psyche story offers us a beautifully observed developmental psychology that can sustain a resistance based in the love of partners as equals, and the Isis episode offers us a religious stance based on the authority of an ethical voice rooted in the powers of women as loving sexual partners and as mothers in relationship to those they love and who love them.

Our interest in the Cupid and Psyche story arose from contemporary research into the rather different pattern of psychological development in boys and girls. Psychologists have observed for some time that boys are more likely than girls to show signs of emotional trouble in early childhood – "more prone to depression, learning and speech disorders, and various forms of out-of-control and out-of-touch behavior."[34] In contrast, girls, hardier in childhood, show a resiliency to stress that is at risk at adolescence:

> The sudden high incidence of depression, eating disorders ranging from anorexia to obesity, problems in learning and destructive behavior among girls at adolescence parallels the heightened risk to boys' resiliency in the late years of early childhood, roughly around the age of five – the time Freud marks as the Oedipal crisis.[35]

Various explanations for this disparity, ranging from biological differences to socialization, have been offered, but research with girls pointed to a second, repeatedly confirmed observation. A single confiding relationship, meaning a relationship where one can speak one's mind and heart, offers the best protection against most forms of psychological problems, especially in periods of stress. The risk that girls face in adolescence and will name explicitly is loss of such a relationship. In adolescence, "girls often discover or fear that if they give voice to vital parts of themselves, their pleasure and their knowledge, they will endanger their connections with others and with the world at large."[36]

Comparable research into four- and five-year-old boys reveals a remarkable sensitivity to the human world and an ability to read the feelings of their parents, including emotions that are withheld.

> "Mummy," four-year-old Jake said one morning to his mother, Rachel, "you have a happy voice, but I also hear a little worried voice." By listening to her voice, he registers her happiness and also her anxiety. "He is my barometer," Rachel says.[37]

When Alex, Nick's father, expressed his remorse for having "lost it" and hit Nick the previous day, Nick, age five, said to his father: "You are afraid that if you hit me, when I grow up I'll hit my children." Alex, who had been hit by his father, had vowed to break the cycle. Nick, his son, articulates his fear.[38]

It may be traumatic for boys that patriarchal conceptions of masculinity require such relationships to be broken relatively early (in contrast to girls), imposing on men what Suttie called "the taboo on tenderness."[39] When good therapists address these issues later in such men's lives, a loving, confiding relationship once again proves crucial to enabling these issues to be faced.[40]

These contemporary observations suggest that girls, more robustly than boys, hold onto a voice rooted in relationship because they face pressures on this voice later in life, at adolescence rather than in early childhood, and consequently, with a greater capacity for resistance. It is this voice of resistance that has come to interest us not just as a contemporary phenomenon but as a long-standing human possibility, one particularly evident historically in the resistance of Roman women to the forms of patriarchy imposed on them. In the Cupid and Psyche story, we find a remarkable artist's sensitivity to this developmental strength in girls growing into women, in particular, as they face the demands of patriarchy that they conform to the idealized images of women who comply with these demands or be denigrated and dismissed as bad women. There can be no clearer example than Augustus's *Lex Julia de adulteriis coercendis*, which explicitly divides women into good idealized patriarchal women, who fulfill their marital obligations by not engaging in adultery, and bad women, who transgress these obligations and either are subject to severe criminal penalties (exile to an island, and eventually death through the gruesome "sack") or denigrated to the class of prostitutes. The unredeemed world of the *Metamorphoses* is very much the world of the *Lex Julia*: a highly patriarchal world, in which, as Apuleius recounts at length, not only is adultery common but so too are related forms of violence. In contrast, the Cupid and Psyche story reveals a psychological potential for resistance to such patriarchal demands, a resistance that was, as we have seen, quite common even in the Roman world. In the Romanized world of North Africa, at the time when Apuleius was writing his novel, Psyche was a common name for girls.[41]

The Cupid and Psyche story appears in the middle of the novel.[42] It is narrated by an old woman who cooks for the bandits who have abducted Charite from her family just at the point when she is to marry Tlepolemus.

Charite has a nightmare about the death of her lover and comes to the old woman in tears, seeking comfort. The old woman says that

> daytime dreams are untrue; and what's more important, night-time dreams generally foretell the opposite of what actually happens. So weeping or being beaten, or sometimes even being murdered, is a promise of money and profit, whereas smiling or stuffing yourself with sweetmeats or meeting a lover is a sign that grief or illness and all sorts of other misfortunes are in store. (p. 71)

To take Charite's mind off her troubles, the old woman tells her "a pretty fairytale, an old woman's story" (p. 71), the story of Cupid and Psyche.

The story opens in the traditional fairy tale manner, and we tell it here following E. J. Kenney's translation. There was once a city with a king and queen who had three beautiful daughters. The two eldest were very fair to see, but not so beautiful that human praise could not do them justice. The beauty of the youngest, Psyche, was so remarkable that no human speech could do it justice. Indeed, citizens and foreigners in larger numbers were drawn together by the fame of such a sight, struck by the peerless beauty, and putting right thumb and forefinger to their lips they offered her worship as the goddess Venus. Meanwhile, the news spread to nearby cities and regions that the goddess born of the blue depths of the sea has made public her godhead by mingling with mortal men, or at least that from a new fertilization by drops from heaven, the earth, not the sea, had grown another Venus in the flower of her virginity. Now crowds of people came from long distances to view this wonder, no longer visiting the traditional sites for the worship of Venus. It was to Psyche, rather, that prayers to Venus were addressed, and in her human shape that the power of the goddess was placated. When she appeared each morning it was the name of Venus, who was in fact far away, that was addressed to her, propitiated with sacrifices and offerings; and as she walked down the streets crowds of people adorned her with garlands and flowers.

Venus herself responded to this outrageous transference of adoration from her to a mere mortal with violent anger and indignation, and she called forth her son Cupid, "that most reckless of creatures, whose wicked behaviour flies in the face of public morals" (p. 73), to punish Psyche by making her fall in love with some degraded creature.

Psyche, meanwhile, took no joy in her beauty, as no one wished to marry her: "Though all admire her divine loveliness, they did so merely as one admires a statue finished to perfection." Her less beautiful sisters had long since been married to rich, royal suitors, but Psyche was left at home, "mourning her abandoned and lonely state, sick in body and mind, hating this beauty of hers which had enchanted the whole world." Finally, her father consults the oracle of Apollo at Miletus, who responds that his daughter must be exposed on a mountain peak in "funeral wedlock ritually arrayed," awaiting "[n]o human son-in-law" but "something cruel and fierce and serpentine" that, "borne aloft on wings," plagues even Jove himself. With great sadness and weeping, the father and mother prepare to take Psyche to a mountain peak. Psyche is led forth, "a living corpse," and addresses her parents: "Only now is it given to you to understand that it is wicked Envy that has dealt you this deadly blow. Then, when nations and people were paying me divine honours, when with one voice they were hailing me as a new Venus, that was when you should have grieved, when you should have wept, when you should have mourned me as already lost" (pp. 74–5). After this speech, Psyche leads the procession to the summit of a mountain, where she is left, fearful and trembling.

Once he sees Psyche, Cupid disobeys his mother's command to punish her by making her fall in love with a low creature. Falling in love with her himself, he has "the gentle breeze of softly breathing Zephyr, blowing the edges of her dress this way and that" (pp. 75–6) carry her gently to the verdant valley below. Psyche sleeps, and wakes to see a beautiful garden and palace. She enters the palace, and is told by a disembodied voice that all her wants will be attended to by servants – sleep, a bath, a delicious meal – and with music, a singer with a lyre followed by a choir of voices.

Psyche goes to bed. When night is advanced, she hears a gentle sound. Alone and "fearing for her virginity, Psyche quailed and trembled, dreading, more than any possible harm, the unknown." Invisible to her, Cupid enters, has sex with her, and leaves before sunrise. Invisible voices minister to "the new bride's slain virginity," and over time "as is usually the case, the novelty of her situation became pleasurable to her by force of habit, while the sound of the unseen voice solaced her solitude" (pp. 78–9).

Cupid now speaks to Psyche about the mortal danger from her two sisters who, having heard from their parents of what happened to Psyche, want to visit her. He tells her that he can be with her only on condition that she does not try to see him or speak about their love. When Psyche, lonely and depressed, pleads to see her sisters, Cupid reluctantly agrees, warning her that "she must never be induced by the evil advice of her sisters to discover what her husband looked like, or allow impious curiosity to hurl her down to destruction from the heights on which Fortune had placed her, and so for ever deprive her of his embraces." Psyche's sisters, seeing her magnificent surroundings, envy her good fortune and question her about her husband. Psyche, who has never seen her husband, dissimulates that he is a handsome young man. Cupid again warns Psyche, now pregnant, not to speak to her sisters about their secret, telling her if she divulges it, the child will be mortal; otherwise, divine. The sisters return and hear from Psyche, who has forgotten her earlier story, that her husband is a middle-aged merchant. Convinced she is lying and consumed with envy, they tell that her unseen husband is, as the oracle foretold, "an immense serpent, writhing its knotted coils, its bloody jaws dripping deadly poison, its maw gaping deep, if only you knew it, that sleeps with you each night" (p. 85). They persuade her to kill him before he devours both her and the child.

Night comes, and with it her husband who, after making love falls into a deep sleep. Psyche takes the knife and oil lamp that she has concealed, preparing to kill him. But when she looks at him under the light, she sees not a monster but a beautiful young man. Curious as ever, she plays with Cupid's arrows, one of which pricks her finger, drawing blood:

> Thus without realizing it Psyche through her own act fell in love with Love. Then ever more on fire with desire for Desire she hung over him gazing in distraction and devoured him with quick sensuous kisses, fearing all the time that he might wake up. (p. 88)

Oil from the lamp now falls on Cupid, who wakens suddenly and accusing Psyche of breaking her promise, takes off into the sky. Psyche manages "to seize his right leg with both hands, a pitiful passenger in his lofty flight, trailing attendance through the clouds she clung on underneath, but finally in her exhaustion fell to the ground" (p. 89). Cupid tells her that as punishment for breaking his prohibition on seeing him, he will leave her.

Psyche grieves as she watches her beloved husband depart. She tries to throw herself suicidally into a stream, but the river bears her unharmed on his current and places her on the bank. The country god Pan advises her not to yield to grief, but rather strive to earn Cupid's love, "young wanton and pleasure-loving that he is, through tender service" (p. 90). Psyche worships Pan's saving power, and pursuing Cupid, comes to the cities of her two sisters, deceitfully telling each sister that Cupid now wishes to marry her and that she should go to the mountain top where she would be carried by the wind to Cupid. In fact, they plunge to their death.

Meanwhile, Cupid, groaning in pain from his wound, returns to his mother's chamber. Venus rebukes him for his disobedience and storms out. Both Ceres and Juno question her reasons for such rage, asking "Aren't you condemning in your fair son your own arts and pleasures?" (p. 93).

Psyche travels the world in search of Cupid. Meeting with a refusal of help from Ceres and Juno, she finally comes to Venus herself, who flies at her with rebukes and beatings and then sets her several tests. In the first, Psyche must sort various kinds of seeds that have been mixed together. A compassionate ant, seeing her plight, calls on fellow ants to separate the seeds, which they do, meeting Venus's initial trial. Returning from a banquet, Venus refuses to believe that Psyche did this on her own, saying that only Cupid could have helped her.

The lovers are now kept in separate rooms in the same house, and Venus sets her second test: Psyche must get a golden fleece from wild and dangerous sheep that wander in a certain wood. She is about to throw herself into a river when a reed tells her that the fleece can safely be gathered from the branches on which it is caught. Venus responds that Psyche's meeting this second trial can only be because of help from Cupid. She sets a third test: Psyche must secure water from a certain mountain stream. She comes to the mountain stream and sees that the task is impossible, but is helped now by Jove's eagle who takes the urn and fills it with the mountain water.

Venus sets Psyche a fourth and final test: She gives her a casket, which Psyche must carry to the underworld, presenting it to Proserpine, goddess of the underworld, with the request that she put in a little of her beauty. Psyche, despairing, prepares to throw herself from a tower when the tower tells her how to enter the underworld and secure entrance to the presence of Proserpine to meet the test. She follows the directions and brings the casket back to the light of day, but succumbing "to her reckless curiosity," (p. 104) she opens the casket and finds not beauty but an infernal sleep, which overcomes her.

At this point, Cupid, his wound now healed, "could no longer bear to be parted for so long from Psyche," and he flies to her rescue, "wiping off the sleep and replacing it where it had been in the box." He instructs her to take the casket to his mother, as he would appeal to Jupiter, his father. "Eaten up with love, looking ill, and dreading his mother's new-found austerity," Cupid pleads his cause with Jupiter who kisses his son, and though he blames him for compromising even his own reputation "in defiance of the laws, the Lex Julia included," he agrees to help. At a meeting of all the gods, Jupiter tells Venus that, by his will, the marriage of Cupid and Psyche will be one of equals: "I shall arrange for it to be not unequal but legitimate and in accordance with civil law" (p. 105). Psyche is brought to heaven and made immortal. Cupid and Psyche are married "with all proper ceremony, and when her time came there was born to them a daughter, whom we call Pleasure" (p. 106).

Psychologists have seen the story of Cupid and Psyche as affording insights into love and the soul.[43] We are riveted more particularly by its insights into the struggle for love under patriarchy, where gender idealization and denigration disrupt intimate relationships for both women and men. The story is certainly as much about Cupid as it is about Psyche, let alone the relationship of both of them to Cupid's patriarchal mother, Venus, and of Psyche to her patriarchal sisters.

Psyche, a young woman, comes to the point in development when girls confront stresses they have not previously known: in particular, the demands of patriarchy as they bear on their relationships to men. Psyche's distress is at her own idealized objectification as "the new Venus," which cuts her off from any possibility of intimate relationship. Venus's rage at Psyche for displacing her is enacted through Cupid, her son, whom she regards as an instrument of her authority. He resists because he falls in love with Psyche, but nonetheless enforces on her what he takes to be the demands on women under patriarchy: They must not see their husbands as persons, and they must not speak of what they know of their husbands through experience, in this case, his tenderness – which is at odds with his public image. What moves Cupid from this patriarchal stance is Psyche's resistance to these demands, because such taboos on seeing and knowing disable her from loving him as the tender, beautiful young man he is. Because of such taboos, Psyche has no access to a body-based experience of truthful voice in intimate relationship, but is psychologically vulnerable both to depression and to the promptings of her envious sisters.

It is only when Psyche breaks the taboo on seeing that she falls in love, not with the mythological Cupid but with the man she sees and knows. And this rooted experience does not end but rather impels her continuing journey of resistance. Her search for the love of Cupid will require coming to terms with the place of his patriarchal mother in his life. The four trials to which Venus subjects Psyche mark the stages of her struggle for an intimate relationship with Cupid. While the struggle is ostensibly with Venus, the real protagonists are Psyche and Cupid; he himself overcomes his terrors of relationship, defying his mother and moving experientially to help Psyche meet her trials, explicitly with the fourth test, perhaps implicitly (as his mother suspects) with the earlier three as well. What Psyche falls back upon, as she contemplates her almost comically recurrent suicide attempts, is a sense of nature and what nature tells us about the place of loving relationship in the human order of things. Once she breaks free of the idealization and denigration and the dissociation from experience that sustain the disruption of intimate relationships, she is prepared to enter into an equal marriage and become the mother of a daughter named Pleasure.

It is illuminating to contrast Vergil's Aeneas with Apuleius's Cupid, a contrast Apuleius probably intended his Roman readers to make. Both Aeneas and Cupid are, in the *Aeneid*, very much the tools of their patriarchal Roman mother (Venus), who strategically uses Cupid sexually to attract Dido to Aeneas, but ultimately (in contrast to Juno) approves Aeneas's abrupt breaking of relationship to Dido when patriarchal duty so demands. It is only Juno in the *Aeneid* who sees the equal marriage of Dido and Aeneas as a fitting resolution to the legacy of Troy. In the *Metamorphoses*, Apuleius shows a Cupid who resists his mother's demands and falls in love with Psyche, who will not accept the dissociation central to patriarchal love or married life. It is the pressure of this young woman's love and the responsive chord she strikes in him that makes psychologically possible their common resistance. The end of the story could not be more different from Jupiter's role in the *Aeneid*: Jupiter in the *Metamorphoses* calls forth an equality in marriage between Psyche and Cupid and suggests that the new map of love, which their struggle reflects, renders obsolescent the Love Laws, including the *Lex Julia*, that sustain, at the expense of love, a patriarchal order.

The developmental psychology implicit in Apuleius's telling of the story of Cupid and Psyche makes sense not only of the resistance of Roman women to patriarchy but also of the continuing form of such resistance today. What makes Apuleius so remarkable is that he came, presumably through his relationships with women, to see the crucial place of women's strengths in resistance to patriarchal demands. How was this possible in so patriarchal a culture as the Roman Empire of the second century? To make sense of such resistance, the developmental psychology of the Cupid and Psyche story must be understood in relationship to the Isis narrative of Book 11 of *Metamorphoses*.

The cult of Isis plays the role it does in the conversion of Lucius/ Apuleius because among religions in the second-century Roman Empire, it uniquely spoke to women's experience as lovers, mothers, and moral agents – having an authority of voice outside and under the radar of patriarchy, including a role in the rituals of the religion as priestesses. Isis was the sister and lover of Osiris, killed and dismembered by his brother Seth (symbolized by the ass), with body parts spread over Egypt. Isis gathers the fragments of her lover except his penis, which is lost, and brings him back to life and wholeness through her powers of sexual love, her own powers replacing the lost member, as she literally resurrects her husband through the sexual erection she, mystically, makes possible.

The hymns to Isis that have come down to us reflect the syncretism of the period: Isis appears under other names, as Demeter/Ceres (as Pater notes in his essay on Demeter), Aphrodite, Venus, and so on. While her worship called for sexual abstinence for certain periods, she is, in contrast to Diana and Cybele, a sexual goddess whose powers are shown in sexual relationships and call for the equality of women and men: "thou didst make the power of women equal to that of men."[44] We know that the condition of women in Egypt was markedly freer and more equal than in ancient Greece or Rome, and women ruled in Egypt, notably, in the Ptolemaic period, a fact that shocked Romans (see our discussion of Cleopatra in Chapter 2). The Isis religion, in the form that enjoyed appeal within the Roman empire (Osiris being replaced by Sarapis), dated from the early Ptolemies, combining, syncretically, Greek and Egyptian elements. Its roots, however, lie in an Egyptian experience of women's lives that obviously had broader appeal, as the appeal of the Isis religion to Greeks and Romans shows,[45] not to mention the responses of Caesar and Antony to Cleopatra or of Aeneas to the Carthaginian Dido.

There have been very few religions that were not patriarchal, which means that the study of the Isis religion may be particularly helpful in understanding their distinctive contribution. In fact, the *Metamorphoses* is one of our best sources on the Isis religion and is always treated as such in serious discussions of its terms and conditions.[46] Book 11, for example, offers a quite detailed narrative of its central rituals, including references to its mysteries, about which, consistent with the vows of secrecy of mystery religions, we are never told. We only know they existed, and that they included rituals of death and resurrection that were common features of all mystery religions in the ancient world. But we believe that the *Metamorphoses* affords, as well, a deeper insight into how and why the Isis religion had the appeal it did for a highly civilized Roman man and artist like Apuleius, enabling him to come to the remarkable insights we have discussed in the story of Cupid and Psyche.

No once-patriarchal man could have written the Cupid and Psyche story as the revelatory account of developmental psychology it is unless he had come into an unusually close, intimate relationship to non-patriarchal, resisting women. What the Cupid and Psyche story preserves is the narrative of a young woman's resilient resistance to the objectifying demands of patriarchy and her willingness to break the taboo on seeing, knowing, and speaking of her intimate experience with her husband. As the myth of Cupid and Psyche makes clear, she does not fall in love with him until she breaks this taboo. What makes her resistance sustainable is ultimately its power to elicit a comparable resistance in the man she loves. The unusual character of Apuleius's relationship with Pudentilla may have sparked this insight, but it also may hinge on the way he came to understand and make sense of this experience as enacting or reenacting the central mystery of the Isis religion: Through the sexual love of Isis, the dismembered Osiris (Sarapis) is brought back to life and wholeness.

The power that the Isis religion gives to women's sexual love suggests an awareness of how psychologically fragmented men are by the battles they engage in. The Dido-Aeneas episode in the *Aeneid* reveals this psychology starkly. What differentiates Psyche from Dido is her resistance to dissociation in herself. Like Isis, she restores her lover to psychic wholeness. Psyche is as despairing and suicidal when Cupid abruptly leaves her as Dido was when Aeneas abandoned her. But Apuleius shows as well the psychological strengths in young women that enable them, more easily than young men, to resist the tragic terms that patriarchy imposes on their love. By holding onto and pressing their love through seemingly hopeless trials and tests, they elicit even from such men a resistance not otherwise psychologically possible. As Psyche will break Cupid's taboo on seeing him or speaking about their love, so Cupid will stop hiding his tenderness and his love.

Ancient religions, like religion generally, addressed the great issues of a human life lived, as it is, in self-consciousness of the three experiences that touch us as mysterious and transcendent: the mysteries of birth, of love, and of death. The Isis religion, however, offers us one of very few examples of such a religion that addresses these questions through the experience of women as wives and mothers and also accords religious and ethical authority to voices arising from such experience. The sense Apuleius makes of this religion may be what enables him, as a Roman man and artist, to align his own creative voice with the voices and experience of non-patriarchal women. The result is the remarkably critical stance he takes in the *Metamorphoses* on the lives Roman men and women lived under patriarchy, as well as the possibility he sees for redemption through the psychology illuminated by the Cupid and Psyche story and the religion of Book 11.

The two narratives are variations on a common theme: Both the psychology and the religion suggest that there can be no truthful or authoritative voice on the three great questions of religion unless we take seriously the experience and voices of women, speaking under the radar of patriarchy. Patriarchy bears most heavily on men (consider Aeneas) and on women only to the extent that they either get in its way (Dido) or are necessary to achieve its ends (Venus as a patriarchal mother in both the *Aeneid* and the *Metamorphoses*). It leaves other women alone, living under its radar. The story of Cupid and Psyche is thus told by an old mother to a younger woman as "an old woman's story,"[47] an old-wives' tale drawing on experiences of love that women know and often keep to themselves, but under certain conditions will impart to younger women.

Both the old woman and Charite, to whom she tells the story, commit suicide, and so we know that such knowledge cannot save women from the ravages of patriarchy when they are caught up in its demands. We suggest that the importance for Apuleius of the Isis religion is that it gives him a sense of voice in himself (under his patriarchal armor, so to speak) that is more truthful and more authoritative than the voice of patriarchal manhood. Isis offers him a loving relational understanding of and pity for the human voice that has been silenced by what patriarchy had made of him, a golden ass.[48] What is said of many terrible men may be true of Lucius/Apuleius the ass, that only a mother could love them. Isis appears to him in Book 11 as such a mother, her love recognizing the human voice still alive in him, a trusting confidante who makes possible "the rebirth of my tongue."[49] Apuleius thus appeals to a relational capability, a capacity to read and respond to the human world that patriarchy traumatically disrupts in boys at a young age and silences in girls when they become young women. It is this natural world that offers resources for the resistance to patriarchy, including men caught up in its demands.

A maternal love had been offered to Lucius earlier in the novel by Byrrhena, his mother's friend, who extends him both the hospitality of her house and good advice, both of which he ignores, much to his cost (pp. 23–5). The possibility of redemption is, Apuleius suggests, always available, but Lucius is at this point not open to such love. It is only at the lowest point of his life-as-ass, after being treated as a sexual tool by "a certain noble and wealthy lady" (p. 184), that he opens his heart and mind to Isis. Is this a comic image of the sexual union of the dismembered Osiris/Sarapis and Isis? Its place in the narrative suggests as much.

The divine authority accorded a loving wife and mother is at the heart of the appeal of the Isis religion for Apuleius and probably many other Roman men and women of his period. The questions of birth and death are answered as corollaries of what such love makes possible, the birth of pleasure and the resurrection of the dismembered dead into wholeness in a fully human life. If the birth of tragedy arises in the shadows cast by patriarchy in the Athenian democracy,[50] Apuleius radically questions the force patriarchy exerted over the lives of Roman men and women. His narrative offers a psychology and religion in service of this critique, which takes the form of ribald comedy.

Apuleius thus questions the Roman belief in the inexorable force of Fate over human life, identifying the love embodied in Isis and in Psyche as a form of grace that can release patriarchal men, like the man Apuleius once was, from the belief that nature condemns us to the violence and lovelessness of a life lived under patriarchy. While it was Lucius/ Apuleius's curiosity that led him astray, it was also curiosity that led him to discover the possibility of metamorphosis or transformation, and curiosity is Psyche's notable trait. Apuleius probably shared Plutarch's worries about a wayward curiosity that did not serve any scientific or moral end,[51] but the overall trajectory of *Metamorphoses* suggests that, on balance, curiosity is redemptive, pressing us to ask questions that may enable us to know the sources of our depression and making possible a turn, a conversion, to a life lived in love. What we can come to know is that our belief in Fate confuses a cultural form, patriarchy, with nature. Nothing in nature requires us to live out such violence and tragedy. We can resist, as free persons, if we open ourselves to the loving relationships that make resistance possible and fruitful.

Our study of Apuleius's *Metamorphoses* thus shows us that in the second-century Roman Empire, there was an opening through an anti-patriarchal religion to women's authority and voice, leading to astonishing insights into the possibility of a human love not tragically corrupted by idealizations and illusions. A century that had experienced the tragedy of Hadrian's fatally flawed love for Antinous was a ground for such insights, and even the Christianity of the period, as suggested by Pater, may have had features more aligned with the voices and experiences of women. That understanding of Christianity was, in the late fourth century, shifted in a decisively patriarchal direction by Augustine of Hippo.

# 5  Augustine on Conversion

A radical shift separates the Christianity of the second century from that
of the end of the fourth century, and no figure was more powerful in
engineering this shift than Augustine of Hippo. The backdrop, decisively
influential on the thought and life of Augustine, was the political decline
of the Roman Empire itself, marked not only by bloody civil wars over the
succession but also by the decisive political power of the Roman armies.
As the armies proved increasingly unable to contain the barbarians on the
borders of the empire, Rome was sacked in 410. This event shocked the
Roman world and led to Augustine's work on *The City of God*, explaining
why the Catholic Church was not responsible for this catastrophe.[1]

Christianity had been a distinctly minority religious preference in the
second century. Although it grew steadily after that,[2] its dominance in
the fourth century was due to two remarkable developments: first, the
decision of Constantine in 311 that Christianity was to be the established
church of the Roman empire, receiving massive state support and patronage continuously from then onward (except for the brief three-year reign
of Julian the Apostate); and second, the decision of Theodosius in 391
that all pagan practices were to be repressed and that the state would use
its coercive powers to support orthodox Christian views over heresies.[3]
When Augustine converted to Christianity in 386, he was not sacrificing
his earlier ambitions for success in the Roman political world, for he
had learned from the example of Bishop Ambrose of Milan that a bishop
exercised significant powers over the emperors and that the church could
use the power of the state to enforce its orthodoxy.[4]

When he became Bishop of Hippo, Augustine was often successful in
appealing to imperial power to enforce his views over his enemies, including the heretical Donatists early in this career and later the heretical
Pelagians.[5] The great importance of Augustine in the history of church-
state relations was his justification of the use of state power in such ways

on religious grounds. His theory of persecution would justify the inquisitorial powers of the Catholic Church in the Middle Ages and later, a view that was only fundamentally reexamined and repudiated by Vatican II in 1967.[6] And it was the refutation of this theory by Pierre Bayle and John Locke, among others, that was decisively important in the development of the institutions of constitutional democracy in which the argument for toleration has been of fundamental importance.[7]

At the heart of Augustine's theory of persecution lies his distinctive contribution to Christian theology, his doctrine of original sin. His views on this matter can be freshly understood by counterposing his conversion to Christianity to Apuleius's conversion to the religion of Isis. As we have noted, Apuleius and Augustine were both North African Romans and shared an education in classical philosophy as well as common ambitions and achievements as rhetoricians/lawyers. They also shared a common sense of crisis about the lives they had once led as privileged Roman men, both highly sexual. They took quite different paths, however: Apuleius into a new kind of loving relationship with a woman, Augustine into celibacy. At the center of Augustine's different path lie his views of women.

In this connection, a Catholic nun, Karol Jackowski, recently traced the "Catholic Church's obsession with legislating sexual morality" to

> the thinking of Augustine. His most famous prayer appears to be the tormented prayer of the Catholic priesthood still: "Lord, make me chaste, but not yet." And while some church historians tend to minimize and even deny Augustine's obsession with sex, I find that his teachings prove otherwise. One has only to look at Augustine's writings (especially on original sin and the seductive nature of woman) to see that this is clearly a man who could not, without anguish, stop thinking of sex, and could not stop blaming women for his misery.[8]

Jackowski points to Augustine's quite remarkable, highly mythologized reading of the Adam and Eve narrative, a narrative that is "[t]he cornerstone of current Catholic moral theology on sex and the subordinate nature of woman."[9]

There are two roads into Augustine's pivotally important thought on this matter: first, his interpretation of the Adam and Eve narrative in *The City of God*,[10] which links a negative view of sexuality with misogyny (as Jackowski observes); and second, his highly introspective exploration of his psychological development from boy to sexual man to celibate priest and bishop in *The Confessions*.[11] Both accounts support

Jackowski's diagnosis of the close linkage between a negative view of sexuality and a misogyny that Thomas Aquinas assumed and codified as natural law.

Augustine's interpretation of the Adam and Eve narrative places Eve in the more responsible position and in essence holds her inferiority responsible for Adam's disobedience, the Fall, exile, and the taint of original sin. In Augustine's telling, the serpent "had a deceitful conversation with the woman – no doubt starting with the inferior of the human pair so as to arrive at the whole by stages, supposing that the man would not be so easily gullible, and could not be trapped by a false move on his own part, but only if he yielded to another's mistake." It is this misogynist view of women's intrinsic inferiority to which the Fall is attributed. Prior to this moment, Adam and Eve had not, for Augustine, experienced sexuality in the way humans now do, but a man could will erections for procreation (when needed), without any lust, just as some extraordinary people can wiggle their ears at will or even pass air musically "without any stink." The mark of the Fall, indeed its punishment, is the way sexuality now operates: "[T]otally opposed to the mind's control, it is quite often divided against itself," that is, feeling sexual desire when one does not want to feel it, and not feeling such desire when one wants to feel it. Indeed, Augustine points to the intensity of our sexual experience as a mark of our loss of rationality:

> This lust assumes power not only over the whole body, and not only from the outside, but also internally; it disturbs the whole man, when the mental emotion combines and mingles with the physical craving, resulting in a pleasure surpassing all physical delights. So intense is the pleasure that when it reaches its climax there is an almost total extinction of mental alertness; the intellectual sentries, as it were, are overwhelmed.[12]

Thus sexuality and the experience of pleasure per se become demonized.

Augustine rests his case on an experience he assumes to be universal: sexuality as a natural object of shame because it involves such loss of control, including control of our rational faculties:

> In fact, this lust we are now examining is something to be the more ashamed of because the soul, when dealing with it, neither has command of itself so as to be entirely free from lust, nor does it rule the body so completely that the organs of shame are moved by the will instead of by lust. Indeed if they were so ruled they would not be *pudenda* – parts of shame.[13]

Accordingly, the only proper form of sex is that which is done with the controlled intention to procreate. Sexuality without procreation or independent of such intention was, for Augustine, intrinsically degrading – a view he bequeathed to the Catholic Church.

This argument, naturalistically interpreted, rests on a rather remarkable fallacy. Augustine cites two observations about human sexual experience: first, humans insist on having sex alone, unobserved by others, and second, humans cover their genitals in public. He argues that the only plausible explanation is that humans experience sex as degrading. The pleasure of sex thus becomes shameful, something to be avoided or hidden.

Assuming, for the purposes of argument, the truth of Augustine's anthropological assumptions,[14] it does not follow that humans find sex intrinsically shameful. These facts are equally well explained by the fact that people experience embarrassment in others witnessing their pleasure, not shame in the experience of sex itself. Shame is an emotion distinguishable from embarrassment, signifying a wound to one's pride or self-esteem. Embarrassment is experienced when a matter is made public that properly is regarded as private.[15] The twin facts adduced by Augustine are, indeed, better explained by the hypothesis of embarrassment, not shame. Surely, many people experience no negative self-evaluations when they engage in sex in private, which is what the hypothesis of embarrassment, not shame, would lead us to expect. For example, people may experience pride in knowing that other people know or believe that they are having sex (the recently married young couple). There is no shame here, but there would be embarrassment if the sex act were actually observed.

That people would experience such embarrassment reveals something important about human sexual experience, but it is not Augustine's contempt for the loss of control of sexual passion. Sexual experience can be a profoundly personal, spontaneous, and absorbing experience in which people expose fantasies and vulnerabilities that cannot brook the presence of an external observer. That humans require privacy for sex relates to the nature of the experience; its pleasure is not intrinsically degrading.

Augustine's view, as Jackowski argues, can be explained by the misogynist assumptions he brings to his interpretation of the Adam and Eve story. To Augustine, women's inferiority accounts for the Fall, and our sexuality is tainted by its association with woman as temptress. Indeed, our sexuality is, on this view, punishment for the Fall, the lapse of control reminding us of our primal disobedience. There is nothing interpretively inevitable in the approach to the Bible that Augustine takes, as Elaine Pagels has made clear.[16] There is, for example, the approach of

Irenaean theodicy which, in order to deal with the problem of evil, does not construe an original state of perfection and then fall, but interprets the Adam and Eve story in terms of humankind's gradually growing into a sense of adult ethical responsibilities, learning from mistakes and developing over time new progressive insights into ethical demands.[17] Augustine brings to the narrative a misogyny that he then finds confirmed by his interpretation of it.

The psychological roots of this misogyny can be seen in the terms in which Augustine narrates his own move from sexually active man to celibate priest, a move in which his mother Monica (a pious Catholic) plays a decisive role. He tells us in *The Confessions* that he had a loving affair with a woman with whom he had a son, Adeodatus: "she was the only girl for me, and I was faithful to her" (p. 53). She was not, however, a woman of a class Augustine could marry, and he separated from her so that he could marry within the terms of the patriarchal order of the time. Monica had arranged a suitable marriage for her son, but since the girl in question would only be of age in two years, he had taken another woman as his mistress. Augustine's words for the separation from the woman he loved convey the traumatic nature of this break: "My heart which was deeply attached was cut and wounded, and left a trail of blood" (p. 109).

Augustine contrasts such sexual attachments to illiterate women with his friendships with men, characterized by conversations of highly literate equals, a model for the intense friendships that he finds fulfilled in his relationships to fellow monks following his conversion. One of the reasons he gives for coming to think of sexuality as only for reproduction is that he can imagine a companionate relationship based on intellectual equality only with a man: "[I]f God had wanted Adam to have a partner in scintillating conversation he would have created another man; the fact that God created a woman showed that he had in mind the survival of the human race."[18]

One woman who fell outside this mold was his mother Monica, who, though probably illiterate, conversed with her son about neo-Platonic philosophy, urging him to convert to Catholicism.[19] The marriage of Monica to Patricius, Augustine's father, had been, like other such marriages, an arranged affair, probably when Monica was quite young. Like other Roman men of his station, Patricius was unfaithful to Monica, and Augustine writes at some length of his father's violence, which he accepts, along with her servitude, admiring his mother's forbearance in dealing with her husband and her ability to calm him down:

> She knew that an angry husband should not be opposed, not merely by anything she did, but even by a word. Once she saw that he had become calm and quiet, and that the occasion was opportune, she

would explain the reason for her action, in case perhaps he had reacted without sufficient consideration. Indeed many wives married to gentler husbands bore the marks of blows and suffered disfigurement to their faces. In conversation together they used to complain about their husband's behaviour. Monica, speaking as if in jest but offering serious advice, used to blame their tongues. She would say that since the day when they heard the so-called matrimonial contract read out to them, they should reckon them to be legally binding documents by which they had become servants. She thought they should remember their condition and not proudly withstand their masters. The wives were astounded, knowing what a violent husband she had to put up with. Yet it was unheard of, nor was there ever a mark to show, that Patrick had beaten his wife or that a domestic quarrel had caused dissension between them for even a single day. (*Confessions*, pp. 168–9)

Passages of this sort bespeak Augustine's sensitivity to his mother, but also his (and her) acceptance of her plight under patriarchy. On the one hand, Augustine insists that we see the violence of husbands to wives in Roman marriages, just as elsewhere he reveals how common were the beatings of boys like himself by his teachers, beatings at which "our parents laughed" (p. 12). On the other hand, Augustine admires not only his mother's close study of her husband's violence, including its trigger by verbal insults, but also her skill in concealing its effects and lowering its incidence.

In this, Monica may have drawn on her religious piety, centered on the Jesus of the Gospels. Jesus' teaching on nonviolence in the Sermon on the Mount, Matthew 5–7, resonated with the experience of many women under patriarchy:

You have heard that it was said 'An eye for an eye and a tooth for a tooth.' But I tell you not to resist one who is evil. But if anyone strikes you on the right cheek, turn the other to him as well. If anyone wants to sue you and take away your tunic, let him have your cape, too. If anyone presses you into service to go one mile, go with him two. Give to him who ask you for a loan, and do not refuse one who is unable to pay interest. (Matt. 5:38–42)

The text is then followed by,

You have heard that it was said 'You shall love your neighbor and hate your enemy,' but I tell you to love your enemies and pray for those who misuse you. In this way you will become sons of your heavenly Father, who causes the sun to rise upon both good and evil men, and sends rain to just and unjust alike. If you love only those who love you, what reward have you? Do not the taxgatherers do the same?

> And if you greet only your brethren, what extra are you doing? Do not the heathen do the same? Be true, just as your heavenly Father is true.[20] (Matt. 5:43–48)

The familiar King James Version translation of 5:48 is: "Be ye therefore perfect, even as your Father in heaven is perfect."[21]

The mandate "not to resist one who is evil" but rather to "turn the other [cheek]" illustrates what Jesus means by telling his disciples "to love your enemies." Such demands are extended by the injunction against judging others:

> "Do not sit in judgment, lest you yourself be judged, for you will be judged by the same standard which you have used. Why look at the splinter in your brother's eye, if you do not take notice of the beam in your own? How dare you say to your brother, 'Let me take the splinter out of your eye,' when all the time there is a beam in your own eye? Casuist! First remove the beam from your own eye, and then you will see clearly in order to remove the splinter from your brother's eye."[22] (Matt. 7:1–5)

As the propensity to violence under patriarchy turns on insults to one's manhood, the power of this sermon lies in laying the groundwork for an alternative response.

Augustine's growing admiration for both his mother's life and her religion makes sense against this background. It accords her experience and voice a remarkable authority in an otherwise highly patriarchal Roman culture, including an emotional intelligence in discerning what incites the violence of patriarchal men. If Augustine comes to resist Roman patriarchy at all, it is clearly through his mother. On the other hand, since her resistance never fundamentally questions her servile role and the violence of her marriage, which are seen as in the nature of things, her son's Christianity, learned from his mother, never extends beyond her understanding. He absorbed the inferior position of women from her; indeed, his reading of Adam and Eve reflects her view. What greater authority could there be for his misogyny than the view of his own admirable mother? – he may well have thought.[23]

In his psychoanalytically informed biography *Augustine of Hippo*, Peter Brown frames the trajectory of Augustine's development in terms of his ambivalent relationship to his mother – fleeing from her[24] but drawn deeply back to her highly personal religion of Christian piety. Her piety centered on the sense of her "heroes, as a man 'predestined,' the course of his life already ineluctably marked out by God." Her religious psychology was at the root of one of her son's most influential beliefs, "Augustine's grandiose theory of predestination: and, as with so many very clever people, such simple roots were all the stronger for being largely unconscious."[25] God's love for Augustine is modeled on that of his mother: "[S]he loved to have me with her, but much more than most mothers."[26] His family was one of moderate means (support for his education and ambitions came from patrons). His parents, both father and mother, were clearly themselves highly ambitious for their remarkably gifted son, who, fired by their ambition for him, would rise very high in the hierarchy of both the Roman church and state of his period.

Augustine condemns his father's ambitions for him and claims for this reason that he cannot be his true father (only God the father can be).[27] Such condemnation reflects the hostile edge in father and son relationships quite common under Roman patriarchy. Augustine would come into financial independence (his father dying when he was sixteen)[28] only at his mother's death, at the time of his conversion. Such extended dependence creates a prolonged psychosexual adolescence. Augustine had a sexual life, but he was drawn to the Manicheans, whose views were more sexually ascetic than those of Christians. And ultimately, at his conversion he argues that asceticism is the preferred path to God. One thinks, in this connection, of Anna Freud's observations about "the asceticism and intellectuality of adolescence."[29]

Again his father comes into the picture. Augustine paints a telling scene revealing his father's pride at the bathhouse in his son's "showing signs of virility and the stirrings of adolescence, [at which] he was overjoyed to suppose that he would now be having grandchildren and told my mother so" (*Confessions*, pp. 26–7). The response of Monica could not have been more chilling:

> [S]he shook with pious trepidation and a holy fear. . . . Her concern (and in the secret of my conscience I recall the memory of her admonition delivered with vehement anxiety) was that I should not fall into fornication, and above all that I should not commit adultery with someone else's wife. (p. 27)

Monica's "vehement anxiety" suggests a wish for her son to repudiate his father's example and reflects her own experience of life with Patricius, the lack of love, his adultery and his violence. Augustine's asceticism would go much further than his mother's, to a repudiation of sexuality itself, but we can also see here the grounds of his search for a loving father, a search that would lead him to God.

Gandhi, as a child, similarly tries to outdo his pious mother, exceeding her in his commitment to nonviolence.[30] But with Augustine, the role of loss is more central: the loss of the woman he sexually loved, the death of his mother following his conversion, and also the death of his son,

Adeodatus, and close friends for whom he deeply grieved, as he tells us at length.[31] And in these losses, we also see the grounds for his repudiation of sexual love and his turn to God.

Augustine, a philosophical rationalist, had turned to Christianity only when he had found a way, through neo-Platonism,[32] to make personal sense of the Christian immaterial conception of God as an inner voice, the voice of a perfectly sensitive and responsive lover to whom *Confessions* is passionately addressed, but a lover decidedly without a body. (Porphyry wrote of the leading neo-Platonist Plotinus that he "seemed ashamed of being in the body.")[33] It is striking in this connection that Augustine, like Descartes (the father of the mind/body dualism in modern philosophy) later, had been at one point a philosophical skeptic – and he anticipated Descartes by finding a way out of global skepticism by a form of the *cogito* argument.[34] Augustine could believe in his mother's God only when, philosophically, he could make sense of the Christian God in such terms and when Ambrose of Milan had given him a living example of a Christian cleric who exercised responsible political authority and made metaphorical interpretive sense of both the Old and New Testament in integrated Christian terms.[35] In this way, Augustine came to the conviction underlying his conversion: that Bible interpretation was the basis for ultimate authority in religious and ethical matters. What compelled him, at the moment of conversion, were the epistles of Paul, in particular *Romans*, texts that he construed as requiring celibacy as the only way of hearing God's voice within, and later as requiring original sin and the interpretation of the Adam and Eve narrative previously discussed.[36]

The Bible interpretation in question had been reasonably contested by Christians before Augustine and would be contested by even more Christians after Augustine.[37] But our interest here is in the personal and political psychology that led Augustine to make the interpretive moves he did and in why those views were so hegemonically dominant for so long. Why, once he arrives at a conception of an immaterial lover/God, does that lead him associatively (certainly not logically or philosophically) to celibacy?

In *The Confessions*, Augustine tells a story in which he identifies his sexual experience as what kept him from the love of God.[38] God, the addressee of *Confessions*, is the most satisfying and absorbing of lovers. With God, Augustine lives in the most confidential, trusting, and loving of relationships: "physician of my most intimate self".[39] The sensuality of his love is unmistakable:

> Yet there is a light I love, and a food, and a kind of embrace when I love my God – a light, voice, odour, food, embrace of my inner man, where my soul is floodlit by light which space cannot contain, where there is sound that time cannot seize, where there is a perfume which no

breeze disperses, where there is a taste for food no amount of eating can lessen, and where there is a bond of union that no satiety can part. That is what I love when I loved my God. (*Confessions*, p. 183)

Why only with God? As Augustine tells us, his heart had been deeply attached to a woman, the unnamed concubine of the *Confessions* with whom he had a son. In leaving her, his heart "was cut and wounded," leaving "a trail of blood." Behind this cutting was his mother, idealized and asexual, and this division is apparent when he insists at the end of his *Confessions* that a woman has "an equal capacity of rational intelligence," undermined "by the sex of her body," which "is submissive to the masculine sex" (see p. 302). The turn to God as his lover signals a rejection of both sexuality and submission – qualities he associates with women, in the search for a love contaminated by neither and also impervious to loss.

It is quite consistent with this interpretation that Augustine in *The City of God* should offer one of the first serious and profound criticisms of Roman imperialistic violence as, more often than not, unjust both in its ends and means, giving rise to the just war traditions of Western thought.[40] Monica never fundamentally questioned the Roman patriarchy she assumed to be in the nature of things. She arranged her son's marriage to an appropriate girl to ensure his upward mobility, even at the expense of giving up his relationship to the woman he sexually loved. Augustine shows himself to be a good son when he accepts his mother's patriarchal demands, though in the honesty of his confessions, he tells us that it broke his heart.

At the beginning of *Confessions*, he admits that before his conversion he adored the Dido-Aeneas episode in Vergil's *Aeneid* (see *Confessions*, pp. 15–16). In his conversion, he reenacted this story, repudiating the woman he loved to fulfill the patriarchal demands of his mother. Unlike Venus, Monica is a pious Christian woman, more of a critic of Roman patriarchal violence, although at best a partial one. Her son, who comes to God through her and often refers to God as "this dearest mother" (p. 257), is also at best a partial critic of Roman patriarchy. Augustine's love for his mother was conflicted, and she, at one point, threw him out of her house because of his Manichean views, relenting subsequently but weeping constantly over his obduracy (pp. 49, 56, 80–2). In embracing celibacy, Augustine ultimately outdoes his mother in piety, but the break with sexuality leaves in him a darkness both visible and akin to that of Vergil's Aeneas.

When patriarchal demands impose on men such traumatic disruptions of real relationships, their legacy is a personal and political psychology that covers over and rationalizes the loss in terms that cannot be questioned, terms linked to the establishment of manhood and enforced through shame. Men like Augustine, who have visited such wounds on their own psyches, can justify violence against anyone who might question or challenge the price they have paid for their manhood. Thus Augustine, himself once a Manichean, confesses at the time of his conversion: "What vehement and bitter anger I felt against the Manichees!" (p. 160; see also p. 254).

Augustine thus plays the patriarchal Roman hero of his confessional narrative in much the same way as Aeneas does in Vergil's epic. Aeneas is a heroic man because he leaves the woman he loved to fulfill his divinely ordained mission. At a time when the western Roman empire is near its end, Augustine tells a story of his own heroism, shown by his abandonment of the woman he loved and of his sexuality in God's service. Since Augustus, the Roman empire had lived under an autocratic political system in which both political and religious authority were concentrated in the emperor. Since Constantine, the emperors had been for the most part Christian and exercised the same authority over Christianity as their predecessors had enjoyed over Roman pagan religion. Augustine works within the framework of this autocratic conception, calling for a heroic form of religious and political leadership, namely, a celibate male priesthood that will support such a patriarchal conception of authority even when the empire collapses, as it does during his lifetime. A member of this celibate male priesthood is "the soldier of the heavenly host" (p. 206), underscoring the militaristic model absorbed from Roman politics. What makes such a soldier possible, whether Aeneas or Augustine, is the renunciation of sexual love.

Augustine is not the first or last sexually conflicted man of genius who turned to celibacy as the only way to free himself from patriarchally framed relationships to women. Tolstoy and Gandhi also turn to celibacy for such reasons.[41] What is striking in such men is that they can extend critical ethical thought to many areas, though not to the patriarchal assumptions governing their most intimate sexual lives, feelings, and relationships. These they accept as in the nature of things, or in the nature of sexuality. It is important to take seriously the suffering that patriarchy inflicts on men as well as women, in particular, highly sensitive, ethically demanding men who experience sex under its terms as lacking the companionship they associate with friendship and the affection of equals.

We also must appreciate that the psychological basis for such sensitivity in men such as Augustine, Tolstoy, and Gandhi is often a close relationship with an idealized and religious mother or maternal figure. However, because the religion of such mothers itself rests on the idealization of asexual women and denigration of sexual women, it does not fundamentally challenge the terms of patriarchy but works within its framework. The consequence for their sons is that like their mothers, they fail to resist patriarchy. Instead, the turn to celibacy often announces a new, more demanding form of patriarchy – one, in Augustine's case, that establishes an exclusively male, autocratic priesthood. This is the ultimate form of religio-ethical patriarchy: a rule of male, celibate priests to whom all others are subordinate. Its rationale is a misogyny, as Sister Karol Jackowski discerns, a misogyny that, in Augustine's case, he learned from his patriarchal mother.

Augustine clearly knew Apuleius's work well, both his philosophical writings and his novel *Metamorphoses*: "No post-classical Latin author has such a place in Augustine's writings as Apuleius."[42] There is good reason to think that Augustine may have modeled his *Confessions* on Apuleius's novel, as the same genre of an autobiography of religious conversion, albeit not fictionalized. Certainly, the text of the *Confessions* uses imagery that is self-consciously Apuleian: When Augustine describes himself as "in love with love" (p. 35), he echoes the scene in the Cupid and Psyche story where Psyche "fell in love with Love,"[43] and his imagery of God's love is Cupid's arrow, "the arrow of your love" and "you pierced my heart."[44] Augustine's condemnation of undisciplined curiosity again echoes the similar theme in Apuleius,[45] but the borrowings are more than stylistic and thematic. *Confessions* is a highly personal, autobiographical narrative of conversion, as is *Metamorphoses*. Both are organized around the question of love, indeed are, in their different ways, love stories: their narratives move from sexual obsession to love, in Apuleius from animal to human, in Augustine from sex with women to the love of God. The Cupid and Psyche story is as central to Apuleius's novel as the coming to God's love as perfect lover is in Augustine. Augustine centers the psyche, as does Apuleius, in love: "My weight is my love" (p. 278).

Once we see these works as so similar, we can see as well their stark differences, which were of enormous consequence for the direction of Western culture for over a millennium and well beyond. Whereas Augustine's conversion is rooted in his relationship to his highly idealized, asexual mother, Apuleius recovers his humanity through the sexual love of a woman who was his equal. It is striking that to the extent Augustinian Christianity incorporates an image of motherhood in its conception of divinity, it is through the asexual Virgin Mary, based, it has been plausibly suggested, not on the mystery religion of the highly sexual Isis but on the asexual Cybele and her violent cult of sexually self-mutilated acolytes.[46] The consequence of such idealization is not to contest patriarchy but to reinforce it.

It is important, particularly at the present moment, to recapture the sense of a period, crucial in the development of human culture, when there was an awareness of open choices between two paths to a fully human life – that of Apuleius and that of Augustine. We reject the view of late Roman sexuality that conveys the impression that there was an uncontested tendency, both philosophical and religious, to an ascetic conception of human sexuality.[47] Even the best historians of this period have been blinded by the hegemonic power of the Augustinian conception to read back into history an inevitability that simply was not there. The Augustinian conception was remarkably successful, but not because it was reasonable and certainly not because it reflected the dominant views of sexuality of classical philosophers or of Judaism, on which Christianity claimed to be based.

The relationship of Christianity to its Jewish origins has always been a tense and ambivalent one,[48] arising against the background of ethnic prejudice against Jews in the ancient world of Hellenistic Egypt.[49] The specifically Roman hatred of the Jews developed in the wake of the two wars against them and was expressed in "a response to rebellion . . . unique in Roman history,"[50] depriving the Jews of a homeland and leading to the diaspora. The Roman patriarchal psychology of violence, triggered by threats to male honor, needed scapegoats to legitimate its atrocities. This psychology found such a scapegoat in the Jews, unleashing on them forms of violence and marginalization unusual even for Romans, rationalized in terms of hostile attitudes to the religion as such. These wars completely changed not only the relationship between Rome and the Jews but also Judaism itself. No longer could Judaism center its rituals on the Jerusalem Temple, which the Romans had destroyed, building on its site, under Hadrian, a pagan temple to Jupiter (Aelia Capitolina).

With the destruction of the Temple, Christianity – in origin a Jewish sect – was increasingly dominated by Paul's mission to the Gentiles. The fact that many Jews did not accept Christianity posed a standing challenge, especially in the early period when Christianity was a proselytizing religion that competed for believers with the wide range of religious and philosophical alternative belief systems available in the late pagan world. Because Christian missionaries increasingly centered their work on Gentiles (non-Jews), there was also a powerful incentive for Christians to distinguish themselves from the Jews, whom Romans now held in disfavor, and indeed to absorb into Christianity Roman anti-Semitism, claiming themselves thus to be more Roman than Jewish.[51] Augustine played an important role in rationalizing such a distinctively Christian anti-Semitism. As we shall see, it was his view of sexuality (as intrinsically problematic) that led him to interpret so negatively the role sexuality played in Jewish life.

The ascetic Augustinian sexual views were, in fact, sectarian and extreme even when adopted, rendering naturalistic features of human sexual experience as marks of demonic possession.[52] Augustine's preoccupation with Apuleius makes sense from this point of view, as Apuleius in *Metamorphoses* converts to a god who is a sexual and caring woman, endorsing a view of sexual love that is redemptive. The Christian attack on pagan culture was significantly focused on the idea that the divine could be sexual, and more particularly on goddesses such as Aphrodite and Isis. For Augustine, the critical point is made at great length in *The City of God* in the form of an attack on Apuleius's claim that daimons/personal gods intermediate between the high God and human experience, for such gods are, Augustine argues, in fact demons, devils.[53] Nothing is more appalling for Augustine than the rituals of pagan cults of mothers (remembered from his pre-Christian days) with their "disgusting verbal and acted obscenities."[54] What strikes us about these rhetorical rants is not only their rather posed mockery but also their underlying sense of horror and fear, centered on sexual experience in general and the sexual experience of women in particular.

The hegemonic triumph of Augustinian Christianity introduced anxiety into the heart of human sexual experience, an anxiety based on an acceptance of patriarchy as in the nature of things. E. R. Dodds wrote a classic book on the anxiety he found to underlie late Roman pagan and Christian thought. We understand that anxiety to receive its fullest and most lasting expression in the Augustinian introduction of the patriarchal script of sexual love as tragic into the heart of sexuality itself.[55] It is an anxiety still too much with us.

Augustine writes of his struggles before conversion as "refusing to become your soldier"[56] so that conversion, when it occurs, places him finally in an appropriately patriarchal relationship to God as a man-soldier. The celibate priest is a new Aeneas, hardened as men must be to the battles required in God's service against His enemies.[57] It is surely not surprising that this psychology would show itself, in Augustine's case, by his making the most historically important arguments in the Christian tradition for the religious intolerance of heretics and for Christian anti-Semitism, arguments remote from the letter and spirit of the Gospels (as earlier and later Christian advocates of toleration observed).[58] We have described the dissociative processes that make such intolerance possible and appealing. If one can justify shutting down the forms of sexual intimacy through which human beings experience loving connection, care, and mutual responsiveness, one is well on the way to shutting down the psychological basis for ethical reasoning and experience, making possible the acceptance of stereotypes that dehumanize and thus rationalize atrocity.

We have seen the force of such stereotypes in Augustine's interpretation of the Adam and Eve story, which plays a crucial role in his conception of human nature as flawed by original sin. His support for the use of Roman imperial power to repress heresy is rationalized in terms of this flaw, requiring coercive power to keep people from making the mistakes, including mistakes in belief, that they cannot avoid on their own. We stress, in this connection, that in contrast to Ambrose, Augustine never resisted repressive imperial policies.[59] As a modern critic of Augustine acidly observes:

> Augustine never challenged any imperial authority. After his return to Carthage in 416, he showed that he knew where authority lay, and in his last years chose to curry favor not with the wealthy aristocrats he had sought out in the 390s and 400s, but now with the hard men: the military and political enforcers Rome sent to Africa.... In his last years, Augustine resembles nothing so much as one of those pious churchmen of Francoist times, leader of a state-promoted church, followed prudently by many, despised quietly by some, and opposed fiercely by a remnant quite sure of its own fidelity to a truer church.[60]

It is the crucial role of gender stereotypes in Augustine's thought that explains the sense of insulted manhood that he displays at any dissent from Catholic religious orthodoxy and his willingness to use and rationalize violence in repressing such dissent. Such propensities to violence are of a piece with his expression of rage at pagan rituals of mother goddesses and his legitimation of Christian anti-Semitism, imposing a servile political status on Jews because, as he put it "The Jew is the slave of the Christians."[61] Key to this psychology is the repressive violence directed at sexual voice and the view of pleasure itself as demonic. The study of Augustine becomes riveting for us because it displays so clearly how important the repression of sexual voice has been in both the construction and transmission of structural injustice, rationalizing violence in terms of gender stereotypes that themselves rest on the repression of sexual voice.

By carrying patriarchy into his own sexuality, Augustine initiates what becomes an influential cultural pattern of religious intolerance that represses any voice that does not conform to patriarchal authority. By repressing his own sexual experience, he renders himself psychologically armored against the reasonable claims of a voice that would contest his views and justifies the use of violence in the service of this repression. This psychological dynamic also explains why the free sexuality of women should have become so demonized under the Catholic Roman emperors. The movement over time to increasingly severe penalties for adultery culminated in the provisions of Constantius and Constans in 339, which not only called for strict enforcement of the law against adultery but also decreed that adulterers be punished "as though they were manifest parricides."[62]

Augustine himself offers a telling introspective account of the larger significance of the repudiation of sexual pleasure in his life. It is not merely sexual pleasure that he disowns, but he discusses as well the need for correlative restraints on the pleasures of food and drink, of smell, of hearing, and of seeing. Such restraints lead, finally, to attacking both the arts (including the theater) and even curiosity itself. If Apuleius called in the Cupid and Psyche story for breaking the taboo on seeing and speaking as key to the possibility of sexual love, Augustine calls, in contrast, for instituting a more radical taboo, namely, on sexual pleasure itself. What follows is what we have come to expect – a shutting down of the very sources of our relational intelligence and imagination, including our ethical intelligence. The repudiation of sexual pleasure is thus at the root of what was so dangerous in the personal and political psychology Augustine exemplifies and defends: its dissociation from real relationships and its underlying propensity to a violence – no longer controlled by ethical intelligence – against those persons or groups who threaten the legitimacy of one's repudiation.

We have seen this dynamic in patriarchal psychology before, namely, in Roman patriarchy and in Vergil's exploration of its psychology. This psychology requires enemies, and the disassociation makes it easier to dehumanize them and thus to rationalize unjust violence against them. In contrast to traditional Roman patriarchy and to Vergil's Aeneas, Augustine thought love was the central issue of a truly human life and, as we have noted, criticized Roman violence and developed an alternative Christian theory of just wars. But his search for love was compromised by something quite different. Because he uncritically carried Roman patriarchy into the very heart of human sexuality, he made psychologically possible a dissociation that would wreak violence on any critic of its imperial demands.

It clarifies this Augustinian psychology, so influential on Christian thought (Catholic and Protestant), to consider Martin Luther's recognition that Augustine's innovations in theology were motivated by a repudiation of relationship.[63] When Luther, himself an Augustinian monk, came to question celibacy as a requirement for the priesthood,[64] he framed his general argument in a letter to his father. Luther's father had objected to his taking vows of celibacy because, he argued, his son did not fully understand how important sexuality was or would be to him.[65] Luther had come to believe that his father was right – that his taking of the vows signified a failure to stay in real relationship and was based, in fact, as his father argued at the time, on "an illusion and deception."[66] The implicit contrast is between Luther's relationship to his real father (who knew his son in some respects better than he knew himself) and his relationship to God as the mythologically idealized father whom Luther had believed required celibacy. Luther thus frames his argument against celibacy as a requirement for priestly authority in terms of a return to real relationship, including a direct, unmediated relationship with God, repudiating the psychology of loss and idealization that he had earlier accepted. His implicit critique of the Augustinian psychology, which he had lived as a celibate monk, was that it arose from a traumatic breaking of personal relationships, a psychic loss that showed itself in a dissociation from experience and an idealization that covered over the loss. The consequence was a kind of motivated stupidity.

A former Catholic priest, Eugene Kennedy, has recently explored another dimension of this Augustinian psychology, namely, the idealization of mothers as asexual and the denigration of sexual women. Consistent with the views of Sister Jackowski, Kennedy argues that the psychology of celibacy in Catholic priests often reflects intense, highly idealized relations to their mothers and a lack of real relationships either with them or with women generally. The patriarchal authority of the priesthood in matters of gender and sexuality[67] covers a history of loss and wounded sexuality.

The force of idealization in this psychology is powerfully apparent in the way Thomas Aquinas brings Augustine's view of sexuality center stage in his argument for a celibate male priesthood. It was one of Thomas's controlling ambitions to show, through what he thought the best science and philosophy available (Aristotle's), that the final perfectionist ends of living could only be understood, recognized, and pursued by a clergy freed from a sexual life that would distract them from the philosophically demanding metaphysical argument that alone enabled one to know and find God. The role sexuality plays for Thomas is solely one of propagation because sexuality is for him so epistemically problematic (as he puts is, "the enjoyment of corporeal delights distracts the mind from its peak activity").[68] It could be redeemed only by producing offspring who would support a society in which a celibate clergy would pursue the ultimate perfectionist value of knowing God. In the next chapter, we consider the consequences of this psychology in the church's response to the contemporary priest sexual abuse scandal.

# Part Two

Resistance Across Time and Culture

# 6 *Resistance: Religion*

We turn now to the closer study of resistance to patriarchy, beginning with the sources of and the difficulties of such resistance within religions wedded to patriarchal forms. Christianity becomes our prime example because of the tension between the historical Jesus and the Augustinian tradition that became hegemonic in Europe for well over a millennium. The virulent anti-Semitism that in part reflects Augustine's characterization of the Jews as "carnal Israel" heightens this tension and suggests the role that sexuality plays in this story. And so does the growth of modern constitutional democracy, represented by Bayle and Locke, who as radical Christians questioned intolerance. We will consider the Quakers who objected to slavery, the American abolitionist feminists who identified racism and sexism as interlocked evils, and Martin Luther King, Jr., whose campaign against injustice was based on an appeal to nonviolent resistance. In the contemporary priest sexual-abuse scandal, we see the legacy of celibacy, and we end with a former Catholic priest, James Carroll, who tells a powerful life story that moves in the opposite direction from that of Augustine, from celibacy to sexual love and from resistance to unjust war to a rejection of Christian anti-Semitism.

The growing evidence offered by feminist scholars indicates that the orthodox Christian tradition repressed the texts of the early Christian period that contested its patriarchalism.[1] Among such texts are those of Gnostic Christianity that were driven underground in the 2nd century, some of which include doctrines and practices that may well have been influenced by the Isis cult.[2] These doctrines approach God as mother or feminine and illuminate a conception of religious insight that resembles what we might today consider a kind of psychoanalytic self-knowledge together with practices that include women as priests. If an anti-patriarchal resistance is part of our psychological nature, it is also part of our religious heritage.

## 1. THE HISTORICAL JESUS

The contemporary scholarly consensus portrays the historical Jesus as a pious, learned Jew of his culture and period, acutely conscious of the prophetic tradition of moral protest that he elaborates. His life had analogues in his period (Honi, Hanina, and others), and his teachings were largely within the range of views current in intertestamental Judaism,[3] including the influence of Hillel.[4] One feature of such pious Judaism is that it focuses on a trusting relationship to God as a loving, caring person, in contrast to the theological propositions of later Christian belief.[5]

Geza Vermes shows, in this connection, how in addressing God, Jesus avoids "the divine epithet, 'King'" predominant "in ancient Jewish literature"; rather, "the Synoptic Gospels depict him as addressing God, or speaking of him, as 'Father' in some sixty instances, and at least once place on his lips the Aramaic title, *Abba*." God is addressed as an approachable, solicitous, and loving father, one concerned above all with staying in a relationship to his erring children and to outcasts, otherwise despised.[6] To a query about his joining a meal given by a publican and attended by many of his colleagues, Jesus justified his presence by identifying his host and his host's colleagues as those who are spiritually ill and in need of a physician (Mark 2:17; Matt. 9:12; Luke 5:31). There is also a specific report that he allowed a prostitute ("a woman of the city who was a sinner"; Luke 7:37, 39; cf. Mark 14:3; Matt. 26:6–7) to anoint him. Jesus' practice of accepting the companionship of the despised was sufficiently common knowledge to endow him with the name "friend of tax-collectors and sinners" (Matt. 11:19; Luke 7:34). If his mission as healer and exorcist was for the sick and the possessed, he understood himself primarily as bringing God's love to those in the most spiritual need: "I came not to call the righteous, but sinners" (Mark 2:17; Matt. 9:13; Luke 5:32). His overriding concern was with the miserable and helpless: "I was sent only to the lost sheep of the house of Israel" (Matt. 15:24); "Go to the lost sheep of the house of Israel" (Matt. 10:6). As Vermes expresses the point:

> [Jesus] is depicted in the Synoptics as the compassionate, caring, and loving pilot and shepherd who, imitating the merciful, caring, and loving God, guides those most in need, the little ones (Matt. 18:10), the sinners, the whores, and the publicans, toward the gate of the Kingdom of the Father.[7]

Jesus' sense of God, as loving and caring father of his erring children, was interpreted by the Jewish philosopher Martin Buber as a model for love in an I-Thou personal relationship:

and now one can act, help, heal, educate, raise, redeem. Love is responsibility of an I for a You: in this consists what cannot consist in any feeling – the equality of all lovers, from the smallest to the greatest and from the blissfully secure whose life is circumscribed by the life of one beloved human being to him that is nailed his life long to the cross of the world, capable of what is immense and bold enough to risk it: to love *man*.[8]

Buber construes this relationship to God as a loving father as one of equality and reciprocity: "[E]veryone can speak the You and then becomes I; everyone can say Father and then becomes son; actuality abides."[9] How are we to understand the sense in which Buber, interpreting Jesus, suggests that what under patriarchy is a form of hierarchy (father-child) can be a loving and caring relationship of mutual actuality? Both Buber and Jesus are surely contesting the patriarchal framing of the relationship, for if *even* the father-son pairing must ultimately be understood as in developmental service of a relationship of equals, then hierarchy must yield to relational care, sensitivity, and concern – including concern for voice – in all relationships.

Buber's reading of Jesus clarifies the remarkable role women play in his life and ministry in ways that are, if anything, very much in tension with patriarchal conceptions of gender. In the Synoptics, Jesus is pictured as showing reserve verging on hostility toward his family, including his mother Mary. Mark (3:21) bluntly reports that his family held him to be mad, to the point that they wanted forcibly to remove him from his public ministry. Elsewhere we are informed that his mother and brothers expected preferential treatment from Jesus – for example, that he would interrupt his teaching when they arrived. Jesus rejected such treatment: "Who are my mother and my brothers?" he asked. Pointing to his disciples, he declared them, metaphorically, his "mother" and "brothers" (Mark 3:31–35; Matt. 12:46–50; Luke 8:19–21). Further, although Jewish men, including holy men, were expected to marry, everything points to Jesus as an unmarried celibate man, including Matthew 19:12 ("eunuchs such as make themselves eunuchs with a view to the kingdom of heaven").[10] In these respects, Jesus does not conform to a patriarchal conception of gender – he refuses to accept the authority of his own family of origin and does not define himself by his authority within a family.

Perhaps as a result, Jesus takes a remarkable interest in women as persons, and they take an interest in him. Women were not only disciples,[11] but among the most faithful of his disciples, holding onto their relationship to him in a way that men did not. While male disciples abandon

Jesus after his arrest or even deny him (Peter), women are with him at his death, as Mark recounts:

> Now there were also women, looking on from a distance, among whom were Mary from Magdala, Mary the mother of James the Younger and Joses, and Salome, who, when he [Jesus] was in Galilee, followed him and served him, and many other [women] who had come up with him to Jerusalem [for the feast of the Passover] (Mark 15:40–41).[12]

Moreover, it is to a group of these faithful women at his tomb that resurrection experiences are first granted, only to be initially disbelieved by the terrified male disciples (see Mark 16:1–14; cf. Matt. 28:1–10; Luke 24:1–49). The interest of women in his teaching is portrayed as engaging their intelligence, and Jesus defends Mary's listening to his teaching from her sister Martha's insistence that he tell Mary to help her in the womanly tasks of serving (Luke 10:38–42).

Jesus teaches and ministers to women in ways that speak to their subjective experience, including their suffering as women, even when traditional outcasts. The experience of women as equally subject with men to God's loving attention is a frequent focus of both his parables and judgment sayings.[13] as well as of his ministering concern. Thus, Jesus cures the daughter of a Syrophoenician woman, though as a foreign woman she would normally be supposed to be an unclean Gentile with whom a Jewish man should not talk (Mark 7:24–30; cf. Matt. 15:21–28); he cures Peter's mother-in-law (Mark, 1:29–31; cf. Matt. 8:14–15; Luke 4:38–39); he heals a crippled woman on the Sabbath (Luke 13:10–17); he cures a woman suffering from menstrual flows, who, though ritually unclean, touches him, then brings the daughter of Jairus back to life (Mark 5:21–43; cf. Matt. 9:18–26; Luke 8:40–56); and he is so moved by the grief of the widow of Nain that he brings her son back to life (Luke 7:11–17).[14] Jesus also accepts and defends as blessed a sinning woman (most likely a prostitute) who has anointed and kissed his feet (Luke 7:36–50) and speaks at length to a ritually unclean sinning woman from Samaria at a well and brings her to faith (John 4:7–42).[15] The conversation with the woman at the well displays unusual openness and interest as well as capacities of psychological penetration, as Jesus speaks "to a woman whom he had never met before and appear[s] to know everything about the emotional chaos of her life … images which cannot be dispelled by scholars calling into question their historical plausibility."[16]

Jesus is of course a man, but the interpretive issue raised by his attitude to women is his critical position to patriarchy. Certainly, his defense of the woman taken in adultery calls for skepticism about one of the roots of patriarchal violence, namely, violence against women who transgress the demands placed on their sexuality (John 8:1–11). As one careful student of the historical Jesus concludes, his teaching, at a minimum, "entailed a certain reformation of the patriarchal structure of society."[17] The truth may be even more radical. Contemporary feminist Bible scholars urge us to take seriously the degree to which Jesus's critique of patriarchy was diluted by the sexism of his later followers. Such followers, including Paul (who had had no personal relationship to Jesus, unlike his disciples), ministered largely to highly patriarchal Greco-Roman audiences of potential converts and may have chosen as canonical texts and traditions those closer to the patriarchal assumptions of their audiences. If so, a reasonable case may be made that the historical Jesus's critique of patriarchy was much more profoundly radical than those of his followers like Paul.[18]

One way of understanding the roots of what is ethically radical in Jesus is to relate his attitude to women to his conception of God, which is itself remarkably anti-patriarchal. Jesus always speaks, as we have seen, of God as a loving father, but as Buber's interpretation of Jesus shows, his understanding of the relationship is one of reciprocal love and care. Jesus's thought on this point is traditionally Jewish: Moses asks God: "Did I conceive all these people? Did I give birth to them, that you should say to me, 'Carry them in your bosom, as a nurse carries a sucking child,' to the land that you promised on oath to their ancestors" (Numbers 10:11).[19] Isaiah not only describes the human response to God in terms of a woman in labor (Isaiah 12:8, 21:3, 26:17), but describes God's prophetic love in such terms as well: "I will cry out like a woman in labor,/I will gasp and pant" (42:14).[20] A Qumran hymn speaks of God's love as maternal: "And as a woman who tenderly loves her babe, so does Thou rejoice in them."[21] Consistent with this Jewish way of thinking, all the important features that Jesus ascribes to a loving God are exactly those that Sara Ruddick describes as maternal care, a loving care that holds onto a relationship to another, despite frustrations and disappointments, to serve the ends of love – protection, growth, and ethical acceptability.[22]

Jesus shows his loving care to sinners who have not yet repented and defines his life and teaching in terms of never breaking relationship to those who have failed his hopes for them. He defines the value, indeed the power, of love as a willingness to stay in relationship, above all when the beloved fails one. Jesus starts, it seems, from the microcosm of caring love that Sara Ruddick describes and then writes such loving care into an ethics and religion based on God's love for his recalcitrant children. The history of their advances and digressions as a people is interpreted through the prophetic tradition, which Jesus assumes and elaborates. We can never know what jolted Jesus to move from microcosm to macrocosm, but if, as historians believe, his father Joseph was dead by the time of Jesus's ministry,[23] the loss of a beloved father who imparted to his son a God of maternal care may figure in the tensions that propelled him from his family to his public ministry. As Buber shows, Jesus redefined the scope of ethical concern between and among persons, made in God's image, as a loving concern that is equally available to all persons, certainly to women at least as much as men. As Erik Erikson, the psychoanalyst and historian, perceptively observed: "[O]ne cannot help noticing, on Jesus' part, an unobtrusive integration of maternal and paternal tenderness."[24]

Consider from this perspective Jesus's teachings about nonviolence, namely, the Sermon on the Mount (Matt. 5–7). There are compelling reasons for believing that the historical Jesus could not have meant Matthew 5:38–42 ("if anyone strikes you on the right cheek, turn the other to him as well") to forbid the role that the principle of self-defense plays in criminal law. As David Daube has argued, Jesus invokes "an eye for an eye" not as a principle of criminal law but in terms of the developing tradition of Jewish civil law, in which varying monetary damages were assigned for different kinds of injuries. Jesus does not question this tradition as applied to injuries, but rather questions the view it extends to insults as well, including the Near Eastern insult of striking the right cheek with the back of the hand.[25] Perhaps, as Joachim Jeremias argues, Jesus is not speaking of a general insult but "of a quite specific insulting blow: the blow given to the disciples of Jesus as heretics."[26] In any event, Jesus is addressing "the urge to resent a wrong done to you as an affront to your pride, to forget that the wrongdoer is your brother before God and to compel him to soothe your unworthy feelings; and it advocates, instead, a humility which cannot be wounded, a giving of yourself to your brother which will achieve more than can be achieved by a narrow justice."[27]

In light of Daube's analysis, we can interpret Matthew 5:43–44, "You have heard that it was said 'You shall love your neighbor and hate your enemy,' but I tell you to love your enemies and pray for those who misuse you," in terms of Jesus's rejection of the Essene teaching that commanded such hatred.[28] Paradoxically, the Essenes accepted a teaching of nonretaliation analogous to that of Jesus, but that teaching was a strategic expression of apocalyptic faith that, at the last judgment, God himself would wreak vengeance on such hated enemies of the light.[29] John the Baptist, Jesus's mentor, may have been associated with the Qumran Essenes, but the fact that his message, like that of Jesus, appealed to the entire Jewish people, including sinners, suggests that by the time he appears in the Gospels, John was no longer a member of the secretive, monastically self-isolated sect.[30] Both John and Jesus may have been celibate men, like the Essenes, but Jesus, unlike the ascetic John, embraced open table fellowship with all as a distinctive feature of his ministry, a "bon vivant existence with robbers and sinners . . . more scandalous and ominous than a mere matter of breaking purity rules dear to . . . the Pharisees."[31] The sense of scandal is captured at Matthew 11:19: "For the Son of Man came eating and drinking, and you say: 'Behold an eater and drinker, a friend of toll collectors and sinners.'"[32] Accordingly, what distinguishes Jesus's commands "not to resist one who is evil" and "turn the other [cheek]" is the way he grounds its motivations in an inclusive caring love that here asks men in particular to question the force in their lives of the Mediterranean honor code, whose demands require that insults to manhood be met with violence.[33]

The historical Jesus, in his teachings on nonviolence, thus was asking men to question the role that patriarchal honor played in defining their sense of manhood. As we have seen, one of the remarkable features of Jesus's life and teaching was his ethical sensitivity to the plight of women the honor code condemned, women against whom violence, threatened or unleashed, was considered legitimate. Thus his defense against stoning of the woman taken in adultery (John 8:1–11). The incident of the adulteress is put in particularly poignant terms as Jesus exposes a culture of male hypocrisy with a voice they do not usually confront:

> Then the scribes and the Pharisees led forward a woman who had been caught in adultery, and made her stand there in front of everybody. "Teacher," they said to him, "this woman has been caught in the very act of adultery. Now, in the Law Moses ordered such women to be stoned. But you – what do you have to say about it?" (They were posing this question to trap him so that they could have something to accuse him of.) But Jesus simply bent down and started drawing on the ground with his finger. When they persisted in their questioning, he straightened up and said to them, "The man among you who has no sin – let him be the first to cast a stone at her." And he bent down again and started to write on the ground. But the audience went away one by one, starting with the elders; and he was left alone with the woman still there before him. So Jesus, straightening up, said to her, "Woman, where are they all? Hasn't anyone condemned you" "No one, sir," she answered. Jesus said, "Nor do I condemn you. You may go. But from now on, avoid this sin." (John 8:3–11).[34]

There is a Socratic inwardness in Jesus's questioning of these men (exemplifying the principle of Matt. 7:1–2: "Do not sit in judgment, lest you yourself be judged, for you will be judged by the same standard which you have used"), one that lays bare what otherwise they repress. Their inability to answer Jesus as he turns from them, "drawing on the ground with his finger," exposes the silences in the male psyche enforced by the demands of the honor code. That code wreaks havoc, of course, on any woman who deviates from its demands, as the stoning of an adulteress shows. Jesus's ethically rooted forgiveness in this case may have been so threatening to the sexism of the early church that it was not accepted into the canon until a more tolerant period.[35] Its profound interest to the present argument is how, combined with the prohibition on violence between men in Matthew 5:43–44, it confronts us with the ways in which patriarchal conventions depend on a violence unleashed by any threat to its gender stereotypes, whether violence against women or violence between men. In both cases, Jesus shows how such violence rests on the repression of a free ethical voice.

No aspect of Jesus's life and teaching was more important than his own insistence on the free ethical voice that, consistent with the tradition of the prophets on which he relied,[36] he himself developed and displayed with an authority that "astonished" his audiences, "for he taught them as one that had authority, and not as the scribes" (Mark 1:22).[37] The historical Jesus may have regarded himself as an eschatological prophet like Elijah,[38] discovering his own prophetic voice in relationship to a conception of a God whose loving care inspired that voice. Jesus's approach to disagreement with his teaching or his actions was that of a teacher; when such disagreement expresses itself in the political violence that ultimately ends his life, he asks poignantly: "Are ye come out as against a thief with swords and staves for to take me? I sat daily with you teaching in the temple, and ye laid no hold on me" (Matt. 26:55).[39] Like Socrates, who in his method of indirection and introspective inwardness he resembles, Jesus dies for his beliefs and teachings – himself the victim of political violence directed against a voice interpreted as challenging the terms of Roman law that "instigators of a revolt, riot, or agitators of the people" were to be "either crucified, thrown to wild animals, or banished to an island."[40]

Roman political authority, as we have seen, rested on a conception of manhood that made possible a military life which legitimated aggressive war, imperial rule, and the enslavement of defeated peoples on which the Roman imperium and economy depended.[41] Pontius Pilate, the Roman governor of Judea who condemns Jesus to death, probably at the insistence of the Sadducee temple officials who were complicitous with Roman rule, exemplifies a servile devotion to his superiors, contempt for the people he ruled, cowardice, and cruelty.[42] Jesus may have been just as critical of the forms of patriarchal violence in Jewish culture, including those that would later develop into the violence of the Zealots in the First Jewish Revolt (66–70 C.E.), to which the Romans would respond within 40 years of Jesus's death with the destruction of the Second Temple in 70 C.E.[43] The death of the historical Jesus thus exemplifies what may have been one of his distinctive teachings: that a free ethical voice is the antithesis of patriarchal manhood.

## 2. THE JEWS AND CHRISTIAN ANTI-SEMITISM

Why the Christian obsession with the Jews? On the basis of the Augustinian legitimation of religious persecution, politically entrenched conceptions of truths had become the measure both of standards of reasonable inquiry and of those who could be considered reasonable inquirers. Such political enforcement of a conception of religious truth immunizes itself from independent criticism based on reasonable standards of thought and deliberation. In effect, the conception of religious truth, though perhaps having once been shaped by more ultimate considerations of reason, ceases to be held or to be understood and elaborated on the basis of reason.

A tradition that loses the sense of its reasonable foundations will stagnate and depend increasingly for allegiance on question-begging appeals to orthodox conceptions of truth and the violent repression of any dissent from such conceptions, treating that dissent as a kind of disloyal moral treason. The politics of loyalty rapidly degenerates into a politics that takes pride in widely held community values solely because they are community values. Standards of discussion and inquiry become increasingly parochial and insular and serve only a polemical role in the defense of such values; indeed, they become increasingly hostile to any reasonable assessment in light of independent standards.[44]

Such politics tends to degrade to forms of irrationalism in order to protect its now essentially polemical project: Opposing views are suppressed, facts distorted or misstated, thought disconnected from ethical reasoning, and ultimately, deliberation in politics is denigrated in favor of violence against dissent and the glorification of such violence. Paradoxically, the greater the tradition's vulnerability to reasonable challenge, the more likely it is to generate forms of political irrationalism, including scapegoating of outcast dissenters, in order to secure allegiance.

This phenomenon illustrates the *paradox of intolerance*.[45] A certain conception of religious truth is originally affirmed as true and politically enforced on society at large because it is taken to be the epistemic measure of reasonable inquiry (i.e., more likely to lead to epistemically reliable beliefs). But the consequence of the legitimation of such intolerance for alternative conceptions is that standards of reasonable inquiry, outside the orthodox measure of such inquiry, are repressed. In effect, the orthodox conception of truth is no longer defended on the basis of reason but is increasingly hostile to reasonable assessment in terms of impartial standards not hostage to its own conception. Indeed, orthodoxy is defended as an end in itself, increasingly by nonrational and even irrational means of appeal to community identity and the like. The paradox appears in the subversion of the original epistemic motivations of the Augustinian argument. Rather than securing reasonable inquiry, the argument now cuts off the tradition from such inquiry. Indeed, contradicting and frustrating its original epistemic ambitions, the legitimacy of the tradition feeds on irrationalism precisely when it is most vulnerable to reasonable criticism. Thus the sense of paradox in such epistemic incoherence.

The history of religious persecution amply illustrates these truths, and no aspect of that history more clearly so than Christian anti-Semitism. In his recent studies of anti-Semitism,[46] the medievalist Gavin Langmuir characterizes as anti-Judaism Christianity's long-standing worries about the Jews because of the way the Jewish rejection of Christianity discredited the reasonableness of the Christian belief system in the pagan world. Langmuir argues that the Christian conception of the obduracy of the Jews and the divine punishment of them for such obduracy were natural forms of anti-Judaic self-defense, resulting in the expulsion and segregation of Jews from Christian society that expressed and legitimated such judgments.[47] In contrast, he calls anti-Semitism proper the totally baseless and irrational beliefs about ritual crucifixions and cannibalism of Christians by Jews that were "widespread in northern Europe by 1350."[48] Such belief led to populist murders of Jews that were usually, though not always, condemned by both church and secular authorities. The irrationalist nature of these beliefs requires, Langmuir suggests, a distinguishing name, *chimeria*, suggesting, from the Greek root, "fantasies, figments of the imagination, monsters that, although dressed syntactically in the cloths of real humans, have never been seen and are projections of mental processes unconnected with the real people of the outgroup."[49]

Langmuir suggests, as does R. I. Moore,[50] that the development of anti-Semitism proper was associated with growing internal doubts posed by dissenters in the period 950–1250 about the reasonableness of certain Catholic religious beliefs and practices, and the resolution of such doubts by the forms of irrationalist politics associated with anti-Semitism – often centering, for example, on fantasies of ritual eating of human flesh that expressed underlying worries about transubstantiation. The worst ravages of anti-Semitism illustrate the paradox of intolerance. Precisely when the dominant religious tradition gave rise to the most reasonable internal doubts, these doubts were displaced from reasonable discussion and debate into blatant political irrationalism based on chimeria against one of the more conspicuous, vulnerable, and innocent groups of dissenters.

Langmuir's distinction between anti-Judaism and anti-Semitism proper is an unstable one. Both attitudes rest on conceptions of religious truth that are unreasonably enforced on the community at large. Beliefs in obduracy are not as unreasonable as beliefs in cannibalism, and segregation is not as evil as populist murder or genocide. Yet both forms of politics are, on grounds of the argument for toleration, unreasonable in principle. More fundamentally, anti-Judaism laid the corrupt political foundation for anti-Semitism. Once it became politically legitimate to enforce at large a sectarian conception of religious truth, reasonable doubts about such truth were displaced from reasonable discussion and debate to the irrationalist politics of religious persecution. The Jews have been in the Christian West the most continuously blatant victims of such politics, making anti-Semitism "the oldest prejudice in Western civilization."[51]

Building on Langmuir's insights, our argument can more deeply explain both the resistance of the Jews to Augustinian orthodoxy and why that orthodoxy turned on them so viciously, with such catastrophic consequences in 20th-century Europe. Within our framework, it was Augustine who, building on the Roman anti-Semitism that flourished in Rome after the Jewish wars, rationalized a distinctively Christian anti-Semitism. Augustine's marking of the Jews as "carnal Israel" is not incidental to their persecution. We could go further and argue that the Jews provided a remarkable example, within limits, of a resistance grounded in the protection of intimate personal life, including sexual love and relationship. In the Judaism before the diaspora, the Temple priesthood was not celibate. Celibacy was advocated only by sects, like that of Qumran, opposed to dominant Jewish belief and practice. After the diaspora, temple rituals and the associated priesthood play no role in rabbinical Judaism, as Jewish belief and practice increasingly centers in the home and in synagogues where the Hebrew Bible is studied under rabbis, meaning teachers, chosen by believers. Like other Jewish men, rabbis marry and have family lives. Sexual love and family relationships are at the center of Jewish belief and practice, including religious commandments for husbands to give pleasure in sex to their wives on the sabbath.[52]

Thus, as we have seen, Martin Buber explicates the Jewish experience of God in terms of a relational and loving care and sensitivity of one human, made in God's image, to another. Since Jews do not believe in an afterlife, there is little temptation to denigrate the pleasures of this world in light of the next.[53] While Jewish women in the diaspora were not permitted to be rabbis, they played, in contrast to many Christian women, powerful roles not only in their families (including family religious life) but in business, as Jewish men were expected to study Talmud. Under the anti-Semitic laws in Christian Europe, Jewish men were also excluded from many forms of profession, including the military, which further accentuated the cultural differences between Jewish and Christian conceptions of manhood and womanhood.[54]

Jewish resistance to Augustinian Christianity can in part be explained as a resistance to Christianity's denigration of sexual life and relationships. The Jews objected as well to many theological views of the hegemonic Christianity that enveloped them – for example, the trinity, the virgin birth, Jesus as the incarnation of God, an afterlife, and the like – beliefs that would have struck many Jews of the period of Jesus as forms of pagan belief, inconsistent with the ethical monotheism of the Hebrew Bible. But the role these beliefs played in legitimating Augustine's disavowal of sexual love and relationship may explain the tenacious resistance of Jews, a resistance maintained against extraordinary pressures and constraints. The joyous eroticism of the Song of Songs in the Hebrew Bible is the antithesis of Christian asceticism. The Hebrew Bible's anti-mythological narratives (contesting the mythological religions around them),[55] as well as its anti-idealizing narratives (for example, the remarkable rendering of human frailty before the ethical demands of God), require an artistry that prefigures the novel.[56] To Robert Alter, the ancient Hebrew writers invented a narrative art in order to capture their view of life as lived "under God, in the changing medium of time, inexorably and perplexingly in relationship."[57] Even the leaders God favors (for example, David) are notably flawed, highly sexual, and subject to betrayal and loss[58]; and God also has his frailties (anger, for example).[59] The refusal of God to permit Abraham's sacrifice of his son[60] bespeaks a larger view of the ethics of loving relationships in the family that rejects not simply human sacrifice but more specifically the sacrifice of children – a Jewish view that would explain why the orthodox Christian view of God's sacrifice of his son would, to say the least, not appeal to Jews. Idealization arising from loss – a feature of Augustinian orthodox Christianity – would also be questioned by Jews as antithetical to the religious and ethical demands of a loving God and to a life lived in relationship and in time. Indeed, the Jews, for these reasons, may be the first example in human history of such a long-lasting resistance group, clarifying how important such associational activity is to the power and persistence of such resistance.

Historical Judaism, like most religions and cultures that we know of, embodied patriarchal features. Its exclusion of women from study of the Torah established, at the core of the religion, a patriarchal hierarchy, rationalized on explicitly sexual grounds: "Anyone who teaches his daughter Torah, teaches her lasciviousness."[61] Although the starkly homophobic prohibitions of Leviticus 18:22[62] and 20:13[63] are today understood, by Jewish Bible scholars among others, as applicable only in certain places and circumstances, the historical tradition of rabbinical Judaism did not qualify its homophobic teaching.[64] On the other hand, the celebration of the sexual body and the antiheroic conception of manhood placed Judaism in opposition to the dominant patriarchal conception of Christianity. Furthermore, the appeal to values that underlie the growing internal criticism by Jews of both the sexist and homophobic features of their historical tradition has supported changes that have been more difficult certainly for Augustinian Christianity.[65]

Because Jewish resistance took the form of defending both the sexual body and an antiheroic conception of manhood, Augustinian Christianity, centered in the repression of sexual voice, turned on the Jews with repressive force. The role of grace in Augustine's thought arises from the doctrine of original sin that he finds in the Adam and Eve narrative. The Pauline attack on the role of law in Judaism, which subjects sexual love to ethical constraints, arises from what Jews found so unreasonable, the rejection of sexuality because it blocked access to God.[66] The Jews accept no such doctrine of original sin because God is known through, among other human blessings, the pleasures of sexual love. The role of law is to address our rational autonomy, offering reasonable constraints within which we should pursue this pleasure. From a Jewish standpoint, it is the Christian repudiation of sexuality, unreasonable and difficult to comply with, that explains the role of grace in Pauline/Augustinian Christianity: Only God's love (His grace or gift to us) makes such asceticism possible. Augustine's search in *The Confessions* for a more perfect lover, which he finds in an incorporeal God, makes sense against this background.

When the Jews rejected this conception of God, their view stood as a stinging rebuke to Augustinian Christianity, and Augustine took the sharpest objection. He made his point in terms of "carnal Israel," explaining that "the Jews . . . prove themselves to be indisputably carnal."[67] Yet his ire more repressively targeted heretical Christians (the Donatists and the Pelagians); in contrast to Chrysostom and Ambrose, Augustine called for an end to violent assaults against synagogues, Jewish property, and Jewish persons, which he did not when it came to pagans or Christian heretics. But he wanted the Jews to survive only on terms of subordination, which would make of their obduracy an example to all others.[68] He thus called for a legally enforced moral slavery of the Jews, the degradation of a whole class of persons to servile status (including limits imposed on access to influential occupations, intercourse with Christians, living quarters, and the like) justified, as it expressly was by Augustine, in terms of a legitimate slavery.[69]

This cultural background of enforced moral slavery was then supported by orthodox Christianity (both Catholic and Protestant) and can explain the development of the more lethal forms of anti-Semitism in the modern period. Augustinian intolerance was highly patriarchal and thus gendered. The repression of sexual voice in himself made Augustine extraordinarily sensitive, as a patriarchal man, to any questioning of the terms of his repression, and no group raised such questions more forcefully than the Jews – hence "carnal Israel." Augustine, however, operated within an ethical system that imposed Christian limits on the persecution of the Jews.

In the modern period, Hitler accepted no such limits. Inspired by Nietzsche's hatred of Christianity (much deeper than any animus against the Jews)[70] and expounding a crackpot racist science, he popularized an aggressive form of political anti-Semitism that drew its appeal from the highly patriarchal form of European anti-Semitism inherited from Augustine. For an anti-Semite like Hitler, Jewish resistance in matters of sexuality and gender became the target of his genocidal rage, a rage stoked by the humiliation of German manhood at Versailles[71] and directed at the traditional scapegoat for such reverses, the Jews, whose resistance insulted German manhood.[72]

No group had responded with more enthusiasm to emancipation and the promise of political liberalism than the Jews of Germany and Austria-Hungary.[73] The problem, however, was that what counted as political liberalism was fundamentally flawed. For one thing, Augustinian Catholic and Protestant Christianity – despite its history of anti-Semitism – continued to enjoy state support and endorsement. For another, the dominant conception of manhood remained highly patriarchal, formed on classical models like Aeneas in politics and military life and Augustine in religion. There is a fundamental contradiction between democratic liberalism with its central conviction of equal voice and patriarchy with its hierarchical arrangement of authority (father/priests over sons, daughters, and wives). The enthusiasm of the Jews for this form of liberalism thus carried within it very real dangers, because that liberalism rested on a patriarchal conception that could easily turn on them, as it had throughout the history of Augustinian Christianity.

Perhaps the worst danger was that successful assimilation to such a political and religious culture would compromise the very resistance of the Jews to its unjust demands. In fact, we offer in the next chapter a close study of Freud that illustrates how his most creative insights into human psychology came to be compromised in this way. Freud himself puzzled over the ferocity of the political anti-Semitism that he saw gathering force in Germany and Austria, observing that the more Jews assimilated to German culture and thus the less the differences between Jews and non-Jews, the more ferocious the anti-Semitism, with the irrationalism of anti-Semitism expressing "the narcissism of small differences."[74] What Freud did not see was the patriarchal strand in anti-Semitism, which we have traced back to Augustinian orthodoxy, namely, that it arose from the traumatic renunciation of sexual love and connection, a renunciation both part of and necessary for the heroism of manhood, whether in politics or in religion. Freud could not see the problems in this patriarchal conception, including its dangers to the Jews, because under the pressure of assimilation, he had come to integrate a form of it into his psychology.

Such assimilation is made possible by the loss of historical memory, memory that is often required for resistance. For many lovers of art, Christian and non-Christian, it is difficult to remember the cultural roots of Christianity in the anti-Semitic construction of the Jews as the slaves of Christians. Handel's masterpiece, *The Messiah*, taken at face value as a retelling of the basic Christian narrative of tragedy and triumph, builds toward the "Hallelujah" chorus. But recent scholarship reminds us that this joyous chorus may in fact have been theologically written and understood as celebrating the defeat of the Jews by the Romans, a defeat which marked for Augustinian Christians the legitimation of Christianity over the Judaism it supplanted and supposedly fulfilled.[75] It deepens our critical understanding and appreciation of *Messiah* to recover our historical memory of its place in the history of triumphalist Augustinian Christianity, including its anti-Semitism. We better understand its power and appeal both when it was written and for later generations, but we also are better able to understand critically and to resist, certainly today, the role that anti-Semitism has played in the appeal of Christianity. We love the arts no less when we come to understand that their appeal to our psyches may be compromised by assumptions we should both acknowledge and question. Otherwise, we fail to understand and deal with the depth of anti-Semitism in our cultural heritage, which of course includes the arts.

What made political anti-Semitism so powerful in Germany and Austria was the highly gendered form that Hitler drew upon, including the romantic nationalism, rooted in anti-Semitic stereotypes and in Richard Wagner's operas, that so inspired him.[76] It was also an anti-Semitism that Hitler strategically fomented as the experience of traumatic loss and defeat in World War I fueled a psychology that created an enemy within, a scapegoat, whose fault was resistance and history of resistance to dominant arrangements. The shame of humiliated manhood expressed itself in the violence and the glorification of violence in Hitler's fascism. And as James Gilligan reminds us, Hitler came to power on the campaign promise to undo the shame of Versailles. He modeled his politics on the fascism that Mussolini had invented in Italy, a fascism self-consciously based on a revival of Roman politics and religion, and took on the role of an autocratic Roman emperor. Ancient Roman patriarchal psychology is thus very much in play in these modern developments.

Theodore Herzl saw the looming danger of political anti-Semitism in European politics early on at the time of the Dreyfus affair. He called for a political resistance, Zionism, and a liberal Jewish state where Jews could live as equals, not dependent on the flawed liberalism of France, Germany, or Austria.[77] Hannah Arendt understood, before it was too late, the genocidal intentions of German fascism and fled to Paris and then to the United States, writing her pathbreaking study *The Origins of Totalitarianism*.[78] When she subsequently raised the issue of resistance, asking why there had not been more of it by Jews and particularly by the Jewish councils in Europe,[79] the response was incendiary – as if broaching the subject was itself an atrocity. Yet neither Herzl nor Arendt saw the role of patriarchy in the political anti-Semitism they otherwise so shrewdly anticipated and resisted.

In this regard, we find it instructive that the most notable forms of Christian resistance to fascist violence did not come from a reading of religious texts, let alone from theology. For example, Dietrich Bonhoeffer initially thought that Christian texts required pacifism.[80] The change in view that led him to join the plot to kill Hitler arose from the call of lived experience, leading him "to see the great events of world history from below, from the perspective of the outcast, the suspects, the maltreated, the powerless, the oppressed, the reviled – in short, from the perspective of those who suffer."[81] Among those experiences were his relationships within his family, in particular with his mother and grandmother who saw Hitler's anti-Semitic policies as an outrageous breach of long-standing relationships in daily life. And his brother-in-law, a leader of the plot to kill Hitler, confronted Bonhoeffer with the genocidal reality of Hitler's programs.[82]

Similarly, nothing in the Huguenot theology of the French minister Andre Pascal Trocme called for pacifism in general or active resistance to the enforcement of Hitler's anti-Semitic programs in Vichy France. Instead, Trocme's relationship with his mother and with his Italian, rather non-religious wife, who took Jews in and saw that Jewish children were given refuge, encouraged him to take the prominent role he did in resisting Hitler's anti-Semitic programs.[83]

These examples suggest that resistance becomes psychologically possible when the human psyche finds its voice in experiences of ethical presence in relationship to other loving, attentive persons and their voices. It is when humans hold on to the truth of that ethical voice in relationship that they come to question and reject conceptions and practices that not only are false by that test but also *require* the suppression of truthful voice. What underlies the psychology and ethics of resistance is the voice of the psyche revolting at conceptions and practices that rest on lies and must, to survive, kill one's sense of relational truth and presence. The resistance we saw in the Cupid and Psyche story makes this point exactly.

## 3. THE ARGUMENT FOR TOLERATION

### i. Christian Resistance: Bayle and Locke

Historically, the most influential resistance to Augustinian intolerance came from within Christianity, in particular the argument for toleration stated in variant forms in the late 17th century by Pierre Bayle and John Locke[84] that laid the foundations of modern democratic constitutionalism. The context and motivations of the argument were those of radical Protestant intellectual and moral conscience, reflecting on the political principles requisite to protect its enterprise against the oppressions of established churches, both Catholic and Protestant. Often, such arguments appealed directly to the spirit of the Gospels, questioning the highly patriarchal interpretive traditions (including Augustinian orthodoxy) that had corrupted their meaning.[85]

Both Bayle and Locke call for a democratic equality in the interpretation of the Gospels, implicitly questioning the role a patriarchal priesthood had played in interpreting Christianity since Augustine. Moreover, both of their lives and works bespeak a resistance to the violence that Christian intolerance incites and its effects on intimate personal life. Bayle, for example, "suffered the worst blow of his life" when his brother, arrested for Bayle's publications in his stead, died in prison from appalling conditions because of his refusal, at the insistence of a Jesuit, to abjure his Protestantism.[86] And Locke's reading of the Adam and Eve narrative was less patriarchal than that of orthodox Christianity,[87] reflective perhaps of his own parents and their relationships to him.[88] Both Bayle and Locke were outsiders not only to Catholicism but to conventional patriarchal family life; neither married (Locke very likely was homosexual in orientation).[89] Both advocated the principle of toleration as a way of questioning and delegitimating Augustine's rationale for the use of political power in religious persecution.[90]

Their enterprise of toleration arose from a moral ideal of the person and the need to protect that ideal from political threat. The ideal was of respect for persons in virtue of their moral powers both rationally to assess and pursue ends and reasonably to adjust and constrain their pursuit of ends in light of the moral status of other persons as bearers of equal rights. The threat to this ideal came from the political idea and practice that the moral status of persons was not determined by the responsible expression of their own moral powers but, rather, by a hierarchical structure of society and nature in which they were embedded. That structure, classically associated with orders of being,[91] defined roles and statuses in which people were born, lived, and died and specified the responsibilities of living in light of those roles.

The political power exerted by this hierarchical conception was manifest not only in the ways people behaved but also in the ways it penetrated into the human heart and mind, framing personal, moral, and social identity in its terms. The hierarchical structure – religious, economic, political – did not need to rely on massive coercion precisely because its crushing force on human personality had been rendered personally and socially invisible by a heart that felt and a mind that imaginatively entertained nothing that could render the structure itself an object of critical reflection.

In light of the moral pluralism made possible by the Reformation, liberal Protestant thinkers subjected the political power of the hierarchical conception to radical ethical criticism. Both Bayle and Locke argued as religious Christians, and their argument arose as an intramural debate among interpreters of the Christian tradition about freedom and ethics.[92] An authoritative Pauline strand of that tradition had given central weight to the value of Christian freedom. Like the Jewish tradition from which it developed, it had a powerful ethical core of concern for the requisites of moral personality; Augustine of Hippo thus had interpreted the trinitarian nature of God on the model of moral personality, that is, the three parts of the soul – will, memory, and intelligence. Indeed, the argument for toleration arose from an internal criticism by Bayle of Augustine's argument for the persecution of the heretical Donatists; to wit, Augustine had misinterpreted central Christian values of freedom and ethics. The concern was that religious persecution had corrupted ethics and also, for this reason, the essence of Christianity's elevated and simple ethical core of a universal brotherhood of free people.

The argument for toleration was a judgment of and response to perceived abuses of political epistemology. The legitimation of religious persecution by both Catholics and Protestants (drawing authority from Augustine, among others) had rendered a politically entrenched view of religious and moral truth as the measure of permissible ethics and religion, including the epistemic standards of inquiry and debate. By the

late 17th century when Locke and Bayle wrote, there was good reason to
believe that this view, resting on the authority of the Bible and associated
interpretive practices, had assumed contestable interpretations of a complex historical interaction between pagan, Jewish, and Christian cultures
in the early Christian era.

The Renaissance rediscovery of pagan culture and learning reopened
the question of how the Christian synthesis of pagan philosophical
and Jewish ethical and religious culture was to be understood. Among
other things, the development of critical historiography and techniques
of textual interpretation had undeniable implications for reasonable
Bible interpretation. The Protestant Reformation both assumed and further encouraged these new modes of inquiry and encouraged as well
the appeal to experiment and experience that were a matrix for the
methodologies associated with the rise of modern science.[93] These new
approaches to thought and inquiry had made possible the recognition
that there was a gap between the politically entrenched conceptions of
religious orthodoxy and the kinds of reasonable inquiries that the new
approaches made available. The argument for toleration thus arose from
a recognition of this disjunction between the reigning political epistemology and the new epistemic methodologies.

In light of the new modes of inquiry, prevailing conceptions of religious truth were often seen to rest not only on the degradation of reasonable standards of inquiry but on the self-fulfilling degradation of the
capacity of persons reasonably to conduct such inquiries. In order to
rectify these evils, the argument for toleration forbade, as a matter of
principle, the enforcement by the state of any such conception of religious truth. The scope of legitimate political concern must, rather, rest
on the pursuit of general ends such as life and basic rights and liberties,
including the right to conscience. The pursuit of such goods was consistent with the full range of ends that free people might rationally and
reasonably pursue.[94]

## ii. Jewish Resistance: Spinoza

Yet another form of the argument for toleration was developed in the
Netherlands by Baruch Spinoza, somewhat earlier than the arguments
of Locke and Bayle. For Spinoza, the argument was grounded not in a
radical Protestant sense of Christian conscience, but in a more secular
conception of the inalienable right of philosophical reason, which would
extend to all persons capable of such reason, whether theist or atheist.[95]
Spinoza had been a learned member of the Jewish community of Amsterdam, but his interests in secular philosophy, inspired by the study of

Descartes, led to his excommunication in part because his views on Bible interpretation led him to question traditional Jewish beliefs and rituals.[96]

Spinoza's development of the argument for toleration is remarkable not only for its more secular character and more expansive protection (even of atheists) but also because of its later role in Enlightenment thought and practice. Spinoza's position, subsequently interpreted as grounding a right of sexual freedom and even the rights of women,[97] led Jonathan Israel to argue that Spinoza had initiated a more radical Enlightenment that was compromised and even covered over by the more moderate forms of Enlightenment thought sponsored by Locke and Bayle.[98] What strikes us is the plausible psychological connection between Spinoza's much more contemporary understanding of the principle of toleration and his sense of the embodied self that arose from his Jewish background. He may have been a Jewish heretic,[99] but his distinctive philosophical doctrine, the unity of the mind and the body,[100] arose, we suggest, from a revulsion at the form of mind-body dualism that Descartes, a believing Catholic, had developed to support the consistency of the emerging science with traditional Catholic doctrines, including the immortality of the soul.[101] Though Spinoza was, in fact, a forbiddingly metaphysical thinker, many people today find his thought surprisingly modern and contemporary.[102]

Finally, Spinoza, like Locke and Bayle, never married,[103] and he became a more radical outsider to the religion of his birth than Locke and Bayle, both of whom remained believing Protestants. We wonder if Spinoza's more extreme outsider status to both the dominant patriarchal family life and religion of his time may not explain how and why he gave the argument for toleration a more muscular and expansive interpretation, in his hands questioning the use of state coercion on sectarian religious grounds against the inalienable right of philosophical conscience.

## 4. ETHICAL RELIGION AND CONSTITUTIONAL RIGHTS

Within the framework of Christian religious belief, notable arguments have been and are being used to advance both the theory and practice of justice under law. Key examples in the United States are the arguments of radical abolitionists including the abolitionist feminists in the pre–Civil War period and those of Martin Luther King as the leader of the Civil Rights movement in the 1960s. The democratic equality called for by Locke and Bayle in interpreting Christianity has now been broadened to include women and men and all races and ethnicities. Increasingly, these forms of Christian resistance give prominence not only to women's voices and experience, but also to the voices of men who take such women seriously. In this section of the chapter, we examine the structure of such arguments before making some general observations about their role in advancing the values of a constitutional democracy.

## i. Radical Abolitionism

When William Lloyd Garrison attacked colonization as based on cultural racism in his book *Thoughts on African Colonization*,[104] it was not only through abstract argument but also through his experience in Boston of the black religious community, "the call sounded with emotional depth in the African Meeting House as he had never heard it sound before."[105] Later, on hearing the black woman preacher Maria Stewart, he heard a voice he "knew so well from his mother."[106] Garrison was inspired by the life and teaching of Jesus of Nazareth,[107] and it was his growing sense of the ethical importance of speaking and hearing this voice that seemingly explains his nonviolent resistance: a stance that also attracted many of the radical women who collaborated to momentous effect with him. Garrison and the women were attracted to the position of nonviolence as a reasonable interpretation of Matthew 5:38–39, because they had become increasingly aware of and skeptical of the role played by patriarchal gender roles in the violence unleashed against voices raised in protest against slavery and racism. In 1835, Garrison himself was famously dragged by a rope through the streets of Boson and beaten, his life under threat, by a lynch mob for his radical abolitionist views.[108] His patient endurance of such violence was very much inspired by the abolitionist women who had accompanied him; as he put it, "Such a mob– 30 ladies routed and ... demolished by 4,000 men." Garrison had earlier addressed the "mob," who were disrupting an abolitionist meeting, in terms that bring out how far his antislavery arguments had become for him a criticism of the conventional understanding of manhood:

> [H]is lame joke, "If any of you gentlemen are ladies in disguise ... give me your names ... and you can take your seats in the meeting" further dramatized the issue as one that pitted Christian meekness against established power, feminine sentiment against masculine patriotism, with Garrison identified with the women.[109]

The importance of this issue to Garrison is further dramatized by his public resistance at the World Anti-Slavery Convention in London in the summer of 1840 to the convention's rule, adopted despite the strong objections of some American leaders, that only male delegates could be seated. Garrison, in protest, sat in the galleries with women, including Lucretia Mott and the young wife of an antislavery leader, Elizabeth Cady

Stanton. There began the conversations and an association that would lead, eight years later, to the emergence of political feminism at Seneca Falls, New York, in 1848.[110]

Garrison's critique of slavery and racism thus entailed a questioning of the role of gender stereotypes.[111] His growing commitment to nonviolence tracks closely his sense that the enormity of the evil of American slavery and racism required not only men, such as himself and the ex-slave Frederick Douglass whom he early recognized and supported,[112] to resist the violent demands of patriarchal manhood; that enormity required resistance from women as well. The importance of supporting the voice of women was brought home to Garrison by a woman of the North (Lydia Maria Child) and two women of the South (the Grimke sisters, Angelina and Sarah) whose commitments to nonviolent resistance reflected a growing sense of free ethical voice displayed in pathbreaking works of ethical criticism that linked unjust racial and gender stereotypes.[113]

The nonviolent resistance of both Child and the Grimke sisters also reflects their own struggles as women. Child had won popularity and respectability by editing the nation's first children's magazine and publishing two best-selling domestic advice books. Under the catalytic influence of a meeting with Garrison in 1830 (a meeting she later described in the terms of religious conversion), Child began to study American slavery. In 1833, just after the prestigious *North American Review* ranked her as America's preeminent woman writer, she forfeited her literary reputation – and her livelihood – by publishing *An Appeal in Favor of Americans Called Africans*, her book on American cultural racism, which included an indictment of anti-miscegenation laws in Massachusetts and elsewhere.[114] Nonetheless, Child continued to speak in her own voice, writing an early study of women's rights and advancing the publication of Harriet A. Jacobs's *Incidents in the Life of a Slave Girl, Told by Herself,* which recounted Jacobs's experience of and resistance to sexual exploitation.[115]

The ethical journey of Angelina and Sarah Grimke was equally remarkable. With the support of Garrison at crucial points,[116] they spoke in public (something which Child never dared to do)[117] about aspects of southern life under slavery not previously exposed and revealed how patriarchal gender roles were brought to bear in the repression of women's ethical voices in both the South and the North. Born and raised in a leading South Carolina slave-holding family, the Grimke sisters exemplified the force of moral revolt and self-exile from the South's violently polemical culture and clarified the ethical foundations of such revolt in women's experience.[118] They self-consciously stated the case for abolitionist feminism that would later be developed by Lucretia Mott and Elizabeth Stanton into an independent women's movement as well as by the ex-slaves Sojourner Truth and Harriet Jacobs, who deepened the abolitionist feminist analysis of the common roots of American racism and sexism.[119] Sojourner Truth's "Ain't I a Woman?" exposed as never before the lies and distortions in the conception of white womanhood, and Harriet Jacobs underscored the self-imposed blindness of the wives of slaveholders to what was going on in their households.

Sarah and later Angelina Grimke felt impelled to leave the South to express their opposition to slavery as an institution in general and to their own family's commitment to the institution in particular. Both initially gravitated to a Quaker expression of their antislavery views, but their growing moral independence led them into more radical forms of antislavery activism. The negative northern response prompted both women to reflect on the analogy between race and gender as the objects of prejudice. No abolitionist of their generation carried the analysis further.

Like Child, the Grimke sisters objected not only to American slavery but to its underlying moral pathology, American racism, which Angelina called "the monster Prejudice"[120] or "that American Juggernaut, Prejudice."[121] The extraordinary power of their analysis for their generation lay in the intimate knowledge that they, children of a slaveowning family, brought to it. No aspect of that knowledge more shocked their northern audiences than their testimony as to the tyrannies of women slaveowners.[122] The public image of the character of southern women, "their gentleness and love... suavity," was, on their testimony, "the paint and the varnish of hypocrisy, the fashionable polish of a heartless superficiality."[123] The place of southern women upon what a pro-slavery advocate, Louisa McCord, had called "the high pedestal where God has placed her"[124] was indeed, as pro-slavery thought had insisted,[125] central to the repressive culture that sustained and indeed idealized southern slavery. The abolitionist criticism of that culture, the Grimke sisters made clear, must extend to the role played by the pedestal and its ideology of separate spheres of gender in the obfuscation and rationalization of injustice.

The Grimkes thus began serious American criticism of the linked political evils of racism and sexism. They did so on the basis of an anti-patriarchal conception of Bible interpretation that not only rejected the misogynist interpretation of the Adam and Eve narrative but also called for women to exercise their moral powers in the interpretation of the Bible, independent of what they argued was the patriarchal reading that had come to dominate Christianity.[126] In this respect, they followed the path of Anne Hutchinson who, two centuries earlier in Puritan Massachusetts, was found guilty of heresy and insubordination for interpreting the Bible on her own, challenging the authority of the male clergy by claiming, in the antinomian tradition, a direct, unmediated relationship with God.[127]

### ii. Martin Luther King, Jr.

Martin Luther King must be understood both as a person in himself who came to a powerful stance of resistance and as the leader of the nonviolent mass movement of protest for civil rights that he inspired.[128] More specifically for our purposes here, King is important for two reasons. First, he came to see the social movement that he led as a reformation and great awakening within Christianity that challenged the traditional religious, ethical, and political authority of the Christian churches in terms of a certain reading of Jesus of Nazareth. Second, he was a major 20th-century leader of the struggle within the United States against the structural injustice of racism, a struggle that could be traced to the pre–Civil War radical abolitionist movement. Despite his advocacy of nonviolence, King always accepted the right of self-defense[129] and was a lifelong skeptic of pacifism. He was a Baptist preacher very much within the Protestant tradition, and – after much struggle over his vocation – a preacher in a black church in the deep, racist South. His originality lay in the prophetic ethical voice he found within this role, a voice that energized a remarkably disciplined social movement and spoke to the conscience of the nation as no black voice ever had.

   The key was nonviolence. Given that King was not a pacifist (unlike Gandhi whose successful nonviolent strategies he carefully studied), it is important to understand how a strategy of nonviolence recommend itself to him. King came to nonviolence both through the developmental psychology that gave rise to his sense of religious vocation and through his theological studies of what made religion valuable. His nonviolent stance almost certainly found its inspiration not in his father's patriarchal voice but in the voices and loving care of his grandmother and mother, reflecting the long tradition of identification of Baptist black women with Jesus of Nazareth.[130] His theological studies had brought him to personalism, the view that what is valuable in religion is the sense of persons made in God's image who find themselves in loving, caring relationships with the individuality of other persons. This psychology and ethics of religion was highly relational, attuned to the impact of one's voice on the audience, whether an audience consisting of those in a movement one leads or an audience addressed by that movement. King came to nonviolence as an experiment that shocked and disturbed him, given that it carried him into an unanticipated role and burdened him with responsibilities he had never imagined.

It was important, in this connection, not only that the famous Montgomery bus boycott began in the 1955 refusal of a woman, Rosa Parks,[131] to obey the laws governing segregation on buses, but also that its initial groundswell of support came spontaneously from women and that women were disproportionately involved in the boycott itself.[132] This ethical leadership of women had become so conspicuous that when black male leaders of Montgomery first met to discuss tactics, some urged keeping their names secret. E. D. Nixon, a railroad porter, exploded in rage at their timorousness in comparison to the courage of women:

> "Let me tell you gentlemen one thing. You ministers have lived off their wash-women for the last hundred years and ain't never doing anything for them.... We've worn aprons all our lives.... It's time to take the aprons off.... If we're gonna be mens, now's the time to be mens."[133]

Nixon thus challenged black men to be men, not in opposition to women but by joining their resistance. Constance Baker Mottley, an NAACP lawyer during this period, notes in this connection that, as regards nonviolence:

> [King] sometimes had problems with young men who believed that violence was the answer, but. . . [w]hen he preached nonviolence to the largely elderly females in those Birmingham churches at night, King was preaching to the converted.... They were always there, night after night. Strong black women had always set the tone in Southern black communities.[134]

In response to Nixon's taunts, King was clear that "I don't want anyone to call me a coward"[135] and urged all the leaders to act openly under their own names. His remarks led to his being elected president of the Montgomery Improvement Association, which would coordinate the boycott and engage in negotiations over the demands of blacks. But it is of particular interest to us that this road entailed a willingness on the part of men to join openly with women in a moral sensibility that readily could be read as feminine and thus to put their manhood on the line. In this sense, it was not possible to challenge racism without also taking on the gender norms and values that would silence the voice of protest.

Speaking at a meeting at a Holt Street church, King was faced with a crowd of thousands. His speech provides a powerful summation of some of his key arguments. He began by stating:

> We are here in a general sense, because first and foremost – we are American citizens – and we are determined to apply citizenship – to the fullness of its means. . . . But we are here in a specific sense – because of the bus situation in Montgomery. The situation is not at all new. The problem has existed over endless years. Just the other day – just last Thursday to be exact – one of the finest citizens in Montgomery – not one of the finest Negro citizens – but one of the finest citizens in Montgomery – was taken from a bus – and carried to jail and arrested – because she refused to give up – to give her seat to a white person.[136]

As King's speech progressed, the crowd cheered and applauded, stamping their feet with a noise like thunder that "shook the building and refused to go away . . . pushing the call-and-response of the Negro church service past the din of a political rally and on to something else that King had never known before."[137] Perhaps daunted by the force of what he had unleashed, he turned to the pitfalls of using force in their boycott:

> Now let us say that we are not here advocating violence. We have overcome that. . . . I want it to be known throughout Montgomery and throughout this nation that we are Christian people. The only weapon that we have in our hands this evening is the weapon of protest. If we were incarcerated behind the iron curtains of a communistic nation – we couldn't do this. But the great glory of American democracy is the right to protest for right.

King offered as a further reason for nonviolence the need for civil rights protesters to distinguish themselves from the violence of the Ku Klux Klan:

> There will be no crosses burned at any bus stops in Montgomery. There will be no white persons pulled out of their homes and taken out on some distant road and murdered. There will be nobody among us who will stand up and defy the Constitution of this nation. My friends, I want it to be known – that we are going to work with grim and bold determination – to gain justice on the buses in this city. And we are not wrong. We are not wrong in what we are doing. If we are wrong – the Supreme Court of this nation is wrong. If we are wrong – God almighty is wrong.

King thus fused the cutting edge of his ethical faith to the hearts of his audience: "If we are wrong – Jesus of Nazareth was merely a utopian dreamer and never came down to earth! If we are wrong, justice is a lie." His soaring, indignant, inspired conclusion drew on the cadences of the Bible: "And we are determined here in Montgomery – to work and fight until justice runs down like water, and righteousness like a mighty stream!" The prophet Amos, the herdsman prophet, along with Isaiah, was his authority on justice.[138]

In the Holt Street speech, King found his prophetic ethical voice in relationship to the voices of his audience, discovering in this process, it would seem, the power and appeal of nonviolence. He came rather accidentally to his leadership position through his response to a challenge that asked men to measure up to the example of women. When King, as a man and Baptist preacher, brought nonviolence into the center of a movement of mass social protest, he aligned himself with an experience that women understood intuitively. He thus spoke to women about the moral authority of their own experience, empowering them to act on that experience in new ways and new contexts that challenged traditional gender roles.

No small part of the appeal of the prophetic ethical voice discovered at the Holt Street meeting was the recognition by black women in the audience of what they believed already and now understood to have a wider scope, applicability, and resonance. Like Constance Baker Motley, Andrew Young, a leading figure in King's movement, observed that getting black men to accept nonviolence was always more of a struggle:

> Throughout the movement, the men were usually the last to become involved, always using the reason that they didn't believe in a non-violent response to violent provocations. This was more an excuse than anything else. I began challenging the men as they went into the pool halls and bars, attempting to shame them for letting the women and children carry the movement. . . . Finally the men realized that their presence was essential. . . . Women and the elderly had borne the brunt of our demonstrations for far too long.[139]

But King was also speaking in a voice that challenged traditional manhood, including black manhood. His challenge appealed to two kinds of arguments, constitutional and religious.

Constitutionally, he took on board the remarkable successes of the NAACP's litigation strategy, arguing that African-American protest rested on a more reasonable understanding of American constitutionalism than that held by its racist opponents, a fact shown by its appeal to the constitutional right to protest. By anchoring his movement for justice in nonviolence, King underscored the basis of his movement in an ethical voice, supported by constitutional principles of free speech. Indeed, under the impact of his movement, such principles were held by the Supreme Court to include conscientious dissent, requiring such dissenters to be protected by the state.[140] Because the police in Birmingham and Selma were conspicuous agents of state violence against conscientious dissenters, Americans during this period came increasingly to see that King's movement rested on constitutional principles.

Religiously, King appealed to the ethical voice of Jesus, within the Christian tradition. He was striking a chord he was to repeat throughout his career, by suggesting that the racist persecution of African-Americans was in principle the same atrocity as religious persecution, including the persecution not only of Puritans that drove them to New England but also of Christians under the Roman Empire.[141] King and his social movement thus signified an ethical reformation of Christianity against its corruptions as much as a movement for justice under American constitutional law.

In anchoring a mass movement of resistance in nonviolence, King took on the codes of male honor. We saw earlier that a plausible interpretation of Jesus's injunction "if anyone strikes you on the right cheek, turn the other also" (Matt. 5:39) is an ethical skepticism about the ways in which insults to male honor trigger violence. King essentially rediscovered or reinvented this interpretation, one that would have great appeal to black men of the South who had suffered for centuries under a racist regime of white male violence, including lynchings, directed at black threats to white male honor. It also appealed to African-American constitutionalism, which had come so far under the leadership of the NAACP by an insistence on pressing its constitutional rights of free speech and protest. By centering a mass social movement in nonviolence, King made central to the democratic experience of African-Americans in general the exercise of their constitutional rights to protest that had hitherto figured largely only in the protest of black elites, including black lawyers and intellectuals.

King's most successful experiments in ethical voice were the Montgomery boycott, Birmingham, leading to the Civil Rights Act of 1964, and Selma, leading to the Voting Rights Act of 1965. Apart from drawing on the achievements of African-American constitutionalism (the Montgomery bus boycott was one year after *Brown v. Board of Education*), the appeal of King's nonviolent voice also drew importantly upon the role of the black churches in the South. On the one hand, his insistence on a nonviolent voice protesting the structural injustice of racism brought him into the very center of developing principles of American constitutionalism, including not only the recognition of the evil of racism as a violation of the Equal Protection Clause of the Fourteenth Amendment but also a muscular, speech-protective interpretation of the First Amendment, which the movement used, tested, and extended.[142] On the other hand, the authority of his voice drew upon an interpretation of nonviolence in the life and teachings of Jesus, in particular the Sermon on the Mount,[143] that justified participation in nonviolent civil disobedience as an ethical and religious duty. King's voice gave an ethically compelling sense to Jesus's injunction, "Love your enemies" (Matt. 5:44), to which he appealed as early as 1957 as the proof text for the demands of his movement. As he put the point:

> So this morning, as I look into your eyes, and into the eyes of all my brothers in Alabama and all over America and over the world, I say to you, "I love you. I would rather die than hate you." And I'm foolish enough to believe that through the power of this love somewhere, men of the most recalcitrant bent will be transformed. And then we will be in God's kingdom.[144]

"I look into your eyes" captures both the intimacy of King's prophetic ethical voice and its direct appeal to conscience. Much of his audience would have been black women of the South, and King connected with them. His view of religion was very much his own, so different from the role of the black churches in the past that it was questioned not only by the white clergymen who criticized the Birmingham campaign but by black ministers as well.[145] He certainly worked within the patriarchal assumptions of the Baptist church, but he also challenged these assumptions. The fact that a black man and a minister was doing this was not inconsequential. Under the impact of King's voice, black women claimed the moral and political agency of mass protests, with all of the attendant risks and challenges, not least to their sense of themselves as women.[146] The intimacy of King's voice ("I look into your eyes") invited a relationship between a man and a woman that empowered both as moral and political agents.

Only now, in the light of the feminist project to recover women's roles in history, can we appreciate more fully the part played by black women, not only in demonstrations throughout the South but also in leadership roles.[147] These women included, among many others, Ella Baker,[148] Septima Clark,[149] Diane Nash,[150] and Fannie Lou Hamer.[151] King was enough of a patriarchal man to maintain the Baptist tradition that top leadership be kept in the hands of men, and some of these women – notably Ella Baker – resisted him on this and other points. The patriarchal problem was not just King's, of course; it was endemic in the Civil Rights movement. In fact, the ethical empowerment of women through participation in the Civil Rights movement led them to question its patriarchy and patriarchy generally, both as an aspect of racial intolerance and as an injustice in itself.[152]

The ethical voice that energized mass political protest also gave a strengthening resonance to white Southerners who had seen the role that racism played in the South's political and economic backwardness.[153] King always emphasized how much blacks and whites shared in the South, the "network of mutuality"[154] or "single garment of destiny" that tied them to one another's lives, not only in economic relationships but also sometimes as children in playgrounds, sometimes as black caretakers in white homes, sometimes in easy social and even sexual relationships or in clandestine visits of whites to experience black dance or music. The dominant racist ideology required that such relationships not be recognized or accorded significance. King's ethical voice raised exactly the questions that – when heard – destabilized the hegemonic power that southern ideology had enjoyed for so long. What the nonviolence of the movement brought out with such clarity, when its moral dramaturgy was most successful, was that it was unjustly repressive violence – including the violence of public officials – that held this ideology in place.

King's appeal, both northern and southern, thus drew upon something that American whites and blacks deeply shared, namely, a commitment to constitutionalism and a religion that was broadly Judaeo-Christian. His voice carried great authority for African-Americans and Americans generally, showing that ethical protests were not peripheral or marginal but a manifestation of core political and religious values. His insight that nonviolence was a way of working through racism's psychic injuries led to a strategic disarmament: By disarming themselves of violence as a means to act out their hatred and eradicate shame, African-Americans found an ethical voice to express feelings that might otherwise have seemed to compromise manhood. These feelings were deeply, centrally human and connected them to other Americans through what King unashamedly called love: "I love you. I would rather die than hate you."

That King's voice would be silenced by assassination and the movement he led would be contested in the name of black power underscores the volatile gender dynamics still playing out in this protest against racial injustice.

### iii. Religion and the Values of Constitutional Democracy

The advocacy of the pre–Civil War radical abolitionists and that of Martin Luther King illustrate the transformative power and appeal of free ethical voice, speaking out against injustices that affront the values of constitutional democracies. These historical examples are notable in that the voice of protest, while based on specifically Christian sources, is as strongly critical of the views of established Christian churches as it is of conventional politics. In *The Letter from Birmingham Jail*, King challenged the complacency of churchmen[155] who refused to take action against the violence that enforced southern racism. The ethical power and appeal of the radical abolitionists and King are distinguished by the way in which they found their free ethical voices at precisely the point where the violence deployed in support of injustice appeared to be so close to hand.

The radical abolitionists had confronted the patriarchal institutions of Christianity precisely because such institutions rested on structural injustice. By denying ethical voice to over half the human race, such institutions clearly disfigured democratic politics and ethics. King's arguments for nonviolent resistance directly countered the norms and values of patriarchal manhood, further empowering the moral agency of both women and men.

## 5. THE LEGACY OF CELIBACY

### i. The Priest Sexual Abuse Scandal

Augustine's argument that led to the Catholic view of sexual morality, defended by Thomas Aquinas in the 13th century and by the new natural lawyers in the 21st century,[156] rested on the highly patriarchal conception of sexuality of his age. It combined misogyny with men's sexual desire for partners (women or men) over whom they could exercise control. Augustine himself turned to celibacy as the only way he could experience the loving voice of God. We observed in his progression from boy to sexual man to celibate priest a psychology of loss, dissociation, and denigration of women. Conceiving himself as God's lover and soldier, he exemplified a militant manhood that expressed itself in arguments for Christian intolerance. This darkening of ethical intelligence and the underlying psychology are currently reflected in the priest sexual abuse scandal.

There are demographic and other reasons that can explain why celibacy seemed for many a reasonable choice long after Augustine, including the Christian institution of oblation, which allowed families to donate children to monasteries. A church that recognized no legitimate form of population control thus provided a legitimate outlet for children, reducing pressure on scarce resources and keeping estates undivided.[157] These reasons, including the practice of committing children to celibacy long before maturity, were contested even at the time as they were to be later, notably by Christians themselves. Luther led a reformation on the basis of what he analyzed as the church's corruptions of true Christian belief, and one of those corruptions was the role celibacy played as a requirement for the priesthood.

Luther's critique of celibacy remains worthy of study both because of his analysis of the costs of breaking relationships and because of his insights into its consequences for the religious life of the celibate priest – a dissociation that makes possible "a wilderness of lies," a permanent immaturity (monks who are "boys their whole life long"), an unjustified arrogance in "utterly godless university faculties," and a failure to acknowledge that "[t]here is never less chastity than in those who vow to be celibate."[158] Luther alludes, in this connection, not only to rampant sexual fantasy and masturbation[159] but, elliptically (and homophobically), to homosexual sex. The consequence of such celibacy is "that you lose your body and soul," degenerating into a "servitude to the belly."

Today, the internal critique of a celibate male priesthood has two dimensions: first, the arguments within Catholicism over whether its clergy should, as in other Christian religions, be able to marry and also whether women should be included; and second, growing public understanding of the depth and legitimacy of gay/lesbian sexuality, a view that removes a rationale for choosing celibacy that may once have made sense. We are here particularly concerned with the latter question.[160]

One of the distinguishing features of Catholicism's priesthood was that it gave gay men a life outside of marriage and an identity of great dignity. Under conditions of violently repressive homophobia, Catholicism offered positions of respect to people whose lives would otherwise have gone much less well. As our views on sexuality have changed, the appeal of Catholicism's celibate priesthood is no longer the same. Once we see sexuality as a feature of our moral individuality, the positions of Augustine and Thomas Aquinas lose their appeal. If the purpose of sex is not simply propagation, homosexuality can take its place among other sexualities. The traditional rationale for celibacy and monastic life is correspondingly lost.

Once we have come to this understanding, we can see why a wounded sexuality would increasingly lead men into the priesthood. The former priest Eugene Kennedy argues that this wounded sexuality may serve today to rationalize views on sexuality and gender that are untenable on internal religious grounds, distorting the word of God.[161] The increasingly homophobic character of Catholic moral theology is not in line with its traditional Thomism, which did not particularly target gays and lesbians but condemned equally all forms of nonprocreative sex. Catholicism, thus understood, never romanticized marriage, thinking, as Jesus of Nazareth apparently did, that the ultimate values of living lay else-where – in learning, teaching, charitable service, and knowing God.[162] Against this historical background, many contemporary Catholics find the church's increasingly strident sexist, homophobic views on issues of sexual morality objectionable – un-Christian, if you will.[163]

There are always choices to be made within a tradition as rich and complex as Roman Catholicism about which strand to follow, which to reject. Vatican II showed that there is great courage, honesty, and integrity within Catholicism and that there are within Thomism, in the spirit of Jacques Maritain and John Courtney Murray, resources to rethink and reasonably change anachronistic moral teachings. But the choices of the papacy on issues of sexual morality conspicuously fail this test, and the contemporary school of thought, new natural law, has rationalized the church's modernist homophobia.

It has probably always been the case that higher percentages of gays went into the Catholic priesthood.[164] Largely because of the church's increasingly homophobic stance on public issues, however, their position today is fraught with more destructive forms of denial than have perhaps ever existed before – and thus less capacity to resist the temptations the priesthood puts before them.

The feminist movement was energized by women speaking out against abuses that had been considered too shameful to mention, where the very act of revealing what had happened would lead one to be labeled a bad girl or woman. Gay men and lesbians subsequently found their voices through similar protest. And it is against this backdrop that we understand the courage of those who have broken silence about their sexual abuse by priests. The patriarchal culture of the Catholic church, where priests are called fathers, had relied on its authority to silence or disparage any voice that would reveal what was going on. Priests who abused children were quietly transferred from one diocese to another in a collusion that went up the hierarchy, a collusion often rationalized in religious terms. The men who overcame their shame in revealing their experiences of sexual abuse by priests thus broke a patriarchal taboo. The church's response has been in part to defend patriarchy on grounds of homophobia.

In his recent book, *Our Fathers*, David France explores this dyna-mic.[165] He reports research showing that outside the Catholic clergy: "[p]roportionately, there are no more pedophiles or ephebophiles among gays than among straights. In fact, all available data show that men and women who live openly as gays account for less than one percent of sexual assaults on minors." For an explanation of the prevalence of such abuse among priests, France turns to data suggesting that men who themselves had been traumatized by sexual abuse "entered the priesthood in disproportionate numbers, searching for external regulations for their sexuality and intimate relationships."[166]

Such grounds for celibacy would then explain both the rampant sexual abuse by clergy of children (pedophilia) and teenagers (ephebophilia) and the nature of its denial. The church's condemnation of gay/lesbian sexuality adds to the effects of traumatic abuse in repressing sexual voice by rendering it literally unspeakable, further fostering denial and dissociation. The church also provides priests with a language of justification. One abusive priest, Gilbert Gauthe, "told the [male] victims he was doing God's work when he forced himself into them"; another, Robert V. Meffan, sexually abused young girls, in order, as he put it, "to get them to love Christ even more intimately and even more closely."[167]

Even responsible, mature gay men were drawn into the web of lies and self-deception. Father George Spagnolia knew he was gay from age ten, but had kept his vows of celibacy until middle age, when he had an affair with another man; he was later to deny having any consensual adult relationships and when publicly revealed as a liar, responded defensively: "I had no concept of it being a lie. No concept at all. It's not the first time that I had said it, and it's almost like you say something enough times you begin to believe it yourself."[168] An introspective gay priest, Neil Conway, compares his struggles with those of Tosca in Giacomo Puccini's opera, who had lived for art and love, only to be crushed by a police state. Conway describes his dissociation, including his awareness of living in two worlds:

> There's a famous Tosca aria where she's trapped and she goes, 'God, you know my life is art, my trade is art and love.' I want to say: I was ordained a priest as a young man who was still a young boy – fourteen years old – emotionally and sexually. And I learned how to get what I thought I needed in the priesthood, doing what a priest does. Tosca says, 'Look what has happened to me!' I was in love with my life, and at the same time I was in trouble right away, as soon as I stepped off the box. . . . I thought the way a fourteen-year-old does, so I reverted to the age of fourteen in my behavior. I don't want to overdramatize this, but in therapy they always ask: Did you feel part of you was hovering over the event? Yes! Yes! That was it! I was able most of the time to block it out. I lived in two worlds"[169]

There comes a point when a culture, resting on the repression of sexuality, kills the capacity to read the human world, including one's own inner world. Once thought becomes disconnected from emotional truth or presence in relationship, one can no more read the emotions of others (the abused children and teenagers) than one's own. We see the costs of this in the parents who chose to disbelieve their children's reports of sexual abuse by priests, rather than to believe a priest could have done such a thing.[170] Such mothers or fathers are as dissociated from themselves as they are from their sons. It is not surprising that some of the fathers of abused boys had themselves been abused by priests as children.[171] One way the problem is rationalized in the priesthood is by appealing to "the father-son relationship that would otherwise be destroyed."[172] The normative paradigm of this relationship for priests is that of priest to child. Idealization again covers loss: a loss of voice in priests who can no longer distinguish truth from lies, a loss of voice in laypersons who can no longer differentiate emotional presence from mythological idealization. As Eugene Kennedy observes, many priests have highly idealized connections to their mothers rather than real relationships to them or women generally.[173]

The threat currently posed to the church by homosexuality is elucidated by the observation that it now scapegoats gays and lesbians in the way it once scapegoated Jews. For Augustine and Thomas, the issue was the embarrassing choice of Jews, co-religionists of Jesus, not to follow Jesus's teaching, rooted as it was in the prophecies of the Hebrew Bible. Correspondingly, what makes gays and lesbians so offensive to the church is that they increasingly choose not to be celibate or to lead false heterosexual lives in the service of convictions that the church upholds. What particularly draws the ire of the Vatican at present are the voices of gays and lesbians calling for constitutional recognition of their human rights as persons, including the right to marriage. In this call, the clash between patriarchy and democracy is exposed.

Mark Jordan underscores "the institutional paradox of a church that is at once so homoerotic and so homophobic."[174] The crisis in the modern church arises from this disjunction, illustrating the paradox of intolerance. Lacking the traditional rationale for celibacy, the church retains its homoerotic character, its absorption in the relationship of father and son, priest and boy, protecting abusing priests, perhaps as wounded children of God, while publicly maintaining an aggressively homophobic stance.

Freud observed of anti-Semitism that its irrationalism lay in its heightening of small, morally irrelevant differences into Manichean stereotypical truths.[175] The Catholic papacy similarly builds upon such differences to paint a dehumanized portrait of homosexuals. The church could reasonably acknowledge what it clearly knows to be true – that homosexuals can be good priests, judged on the basis of merit and contribution. Instead, the church wars on its gay children. The views of the church, as defended by new natural law,[176] are as sectarian as the grounds that rationalized Christian anti-Semitism. Gays and lesbians are thus to modernist religious homophobia what the Jews were to Christian anti-Semitism. And just as Christian anti-Semitism sexualized the Jews as "carnal Israel," so the contemporary Catholic Church sexualizes gays and lesbians, who become not persons but sex acts and intrinsically wrong sex acts at that. This focus on an objectified sexuality serves further to demonize any resistance to or protest of the underlying core of patriarchal practices and values.

How can an otherwise ethical tradition and people become so insensitive to the issues raised by the priest sexual abuse scandal? Such dimming of ethical intelligence reveals a deepening darkness within contemporary Catholicism.

### ii. James Carroll on Resistance to War and to Anti-Semitism

In *An American Requiem*, James Carroll recounts his journey into and out of the priesthood in the latter half of the 20th century, a journey that illuminates our study of resistance within Christianity. Carroll's identification with Augustine could not be clearer or more self-conscious: "I was Augustine" (p. 31, 34). Like Augustine, he was hesitant to join a priesthood that required taking a vow of chastity. Carroll also had a pivotally important and close relationship to this mother; he writes that "images of my mother's beaming face [are] one of my first true memories" and "[s]he is the first source of my pride and self-regard, the virtue of my worldliness. I knew from an early age what a rare woman she was" (pp. 45–6). But he also was sensitive to her emotional underworld, describing her as "a quietly scorned woman," "our own Pieta," and the "Mother of Sorrows herself, a woman privileged to be in pain."

Carroll's narrative, however, unlike Augustine's, is also about his relationship to a loved father. In part, his sense of a religious vocation can be traced to his father, who had been in an archdiocesan seminary for twelve years training to be a priest, when, to the disgrace of his family, he left to marry Carroll's mother. Much of the book is about the tension between father and son that arose from Carroll's resistance as a priest to the Vietnam War, during a period in which his father was an Air Force lieutenant general choosing Vietnamese targets for American bombs.

Carroll attributes his decision to become a priest to his mother: "Especially her. I learned early that to follow my own sexual desire would be to abandon her to a world of power – male power? – that would abuse her. An unspeakable dread surrounded these feelings, so naturally I did not speak of them. Nevertheless, the feelings efficiently packed themselves into the one word, vocation" (p. 56). Like Augustine, he, a sensitive and artistic man, is unsure how to be both a man and a son. A sexual man in a patriarchal culture is primed to see and treat women as sexual objects. When a man, especially a sensitive son, sees women as fully human, it becomes difficult for him to live under patriarchy. Augustine had seen what his mother endured as a "good wife" under Roman patriarchy and opted, finally, not to marry. A similar motivation in the lives of both men is suggested by the observation that Augustine's mother's affection for Ambrose of Milan parallels the affection Carroll's mother felt for priests who responded to her as a person.

Carroll's decision to become a priest was fostered by childhood memories of his mother interacting with Catholic chaplains in Germany: "[The chaplains] forced a new idea of the priesthood on me. The same was true of my mother. With these men, she was extroverted and flirtatious. . . . The chaplains were champions of her court" (p. 69). At the death of Francis Cardinal Spellman, whom Carroll and his parents had known, his mother reminded her son,

> that while so much else in her life as an uneducated, 'unfinished' woman who'd been conscripted into the role of a general's wife had aimed to undercut her, Cardinal Spellman had only affirmed her. Recognizing a rare spirit, and freeing it, he gave her ways to feel proud of herself. Through Catholic councils of military women in Europe and Washington, she found ways to exert leadership and express herself. (p. 198)

Carroll and Augustine are separated from one another by well over a millennium, yet their autobiographies are written by loving sons of mothers they both understand and take seriously. Acutely sensitive to the burdens patriarchy placed on their mothers' lives, they found in the Catholic priesthood a way to live as loving men resisting patriarchal demands. The problem, as we have seen, is that their resistance was itself compromised by these demands, which their mothers assumed as axiomatic. Both men, because of the anti-patriarchal strands in their resistance to the violence of patriarchy, come to take principled stands against unjust wars – Augustine against the imperialistic wars of the Roman republic and empire, Carroll against the Vietnam War. Carroll, however, came to question that Augustinian "standard of [sexual] repression that we [Catholics] called morality" (p. 63), leaving the priesthood to marry and have children and finding his voice as a novelist.

It is consistent with his fundamental questioning of and repudiation of the Augustinian denial he had once accepted that he would later write one of the more important critical studies of Christian anti-Semitism, *Constantine's Sword: The Church and the Jews: A History*. Carroll places Augustine at the center of Christian anti-Semitism[177] and brings his own experience of celibacy to bear on the narrative of Augustine in *Confessions*. We have learned much from Carroll about Augustine's psychology, and vice-versa. Yet the differences can explain both Carroll's repudiation of celibacy and move into loving, sexual relationship as well as his more probing resistance to unjust wars by ostensibly Christian powers. Whereas Augustine always supported the Catholic Roman emperor, Carroll resisted not only the Vietnam War but the pattern of American military adventures in the post–World War II period.[178]

Carroll's respect for his father, including the willingness of father and son to express their disagreement about matters like the Vietnam War while holding onto their love for each other, stands in sharp contrast to Augustine's dismissal. And whereas Monica died at the time of Augustine's conversion, Carroll got to know his mother better in the years following his ordination. He saw her struggle with his public antiwar stance and his father's illness. After spending a night in jail, however, he registered a shift in his perception of her during a telephone conversation in which he asked to talk to his father, but she responded: "'He doesn't want to talk to you *again*!' The pitch of her voice shot up. 'I won't let you do this to him. Do you hear me? I won't permit it. Not you too.'"[179] Her reply countered his image of her as a sorrowing housewife, replacing it with a recognition of her as a powerful figure: "In her tone I heard the fury of a warrior woman. Not my man, you don't! You don't do this to him! Those others might, but not you! Not to mine!" In the future, he would refer to her as his father's "omniscient protector."

Carroll was not attacking his father as such; rather he was contesting patriarchal values. When his mother in effect said, "You're not going to attack the patriarch by attacking the patriarchal war," she became, in Carroll's words, the "omniscient protector" of both. And to speculate, her alliance with the patriarchy may have released Carroll's resistance from whatever restrictions her views of men and priests had imposed. Following his protest of unjust war, he left the priesthood, rejecting celibacy and ultimately taking on the injustice of Christian anti-Semitism.

# 7  Resistance: Psychology

Why is patriarchy so powerful? One reason is that it has profoundly shaped not only our religion and politics but also our very understanding of ourselves, our psychology. We can see the power and consequences of this influence most clearly in a great psychologist, Sigmund Freud, who turned abruptly away from his early insights into the sources and nature of human suffering to a psychology that inscribed patriarchy as in the nature of things. We examine and analyze this development closely, arguing that at a crucial point, Freud's ambition to succeed according to the terms of Viennese manhood against the background of an increasingly aggressive political anti-Semitism distorted, as patriarchy often does, some of his most creative and lasting contributions to human understanding. We show the continuing power of the psychology of Roman patriarchy in modernity as Freud frames his struggles to manhood in terms of the *Aeneid*. We then consider alternative views within psychoanalysis, in particular, those of Sandor Ferenczi and Ian Suttie, who, even in Freud's lifetime, exposed and questioned his confusion of patriarchal culture with human nature, offering a different reading of the relationship between culture and psychology.[1]

Ferenczi and then Suttie located in history, including the history of an individual life, what Freud had naturalized: the identification with the voice or law of the father and the prevalence of aggression or violence. Where Freud saw development or instinct at work, Ferenczi saw trauma and Suttie the breaking of intimate relationship. Deepened by renewed attention to women's voices and experience, by the study of trauma, and by the findings of research in developmental psychology and neurobiology, these insights have led to a paradigm shift – a relational reframing of psychology. With this reframing, we can see how the gender binaries and hierarchies of patriarchy become incorporated into the psyche in the form of splits between mind and body, thought and emotion, self and relationship, which then undermine the potential for ethical resistance.

As we become bound to what is an essentially false story about ourselves, we lose our capacity for resistance. The optimism of this chapter lies in revealing how and why an empirically grounded view of human nature (and thus of both women and men) points to the psychological and neurological grounds of resistance to patriarchal norms and practices.

## 1. FREUD'S OPENING AND CLOSING TO WOMEN

Psyche, the young woman who became an object in Apuleius's *Metamorphoses*, who was forbidden to see or to say what she knew about love, is stage center in *Studies on Hysteria*.[2] In a rush of discovery, Josef Breuer and Freud, its co-authors, lay bare the profound connection between our minds and our bodies by tracing the conversion of psychic pain into physical pain. They describe the process of dissociation, the splitting of the mind so that parts of our experience become absent from our consciousness. And in their treatment of hysterical young women, they discover the power of relationship, the way in which association heals disassociation, the power of the talking or listening cure. They have discovered the power of a confiding relationship and, more generally, the power of association to undo dissociation, unlocking secrets held in the psyche. It is the psychological equivalent of discovering fire.

Like Psyche, the young women of *Studies on Hysteria* were not only victims but also resisters; at one and the same time, they internalized and they broke the taboo on seeing and speaking what they knew about love. The key, Freud's "pick-lock," was to reverse the process underlying the hysteria. Observing that hysterics suffer mainly from reminiscences, he moved their memories out of the body and into language.

When the "lost" or silenced voice of hysteria was found, however, all hell broke loose – to summon the image from the *Aeneid* that Freud would choose as the epigraph for his *Interpretation of Dreams*. He had not been able to move the upper world – his colleagues in medicine and in the university – with the insights of his studies on hysteria; instead he would appeal to the underworld, to dreams, finding in his own dreams the royal road to the unconscious. The path he took is marked by quotations from the *Aeneid*, flagging an identification with Aeneas that provides us with a clue to what follows: the confusion of tongues that Ferenczi, his most beloved and then rejected colleague, was to describe – an identification with the aggressor, the taking on of the voice of the aggrieved or insulted father.

We can see how quickly the discoveries of the *Studies on Hysteria* became burdened with radical implications that may well have frightened its authors. Freud referred to his early women patients as his teachers, and what they taught him gave him insight not only into the workings of the psyche but also into the connections between inner and outer worlds, the psyche and the culture in which it is embedded. In *Studies on Hysteria*, what will subsequently be recognized as the implicit relational knowing of the human infant becomes the knowing that is carried symbolically by hysterical symptoms. In these early, heady days of psychoanalysis, it became the explicit relational knowing of young women and also of their physicians.

In Tennessee Williams's play *A Streetcar Named Desire*, when Blanche is raped by her sister Stella's husband Stanley, she tells Stella what has happened. Stella then tells her friend Eunice that "I couldn't believe her story and go on living with Stanley." The insight of this realization illuminates the history of psychoanalysis: Freud could not believe the story of his women patients and go on living in patriarchy. But the issue from our perspective is even more pointed. The discoveries of the *Studies on Hysteria* had led Freud to see trauma and specifically the traumatizing of sexuality as the *caput nili*, the head of the Nile, the source of neurotic suffering. This is an insight Ferenczi and Suttie will come to, with the trauma read more broadly as a traumatizing of voice and thus of relationship. The traumatized person, experiencing his or her voice as ineffective, as powerless, takes on the voice that carries power and authority. Stella cannot take on Blanche's voice and all it implies within a culture in which Stanley holds the power. Or rather, to take on her voice would mean protesting the culture on ethical grounds.

It may well be that exposing the psychology underlying patriarchy touches a nerve so sensitive that it becomes inflammatory. By this point, we have come to see many reasons why this would be so, reasons having to do with the dynamics of shame and violence, with how closely questions of honor are aligned with questions of gender so that insults to one's honor become insults to one's manhood or womanhood, and with how intricately gender is woven into the body, into language, and into identity and culture. To take on gender, as Virginia Woolf discovered, means to find new words and create new methods, to be sensitive to the processes of association and dissociation at work in the psychology we are seeking to explore and explain.

It was the separation of women from their own stories that initially caught Breuer and Freud's eye: "[H]er love had already been separated from her knowledge,"[3] Freud writes of the woman he calls Fraulein Elisabeth von R. Since women's love is often connected to men's, the seeming conflict between love and knowledge that became the center of this psychological case history also raises a series of larger questions: Is it possible to know and also to love? Or, more radically, is it possible to love and also not know?

In connecting women with their knowledge, "Freud became a virtual Eve or, more accurately, the serpent in the garden. He was breaking a cultural taboo, undoing a process of initiation by forging a method of inquiry that placed him in direct opposition to the fundamental rule of patriarchy: the claim on the part of fathers to authority."[4] The case of Elisabeth von R. (Ilona Weiss) illustrates these themes. Elisabeth, a young woman of twenty-four, had been referred to Freud for treatment of pains in her legs, which made it difficult for her to walk. The referring physician suspected that her symptoms were hysterical in origin, and Freud's observations confirm this suspicion. When he proposes psychoanalytic treatment to Elisabeth, his suggestion is met with "quick understanding and little resistance." He writes:

> The task on which I now embarked turned out, however, to be one of the hardest that I had ever undertaken.... For a long time, too, I was unable to grasp the connection between the events in her illness and her actual symptom, which must nevertheless have been caused and determined by that set of experiences.... When one starts upon a cathartic treatment of this kind, the first question one asks oneself is whether the patient herself is aware of the origin and the precipitating cause of her illness. If so, no special technique is required to enable her to reproduce the story of her illness. (Studies on Hysteria, p. 138)

At the beginning, Freud suspected that Elisabeth's knowledge was a secret she was keeping from him, but he quickly discovered that she was also keeping the secret from herself. He had come upon dissociation: the splitting of consciousness through which we can hold parts of our experience out of awareness, knowing while also not knowing what we know. Gaps in memory, broken trains of thought, something missing in a causal chain were the clues that alerted him to this process.

Pierre Janet, a pioneering French psychologist in the field of traumatic memory, had relied on hypnosis to unlock the dissociation of trauma; Breuer's way was made easy by his patient Anna O's ability to sink into periods of "absence," thus effectively hypnotizing herself. Freud, never good at hypnosis and facing a patient with "the *belle* indifference of a hysteric,"[5] decided on a more straightforward approach. Proceeding on the assumption that his patient knew everything of pathological significance relating to her symptoms,[6] he would press his hand on her forehead at moments when she fell into silence or claimed that nothing was occurring to her and suggest that in fact she knew. In this way he discovered that Elisabeth's love had become separated from her knowledge, and by reconnecting them, he also came to know what she knew.

Freeing women to speak about love, he was using his pick-lock, his psychoanalytic method, to unlock one of the deep secrets of patriarchy: what daughters know about their fathers, including the secret of father-daughter incest. Trauma, seen by Janet and others to be the bedrock of hysteria, becomes in Freud's understanding a sexual trauma, leading the psyche to dissociate itself from the body, which then becomes the repository of experiences that remain outside of consciousness.

As Freud discovered the power of association to undo dissociation – the associative stream of consciousness and also the touch of relationship – the psyche opened to his investigation. In short order, he learned the indirect discourse of symptoms, and this language led him to understand the mechanism of conversion, how psychic pain becomes physical pain; he discovered the symbolic nature of human consciousness, the force of resistance, and also the power of voice to bring dissociated parts of the self back into relationship.

The difficulty Freud faced in his early work lay in relinquishing the voice of the father; as a physician he had a claim to authority, and yet his method depended on giving up this claim. His authority lay in knowing a way – a method for undoing dissociation – but not the endpoint of the journey. In a stunning moment with Elisabeth, when she breaks off her stream of consciousness, declaring that nothing has occurred to her, he observes her "tense and preoccupied expression"[7] and assures her that something occurred. Perhaps she had not been sufficiently attentive; perhaps she thought that "her idea was not the right one," or she was concerned as to whether it was "appropriate or not"[8]; perhaps she was concealing what had in fact occurred to her because she was reluctant to share thoughts and emotions that felt shameful or unbearable. But in challenging Elizabeth to know what she knew in her body, to connect her voice with her experience, Freud was systematically (and paradoxically) undoing a process of initiation that had led her to take on a father's voice as her own.

The psychology of patriarchy and the psychology of trauma converge at this juncture. The confusion of tongues that Ferenczi identifies as a telltale sign of trauma, the taking on of the aggressor's voice as one's own, becomes the identification with the father that marks the psyche's initiation into patriarchy. But it is not the father per se. Rather, it is an identification with the voice of patriarchal authority (the law of the father) and an internalization of its demands. A developmental process that otherwise can appear adaptive thus contains a darkness at its center, and in that darkness we recognize the loss of voice and the confusion of memory that will make it difficult or impossible to say or even to know what actually happened. Freud's discovery of a method to undo dissociation gave him an entry into what otherwise is a blind spot. The power of psychoanalysis was clear. Freud's dream of aligning his new science with enlightenment and freedom was within his grasp.

He writes:

> I derived from this analysis [of Elisabeth] a literally unqualified reliance on my technique. It often happened that it was not until I had pressed her head three times that she produced a piece of information; but she herself would remark afterwards: "I could have said it to you the first time," – "And why didn't you?" – "I thought it wasn't what was wanted," or "I thought I could avoid it, but it came back each time." In the course of this difficult work, I began to attach a deeper significance to the resistance offered by the patient in the reproduction of her memories and to make a careful collection of the occasions on which it was particularly marked. (Studies on Hysteria, p. 154)

"I could have said it . . . I thought it wasn't what was wanted . . . I thought I could avoid it, but it came back each time." Voice and memory were pressing against restriction; knowledge and emotions held out of consciousness were coming back into relationship. Dissociation was yielding to association. Freud was becoming interested in the impediments to this process. The material split off from consciousness, the "it" that had become separated from the "I," was at once familiar and surprising. "I knew it," Elisabeth said; "I could have told you the first time." And yet she hadn't.

We return to the *Studies on Hysteria* and retrace Freud's steps in the critical period leading to *The Interpretation of Dreams* in order to illuminate how a man as intelligent and sensitive as Freud could in effect lose his bearings. We can see how the sacrifice of a democratic for a patriarchal approach to knowledge blinded him, as it has blinded others, to the point where he lost his capacity for seeing the obvious, or at least what to him should have seemed obvious: the role of trauma in initiating the Oedipus tragedy, the significance of the quotations from the *Aeneid* that appear at this juncture in his writings, and the implausibility of claiming to understand human sexuality while declaring the sexual life of women a mystery. Our larger point in recapitulating this history is to demonstrate how the seductions of patriarchy can constrain the liberatory potential of a science that had discovered a resistance that is psychologically rather than ideologically grounded, arising from our desire for voice and relationship, from our human nature. In this, our psychology is inherently aligned with the requisites and values of a democratic society, just as science itself is intrinsically democratic because its epistemological basis, the source of truth or knowledge, is evidence rather than authority. The irony, of course, is that in adopting a patriarchal stance in an effort to render his work scientific in the eyes of his colleagues, Freud embarked on a path that would lead many people to question whether psychoanalysis could in fact be considered science. But this is not where he began.

Describing Elisabeth, Freud notes her giftedness, her ambition, her moral sensibility, what her father jokingly called her "'cheeky' and 'cocksure'" ways, "being too positive in her judgements and . . . regardlessly telling people the truth."[9] He records what he terms "her excessive demand for love which, to begin with, found satisfaction in her family, and the independence of her nature which went beyond the feminine ideal and found expression in a considerable amount of obstinacy, pugnacity and reserve."[10] He is describing the character of a resister, the qualities Breuer notes in Anna O:

> She was markedly intelligent, with an astonishingly quick grasp of things and penetrating intuition. She possessed a powerful intellect. . . . She had great poetic and imaginative gifts, which were under the control of a sharp and critical common sense. Owing to this latter quality she was *completely unsuggestible*; she was only influenced by arguments, never by mere assertions. Her willpower was energetic, tenacious and persistent; sometimes it reached the pitch of an obstinacy which only gave way out of kindness and regard for other people. (Studies on Hysteria, p. 21)

Yet these stubborn, intelligent, imaginative, morally sensible, independent, and gifted women were suffering from hysterical paralysis, losing the range of their sight and hearing, displaying nervous tics and paralyses, choked by nervous coughing, and suffering most commonly from loss of voice.

Judith Herman in *Trauma and Recovery*[11] and Bessel van der Kolk and his colleagues in *Traumatic Stress*[12] identify loss of voice as the psychic core of traumatic experience, an inability to tell one's story. It is the wisdom of women-centered folktales, such as Cupid and Psyche, in which Psyche has no voice in a relationship until she breaks the taboo on seeing and speaking about love. Neither the old woman who tells the story nor Charite to whom she tells it is able to sustain a voice of resistance; both commit suicide. But such folktales show us that people do not lose their voices; they lose the desire or the courage or the will or the ability to use their voices to tell their stories.

From the beginning, psychoanalysis struggles with this problem of voice. Freud will lose his voice, and this loss will become yoked to the ascendance of the Oedipus story – the quintessential story of the wounded son. In his early work, Freud had been a man resisting patriarchy, and then he found himself at sea. His early case histories, which "read like short stories" and seemingly "lack the serious stamp of science,"[13] in fact reflect a boldness of method whose claim to science lies precisely in their narrative style. In the heady days of discovery, Freud had set out from a position of not knowing, and the evidence he came upon through a process of relationship required that he report the process – hence, the narrative method of the case histories. To capture the relational and responsive nature of his psychoanalytic inquiry, he invented a narrative art for his scientific writing.

The drama of the early case histories is one of relationship. We watch with fascination as Freud and Elisabeth move in and out of touch with each other, finding and losing and finding again, the process of discovery resembling the rhythms of love. "Psychoanalysis is a cure through love," Freud will subsequently write to Jung,[14] and here we see love unfolding. Freud writes of the "deep human sympathy"[15] he feels with Fraulein Elisabeth, although he notes that this in itself does not illuminate the cause of her symptoms. As she comes to connect her love with her knowledge, she connects the pains in her legs with memories of her father resting his legs upon her thighs. She remembers her hidden love for her sister's husband, their affinity for each other, and most shockingly, the thought that came unbidden into her consciousness as she stood at her dead sister's bedside ("Now he is free again, and I can be his wife").[16] The relationship with Freud, his ability to stay in the presence of such thoughts and feelings, releases Elisabeth from a feeling of condemned isolation.[17] As Elisabeth discovers that she can be with herself and also with Freud, as she responds to his interest in what she knows, we see dissociation giving way to association: Knowing replaces not knowing, and the pains in her legs subside.

Freud had come to astonishing discoveries about the human psyche and invented a method to unravel its secrets, a method that freed women like Elisabeth to know and to say what they knew. Moreover, at this point in his development, he not only listened carefully and responsively to what women said in free association but also accorded them ultimate authority in the process of discovering the conflicts underlying their neurotic symptoms, thus undoing the initiation that had led them to substitute a father's voice for their own.

It is astonishing to compare the Freud of this period with the views on women he was soon to adopt and hold basically for the rest of his life.

On the issue of sexuality, he would observe in 1905: "That of women – partly owing to the stunting effect of civilized conditions and partly owing to their conventional secretiveness and insincerity – is still veiled in an impenetrable obscurity."[18] On the question of love, he wrote in 1914: "Strictly speaking, it is only themselves that . . . women love with an intensity comparable to that of the man's love for them. Nor does their need lie in the direction of loving, but of being loved; and the man who fulfills this condition is the one who finds favour with them."[19] On the psychology of women in 1926, "the sexual life of adult women is a 'dark continent' for psychology."[20] On the capacity for ethics, in 1925:

> [F]or women the level of what is ethically normal is different from what it is in men. Their super-ego is never so inexorable, so impersonal, so independent of its emotional origins as we require it to be in men. Character-traits which critics of every epoch have brought up against women – that they show less sense of justice than men, that they are less ready to submit to the great exigencies of life, that they are more often influenced in their judgements by feelings of affection or hostility – all these would be amply accounted for by the modification in the formation of their super-ego which we have inferred above.[21]

Or, in 1933, "women must be regarded as having little sense of justice."[22] Correlatively, in 1930 he observes that "the woman finds herself forced into the background by the claims of civilization and she adopts a hostile attitude towards it."[23]

Freud in this later period could view woman's anatomy as destined to leave her with a sense of inferiority,[24] but earlier, in 1908, he had more radically connected "the undoubted intellectual inferiority of so many women . . . to the inhibition of thought necessitated by sexual suppression."[25] However, his most penetrating investigations of sexuality, including his three contributions to the psychology of love, view the question almost entirely from the point of view of men's interests and ambivalences.[26] Karen Horney observes that Freud's understanding of women mirrors the culture of patriarchy and narcissistically "differs in no case by a hair's breadth from the typical ideas that the [little] boy has of the girl."[27]

How can we understand this remarkable shift in Freud's thinking about women? If we follow the insights of his early work, we see evidence of dissociation: a separation of his love from his knowledge that suggests loss and trauma. In 1896, the year after the publication of *Studies on Hysteria*, Freud's father dies. The following year, he begins his self-analysis, based largely on his own dreams. This is the work where he introduces the Oedipus story, finding in his own dreams the same themes of love for the mother and hatred of the father that he finds in the great tragedies of Sophocles and Shakespeare – seeing them now as universal. In sharp contrast to the method he developed in relationship with his hysterical patients, he moves from a position of not knowing to one that "seized the position of the knower, the interpreter of dreams, the conquistador of the unconscious. He begins to override the voices of others; and we see him becoming embattled with those who disagree with him."[28]

We can see this process starkly both in the dreams analyzed in *The Interpretation of Dreams*, and in Freud's increasingly fraught relationships to women patients. We hear him discrediting women's experience and overriding their claims to knowledge with his own. In effect, we are witnessing a 180-degree reversal. Instead of proceeding empirically and building a theory on the basis of his experience with women, he is trying to fit women's experience into his theory, whether of dreams or sexuality or love or morality. And what we find most interesting are the difficulties he encounters: the places where it does not fit. In essence, to encompass women within his theories of human psychology, Freud has to override gender, voice, and body – as if they were inconsequential psychologically.

Yet Freud's difficulty in fitting women into his Oedipus paradigm has everything to do with gender, with voice, and with the body. For reasons of gender and of anatomy, women stand in a different relationship to patriarchy than do men. If the Oedipus struggle centers on the patriarchal triangle of father, mother, and son, for daughters it poses what Freud will come to call "the riddle of femininity," a riddle he is unable to solve. The riddle of femininity, or more accurately of femininity in patriarchy, arises from the confusing perception that to be a good woman in patriarchy, a woman must become selfless: She must sacrifice her voice for the sake of relationship – a sacrifice that poses a nonsense riddle because psychologically it cannot be solved. Without voice, one is not present; there is no relationship, only the chimera of relationship. The human desire for relationship becomes in itself an act of resistance to loss of voice, meaning to trauma.

We come to a crucial observation. Within a patriarchal order, intrinsically more invested in men's participation and compliance, the initiation of girls typically occurs later than that of boys. As a result, girls are less psychically bound to that order, more able to voice their desire and their struggles for relationship. To the extent that such struggles come to be labeled feminine or feminist or seen as women's struggles, they appear irrelevant to men or compromising to manhood. In this sense, women are more likely to become the informants, more able to break patriarchal silences, to speak and thus to bring into conversation the loss of relationship that lies at the heart of its darkness.

In this light, we can understand why Freud's early connection with women proved so fruitful. Leading him into a darkness, women were revealing what had faint light to it: the dimly illuminated reaches of the psyche, the underworld of patriarchy. And he came to see how fiercely guarded it is, how dissociated from consciousness. In *The Interpretation of Dreams*, we see evidence for this.

Freud presents the "Irma Dream" as the first dream "which I submitted to a detailed interpretation."[29] He had dreamed of a patient, "Irma," whom he had treated for hysterical symptoms. In the dream, Freud takes her aside at a social gathering and reproaches her for not accepting his "solution."[30] He tells her that if she still has pains, it is her fault. When she replies that the pains in her throat, stomach, and abdomen are more severe than he knows, Freud wonders if he may have overlooked some organic ailment. Looking down her throat, he sees a white patch and some grayish scabs formed like the tubinal bones of the nose.

The dream scene then grows crowded with physician-friends, all of them in suitable disguise: Oscar Rie, pediatrician to Freud's children; Breuer, Freud's collaborator in *Studies on Hysteria*; and Wilhelm Fliess, Freud's close friend, in the garb of a knowledgeable specialist with whom he is on the best of terms. Somehow these doctors – all but Fliess – prove to have been responsible for Irma's persistent pains. Indeed, Freud claims that his friend "Otto" has given her an injection.[31]

In a discussion prefacing his interpretation, Freud discloses that Irma's hysterical anxiety symptoms had improved in the course of her analysis, but her somatic pains were still troubling her. The day before, he had met Rie, who (so it seemed to Freud) had criticized him for not curing Irma entirely. Freud had written an account of the case for Breuer, someone whose judgment he valued.

This is the background Freud offers to account for the dream's origins and for the wish it distorts. He interprets the dream image by image, speech by speech, and his association to these memories centers for the most part on his proficiency as a healer. The wish the dream expresses is that Irma's sufferings should be truly seen not as his fault but the fault of others. Conveniently, the friend who had criticized Freud is in the dream an irresponsible, bad physician.

Freud chose to read the dream as one of revenge and self-assurance with respect to his own conscientiousness. He shows us, as Erik Erikson observes, that "[d]reams . . . not only fulfill naked wishes of sexual license, of unlimited dominance and of unrestricted destructiveness; where they work, they also lift the dreamer's isolation, appease his conscience, and preserve his identity."[32]

As Peter Gay has shown,[33] however, Irma is a composite of two of Freud's patients, one of whom, Emma Eckstein, suffered from hysterical symptoms and nosebleeds. Freud had thought the nosebleeds psychogenic and asked Fliess to examine the patient to make sure he had not overlooked a physical ailment. Fliess had come to Vienna and operated on Eckstein. The operation did not relieve the problem, but aggravated it, because Fliess had left gauze in the nose. Freud had been sickened by the episode but tried to protect Fliess from any imputation of negligence and professional incompetence. From this perspective, the dream is, *pace* Freud, not about Freud but about Freud's relationship to Fliess, and the dream seeks to exculpate Fliess (and thus Freud) of any responsibility. What the dream overrides is the traumatic experience and grievance of a woman, Emma Eckstein.[34]

We see here a defensiveness at odds with Freud's responsiveness and sensitivity to Elisabeth von R. The wishes expressed in his dream override both Eckstein's trauma and his own sense of grief at what Fliess had done. The repression of trauma, in a psychologist as sensitive as Freud, would once have alerted him to the loss of voice to which trauma leads. But he is moving to a very different position in relationship to himself and to women. The Irma Dream suggests a readiness to sacrifice women in order to shore up a faltering sense of proficiency within himself – but in sacrificing women or his relationship with women, he is also sacrificing what had been a source of his own creativity.

In *The Interpretation of Dreams* as in the *Three Essays on Sexuality* and the Dora case, both published in 1905, we see a psychoanalysis aligned with patriarchy and Freud taking on the voice of patriarchal authority. The traumatic disruption of personal relationships (the Oedipus complex) along with the loss of relational voice and of memory have become at once facts of nature (of development) and the requisites of civilization (of patriarchy). By 1905, women are identified as at once an insoluble mystery and a problem. Freud, who endlessly rewrote *Interpretation of Dreams* over his lifetime, making changes and additions, never makes any changes to his telling and interpretation of the Dream of Irma's Injection, never is able to tell anything like the truth of what had happened and his own relationship to these events.

We can see the exposed nerve that may have sparked this sudden break in Freud's relationship with his women patients when he writes to his confidante that he no longer believes his theory linking hysteria with sexual trauma. Instead, he focuses on the confusion of fantasy with reality, asserting that there are "no indications of reality in the unconscious, so that one cannot distinguish between truth and fiction that has been cathected with affect."[35] The implication is that with something as charged as sexual trauma, there is no way of knowing what actually happened. The voices of daughters are pitted against the reputation of fathers, and Freud takes what is in effect a hands-off attitude. With this, we see a theoretical shift, a move from speaking about dissociation to speaking about the unconscious, and the difference for our purposes is huge. Dissociated knowledge, split off from consciousness, can be brought into consciousness through association – the discovery of the studies on hysteria. This is what Freud meant when he claimed that the patient knows everything of pathological significance with respect to her symptoms, though she may not know that she knows it. The unconscious, in contrast, is accessible only through interpretation. Thus, we see the origins of a priesthood: the interpreters, the intermediaries who stand between the person and his/her unconscious.

There is an irony here. At the very moment Freud distances himself from the incest stories of his women patients, he places an incest story, the Oedipus story, as the cornerstone of psychoanalysis. Further ironies lie in the psychoanalytic processes we can discern at work. In a letter to Fliess, Freud writes that father-daughter incest had been implicated in all the cases in *Studies on Hysteria*, though in the cases themselves this had been disguised. From what we know, father-daughter incest is far more common than incest between mothers and sons. The shift in emphasis in Freud's theory from reality to fantasy follows a shift in the narrator of the incest story, from the young woman speaking about her experience of an incestuous relationship with her father to the young boy fantasizing about his wish for an incestuous relationship with his mother. By privileging the boy, the wish overrides the reality – or more insidiously, by assimilating the voices of women to his Oedipal theory and focusing on the unconscious, the line between fantasy and reality blurs. We are in the underworld with Aeneas, where "sees" becomes "thinks to have seen," a world of shades and phantoms.

From this point on, Freud's theory will be at risk from women's voices that are not captive to a father's voice or bound to a patriarchal story. Women are said by Freud to have no voice (no self, no judgment) and no relationships (no capacity to love except narcissistically) at precisely the point where their voices would jeopardize the developmental psychology that has become the cornerstone of his theory.

Perhaps more deeply telling, when Freud puts forward his formulation of the Oedipus Complex, the trauma has disappeared. In effect, the developmental story has been silenced. Oedipus's father Laius had sexually abused a young boy. The God Apollo told Laius that retribution would come in the next generation, at the hands of a son of his own. When Laius becomes a father, he enlists Jocasta, his wife, in his plan to protect himself by exposing the child. Jocasta and Laius drive a stake through their baby's feet (hence the name Oedipus, swollen foot) and prepare to leave him on a hill to die. Jocasta gives him to a shepherd to carry out the plan, or perhaps to subvert it – which the shepherd does, setting the plot in motion by taking the child to Corinth, to be raised there by the king and queen as their son.

As Oedipus grows up, the only sign of the trauma is the telltale mark on his body. There is no voice speaking about what happened; he has no memory. When Oedipus learns that he is fated to kill his father and marry his mother, he leaves Corinth in an effort to avert his fate. At a crossroads, he kills an older man in a fit of inexplicable rage and then goes to Thebes, where he solves the riddle of the sphinx and marries the queen, an older woman.

In his formulation of the Oedipus Complex, Freud separates the wishes for incest and murder from the developmental story in which they are embedded, interpreting them as a universal feature of early childhood, instinctively driven by and reflecting the triangulation of family relationships, as well as the prohibitions on incest and murder that are a mark of civilization. It is this nexus of instinct and civilization that makes the Oedipus Complex the seedbed for neuroses and the cornerstone of psychoanalysis.

But we have come to a different understanding.

To recapitulate what we have said so far, at the same time that Freud questions the pervasiveness of incest and disavows the voices of his women patients, blurring the line between reality and fantasy, he places another incest story – the Oedipus story – at the center of psychoanalysis. In *The Interpretation of Dreams*, he shifts his attention from women's experiences of sexual trauma, the focus of *Studies on Hysteria*, to his own fantasies of an incestuous relationship with his mother that involved parricide as well, fantasies reflected in his dreams and in the tragedies of Sophocles and Shakespeare. Concurrently, we see Freud retreat from the psychically intimate, pleasurable, and fruitful relationships that he had established with his women patients. The rush of discovery he experienced in these relationships and the deep human sympathy he felt with the women had become associated with danger and vulnerability and with the risk of appearing gullible, incompetent, or intellectually naïve in the eyes of fathers (the Irma Dream). With the death of his own father, Freud became the father – identification replacing a lost relationship – and with this replacement he becomes the hero of his own story.

To cede authority to women and draw on their experience as a basis for science is to go against the grain of a patriarchal culture. In privileging women's voices over the voices of fathers, Freud was placing his claims to manhood in jeopardy, a danger heightened in the Vienna of his period by the fact that he was a Jew. As a Jewish man, he was caught between the promise of political liberalism and the terrors of an aggressive political anti-Semitism in Austria and Germany, a dilemma Carl Schorske describes in *Fin-de-Siecle Vienna*.[36] Schorske specifically situates *The Interpretation of Dreams* in

> Freud's life-long struggle with Austrian socio-political reality: as scientist and Jew, as citizen and son. In *The Interpretation of Dreams* Freud gave this struggle, both outer and inner, its fullest most personal statement – and at the same time overcame it by devising an epoch-making interpretation of human experience in which politics could be reduced to an epiphenomenal manifestation of psychic forces. (Schorske, p. 183)

Freud regarded his dream book as his most important and path-breaking scientific work. He had discovered the meaning of dreams, their function in the human psyche; he had found that dreams follow a distinctive psychological logic (associative rather than deductive), and that this logic could be deciphered and understood through the dreamer's free associations in psychoanalysis. Schorske shows, however, that the work is both highly personal and political, drawing for its data base on Freud's own highly autobiographical dreams, very much in the spirit of Augustine's *Confessions*, albeit weaving into the story as well *The City of God*.[37]

Schorske argues that Freud's dreams are preoccupied with his own ambitions. For example, he recovers his memories of his father's celebration of "newly triumphant liberalism in the Austria of the 1860's," when

> until the very end of his Gymnasium years, Freud planned – undoubtedly, given his father's values with paternal encouragement – to study law, the royal road to a political career.... In such a context of clear and confident liberalism Freud acquired the political values he retained all his life: partisanship for Napoleon as conqueror of backward Central Europe; contempt for royalty and aristocracy (in 1873 as a senior in the Gymnasium Freud had proudly refused to doff his hat to the emperor); undying admiration for England, particularly for the great Puritan, Oliver Cromwell, for whom Freud, the sexual liberator, named his second son; and above all, hostility to religion, especially to Rome. (Schorske, p. 189)

By the 1890s, however, Austria-Hungary had entered "a seething atmosphere of almost continuous political crisis," in which the lower social strata generated the power to challenge the older elites. Out of the working class sprang socialism; out of the lower middle class and peasantry arose both virulent nationalism and Christian Socialism: "The fall of Vienna to Karl Lueger's anti-Semites in the elections of 1895 was a heavy blow to the bearers of liberal culture, Jew and Gentile"; professionally, the frustrations that had dogged Freud from the beginning of his career "had by 1895 produced a bitterness verging on despair." Wanting to be a research scientist, Freud had been forced into being a physician to cope with his poverty. The most galling insult he had to suffer was his long wait – 17 years in all, where 8 was the norm in the medical faculty – to be given a professorship.

Schorske argues that the trajectory of dreams in *The Interpretation of Dreams* reveals the impact of these events on Freud's sense of his own professional ambitions: his withdrawal from the politics of his youth to the social and intellectual resignation of his maturity, including the form of that withdrawal that Freud creatively forged in this and later works. The Irma Dream focuses, in Freud's analysis, on professional frustration and self-doubt. But his analysis of the Dream of the Uncle with the Yellow Beard – a dream quite nonsensical on its face – reveals the unseemly consequences of the political thwarting of his ambitions and expresses his dream wish that he become the minister who could eliminate his competitors and promote himself to a professorship. Freud does not make clear what the Uncle Dream shows us. Much as he might cultivate resignation in his waking life, the wish to be free of anti-Semitism shows itself in his dreams, including "denigration of, that is, aggression against his Jewish friends and colleagues" (Schorske, p. 188).

In his third extensively analyzed dream (the Dream of the Botanical Monograph), Freud's father enters the picture, opening the gates of memories of childhood and early youth, including the memory of his father's liberalism of the 1860s. Having explored these memories, Freud suddenly introduces the reader "to what can only be called his Rome neurosis" (Schorske, p. 189). Some inhibition held him back from visiting Rome, though he had visited Italy a number of times. In *The Interpretation of Dreams*, he reports four Rome Dreams, dreams which conflate images of Catholic Rome with Jewish ideas and situations. Freud does not analyze them fully, but observes that "the wish to go to Rome had become in my dream-life a cloak and symbol for a number of passionate wishes." He discloses only one of them, the clue to which he finds in Hannibal: "I had actually been following in Hannibal's footsteps. Like him, I had been fated not to see Rome." This idea leads him to the recovery of a childhood scene in which he finds the source of his Rome neurosis.

When Freud was ten or twelve years old (1866–68), his father tried to explain to his son how much liberalism had improved the lot of the Jew. He told Sigmund how, in an earlier time, he had been publicly humiliated by an anti-Semitic thug: "A Christian came up to me and with a single blow knocked off my cap into the mud and shouted: 'Jew! Get off the pavement!'" Upon questioning, Freud discovered that his father had offered no resistance: "'I went into the roadway and picked up my cap,' was his quick reply." Freud was disgusted with such "unheroic conduct," contrasting it with Hannibal's father who "made his boy swear before the household altar to take vengeance on the Romans. Ever since that time, Hannibal had had a place in my phantasies" (Schorske, p. 197).

"To take vengeance on the Romans" defined Freud's sense of heroic manhood. Unlike Gustav Mahler and other creative Jewish men who responded to anti-Semitism by converting to Austrian Catholicism, Freud never did so. He defined his oedipal stance not by rejecting his father's liberalism but by identifying himself as Hannibal-Freud, a Semitic general who would avenge his father's nonresistance against Rome, signifying "the organization of the Catholic church" (Schorske, p. 196) and the Hapsburg regime that supported it.

Freud had chosen to be a scientist, not a politician, however. Intoxicated with Goethe's erotic description of Mother Nature, he had entered the university in science instead of law (Schorske, p. 193). How could he square science with his ambition to be Hannibal-Freud? His view of the matter is suggested by his interpretation of the Revolutionary Dream.

On the day of the Revolutionary Dream, Freud was setting out for a holiday with his family. While waiting for the train, he noticed that Count Thun, first minister of the regime, had stalked onto the platform without a ticket to take the train to the emperor's summer retreat at Ischl, where important Austro-Hungarian accords were to be worked out. Freud was struck by the aristocrat's aplomb, waving the ticket-taker aside and taking a seat in a luxurious compartment. All of Freud's liberal resentment against aristocrats welled up as he whistled a subversive air from Wolfgang Amadeus Mozart's *Marriage of Figaro*: "If my Lord Count is inclined to go dancing,/I'll be quite ready to play him a tune."[38]

The dream on the train arose from this encounter and Freud's feelings of resentment. In the opening scene, Freud is a university student at a gathering, listening to Count Thun belittle German nationalism. He rises in anger in response to Thun's contemptuous remarks. In his analysis of his dream, Freud identifies two Jewish men as physicians who had been important figures in resistance movements. After the outburst of anger, he flees the political scene, trying to get out of town to any place but where "the court would be in residence" (*Dreams*, p. 210). The final scene is in the train station. There Freud finds himself on the platform in the company of a blind man, whom he recognizes in his analysis as his dying father. He holds a urinal for the helpless old man, aware that the ticket-taker would look the other way. Thus, the dream ends.

At the beginning of the dream, Freud, as a kind of prerevolutionary Figaro, confronts the powerful Count Thun on the platform. By his defiance of the count, Freud sees himself as having discharged the commitment of his youth to liberal political activism, a commitment he owed to his father. But he also disavows the role other physicians played in political activism. His flight from political activism ends in the final scene on the platform, which he associates with two episodes in his childhood when his father had condemned him for urinating in his parents' room, saying "This boy will come to nothing." In the final scene of the Revolutionary Dream, the now adult Freud reverses the situation, the son now helping his blind and feeble father in urinating. Freud comments: "You see, I *have* come to something" (*Dreams*, p. 216).

In commenting on this dream and his interpretation of it, Freud recognizes it as essentially about his relationship to his father, in a way that he construes in terms of his own mature political theory:

> [T]he whole rebellious content of the dream, with its *lese majeste* and its derision of the higher authorities, went back to rebellion against my father. A Prince is known as the father of his country; the father is the oldest, first, and for children the only authority, and from his autocratic power the other social authorities have developed in the course of the history of human civilization. (*Dreams*, p. 217, n1)

The Revolutionary Dream moves from political encounter, flight to academia, to the conquest of his father who had replaced Count Thun. As Schorske observes, "Patricide replaces regicide; psychoanalysis overcomes history. Politics is neutralized by a counterpolitical psychology" (p. 197).

Freud was haunted by his father's political liberalism, as is shown in the Dream of Hungary, in which the father appears as a political leader mobilizing Hungarians into liberal resistance, and "how like Garibaldi my father looked on his death-bed."[39] Freud does not comment that this victory was political. Instead, he connects this apotheosis of his father to a universal parricidal impulse, such as the one he identifies in the Revolutionary Dream. The political story has become a psychological story, and the parricidal impulse rather than a response to political tyranny becomes a universal feature of the human unconscious, a manifestation of what Freud construes as an unconscious wish for an incestuous relationship with the mother.

In framing human psychology in the notably truncated terms of his reading of the myth of Oedipus, Freud asserts "that the death-wish against parents dates back to earliest childhood."[40] His father's political resistance then becomes a reflection of Freud's own intrapsychic struggles to kill and replace his father as patriarch. But the relationship between political theory and psychological theory essentially remains unexplored, leaving open the way for the reductionism that will follow: the dismissal of political resistance as derivative, as ideology or "rationalization" of an underlying truth that is apolitical because rooted in the unconscious. And hence universal, and in a developmental sense, original: inherent in the very nature of things.

The shift we make here is to identify this structuring of consciousness as a response to a trauma that, in the experience of boys, typically dates back to the end of early childhood, the time in which Freud locates the Oedipus Complex. Placed within a developmental narrative, the Oedipus myth offers an explanation for a psychology that reflects the dissociation that even in Freud's time had come to be associated with trauma. And also germane to our present argument is a kind of healthy resistance, manifest in the very development of symptoms: the refusal of an ethically resisting voice to go gently into silence. As we were told by Freud and Breuer, the young women suffering from hysteria, the women who, Freud's letters reveal, had experienced incest at the hands of their fathers, resisted the codes of patriarchal womanhood: They were defiant in their moral sensibility, cheeky and cocksure, and when they could no longer speak directly about what they knew through experience, they turned to the indirect discourse of symptoms. The most common symptom of hysteria, the loss of voice, carries the political message: I have been silenced.

Freud's early sense of reaching the headwaters of neurosis lay in finding the source of neurotic suffering in the pathology of fathers, the otherwise respectable men who were implicated in incestuous relationships with their daughters. To ask what explained this "unnatural" turn in the sexual lives and loves of fathers and also to inquire into the silence or complicity of mothers would lead, in our experience, to an explanation at once psychological and political. Yet Freud's political theory, as his interpretation of the Revolutionary Dream makes clear, has nothing to do with liberalism, still less with liberal resistance. Instead, it is a theory that naturalizes patriarchy, which is contradictory to liberal democracy, and its psychology certainly does not explain liberal political resistance, which it devalues as just one among a number of forms of father-son conflict. Schorske asks: "Was there nothing left of Hannibal-Freud, nothing of Figaro-Freud, nothing of Freud the challenger of the count in the Revolutionary Dream?" (p. 200).

For Schorske, the answer lies in the epigraph to *The Interpretation of Dreams*: *Flectere si nequeo superos, Acheronta movebo* ("If I can sway no heavenly hearts I'll rouse the world below" – Fitzgerald translation). The words are Juno's in Vergil's *Aeneid*, at the beginning of Book VII, after Aeneas has abandoned Dido and Carthage and is on his way to Italy. Juno, the wife of Jupiter, had been the divine defender of Semitic Dido and of Carthage. Having failed to persuade her husband Jupiter (the upper world) to join her in supporting the marriage of Dido and Aeneas, she summons from hell (the underworld) a Fury, Allecto, to wreak vengeance on Aeneas by arousing the passions of his enemies. Freud will cite Juno's words again later when he wants to point out the overall significance of his work into dreams. After repeating the quotation, he observes: "The interpretation of dreams is the royal road to the knowledge of the unconscious activities of the mind." And in a footnote he adds that "this line of Vergil . . . is intended to picture the efforts of the repressed instinctual impulses" (*Dreams*, p. 608).

Schorske connects Freud's use of Juno's threat to stir up hell with the socialist Ferdinand Lassalle's use of the same quotation in a political pamphlet, warning that if the Prussian state fails to unite with Italy in opposing the Hapsburg state, the latent forces of national revolution will stir up a political Acheron ("the world below" in the epigraph) (Schorske, pp. 200–1). Freud had dreamt of Lassalle and interpreted the dream as a confirmation of his own fears of coming to grief over a woman, as Lassalle had. In the dream, Freud conquers his own sexual temptation by his understanding of neurosis, while politicians like Lassalle are undone.[41]

Having explored his own past through dream analysis, Freud broke the spell of Hannibal's oath. He actually entered Rome in 1901, nearly five years after his father's death, not "to take vengeance on the Romans" but as psycho-archeologist. He was disappointed and was only moved to enthusiasm by the Rome of antiquity: "I would have worshipped the humble and mutilated remnant of the Temple of Minerva" (quoted in Schorske, p. 202).

Freud's identification of his theory of dreams with Juno's rage in the *Aeneid* suggests to us a yet deeper dynamic in the evolution of his thought from *Studies on Hysteria* to *The Interpretation of Dreams*: namely, the impact of anti-Semitism on his abandonment of his early relationship with women patients and the trajectory of dreams we have now discussed. Freud's interpretation of his own dreams reveals a man acutely sensitive to the effects of anti-Semitism on his ambitions as a man of science, leading him from the liberal resistance of his youth (when he identified with Hannibal) to the patriarchal psychology and political theory he puts forward in *The Interpretation of Dreams*. This sensitivity included something that Schorske does not notice: the highly gendered character of European anti-Semitism, which has, since Augustine, stigmatized the role that both sexuality and gender play in Jewish life. The Jewish acceptance of sexual love as central to religious life led Augustine to see the

Jews as "carnal Israel" (see Chapter 5). The active roles played by Jewish women not only in family life but also in business resisted the gender norms of patriarchy that otherwise prevailed among the European bourgeoisie. But more seriously, the devotion of Jewish men to study and the fact that they were unable for the most part to own property or serve in the military exempted them from the gender roles of patriarchy – and yet within the Jewish community, in its religion as well as in family life, their manhood was affirmed.

Jewish men, in the terms of prevailing stereotypes, were at once effeminate and highly sexed. It is against this background that we can understand Freud's shift from his early relationships to women and the central role he accords to sexuality (seeing the traumatizing of sexuality as the key to psychoneuroses) to his later views, as he breaks confidence with women, in essence breaking relationship and discounting their voices. If the goal is to secure his psychology and gain status within a conventionally patriarchal Christian society, this can be seen as a necessary move. Yet with this break in relationship to women, Freud's methods and his theory change. As he now assumes the patriarchal position of authority – the interpreter of his patient's unconscious – he elaborates a personal and political psychology that conforms much more closely to the dominant culture surrounding him, a psychology that centers on the father-son relationship and accords authority to fathers. In his tripartite division of personality into the it, the I, and the over-eye or superego, the father's voice as internalized becomes the arbiter of conscience, morality, and law.

Certainly, the narrative in *The Interpretation of* Dreams is structured in a highly patriarchal way, as if, contrary to fact, Freud had only a father, when in fact his mother, Amalia Freud, in Peter Gay's description, "was temperamental, energetic, and strong-willed, getting her way in small matters and large, vain of her appearance almost to her death at ninety-five, efficient, competent, and egotistical."[42] This powerful woman figures only marginally in Freud's self-presentation, which suggests the degree to which that presentation was framed in terms of the highly patriarchal audience he meant to address and persuade.

Patriarchy bears most heavily on the voices of men who would reasonably protest its terms. Freud's early relationships to women exposed him to these burdens, especially his efforts to connect women to their own dissociated or split-off knowledge. Moreover, his discoveries focused on the importance of sexuality in human life, a view that placed him at odds with orthodox Augustinian Christianity. Both his alliance with women and his views about sexuality isolated Freud from the patriarchal culture in which he wanted so desperately to succeed, indeed exposed him to ridicule, as not a man but a woman and a Jew, in ways that from the evidence of his dreams clearly stung his manhood.

The crucial piece missing in the puzzle of Freud's development from liberal activist to psychologist of patriarchy is his vulnerable sense of manhood in the increasingly anti-Semitic Vienna of the 1890s, the period of *Studies on Hysteria* and *The Interpretation of Dreams*. Freud's father had trusted in political liberalism, supposing that his son could and would succeed and flourish as he became assimilated to the terms of Austrian liberalism. But the liberalism of his period was itself deeply flawed by its connections to patriarchal religion and its assumption that patriarchy was in the nature of things. And its increasingly robust opponents, polit-ical anti-Semites, were even more grounded in unjust patriarchal con-ceptions, in terms of which the Jews, in particular, were singled out and dehumanized, no matter how much they tried to assimilate to the dom-inant norms and ways of life. Freud was caught between a rock and a hard place; having found his most creative voice as a psychologist in his early relationships to women, his credibility and his manhood hinged on breaking these relationships.

We see an artistic expression of what women meant to Freud during this period in Gustav Klimt's painting "The Kiss."[43] The man, rather desperately holding a kneeling woman's head with his two hands and kissing her on the cheek, is engulfed in a large armoring cloak with a design of rectangles that conceals his body. The woman, however, is alto-gether freer. The gold cover on her side is transparent, showing the shape of her body and her dress with its pattern of circles; her arms weave in and out of the cloak and her feet stick out completely. Her attitude toward the man, his longing and his captivity, is reflected in her languid placing of her arm around his neck, her fourth finger crooked in a casual gesture. She experiences an openness, an ability to move in and out of the gold covering that is unavailable to him. In the title of his painting, Klimt suggests that the man and the woman stand in a very different relation to sexual life.

Freud's letters to Fliess convey his grief and even panic over the loss of his liberal father, and it is plausible that in the wake of this loss, Klimt's portrayal of men's engulfing armor captured Freud's situation. His cre-ative voice – so aligned with women and the release of their sexuality from the aftereffects of trauma – could not find the resonance it required in the culture around him, at least not in those places where he sought it. Even the most creative men, of the highest integrity and intelligence, often cannot bear patriarchal pressures on their honor as men and need to establish their manhood in the eyes of other men. We can see the underlying psychological process quite clearly in *The Interpretation of Dreams*, culminating not in experience or science but in Freud's way of telling the myth of Oedipus, as he breaks relationship and becomes his father or, rather, his patriarchal idea of what his father was or should have been.

In contrast to the Cupid and Psyche narrative where love hinges on seeing and speaking, Oedipus's love for his wife/mother hinges on blindness and ends not in the birth of pleasure but in tragedy and death. It is instructive to note the similarity in the choice that both Psyche and Jocasta face: Both are presented with a conflict between obeying their husband and protecting their child. Jocasta chooses to protect Laius against the oracle's prophecy of parricide by exposing the infant Oedipus, leaving him on a hillside to die. When Psyche, pregnant, is told by her sisters that she is married to a monster who is waiting to devour her and the child, she sets out to kill the monster rather than risk herself and the child. In doing so, she violates her husband's (Cupid's) injunction that she must never try to see him. Yet when she looks at Cupid under the light, she discovers that the choice itself is based on false premises – her lover is not a monster, nor in the end does he become one. Jocasta, following the patriarchal script and giving priority to the father over the child, discovers the tragic consequences for all involved.

In Sophocles's tragedy, as Jocasta warns Oedipus about the dangers of knowing ("no more truth"), the chorus comments to Oedipus about his mother's silence: "Furrows your father ploughed bore you in silence./ How, how, oh how could it be?"[44] Although the question "Anyone on this earth/struck by a harder blow,/stung by a fate more perverse?" remains unanswered, the answer implied is Jocasta – the unspeaking and in the end unspeakable mother, who will appear and reappear throughout psychoanalytic writing well beyond Freud's time. She will become the "object" of object-relations theory, the not-good-enough mother of innumerable case histories, a repository for accusation, blame, and regret.

Yet, again in Sophocles's tragedy, when Jocasta finally does speak of her own experience briefly before strangling herself, it is to ask what happened in what had seemed to be a story of love: She "cried out to Laius, long since dead. She cried out to him, remembering the son that she had borne long ago, the son who killed his father, the son who left her to bear a dread curse – the children of her own son!"[45] Thus, human connection remains a puzzle, and the story of abandonment comes full cycle. Jocasta's tragedy is that twice she fails to perceive the connection between mother and child. Consequently, she suffers for the most part in silence. Although her actions are central to this story about love, her silence becomes, as the chorus says, part of its mystery.

Freud gives us only a truncated narrative of the Oedipus story, omitting its underlying developmental trajectory, and in its absence we see a man, Oedipus, who is blind to his own history, unwilling or unable to see his physical and psychological scars. In a man with as much integrity as Freud, what is so sad and so shocking is not only his betrayal of his connections with women but also, according to Schorske, his betrayal of his father's political liberalism. For us, this betrayal is best seen in the incorporation of a patriarchal voice into the very structure of the psyche in the form of a superego or over-I, an over-voice that in Freud's description is harsher than that of an actual father, by which, in this context, he would seem to mean his own. Thus, Freud does not so much turn away from politics, following Schorske's argument, as write an essentially patriarchal politics into psychology, to much more devastating effect. Liberal resistance to the evils of patriarchy (including anti-Semitism) has, for Freud, no sound psychological basis, as it wars on what he has come to believe is our universal human psychology: patriarchal forms of hierarchy established through the Oedipus Complex and held in place by its resolution, the taking on of a patriarchal voice as one's own. Resistance then becomes a sign of pathology, a form of oedipal acting out – immature and certainly unmanly.

This betrayal of his real father haunted Freud, as he tried to understand his relationship to his father's liberalism and his own attempt to become the liberal hero he thought his father never was. We are struck by the language of heroism in terms of which Freud explores his struggles: Hannibal-Freud, Figaro-Freud, Garibaldi-Freud, and the men he admired as liberal heroes – Napoleon and Cromwell, both great soldiers and imperialists. When Freud allowed himself to consider ending war, which he came to regard as rooted in Thanatos, an instinct as primal in our psychology as Eros, only an international community armed with supreme force came to mind.[46] A figure like Gandhi, who was historically notable by the early 1930s when Freud wrote about war, is not on Freud's radar screen. His patriarchal psychology could make no sense of a Gandhi or nonviolent resistance.

What Freud offers us is a view of civilization. On the one hand, civilization must constrain the sexual love of men in the interest of sublimation (in consequence, "the woman finds herself forced into the background by civilization and she adopts a hostile attitude towards it"). On the other, civilization imposes problematic demands of loving one's neighbor as oneself to control men's "instinctual endowment," including "a powerful share of aggressiveness."[47] Because his psychology reads patriarchy as nature, he does not question why sexual love is for men under patriarchy so problematic, and aggression, including war, so irresistible. There is no space within such a patriarchal psychology for even raising the question of whether the traumatic disruption of relationship (so that people cannot desire what they love, or love what they desire) is what makes male violence and the "universal [by which Freud means men's] tendency toward debasement in the sphere of love"[48] so endemic and pervasive. Both war and tragic love come to seem, as it were, as in the nature of things.

Freud thus reads the history of culture in a way that aligns his patriarchal psychology with civilization, and its discomfort or neurosis is the price we have to pay. His belief that there is no real alternative is shown by the sense he made of one of his most prized possessions, an ancient Egyptian statue of Isis suckling the infant Horus.[49] Freud knew such mother goddesses had once existed, but he argued, following Bachofen,[50] that they expressed a primitive matriarchy that had yielded to civilization's patriarchy.[51] The role Isis plays in Apuleius's *Metamorphoses*, presenting a religion antithetical to hierarchy, whether patriarchal or matriarchal, and one arising within a patriarchal culture as an alternative is not a possibility Freud entertains. And yet he keeps Isis with him. Oddly, he mistakenly supposes that Isis, a sexually loving wife and mother, is the model for the asexual, indeed virginal, madonna of Augustinian Christianity.[52] The authority of a woman's real and sexual love for a man in an equal relationship is thus buried in the familiar patriarchal pattern of idealization and denigration, which Freud assumes to be universal. And in making this assumption, he misses what we have come to see as a clue in the Isis story, a clue the early Freud might have grasped: It is through her sexual love that Isis brings the defeated and dismembered Osiris, her husband, back to life.

Motivating all of this, we have come to believe, is Freud's reenactment of an ancient Roman story he knew all too well: Aeneas abandoning Dido, as the condition for realizing his patriarchal manhood; Augustine repudiating his beloved concubine and even his sexuality in order to become a soldier of God. We are riveted by the analogy in both form and content between Augustine's *Confessions* and Freud's *The Interpretation of Dreams*. In both, sensitive, artistic, highly intelligent men believe they must radically break with women in order to establish their manhood. Augustine turns from sexual love to an ascetic priesthood; Freud never found in his wife, Martha, "a companion . . . for his long and lonely progress toward psychoanalysis" and was moving into sexual abstinence in the decade after *The Interpretation of Dreams*.[53] And in his analytic psychology, Freud turns from his real relationships to his women patients in *Studies on Hysteria* to the essentially deductive, nonempirical, and ultimately incoherent attempt to fit women into the oedipal psychology of his later work. In the process, he comes to the astonishing misogyny of his later work: views on women earlier discussed, which were conventional in the German high culture of his time. In both Augustine and

Freud, such disruption leads to loss and its consequences, idealization and denigration, manifest in their subsequent views on women.

In Freud's case, he arrives at the point where his theory has blinded him to the reality of women's experience – but also to his own experience with women, recorded in his letters and evident in his life. "My dear Frau Lou," Freud writes to Lou Andreas-Salome in 1916, two years after the narcissism paper earlier discussed (that women cannot love): "You are an 'understander' *par excellence*; and in addition you invariably understand more and improve upon what is put before you. . . . [Y]ou come along and add what is missing, build upon it and put what has been isolated back into its proper context."[54] Writing to Marie Bonaparte in 1938, he acknowledges the "self-effacement with which you give your energies to the introductions and popular expositions of psychoanalysis. . . . You claim to be so very ambitious and to long for immortality at any price! Well, your actions testify to a nobler character."[55] As these portrayals contrast with the image of women in Freud's scientific writings, the efforts by women to elaborate Freud's theories, with few exceptions – most notably Karen Horney – perpetuate a central silence.[56]

Yet as we listen to Freud's increasingly insistent claims not to know about women, despite being surrounded by women in his professional as well as his personal life, we hear his gnawing sense of a problem, one arising in part from the very nature of theory construction: "I know that in writing I have to blind myself artificially in order to focus all the light on one dark spot."[57] In part, his claims reflected a society where women's lives were not considered to inform human possibility, a society where virtue for women was equated with innocence and self-sacrifice. But constraints also arose from a conception of objectivity in science that led, as we have seen in the Dream of Irma's Injection, to a series of enforced separations from women, reflected in the way Freud had come to design his laboratory – the analytic situation – on the model of a patriarchal priesthood.

We are not alone in believing that the resulting conception of the authority of Freudian analysts has fundamentally compromised the democratic and emancipatory power of psychoanalysis. Both psychoanalytic theory and its practice have suffered from the largely deserved objections of feminists.[58] And similar objections have come from within psychoanalysis, including some of its leaders, most recently the former editor of the *Psychoanalytic Quarterly*, Dr. Owen Renik.[59] Renik urges a more democratic, egalitarian, and empirical conception of the aims of psychoanalysis, one he also associates with Freud's views and practices in *Studies on Hysteria*. In a similar spirit, Renik also urges rethinking of Freud's position on the universality of the Oedipus Complex.[60] What Freud mistakenly calls universal is, to Renik, a particular experience of family life "by a boy...as desperately competitive...for example, when narcissistic parents pursue their pleasure without consideration for their son's needs" (Renik, p. 153). Renik reports from his clinical work that

> boys whose parents have a happy, passionate relationship and are loving toward their son do not seem to struggle with the Oedipus complex. When domestic conflicts don't create a competitive atmosphere, a boy enjoys a gratifying, appropriate sexual element to his relationship with his mother, is satisfied with it, and doesn't experience his father as being disturbed by it. The boy identifies with his father – not because of a need to identify with the aggressor, but out of a nonconflictual admiration for his father and desire to emulate him. For girls, successful psychosexual development without significant oedipal conflict is perhaps even more common because – in most western European cultures at least – greater latitude for homosexual expression is given to females than to males, so that a girl, even more easily than a boy, can enjoy a measure of normal and appropriate sexual pleasure with both parents. (Renik, 153–4)

We see once again how patriarchy has distorted psychoanalysis in the same way that through Augustine it distorted Christianity. We cannot rectify these distortions without considering both the continuing power of patriarchy and the forms of resistance to it that are called for, including a psychology that addresses these concerns. We note that Renik has written sexuality and pleasure back into a psychoanalysis that, as it turned its back on women, in effect chose analysis over psyche and became, like Freud himself, increasingly wedded to sexual asceticism and abstinence, once proposed as the rule for patients undergoing treatment.

In coming to this understanding of Freud, we were drawn to three quotations from the *Aeneid* that appear in his work at precisely this juncture, as if he were marking his turn through an identification with Vergil's hero. We have already discussed the most famous of these quotations: the epigraph from *The Interpretation of Dreams*: *Flectere si nequeo superos, Acheronta movebo* – "If I can sway no heavenly hearts I'll rouse the world below." The apposite nature of this epigraph for a book on dream interpretation that exposes the underside of the psyche has diverted attention away from the question: What is the source of this line in the *Aeneid*? The line comes from Book VII, where Aeneas and his men, having left Carthage, land safely on the shores of the Tiber. In Book VI, Aeneas had traveled to the underworld in search of his father and in the course of that journey had come upon Dido. In a scene described by T. S. Eliot as "one of the most poignant and civilized passages in poetry,"[61] Aeneas tells Dido that he had not believed the stories that reached him: "I could not believe that I would hurt you/ So terribly by going."[62]

The line Freud takes as his epigraph is from the middle of a long speech by Juno, the goddess who had sought in vain to move the heavens on behalf of Dido and Carthage. Now, with Dido dead and Aeneas moving toward the successful completion of his mission, Juno calls on Allecto, "Grief's drear mistress," to do something about what has happened. Her aim is vengeance, and she addresses this fury "with her lust for war,/ For angers, ambushes, and crippling crimes":

> "... You can arm
> For combat brothers of one soul between them,
> Twist homes with hatred, brings your ships inside,
> Or firebrands of death...
> Break up this peace-pact, scatter acts of war,
> All in a flash let men desire, demand,
> And take up arms."[63]

In the cosmology of the *Aeneid*, this passage provides an explanation for Aeneas's transformation in the course of the epic from pious (*pius*) to savage (*saevus*). His "once kindly ears now blocked by divinely ordained duty," pious Aeneas who left Troy carrying his aged father and leading his small son, the man who fell in love with Dido, will at the end of the epic enact a savage and senseless retribution on Turnus. Juno's appeal to Allecto – her determination that someone redress what transpired at Carthage – is, in fact, a fitting epigraph for the book that inscribes the Oedipus story as paradigmatic, since this is the story that will block Freud's ears, rendering women incomprehensible.

The second quotation from the *Aeneid* occurs in the paper, "Screen Memories," published in 1899 along with the first volume of *The Interpretation of Dreams* (1899/1900). The line from the *Aeneid* is from Book I: *Foran et haec olim meminisse juvabit* – "Some day, perhaps, it will be a joy to remember even these things" (Aeneas to his men, on the possibility that their misfortunes may be favorably remembered).[64] The hope is that memory will be reconstructed and history rewritten, again an apposite quote for a paper showing how one memory can stand in front of and block another that is painful to recall. Freud illustrates this process by recalling a childhood scene of sensual pleasure and transgression that has screened a recollection of adolescence, a reversal of what will be taken as the usual sequence. This observation grips our attention, together with the substance of the memories. Freud begins by describing the childhood scene:

> I see a rectangular, rather steeply sloping piece of meadow-land, green and thickly grown; in the green there are a great number of yellow flowers – evidently common dandelions. At the top end of the meadow there is a cottage and in front of the cottage door two women are standing chatting busily, a peasant-woman with a handkerchief on her head and a children's nurse. Three children are playing in the grass. One of them is myself (between the age of two and three); the two others are my boy cousin, who is a year older than me, and his sister, who is almost exactly the same age as I am. We are picking the yellow flowers and each of us is holding a bunch of flowers we have already picked. The little girl has the best bunch; and, as though by mutual agreement, we – the two boys – fall on her and snatch away her flowers. She runs up the meadow in tears and as a consolation the peasant-woman gives her a big piece of black bread. Hardly have we seen this than we throw the flowers away, hurry to the cottage and ask to be given some bread too. And we are in fact given some; the peasant-woman cuts the loaf with a long knife. In my memory the bread tastes delicious – and at that point the scene breaks off.[65]

Freud clearly knew Apuleius's novel,[66] and the Apuleian references are striking; the grassy meadow filled with flowers, the sequence of sensual pleasure followed by transgression, which in turn is followed unexpectedly not by punishment (the knife) but by a deeper, earthy pleasure (black bread) evoke the tale of Cupid and Psyche. But Cupid and Psyche is an adolescent love story, and its displacement to early childhood suggests a reconstruction or displacement of memory, complicating Freud's account. The memory it screens, however, is one of first love:

> When I was seventeen and at my secondary school, I returned for the first time to my birthplace for the holidays, to stay with a family who had been our friends ever since that remote date. . . . In the family, where I was staying there was a daughter of fifteen, with whom I immediately fell in love. It was my first calf-love and sufficiently intense, but I kept it completely secret. After a few days the girl went off to her school . . . and it was this separation after such a short acquaintance that brought my longings to a really high pitch. . . . [For] a long time afterwards I was affected by the yellow colour of the dress she was wearing when we first met, whenever I saw the same colour anywhere else.[67]

The yellow of the dandelions and the dress links the two memories, but although the color is the same, the feelings associated with it are not.

Freud describes the dandelions as "common" flowers which, he says, "I am, of course, far from admiring today."[68] The little boys snatch the best bunch from the girl, but the flowers themselves are quickly discarded. The girl cries, but her tears are assuaged by the offer of bread, and the boys, their trespass forgiven, partake of the bread as well. The act of defloration has little consequence, and in retrospect what was stolen has little value.

It's the hidden memory that holds the strong feelings, the yellow dress evoking a love Freud has kept secret and intense longings linked with a painful separation – feelings reminiscent of Cupid's hidden love for Psyche, which surfaces after he leaves her. It's hard to make sense of these impressions or of Freud's association to Aeneas in this context, until we recall that Freud at this time is in the process of reconstructing psychoanalysis in a way that seems relevant to the two memories and their sequence.

With *The Interpretation of Dreams*, Freud has abandoned a key insight of the *Studies on Hysteria*. The incest stories told by his young women patients have for the most part been relocated to childhood, reconstructed as Oedipus wishes, construed as a universal childhood fantasy. As the focus of his theory shifts from adolescence to early childhood, an act of theft supplants first love, associated with painful memories. The line from the *Aeneid* begins to make sense: Perhaps someday even this will be remembered with joy. If Freud becomes the conquistador of the unconscious and accomplishes his mission to found a new science, the reconstruction of incest stories as Oedipal wishes will be of no lasting consequence and his suffering will be cast in a new light. But the memory of first love lingers. The suffering Aeneas refers to occurs before he meets Dido, and since it leads him to Dido and intense love, it could be remembered with joy. Poised on the edge of rewriting history, does Freud register a momentary regret, expressed in the screen memory paper by the evocation of Cupid and Psyche? These are our associations, spurred by the extent to which we have become steeped in Apuleius and the hope of a psychology wedded more to pleasure than to tragedy. In any event, the final quotation from the *Aeneid*, appearing two years later in a discussion of forgetting, marks Freud's turn.

The line comes from Book IV, which recounts the love story of Dido and Aeneas, and it provides the text for an illustration of forgetting in *The Psychopathology of Everyday Life*. In the second chapter of this 1901 volume, "The Forgetting of Foreign Words," Freud's interlocutor, a young man of academic background, at first tries to conceal "an obvious gap" in his memory of "the well-known line of Vergil's in which the unhappy Dido commits to posterity her vengeance on Aeneas."[69] The young man then challenges Freud to substantiate his claim that one never forgets without a reason. The line is: *Exoriare aliquis nostris ex ossibus ultor* – "May someone arise from my bones, an avenger," and the indefinite pronoun *aliquis* is the forgotten word. Freud explains that the forgetting serves the function of erasing the person who would become the avenger – in the case of the young man, the child whose conception he fears. His lover has missed her period, and he worries their affair will now be exposed. Unnamed, erased, someone becomes no one; the potential avenger is silenced.

One way to silence an angry woman is to discredit her account of what has happened by construing it as a wish or fantasy. It is also possible to silence a woman by idealizing or degrading her, or drawing her into a different story about love – Oedipus rather than Cupid [Eros] and Psyche. Or perhaps more simply, by making sexual pleasure and material comforts contingent on her not seeing or at least not saying what she knows about love, as Cupid initially does with Psyche. With the shift in his theory, Freud does all of these things. But he is too sensitive and intelligent a man, too much of a naturalist not to record his path. In turning from the *Studies on Hysteria* to *The Interpretation of Dreams*, he is, in effect, leaving Carthage for Rome, and he marks the trail by sprinkling his work at this juncture with quotations from the *Aeneid*.

Thus Freud signals his turn to a patriarchal psychology, framing his own quest for manhood in the terms of Aeneas's journey. The passages he chooses from Vergil convey a mix of hope and fear: angry women seeking vengeance (Juno enraged at Jupiter's failure to honor the marriage of Dido and Aeneas, Dido calling for an avenger) and a ship-wrecked man hoping for redemption (Aeneas hoping his trials will be remembered favorably). No further quotations from the *Aeneid* appear in Freud's writings, but he adopted a defensive stance. The separation from women, however, continued to haunt him in the form of a paradoxical assertion: that in the process of coming to know more about psychology, he has come to know less about women.

The choice by the Romans to make Aeneas one of their founders makes sense in terms of the psychology of patriarchal manhood we have now discussed at some length. The Romans choose a heroic man who had survived a humiliating defeat at Troy because this traumatizing defeat justifies Roman violence. When Augustus undertakes a building program to buttress the patriarchal ideology that justifies his autocratic rule, one of the central buildings is the Temple of Mars the Avenger (Mars Ultor), with a statue of Aeneas carrying his father nearby.[70]

The psychology of Roman patriarchal manhood thus both expressed and legitimated itself in the venerated image of its founder, a man capable of the forms of violence that sustained both the Republic and Empire. Freud frames his own image of manhood in terms of Aeneas, indeed, reenacts Aeneas's journey in his traumatizing break with women. Resolving his sense of crisis at being read as an unmanly Jew, he reads his own experience as universal. The pivotal place he accords the Oedipus Complex, also the story of a wounded man, renders love forever problematic, as men are trapped between the idealization of the women they love and the debasement of the women they desire.[71] The form that the resulting violence takes in Freud is a violence written into his theory, a death instinct that vies with Eros or the impulse toward pleasure and life. But it is also directed toward women in the form of a verbal assault, as Freud describes women in preposterous terms, evoking the same incredulity as Josephus's description of Roman men as though "born with swords in their hands." Women, Freud writes, are reluctant to accept "the fact of their castration." What swords? What castration? That which Freud would never feel free to say about religious or racial minorities he feels quite free to say of women, putting his intelligence on hold and introducing incoherence into his own analytical psychology and also his life, since he continued to work well with brilliant women analysts until his death, including his daughter Anna.[72]

However unconsciously (trauma covering voice and memory), Freud inscribed patriarchy as a law of nature, but was he too sensitive a psychologist not to register the price he, like Aeneas, had paid to uphold the conception of heroic manhood he was unable or unwilling to question. Although two of the three quotations he chose from the *Aeneid* register the voices of angry women (Juno and Dido),[73] what Freud feared in himself, as his dream of Lassalle suggests, was precisely his vulnerability and responsiveness to women, which had led to his most creative voice and work. He made of psychoanalysis, in the patriarchal terms he had come to understand it, as much a bulwark against such pleasure and vulnerability as Augustine's ascetic disciplines. And the mind of the man, once so creatively opened to women's voices and experiences, closed. His views on women have haunted psychoanalysis, but simply to redress the debasement of women, as many psychoanalysts have now done, misses the larger point: Freud's statements about women as incapable of love and morality and having no self display the ravages to his psychology of a by-now deeply rooted patriarchal mindset. But was there an alternative?

## 2. THE ALTERNATIVE PSYCHOLOGY OF IAN D. SUTTIE

In 1935 when Freud was still alive, Ian D. Suttie, a Scottish psychiatrist, published *The Origins of Love and Hate*.[74] Sandor Ferenczi had earlier begun to question the patriarchal structure of Freud's therapy,[75] and Suttie's wife had translated Ferenczi's works from Hungarian into English.[76] Suttie's pathbreaking work, in the spirit of Ferenczi's anti-patriarchal questions, cogently criticized some of the main substantive claims defended in *The Interpretation of Dreams* and Freud's later works. But more to the point, it offered a compelling alternative, including a new conception of the relation between culture and psychology.[77]

Suttie accepted the main methods of Freud's psychoanalysis – free association and transference – but questioned the metapsychological structure of Freud's late works, a structure dividing human psychology into two ultimate principles that are in tension, Eros and Thanatos, love and hate,[78] a tension that, Freud argued, underlies the modern propensity to war and other forms of violence.[79] Suttie argued that there was a more empirically valid and economical way of understanding what we had learned about human psychology from Freud's methods, namely, that there are not two independent principles of human psychology that are in tension, but only one, love. What is at the heart of human psychology, for Suttie, is human relationality, shown in the close relations and emotional responsiveness of mothers and babies in the long period of human infancy. Hate, in contrast, derives from the frustration or breaking of love: The "process of parturition or psychic weaning must be intensely painful even where not aggravated by jealousy of a supplanter."[80] For Suttie, what Freud had theorized as the core of human psychology, the Oedipus Complex where a son breaks with his mother and identifies with his father, was not normative and normal as Freud supposed but a kind of pathological distortion of fully humane functioning, driven by what Suttie characterized as "the 'taboo' on tenderness"[81] – the word *tenderness* adopted from Ferenczi. One consequence of this taboo was the homophobic stigma placed on the expression of love between men.[82]

Suttie's view makes central to an empirically based psychology the role that culture and the transmission of culture over time play in legitimating such breaks in human relationality, in particular, the "[p]atriarchal culture and sentiment"[83] that Freud had naturalized in *The Interpretation of Dreams*. Patriarchy, Suttie argues, is not natural at all but an unnatural distortion of human psychology in the name of a cultural tradition, one that is not only never questioned as such but not even seen as a culture because scientists like Freud have read it as nature (as the place of the Oedipus Complex in Freud's psychology shows clearly).

The cultural tradition to which Suttie gives closest attention is religion in general and Christianity in particular.[84] For Suttie, Christianity, properly understood as a religion of love, "seeks to reconstitute the tender relationship with the human environment which is lost in early childhood"; as such, it "was primarily a system of psychotherapy"[85] aimed at restoring our ability to love. The central problem of a human and humane psychology thus lies in understanding how Christian culture had itself been so distorted by the Roman patriarchy it uncritically absorbed. Orthodox Christianity, in his view, had come to transmit a culture so drenched in patriarchy that it failed any longer even to acknowledge or understand its original psychological and social mission: the restoration of loving relationships between humans.

Suttie identifies Augustine of Hippo as the central figure who shaped the orthodox Christian tradition into a form of patriarchy. It was Augustine who legitimated the view of children as so naturally bad (corrupted by original sin) that violence was appropriate in childrearing and read his own neurotic sexual conflicts (absorbed from Paul) into Christian doctrine. And Suttie points out as well Augustine's pivotal role in the legitimation of Christian violence in religious persecution (against the Donatists, the Pelagians, and the Jews).

If we are to understand and critically come to terms with the corruption of Christianity that has been transmitted to us by Augustinian orthodoxy, we must, Suttie argues, investigate the historical forms of religion (Christian and pagan) that were more rooted in a non-patriarchal sense of human relationality and were pushed aside and repressed by Christian orthodoxy. Among these historical religions Suttie mentions the idea of Jesus as mother,[86] as well as the mother cults of the ancient pagan world, cults that Christianity repressed. The Isis religion, though unmentioned, would certainly fit this picture.

Freud's cultural works are, for Suttie, especially problematic in this connection. Freud is only interested in highly patriarchal historical religions that exemplify his psychology, certainly not in the many mother cults that run against his position of a near-universal patriarchal psychology.[87] For similar reasons, Suttie would regard as problematic Freud's treatment of war and violence as rooted in one of the central principles of our psychology, precisely because it fails to take seriously, let alone investigate, the plausible alternative hypothesis – namely, that these patterns have been uncritically transmitted by the role played by patriarchy in the transmission of orthodox Christianity.

## 3. THE LENS OF GENDER

Beginning in the 1970s, the lens of gender brought into sharp focus a psychology so wedded to patriarchy that the omission of women from its research studies had, for the most part, not been seen, or if seen, had not been considered consequential. It was an omission "so obvious that no one noticed," to borrow a phrase from Arundhati Roy's novel, *The God of Small Things*. That it turned out to be no small thing was the discovery of subsequent research that began with women but quickly extended to girls, to young boys, and to a reconsideration of what had been taken as true about men.[88] Women, enjoined by patriarchy to be selfless, to be responsive to others but to silence themselves, were holding up, it turned out, half of the sky. The long-standing and vaunted divisions between mind and body, reason and emotion, self and relationships, culture and nature, when viewed through the lens of gender turned out to be deeply gendered, reflecting the binaries and hierarchies of a patriarchal culture. Mind, reason, self, and culture were considered masculine and were elevated above body, emotion, relationships, and nature, seen as feminine and like women at once idealized and devalued. These splits revealed a chasm in human nature, a systematic distortion or deformation of both men's and women's natures. The consequence was an argument over which half was better – the masculine or the feminine part – but more deeply, a recognition that the problem lay in the paradigm itself.

In the classical manner of scientific advances, the discrepant data – the evidence that did not fit the reigning patriarchal construction – proved most informative. Thus women's voices were privileged in informing psychologists about aspects of the human condition that by being tagged feminine and associated with women had been at once ignored and devalued. A paradigm shift followed from this research, joining what had been cast asunder. Whereas in the old paradigm women were seen as emotional not rational, as having relationships but no self, and men, conversely, were considered rational insofar as they were unemotional, autonomous in their sense of self, the new paradigm undid the splits. But the old patriarchal values crept back in: "feminine" qualities were taken as modifiers of "masculine" strengths – hence, "emotional intelligence," "relational self," and most recently, "the feeling brain." And perhaps, more significantly, the history was rewritten, erasing the origins of these insights in the different voices of women: different because they were resisting these splits in asserting the relational nature of all human experience. The insight that without voice there is no relationship and without relationship voice recedes into silence became the key to unlocking a paradigm that was falsely gendered, false in its representation of human nature and also human development. As the paradigm shift released voices in both women and men that previously could not be heard or understood, the early insights of Freud were retrieved along with those of Ferenczi and Suttie in a reframing of psychology that came increasingly to focus on the phenomenon of dissociation and the study of trauma. Studies of women, of babies and mothers, and new studies of men led to a remapping of development as starting not from separation but from relationship.[89] And in this light, the requisites for love and the consequences of traumatic loss became clear. All of this work laid the foundation for the psychology we explore in this book.

But it was studies of girls that illuminated more radically a critical intersection in development where psychology comes into tension with the requisites of patriarchy, its gender norms and roles and values. The research highlighted what previously had been taken as part of the natural course of development and showed it to be a process of initiation, the induction of the psyche into patriarchy. The finding that most arrested attention, and one that consequently was often buried, was that girls in entering adolescence showed signs of a resistance, not to growing up but to losing their minds, as one thirteen-year-old put it.[90] The crisis was one of relationship, and the resistance was to the split between voice and relationship. Paradoxically, girls were discovering that their honest voices were jeopardizing their relationships, not only their personal relationships but also their relationship with the culture they were entering as adolescents: secondary school, sexual relationships, economic and social opportunities. The initiation into patriarchy required a sacrifice of relationship, a sacrifice of love.[91]

The trajectory of this resistance was informative, along with the various meanings of the word itself: resistance in the sense of resistance to disease; resistance as political resistance – speaking truth to power; and resistance in its psychoanalytic connotation as a reluctance to discover one's thoughts and feelings, to know what one knows. Longitudinal studies following girls from childhood to adolescence charted a trajectory whereby a healthy resistance to losing voice and thereby losing relationship turned into a political resistance, a protest against the structures of patriarchy, including the equation of selflessness with feminine goodness. This political resistance when it could find no channel for expression turned into dissociation or various forms of indirect speech and self-silencing. Hence the depression, the eating disorders, and the other manifestations of psychological distress that seemed visited on girls at adolescence. When Stella in *A Streetcar Named Desire* tells Eunice that she could not believe her sister and go on living with her husband, she captured the dilemma of women in patriarchy. It was necessary not to believe or to know what was happening in order to join a culture that mandated repression, where, as in Tennessee Williams's play, the streetcar named desire led to the insane asylum.

It is hard now to capture that first elation in discovering that we have within ourselves, within our very nature, the capacities for voice and relationship that are the foundation for love and for democratic societies. In the course of the initiation into patriarchy, girls would come to label an honest voice stupid (or bad or wrong or crazy), and boys would come to see their relational desires and intelligence as babyish, as associated with women and thereby unmanly. And yet, the striking finding of the research with adolescent girls and with four- and five-year-old boys was the evidence of a resistance that was associated with psychological health, a resistance that made trouble in the sense of challenging the necessity or the value of losses that had been taken as in the very nature of things or seen as sacrifices to be made in the interest of growing up and finding one's place in society.[92]

In the 1990s, these insights from studies in developmental psychology were joined by discoveries in neurobiology, heralded by the publication of Antonio Damasio's widely acclaimed book *Descartes' Error: Emotion, Reason, and the Human Brain* (1994). As developmental research had revealed the splits between self and relationships to signal a traumatic disruption of human connection, so neurological studies revealed the split between reason and emotion to signal trauma or injury to the brain. We had, we learned, been wedded to a false story about ourselves, through a process illuminated in Damasio's second book: *The Feeling of What Happens: Body and Emotion in the Making of Consciousness* (1999). Exploring the neurological foundations of consciousness, Damasio distinguished core consciousness or a core sense of self from what he described as the "autobiographical self," the self that is wedded to a story about itself. We are wired neurologically to register our experience from moment to moment in our bodies and in our emotions, like a film running continually inside us, and our awareness of watching this film extends this core consciousness or core sense of self through time and history, leading to memory and to identity. Thus in our bodies and our emotions we register the music, the feeling of what happens.

It can be seen as a sign of the times, the persistence of suspicions regarding the subject of gender or perhaps an incipient recognition of what we come to see when looking through a gender lens, that researchers as brilliant as Damasio and other neuroscientists working at the forefront of their field have been strikingly silent about gender or have scanned their findings for evidence of differences that serves for the most part to reinforce old stereotypes or lend them a seemingly naturalistic grounding. But some of the most illuminating current research, notably studies of trauma, has called into question the sharp division between nature and culture by demonstrating their interactions. These findings take us back to the *Studies on Hysteria;* as psychic pain could convert into physical pain, so trauma can alter neurophysiology.

By bringing the lens of gender to Damasio's distinction between a core self, grounded in the body and emotions, and an autobiographical self, wedded to a story about itself, it becomes possible to understand in new ways the process of an initiation that weds us to a false story about ourselves. Here again the research on girls is instructive, underscoring Apuleius's insight that women can play a crucial role in resisting the Love Laws of patriarchy by challenging the objectification of women, the idealization and denigration, and above all, the prohibitions on seeing and speaking that keep women from trusting or saying what they know through experience about men and love.

A gender lens then hones the perception that this ability in women reflects their different position with respect to initiation into the demands of patriarchy, typically imposed earlier on boys. Because the initiation into its codes and scripts of manhood and womanhood tends to occur at adolescence for girls rather than around the ages of four and five, because it is in adolescence rather than early childhood that girls are pressed to incorporate a father's voice as the voice of moral authority and to live by the law of the father, girls have more resources to resist the trauma, the loss of voice and the dissociation. In fighting for real relationship, women are joined by men who similarly are moved to resist patriarchal constraints on love. It is in this sense that adolescence becomes a second chance for boys, when sexual desire and more intimate relationships with girls may lead them to reveal what they have repressed or hidden, their own intimate voices, their tenderness, their desire for love. And thus to challenge patriarchal constructions of manhood.

As Elisabeth Young-Bruehl observes in a recent essay, Suttie indicated how Freud's bias "against recognizing the mother-infant 'love reciprocity'... put [him] in harmony with the sexist 'law of the father' bias of patriarchal culture generally," resulting in what Suttie described as "the 'specially inexorable repression,' the grudge against mothers and a mind-blindness for love, equal and opposite to the mind-blindness and repugnance that many of his opponents had for sex." Yet because relationality has the deep place in human psychology that it does, resistance has the appeal and hold on it that it does. Young-Bruehl "identifies a taboo – the antifeminist taboo on tenderness – in the heart of psychoanalysis and sees psychoanalysis's history as a struggle over that taboo."[93]

The tenacity of this struggle, the forces marshaled on both sides within psychoanalysis and more generally within the human sciences, along with the incoherence of much of the argument suggest once again that what is at stake are not competing positions within a single framework but a shift in the paradigm, a change in the framework. With this shift, what previously was seen as a resistance to separation or maturation appears instead as a resistance to loss or trauma. The importance of the new research in developmental psychology and neurobiology thus lies in the challenges it poses to the underlying assumptions of the psychology on which patriarchy rests and relies. More specifically, what was taken as human nature or the natural or ideal course of development can now be seen as a distortion of both our nature and our development, a distortion that bears some of the hallmarks of injury or trauma.

We end with the insight that our ability to love and live with a sense of psychic wholeness hinges on our ability to resist wedding ourselves to the gender categories of patriarchy. That this capacity for resistance is grounded in our neurobiology only highlights the importance of a developmental psychology that provides us with an accurate map with which to chart our course. Once we see where we have come from, we also can recognize more clearly the alternative routes we might follow – one marked by Oedipus and leading to the birth of tragedy, one by the resistance of Psyche and Cupid leading to love and the birth of pleasure. It is thus that we join Damasio in the optimism of his most recent book, *Looking for Spinoza: Joy, Sorrow and The Feeling Brain* (2003). Advances in the human sciences have brought us to the point where we can alleviate some of the causes of human suffering, and this guarded optimism suggests that we have within ourselves the capacity to pursue not only life and liberty but also happiness.

Patriarchy's error lies in wedding us, men and women alike, to a false story about human nature and then characterizing our resistance to this story as a sign of pathology or sin. The long-standing divisions of mind from body, thought from emotion, and self from relationships enforce a kind of moral slavery in that they erode a resistance grounded in the core self and cause us to lose touch with our experience. Damasio's research demonstrated how the severing of thought from emotion leaves the capacity for deductive reasoning intact (the ability to deduce thought from thought) but impairs our capacity to navigate the human social world, which depends on an integration of thought and emotion. The associative methods of psychoanalysis were able to break through dissociations that were psychologically induced and/or culturally enforced, leading to a release of voice and a recovery of relational capacities, and imbuing psychoanalysis with a liberatory potential. But it is by looking through a gender lens that we are able to see the problem whole: not as a problem of women or men, or of women versus men, but rather a problem with the framework we have used in thinking about these questions. The artists to whom we now turn anticipated these insights, serving as early warning signals. Their associative methods broke through dissociation and allowed them to see the framework.

# 8 Resistance: The Artists

## 1. WHY ART?

As the darkness Vergil made visible in singing of arms and the man swept across Europe during World War I, artists, and in particular novelists, took up the problem of resistance. Paul Fussell's now classic study *The Great War and Modern Memory*[1] marks the experience of the soldiers as a turning point in the literary imagination of manhood and war, expressed in the quotation from *A Farewell to Arms* that we use as an epigraph to this book: "Abstract words such as glory, honor, courage, or hallow were obscene beside the concrete names of villages, the numbers of roads, the names of rivers, the numbers of regiments and dates."[2] What to Vergil was an understory had become the story.

In the immediate aftermath of the war, five novelists zeroed in on the psychology and culture of manhood and womanhood that had sustained and justified its slaughter. In different ways, they exemplify the power of art and associative methods to undo the dissociations of patriarchy, taking us into an underworld of feeling and thought about which we often cannot speak. Since patriarchy rests on a suppression of voice and a rewriting of history, artists can perform the vital function of speaking the truth and shifting the framework. And if we are right about Vergil and Apuleius, resistance to patriarchy (the love stories of Dido and Aeneas and Cupid and Psyche) is what rivets us in their works, in part because such resistance is so deeply rooted in our psyches.

The novels we consider in this chapter – Ernest Hemingway's *A Farewell to Arms*, James Joyce's *Ulysses*, Edith Wharton's *The Age of Innocence*, Virginia Woolf's *Mrs. Dalloway* and *To the Lighthouse*, and D. H. Lawrence's *Lady Chatterley's Lover* – were written during a period when Freud had inscribed patriarchy into our psychological natures. Yet these artists explore, more truthfully than Freud, a human psychology that struggles with resistance to patriarchal demands. They play the role that artists sometimes do in democratic societies in affording a deeper understanding of the tensions between democracy and patriarchy that are at the center of our concerns in this book. Working under the radar of patriarchy in the guise of fiction, they bring a compelling and touching personal voice to the rendering of our humanity.

We have seen this in Vergil and also in Apuleius, whose *Metamorphoses* or *The Golden Ass* became a prime source for Shakespeare.[3] The resisting women of Shakespeare's comedies, Rosalind in *As You Like It*, Beatrice in *Much Ado about Nothing*, and Viola in *Twelfth Night*, echo Psyche in breaking taboos on seeing and speaking about love. In Falstaff, Shakespeare gives us a comic yet critical portrayal of a man who plays at being a soldier of honor (rendered musically in Verdi's brilliant last opera, *Falstaff*).[4] But the most searing insights into the costs of patriarchal manhood come from Shakespeare's great tragedies. In *Hamlet, Othello, Macbeth*, and *King Lear*, we witness the destruction of noble men whose characters become caught on the hooks of revenge and honor, ambition and patrimony, in part because they initially resist these demands, just as in *Romeo and Juliet* and *Antony and Cleopatra* we witness the deaths of lovers who defy the Love Laws of a patriarchal order.

Shakespeare's contemporary Cervantes was also influenced by Apuleius (as well as by Ariosto and Tasso), and through the character of Don Quixote, he studies the illusions about women on which patriarchal manhood depends (the Don's ideal being Dulcinea of Toboso – in reality, a bawdy country girl, as his servant, Sancho Panza, tells us). The only remotely real relationship in the novel is between the Don and Sancho, marked by the homoerotic attachment between the Don's horse and Sancho's mule. Yet the Don, for all his cracked idealism, also speaks in an anti-patriarchal moral voice when he appeals to Jesus as an exemplar for not turning to violence in the face of insult to honor.[5] In his art, Cervantes registers his disillusionment with heroism, having come to see his courageous career as a Spanish soldier as rooted in the illusions of the patriarchal honor code.

The point about literature, as a study of the psychology of patriarchy, can be made about opera as well. A novel influenced by Apuleius's *Metamorphoses* was one of the sources of Mozart's *The Magic Flute*, in which, contrary to Masonic practice, the heroine Pamina is admitted to the priesthood of Isis and Osiris and leads the hero, Tamino, through his last trials.[6] And Giuseppe Verdi's operas demonstrate the power of music to give voice to the losses underlying tragic manhood and the suppression of love.[7]

Yet a special urgency attends the novels of the 1920s. A generation of young men had been wantonly sacrificed in the heart of what had seemed like civilization; the paralysis of trench warfare and the horrors of mechanized mass slaughter had belied the ideals of heroic manhood. It had become imperative to explore the modes and difficulties of a resistance based on questioning the psychology and culture that had led to the war, and novelists rose to the challenge. In their different ways, the novelists who interest us here came to the recognition that Hawthorne had reached in *The Scarlet Letter*: that "the whole relation between man and woman"[8] was at the crux of the problem. Hawthorne's genius lay in the perception that the tensions between democracy and patriarchy – between the radical Protestant vision of an unmediated relationship with God and the existence of an all-male clerical hierarchy, and between the vision of a true democracy (a shining city on the hill) and the continuation of patriarchal privilege and power – extend into our most intimate lives, where they register as unhappiness. In this light, sexual love or the pursuit of happiness becomes "a lawless passion" and an act of resistance.

*The Scarlet Letter*, written in 1850, is set in the 17th century, a time when, as Hester Prynne observes, "men of the sword had overthrown nobles and kings. Men bolder than these had overthrown and rearranged – not actually, but within the sphere of theory . . . – the whole system of ancient prejudice, wherewith was linked much of ancient principle."[9] Yet in a sentence that has striking contemporary resonance, she says that the realization of a fair and just society hinges on a psychological transformation whereby, "the very nature of the opposite sex, or its long hereditary habit, which has become like nature, is to be essentially modified" and that of woman too. Hawthorne ends his novel with Hester's prophecy of a future time when "a new truth will be revealed in order to establish the whole relation between man and woman on a surer ground of mutual happiness." Since this transformation involves a change in what has come to seem like human nature, it is a task more daunting than overthrowing nobles and kings.

Hawthorne's choice of the name Prynne for his heroine was not accidental. He was familiar with the history of a Mr. William Prynne, a printer living in England in the 17th century who was found guilty of seditious libel for speaking out against Archbishop Laud. Prynne's cheeks were branded with the letters S and L for seditious libeler, but in the boat on the way to the Tower, he made up a poem changing their meaning to *stigmata laudis*, the stigma of Laud, or alternately, *sanctum laudem*, holy prayers.[10] In *The Scarlet Letter*, Hester's A similarly loses its original signification. In fact, the word *adultery* is never mentioned in the novel, and midway through, we are told that many people said the A meant "Able: so strong was Hester Prynne with a woman's strength." In the piercing illumination of Hawthorne's radical vision, love becomes the seditious act in patriarchy, and this insight takes us into the novels of the 1920s.

We begin with the authors who subvert and revise classical epics of heroic manhood – the *Aeneid* and the *Odyssey*. In the spirit of Fussell's study, we examine, from the perspective of our interest in the psychology of resistance to patriarchy, both Hemingway's novel and Joyce's modernist masterpiece. We then turn to Wharton and Woolf, who expose the captivity of women and men in patriarchal societies and families. And we end with Lawrence's *Lady Chatterley's Lover*, described by Doris Lessing in a recent introduction as "one of the most powerful anti-war novels ever written." It is also the novel where the link between sexual love and political resistance becomes most explicit.

## 2. HEMINGWAY'S *A FAREWELL TO ARMS*

As Vergil begins the *Aeneid* with *Arma virumque cano* ("Of arms and of the man I sing"), Hemingway composes the anti-*Aeneid* as "a farewell to arms." In prose so spare as to become poetry, he starts by evoking a life lived in nature:

> In the late summer of that year, we lived in a house in a village that looked across the river and the plain to the mountains. In the bed of the river there were pebbles and boulders, dry and white in the sun, and the water was clear and swiftly moving and blue in the channels.

Into this setting war intrudes, suffocating nature and disrupting its cycles: "troops went by the house and down the road and the dust they raised powdered the leaves of the trees. The trunks of the trees too were dusty and the leaves fell early that year" (p. 3).

*A Farewell to Arms* is written in the voice of an American, Frederick Henry, who well before America's entrance into World War I chose to assist the Allied cause by driving an ambulance on the Italian front. We are never told why Henry volunteered in a European conflict that many Americans thought was not and should not be of concern to them, but as Henry is very much a man's man, presumably it had to do with manhood. His warm, jocular relationships with Rinaldi, the Italian doctor, and with the priest evoke a life whose pleasures lie in drinking and casual sex, mostly with prostitutes. "I don't love," Henry tells the priest (p. 72).

Yet when this American Aeneas meets and falls in love with his Dido, the Scottish nurse Catherine Barkley, he abandons not her but the war. Moving more closely into a relationship, they form a resistance pair united against the patriarchal violence that threatens to engulf them as it does Europe. Hemingway shows us the power of a deeply sexual love to shift the psychology of a patriarchal man, increasingly skeptical of war and violence, thus leading to a farewell to arms, or in the language of the 1960s, a choice to make love not war.

As Catherine's moral intelligence begins to dissolve Henry's rather Roman conceptions of honor and courage, heroism itself takes on new meaning. In a telling exchange when Catherine becomes pregnant and Henry remarks that women always feel trapped biologically, she observes:

> "'Always' isn't a pretty word."
>      . . . ."I could cut off my tongue," I offered.
>      "Oh, darling!" she came back from wherever she had been. "You mustn't mind me." We were together again and the self-consciousness was gone. "We really are the same one and we mustn't misunderstand on purpose. . . . Because there's only us two and in the world there's all the rest. If anything comes between us we're gone and then they have us."
>      "They won't get us," I said. " Because you're too brave. Nothing ever happens to the brave." (p.139)

When Catherine reminds him "They die of course," Henry responds "But only once." When he goes on to give a fuller, rather free quotation – "The coward dies a thousand deaths, the brave but one" – but can't recall where it came from, Catherine says, "He was probably a coward," and then explains,

> "He knew a great deal about cowards, but nothing about the brave. The brave dies perhaps two thousand deaths if he's intelligent. He simply doesn't mention them."
>      "I don't know. It's hard to see inside the head of the brave."
>      "Yes. That's how they keep that way."
>      "You're an authority."
>      "You're right, darling. That was deserved."
>      "You're brave."
>      "No," she said. "But I would like to be."
>      "I'm not," I said. "I know where I stand. I've been out long enough to know. I'm like a ball-player that bats two hundred and thirty and knows he's no better." (pp. 139–140)

Catherine's clear-eyed skepticism about armored Roman courage leads Henry to a frank admission of his own mediocre score in the Roman courage stakes, but in the course of their exchange, they have come to a very different understanding of heroism, where bravery lies in admitting rather than covering fear and vulnerability and where courage becomes less godlike and more human, accessible to both women and men.

It is through the eyes of men that Hemingway shows us the impact of Catherine on Henry's manhood: "You act like a married man," Rinaldi says, "What's the matter with you?" (p. 167). Rinaldi misses his companion in nights of drunken revelry and sex, but Henry is, as he tells Rinaldi, in love. As Henry deserts the army and prepares to flee with Catherine across the lake to Switzerland, he plays billiards with the aged Count Greffi. "I have outlived my religious feeling," Greffi confesses. Henry says, "My own comes only at night." The count responds, "Then too you are in love. Do not forget that is a religious feeling" (p. 263).

Still, the novel ends bleakly. When Catherine dies in childbirth, Henry, in a final act of defiance, brushes aside the nurses who would stop him from entering her room. "But after I had got them out and shut the door and turned off the light it wasn't any good. It was like saying good-by to a statue. After a while I went out and left the hospital and walked back to the hotel in the rain." Without Catherine, his resistance, like their child, has become unviable.

## 3. JOYCE'S *ULYSSES*

In designing *Ulysses*,[11] Joyce deliberately set out to subvert the verities of Homer's *Odyssey*. With consummate skill in comic reversal, he turns Odysseus, the epic hero, into Leopold Bloom, the Irish Jew, and Odysseus's wife, the faithful Penelope, into the unfaithful Molly. The triumph of *Ulysses* lies in Joyce's ability to render Bloom heroic and Molly loving. In doing so, he illuminates a radically different construction of both heroism and love, stripped of idealism and grounded in seeing, in the "ineluctable modality of the visible." As the critical power of Joyce's novel depends on its inversion of the gender assumptions of Homer's narrative, we begin by clarifying what those assumptions are.

Homer's epic poem follows Odysseus on his way home to Ithaca where his wife Penelope and son Telemachus wait for him. Odysseus is a war hero: wily, ingenious, shrewd, and highly intelligent, the soldier and leader who crafted the Greek victory over the Trojans. On his journey home, which takes him years, he has sexual liaisons with remarkable women, notably Circe, Calypso, and the Sirens, all of whom are characterized by their independence (they are not wives or mothers or sisters of men), by their singing voices that men find irresistible, and by their frank embrace of sexuality.

Penelope, in contrast, embodies the ideal of patriarchal womanhood in being, first and foremost, the wife of Odysseus and the mother of his son. She exemplifies the virtues of selflessness and chastity in her steadfast devotion to the husband who has effectively abandoned her. She rejects the proposals of the many suitors who have forced themselves into the absent Odysseus's household, feasting, playing games, seeking his wife as a sexual partner, and threatening the life of his son. Surrounded by these aggressive, violent, insistent men, Penelope first resorts to subterfuge (postponing a decision on their marriage proposals until she finishes a certain complex weaving, which she unravels every evening until her ruse is exposed) and then to outright refusal. Her personality, grown hard from resisting over so many years, has become so adamantine that when Odysseus returns she will not recognize him, even when he has killed the suitors, appears in his proper form, and is acknowledged by Telemachus as his father. Only when he discloses the shared secrets of their marriage bed – things that only he could know – does she emerge from her patriarchal role as protector of her husband's honor and guardian of their son.

In Claudio Monteverdi's stirring opera based on *The Odyssey*, *Il Ritorno D'Ulisse in Patria*, Penelope's longing for the return of her husband is musically and vocally portrayed. What we hear is certainly the fierce love of a proud woman, but a love also shadowed by the woeful recognition that her hero husband left her to pursue a war provoked by an unworthy woman. Penelope sings:

> "Baleful beauty, shameful passion,
> Unworthy of remembrance;
> The seeds of hatred were sown
> Not by blossoms of a face,
> But by the guiles of a serpent,
> A monster is a love that bathes in blood.
> May oblivion disperse
> Such woeful memories."[12]

What Homer portrays as Penelope's heroic fidelity becomes in Monteverdi a more psychologically complex, ambivalent love that will not yield even to her husband until he sues for her love in a way that recognizes her as the intelligent, strategically shrewd, and courageous equal she clearly is.

The *Odyssey* has both patriarchal and anti-patriarchal features. Odysseus is the armored war hero who has abandoned his wife to pursue a war over male honor, followed by a long-delayed return that includes sleeping with other women; Penelope is the faithful patriarchal wife who will heroically hold to her fidelity to her husband and her role in protecting their son, whatever the costs to herself. Yet in its portrayal of the like-mindedness of husband and wife, both of whom are shown to be cunning, tricky, and stalwart, the *Odyssey* also reveals how equal and well-matched and loving a couple they are: "Penelope and Odysseus may operate in different spheres," writes Sue Blundell, "but their close affinity is brought home to the reader time and time again, not least in the similarity of their characters, for both are remarkable for their cunning and perseverance."[13]

The contrasting pair in Joyce's *Ulysses* exemplify as well such like-mindedness, but in the context of a resistance to precisely the patriarchal values that Odysseus and Penelope embody. Under the patriarchal gender code, the Irish Jew, Leopold Bloom, would be read as effeminate and his wife Molly would be labeled a whore. Joyce thus chooses as the hero of his odyssey not a man central to the history of his time but one both marginalized and patriarchally stigmatized: a cuckolded Jew living in Dublin. Odysseus's long and adventurous journey home from Troy to Ithaca becomes Bloom's day spent walking around Dublin and doing what in the world of *The Odyssey* would be counted as nothing. But then Joyce's novel disparages the slogans of war: "Let my country die for me," Stephen Dedalus says (p. 591).

The heroism Bloom exhibits as a domesticated man lies in spending much of his day doing errands for his languorously demanding wife. One of his biggest victories is getting the last kidney at the butcher shop, and even this triumph is unrelated to his efforts. It would be fairly easy for Bloom to play a pathetic figure. The potential for sorrow is all around him – he has lost his son and in a way his wife, too; he seems to get no respect from those around him; he is a Jew in the midst of anti-Semitic Ireland. The greatest misfortunes have already been visited upon him. Yet he seems unable even to conceive of a life less ordinary: His dream is to own a comfortably furnished suburban bungalow. In the end, Bloom's heroism lies, paradoxically, in his unapologetic disinterest in becoming in any conventional sense heroic.

As a result, he is, in this respect, unassailable. We see him as neither heroic nor pitiful because he doesn't see himself that way either. His losses do not wound him or make him any less who he is. He is a man assailed from all sides, inspiring neither fear nor respect from other men. With an almost systematic thoroughness, Bloom loses every single battle in the war for his masculinity. And yet he is not an unhappy man. What prevents him from being one is neither lack of feeling nor a wounded turn toward isolation but precisely the opposite – his openness to the world.

Bloom displays an open curiosity in his desire to see and know everything around him. In his eyes, everything seems worthy of note – the way a woman's hips sway when she is walking down the street, the way a particular cut of meat would taste, what a cat must think, what a woman in labor must feel. He confers importance on the subjects he pays attention to and reveals himself as a man with a deep capacity for love. Bloom loves the fact that he notices and wants to know. His attempt to feel and see what others feel and see is his odyssey. He slays no enemies on the way, but he is, in the end, completely disarming.

Just as when struck physically one's impulse is to strike back, so the infliction of psychological pain provokes hurtfulness in response. Patriarchal manhood becomes an extreme response, mandating a response to injury or insult that often takes the form of violence or violation as a means of eradicating shame and restoring honor. The ability to escape this dynamic is Bloom's triumph. His response to hurt is neither a passive retreat from the world nor an attack upon it. His pain never turns to hate; his own isolation never turns to intolerance. Bloom is unconquered because when harmed he remains unhateful. In this way, through his capacity for engagement, mindfulness, curiosity and love, he remains, heroically, unhurt.

By making Bloom the Ulysses of the novel, Joyce accords moral authority, indeed an anti-patriarchal heroism, to precisely what European anti-Semitism had stereotypically regarded as the effeminacy of Jewish men. Bloom, whom doctors call "bisexually abnormal," is "the new womanly man. His moral nature is simple and lovable." He unabashedly says of himself, "O, I so want to be a mother" (p. 494). And again in contrast to Odysseus, he is no sex tourist. He is loving, but sexually impotent, much more fatherly and caring to Stephen Dedalus than his biological father was. The one scene in the novel where Bloom becomes sexually aroused is at once erotic and touching, since his masturbatory rhapsodizing occurs over the beauty of Gerty MacDowell, the "bird-girl," whose beauty he can see and appreciate even though, as he finally realizes, she is crippled (pp. 348–70).

For her part, Gerty, sad and downcast, is attracted to Bloom, an outcast like herself. The anti-patriarchal character of their attraction is shown by the play of sexual feeling and experience in masturbation, an act that patriarchal Catholicism regards, as Thomas Aquinas put it, as taking "next place" to homicide.[14] Masturbation, arguably the most innocent of sexual acts in the sense of causing no harm, is accorded such condemnation because it threatens patriarchal control.[15] In *Ulysses*, Joyce underscores the expression of sexuality free from such control when he depicts Bloom as coming to sexual climax only in masturbation and ends his novel with Molly's sexual monologue.

Similarly, Bloom's goodness to Stephen and Molly has nothing to do with patriarchy (Stephen is not his son, and Molly is adulterous with other men) but expresses his connection to them through love. Bloom is not just outside patriarchy; he actively resists its violence, which is portrayed in the Catholic Ireland of the novel as a virulent anti-Semitism: "When in doubt persecute Bloom."[16] In counterpoint to this, Bloom's anti-patriarchal gospel is: "I resent violence or intolerance in any shape or form" (p. 643). Of Christian anti-Semitism, Bloom acidly observes: "People could put up with being bitten by a wolf but what properly riled them was a bite from a sheep. The most vulnerable point too of tender Achilles, your God was a jew" (p. 658). Bloom, the Jew, is the moral center of the novel because he exemplifies, for Joyce, the ultimate moral wisdom: "Love, says Bloom, I mean the opposite of hatred" (p. 333).

Bloom's heroism is thus of an opposite character from that of Odysseus or, for that matter, Aeneas. Joyce describes Bloom's partici- pation in a ritual of mourning in the terms Vergil ascribes to Aeneas: he "bent over piously" (p. 103). But Bloom's piety is not that of Vergil's war hero. His rituals are the homely ones of making breakfast for his wife. For a man who has experienced so much loss (the suicide of his father, the death of his son), Bloom is untouched by the violent manhood around him because he is so connected through love to his non-patriarchal wife, to whom he returns at the day's end. The unconventional character of their marriage is marked by how uncompromised their love is by Molly's adulteries, or by the fact that Molly is more successful in her profession, singing, than Bloom is in his. If anything, the patriarchal gender roles are reversed. Bloom's sexual love for his wife, as the core of his resistance to the demands of patriarchal manhood, may well reflect the importance of Nora in Joyce's own life. Joyce – a patriarchally compromised and dissociated young man very much under the influence of Augustinian Catholicism[17] – came through the experience of sexual love with Nora to what Apuleius may have discovered in his relationship with Pudentilla: a new emotional wholeness rooted in relationship.[18]

If Bloom is Joyce's anti-patriarchal Ulysses, Molly is his anti- patriarchal Penelope. She is not sexually faithful to Bloom, and more radically perhaps, she actively pursues sexual desire and pleasure. In her famous monologue that ends the novel, she recalls Bloom's turning from her sexually after the death of their son, "him so cold never embracing me" when "of course a woman wants to be embraced 20 times a day almost to make her look young no matter by who so long as to be in love or loved by somebody if the fellow you want isnt there sometimes by the Lord God" (p. 777). She wonders, as her husband does, "itd be much better for the world to be governed by the women in it you wouldnt see women going and killing one another and slaughtering when do you ever see women rolling around drunk like they do" (p. 778). And she ends her reverie in sexual ecstasy, spurred by the memory of the day she got Bloom

> "to propose to me yes first I gave him the bit of seedcake out of my mouth and it was leapyear like now yes 16 years ago my God after that long kiss I near lost my breath yes he said I was a flower of the mountain yes so we are flowers all a womans body yes that was one true thing he said in his life and the sun shines for you today yes that was why I liked him because I saw he understood or felt what a woman is and I knew I could always get round him and I gave him all the pleasure I could leading him on till he asked me to say yes and I wouldnt answer first only looked out over the sea and the sky . . . and I thought well as well him as another and then I asked him with my eyes to ask again yes and then he asked me would I yes to say yes my mountain flower and first I put my arms around him yes and drew him down to me so he could feel my breasts all perfume yes and his heart was going like mad and yes I said yes I will Yes." (pp. 782–3)

Bloom has become the loving man he is, the moral authority he is in the novel, in relationship to Molly's powerfully voiced sexual love. Molly has sex with men much more like Ulysses than Bloom, but it is Bloom with whom she falls in love and stays in love. Is Joyce – the critic of violent patriarchy – telling us that the man whom women under patriarchy think they want (Ulysses) is not the man they really desire (Bloom)? The novel, which has been written mainly from the point of view and voice of Bloom, turns abruptly at its end to Molly's voice, highlighting the relationship between Bloom and Molly as the core of what sustains each of them.

When Tolstoy, in writing *Anna Karenina*, came to enter and take seriously a woman's sexual interests and voice, he could only carry his investigation so far before his rigidly patriarchal conceptions shut down his sympathies, leading to Anna's suicide and perhaps to his own subsequent mental breakdown and crisis.[19] Joyce, who came so fundamentally to question patriarchal conceptions of sexuality and love, ends his novel not with suicide but with a celebration of a woman's sexual love. The implicit relational psychology of Joyce's *Ulysses* resonates with Apuleius's embrace of the Isis religion and, more specifically, with its key insight: that patriarchally fragmented men can be restored to human wholeness through the love of a woman. The novel thus ends on the most anti-patriarchal of themes, the affirmation of women's sexual voice in love, which we hear in its fully human, unidealized form.

We are reminded that this most powerful of resistance novels, centering itself in Bloom's relationship to Molly's sexual voice and love, elicited the repressive forces of American censorship in the federal obscenity ban that was only removed by the ruling of Judge John M. Woolsey in 1933.[20] Comparable obscenity prosecutions were directed earlier at Walt Whitman's *Leaves of Grass*, not for its frankly homoerotic poetry but for its depictions of the sexual feeling and desire of women for men.[21] Nothing seems more to arouse American repressive ire than the free sexuality and sexual voice of women. We will argue in Chapter 9 that current efforts at such repression bespeak patriarchy's resurgent political power.

## 4. WHARTON'S *THE AGE OF INNOCENCE*

The difficulty of men's resistance to patriarchy is a subject that absorbed Edith Wharton, notably in *Summer* (1917)[22] and *The Age of Innocence* (1920),[23] both written in the shadow of the war. Wharton was living in Paris and traveled repeatedly to the front, receiving the Croix de Guerre for her efforts on behalf of refugees and the wounded. In both novels, men's resistance takes the form of a deeply erotic, loving relationship with a woman who is an outsider to patriarchy: in *Summer*, the mountain-girl Charity Royall, who resists "the deadening process of becoming a lady"; in *The Age of Innocence*, the Countess Ellen Olenska, who returns to the New York of her childhood after fleeing an abusive marriage. In both novels, socially prominent men are moved by love to break the Love Laws of patriarchy. That in the end neither does so picks up on an observation that Ellen makes to Newland Archer when he says that he wants to go with her into a world where patriarchal categories do not exist, "where we shall be simply two human beings who love each other, who are the whole of life to each other; and nothing else on earth will matter." To which she responds, "Oh, my dear – where is that country? Have you ever been there?" (p. 203).

The ubiquity of patriarchy makes it easy to naturalize its categories, to see in them a reflection of human nature, or divine intention, or evolutionary advantage. But all of the artists we consider show us the mistake. Like Hawthorne, Wharton is unrelenting in comparing the structures of patriarchy to a prison that holds humanity captive, above all intelligent and sensitive men. In *Summer*, Charity (her name recalling Charite, the young woman in Apuleius's *Metamorphoses* to whom the Cupid and Psyche story is told) calls the patriarchal household of Lawyer Royall in which she is raised a "prison-house." But it is in *The Age of Innocence* that we see most clearly what is held captive. With the stunning image of fish who go blind from living in the depths of the ocean, Wharton conveys the loss of natural capacities among those immersed in New York's Gilded Age society.

The innocence of this prewar society implicitly contrasts with the experience of the war that will follow, a connection to which her characters are blind. Yet their innocence, as Wharton shows us, is a willed innocence, a hypocrisy sustained and justified by pieties about love and marriage and family, as pieties about heroism and manhood will sustain and justify the war. In case one misses the analogy, Wharton makes it explicit in a scene where the tribe of the wealthy and successful gathers to celebrate its victory in defending its Love Laws:

> It was the old New York way of taking life 'without effusion of blood': the way of people who dreaded scandal more than disease, who placed decency above courage, and who considered that nothing was more ill-bred than 'scenes,' except the behaviour of those who gave rise to them.
>     As those thoughts succeeded each other in his mind, Archer felt like a prisoner in the centre of an armed camp. (p. 235)

In fact, he is at a dinner party.

Newland Archer (the name suggests Cupid) was prepared to marry the patriarchally sanctioned May Welland when he meets and falls in love with May's cousin, Ellen Olenska. The novel surgically explores the patriarchal customs of New York society, customs that are, as Wharton shows, as rigid and controlling as the patriarchy of ancient Rome. These customs hold men like Newland particularly in their thrall.

Although Newland believes in principle that women should be as sexually free to love as men, he persuades Ellen, while acting as her lawyer, not to seek her freedom by divorcing her husband because of the scandal it would bring on her family. Archer and Olenska, however, fall in love, and when his fiancée May, suspecting as much, offers him his freedom, Olenska, having taken on Archer's values and decided not to divorce her husband, tells him to marry May, which he does.

A paralysis sets in as the net closes around Newland. Unable to hide his love for Ellen from her, or from himself, he seeks to break out of his entrapment. When a family illness summons her back from Washington, he arranges to pick her up at the train station and insists that they go away together. "Is it your idea, then, that I should live with you as your mistress – since I can't be your wife?" she asks. Newland is startled by the "crudeness of the question":

> [T]he word was one that women of his class fought shy of, even when their talk flitted closest about the topic. He noticed that Madame Olenska pronounced it as if it had a recognized place in her vocabulary, and he wondered if it had been used familiarly in her presence in the

horrible life she had fled from. Her question pulled him up with a jerk, and he floundered. (p. 203)

He wanted Ellen, but not a mistress; he wanted love but without scandal. As Wharton compares the grid of New York streets to a prison, she shows us the internalization of its confinement. The question that haunts the novel is whether there is a way out of this framework, soon to be shattered by the war.

Wharton, the artist, wants us to see and to feel the pull of honor and loyalty that holds the grid in place. At the same time, she suggests through her imagery that these are among the relics of an ancient patriarchy. When Newland makes one last, desperate attempt to persuade Ellen to go away with him, they meet at the Metropolitan Museum. Sitting in a remote room, "where the Cesnola antiquities mouldered in unvisited loneliness," they stare at the "recovered fragments of Ilium . . . small broken objects – hardly recognizable." Newland listens in chilled horror as Ellen espouses the values that had confined him. She cannot do something that would harm the people who had helped her, the family for whom she had relinquished her quest for love and freedom. Suddenly she asks, "Shall I – once come to you; and then go home?" meaning go home to her husband. Newland wavers, overcome by an "inarticulate despair . . . 'If I were to let her come,' he said to himself, 'I should have to let her go again.' And that was not to be imagined." Yet when she turned to leave, "he followed and caught her by the wrist. 'Well, then: come to me once,' he said," and she agrees (p. 219).

But again, the lovers are thwarted – now by May, who, suspecting that she may be pregnant, tells Ellen that she is. In response, Ellen resolves to leave New York and return to her husband. The love between Newland and Ellen remains unconsummated, but at the dinner party celebrating Ellen's departure, Newland's eyes are finally opened:

[I]t came over him, in a vast flash made up of many broken gleams, that to all of them he and Madame Olenska were lovers, lovers in the extreme sense peculiar to 'foreign' vocabularies. He guesses himself to have been, for months, the centre of countless silently observing eyes and patiently listening ears, he understood that, by means as yet unknown to him, the separation between himself and the partner of his guilt had been achieved, and that now the whole tribe had rallied about his wife on the tacit assumption that nobody knew anything, or had ever imagined anything, and that the occasion of the entertainment was simply May Archer's natural desire to take an affectionate leave of her friend and cousin. (p. 235)

The ideals of marriage and family, loyalty and honor, have been sustained by a tacit agreement not to see or to speak about love, except in the terms of a foreign vocabulary whose usefulness, like that of the Cesnola antiquities, can no longer be discerned. Feeling himself a prisoner in an armed camp, Newland registers in that moment the violence that passes for gentility: a taking of life "without effusion of blood," a killing that leaves no trace.

In her book-length essay *Three Guineas*, written on the eve of World War II, Virginia Woolf makes explicit the connection that Wharton's novel implies: "[T]he public and private worlds are inseparably connected . . . [T]he tyrannies and servilities of the one are the tyrannies and servilities of the other."[24] The tribe that sacrifices love for honor is the patriarchy that will lead the world into war.

*The Age of Innocence* ends with Archer, now old and his wife long dead, visiting Paris with his son. The son reveals that May, at the time of her death, had told him of Archer's sacrifice of Ellen. In appreciation of this sacrifice and reflecting the changing mores of the time, Newland's son has now arranged for his father and Ellen to meet. In fact, she had not returned to her husband but was living alone in a Paris apartment. Newland and Ellen can now be together without inflicting harm. Yet Newland chooses not to see her. His refusal is startling until we realize that he is a man grown accustomed to loss, more comfortable with the illusion than the reality of love. And yet, he is not undiscerning: "[H]e saw into what a deep rut he had sunk. The worst of doing one's duty was that it apparently unfitted one for doing anything else" (p. 246).

Sending his son up to Ellen's apartment alone, Archer sits on a bench. He hesitates a moment before coming to the realization that Ellen and the life in her apartment are "more real to me here than if I went up" (p. 254). He waits until the blinds on her windows have been lowered and then gets up and leaves.

Archer's son is, of course, quite wrong. Archer never decided to separate from Ellen, but was stage-managed into accepting such a separation as the patriarchally required order of things. A man so caught up in the patriarchy of New York's Gilded Age had not been able to resist when he was free to do so, and the woman he loved had herself been so compromised by his lack of resistance that she accepted what he had not questioned when it could have been questioned, potentially to everyone's advantage. Better a life without love than a love without honor – or so a patriarchal man like Archer may have thought. The innocence of the age lay in its ignorance of the costs that honor would exact on the world. As Othello says, "[w]hy should honour outline honesty? Let it go all."

## 5. VIRGINIA WOOLF'S *MRS. DALLOWAY, TO THE LIGHTHOUSE,* AND *THREE GUINEAS*

Virginia Woolf's *Mrs. Dalloway*[25] and *To the Lighthouse*[26] are among the most astonishing and revelatory artistic explorations of the power of patriarchy in the lives of women and men. Like *A Farewell to Arms* and *Lady Chatterley's Lover*, they explicitly evoke the violence and trauma of World War I. Woolf's great plea for resistance to patriarchal violence, *Three Guineas*, written in the 1930s, directly explores what her novels exposed: the patriarchal roots of the fascist violence that would shortly erupt in the cataclysm of World War II. At this point, artistic resistance becomes political resistance, setting the stage for the final chapters of our study. But first, her novels and *Lady Chatterley's Lover*.

What Woolf shows us so astutely in *Mrs. Dalloway* is the trauma of patriarchy, the losses inflicted on women and men. The novel pivots around a woman and a man who never meet – Mrs. Dalloway and Septimus Warren Smith – yet whose lives have been truncated by the patriarchal roles they have played. Mrs. Dalloway, the name capturing her evisceration as patriarchal wife and mother, has in effect lost her voice and her self. It is only in the very last word of the novel that we hear her name, as she finally appears as herself: "There she was: Clarissa." By this point, she has learned of the suicide of Septimus, the World War I soldier, traumatized by the loss of Evans, the comrade he loved.

The loss of love, or rather the relinquishment of love, has similarly traumatized Clarissa. As a young woman, she had been in love with her friend Sally Seton and also with Peter Walsh, a lively threesome joined in their resistance to patriarchy. In choosing to forgo these loves to marry the emotionally constricted Dalloway, she opts to play her required role as the wife of a successful politician, spending her day preparing to give the dinner party that ends the novel. But Mrs. Dalloway is no Leopold Bloom. She is deeply lonely and unhappy, cut off emotionally from her daughter as well as from her husband and from herself. Woolf shows us the underlying psychology of loss that had turned the vibrant Clarissa into Mrs. Dalloway. Both Peter and Sally show up at the party, but in their own ways they too have succumbed. As in *The Age of Innocence*, there is seemingly no way of avoiding the power of patriarchy. But Woolf also alludes to the loss of a story about love that had shown a way out.

In the middle of the day that ends with Septimus's suicide and Clarissa's recognition of her own despair, Woolf suddenly introduces an Apuleian reference. Crossing a busy street in London, Peter Walsh and also Septimus and his wife, Rezia, hear an old woman singing in a public garden, "the voice of no age or sex, the voice of an ancient spring spouting from the earth . . . singing of love – love which has lasted a million years . . . love which prevails, and millions of years ago, her lover" (p. 87). The reference suggests the old woman in the *Metamorphoses* who tells the despairing Charite the story of Cupid and Psyche. But although the subject – love – is unmistakable, the story itself has become incomprehensible, the path of resistance reduced to fragmented syllables.

Long before Judith Herman and other students of trauma had seen the analogies and drawn the connections between the lives of shell-shocked soldiers and battered women,[27] Woolf forged the link in *Mrs. Dalloway*. When the news of Septimus's suicide slices into Mrs. Dalloway's party, she feels for the first time the depth and force of her own despair. She thinks of committing suicide herself, but in the end she resists, emerging finally from the shell of her marriage to appear, at least to herself, as Clarissa. In showing us the different but analogous role that traumatic loss plays in the psychology of the women and men who take up their patriarchal destiny as wives and soldiers, Woolf also hints at the different capacities of men and women to resist and survive such trauma.

*To the Lighthouse*, Woolf's most autobiographical novel, portrays the patriarchal marriage of her remarkable parents, but also, in the character of Lily Briscoe, the role of the artist as resistor – the one who paints the portrait. At the center of Woolf's canvas we see Mrs. Ramsey, a woman so completely identified with her patriarchal role that she has no name, so selfless that she has no self, yet so compulsive in her enactment of the patriarchal narrative that "she was driven on, too quickly she knew, almost as if it were an escape for her too, to say that people must marry; people must have children" (p. 60). The portrait of Mr. Ramsey, off to one side, shows a man physically present but emotionally distracted in the midst of a family life centered on facilitating and supporting his compulsive work on his encyclopedia:

> It was a splendid mind. For if thought is like the keyboard of a piano, divided into so many notes, or like the alphabet is ranged in twenty-six letters all in order, then his splendid mind had no sort of difficulty in running over those letters one by one, firmly and accurately, until it had reached, say, the letter Q. He reached Q. Very few people in the whole of England ever reach Q. (p. 33)

Yet Mr. Ramsey is obsessed with getting to the letter R. The patriarchal burdens weighing on him are such that despite his accomplishment, he is left with a gnawing sense that "he had not done the thing he might have done" (p. 45).

If *Mrs. Dalloway* reveals the shattering effects of trauma on the psyches of women and men under patriarchy, *To the Lighthouse* captures its blighting effects on creativity. Patriarchal violence, the implicit subject of both novels, moves to center stage in Woolf's late essay, *Three Guineas*. Her beloved nephew, Julian Bell, had been killed in the Spanish Civil War in 1937, the year Neville Chamberlain became prime minister of Great Britain. What Woolf came to see, in the rise of an aggressively violent fascism in Spain, Germany, and Italy – a fascism that had killed her nephew – was something Winston Churchill had also seen, leading him to call for resistance before it was too late: namely, that the aggressive violence of fascism was rooted in humiliated manhood. Woolf brilliantly carries Churchill's insight one step analytically further to expose the patriarchal roots of fascist violence and to explore the possibilities for resistance on the part of the daughters of educated (read patriarchal) men.

What makes *Three Guineas* so astonishing is not only Woolf's pathbreaking analysis of the patriarchal origins of fascist violence but also her larger call for a resistance in which women join with men. At issue, she argued, was what Josephine Butler called "the great principles of Justice and Equality and Liberty." Addressing men, Woolf comments:

> The words are the same are yours; the claim is the same as yours. The daughters of educated men who were called, to their resentment, "feminists" were in fact the advance guard of your own movement. They were fighting the same enemy that you are fighting and for the same reasons. They were fighting the tyranny of the patriarchal state as you are fighting the tyranny of the Fascist state. (p. 121).

The same moral and political values justify resistance to both patriarchy and fascism: namely, the values of democracy, "the democratic ideals of equal opportunity for all" (p. 119). Woolf clearly sees and states as well the anti-democratic injustice and violence of what we have called moral slavery, the common patriarchal roots of anti-Semitism, racism, and sexism.[28]

Woolf frames her argument, however, by focusing on "the daughters of educated men" (p. 16), whom she sees as having an independence men do not have, caught up as they are in the great patriarchal processions of British professional and public life (pp. 23–8). This independence reflects the four teachers of women who have historically resisted the patriarchal demands imposed on them: poverty, chastity, derision, and freedom from unreal loyalties. Women's resistance to patriarchy has, Woolf suggests, certain advantages in part because the disadvantages heaped on their resistance – their four teachers – render them more impervious to its seductions and threats. Even the injustice done to women in the area of sexuality ("how great a part chastity, bodily chastity, has played in the unpaid education of our sex") can be reinterpreted to the advantage of women's resistance: "It should not be difficult to transmute the old ideal of bodily chastity into the new ideal of mental chastity – to hold that if it was wrong to sell the body for money it is much more wrong to sell the mind for money, since the mind, people say, is nobler than the body" (p. 99). For this reason, she calls upon women to pledge "not to commit adultery of the brain because it is a much more serious offence than the other" (p. 112).

Woolf anchors her call for women's resistance in a recognition of difference: It is because women are "[d]ifferent ... as facts have proved, both in sex and in education," that "our help can come, if help we can, to protect liberty, to prevent war" (p. 123). Their distinctive strengths can flourish as grounds for resistance if women who gain access through education and the professions form an "Outsiders' Society," finding their own voices as moral agents and speaking in a different voice, a voice nourished by their own "unpaid-for education" – the relational experience and emotional intelligence that would lead women to question and to resist patriarchal demands on men as well as on themselves:

> [T]he Society of Outsiders has the same ends as your society – free-dom, equality, peace; but it seeks to achieve them by the means that a different sex, a different tradition, a different education, and the dif-ferent values which result from those differences have placed within our reach. (p. 134)

Woolf thus concludes by suggesting that women can best help men prevent war "not by repeating your words and following your methods but by finding new words and creating new methods" (p. 170). In doing so, women will refuse the function Woolf had earlier observed them playing in patriarchy, a function to which men had become addicted:

> Women have served all these centuries as looking-glasses possessing the magic and delicious power of reflecting the figure of men at twice its natural size. Without that power probably the earth would still be swamp and jungle. The glories of all our wars would be unknown.[29]

In *Three Guineas*, Woolf seeks to break the hypnotic spell of a patriar-chally rooted male narcissism – the wounded honor or shame that fueled the mass appeal of Hitler and Mussolini.[30] What makes her argument pathbreaking is the way she connects the forms of public and private violence she had examined so sensitively in *Mrs. Dalloway* and *To the Lighthouse* to the aggressive fascism Britain faced in the 1930s, and the importance she accords to this linking of public and private worlds and tyrannies. To examine these connections critically, she urges that "it is time for us to raise the veil of St. Paul and to attempt, face to face, a rough and clumsy analysis" of how the Christian tradition has treated women (p. 153). Finally, in recognizing how far women have come in resistance to patriarchy, she observes how aggressive the response has been to such resistance.

Many of our central points in this book were first stated or at least suggested by Woolf. Once again, we are aware how deeply artists can see into the problematics of patriarchy, even when the religion, politics, and psychology around them are in thrall to its conceptions and institutions. In Woolf's terms, women are, or can be, "a society of outsiders," with perhaps unique insights as to how to stand at once within and apart. In our concluding chapters, we will consider how our general view supports and explains two of her most important suggestions, namely, the critical moral and psychological role of women joining men in resistance to patriarchy and the roots of the reactionary countermoves to such resistance and the advances to which it leads. But now, the most radical of our six novels and also the most explicitly sexual: the novel that Lawrence had originally called *Tenderness* before settling on its more provocative title.

## 6. LAWRENCE'S *LADY CHATTERLEY'S LOVER*

In her introduction to *Lady Chatterley's Lover*, Doris Lessing admits to a sharp change in both her view and her appreciation of the novel. When she first read it "as a young woman," she responded "to Mellors who loved Constance Chatterley for being womanly" and to Mellors as "the perfect, the whole lover," a view some "very vocal feminists" during the 1960s feminist revolution admitted to sharing.[31] There were, however, other feminists, notably Kate Millet,[32] who vigorously criticized the view both of women and of sexuality that the novel expressed, zeroing in on the "quasi-religious . . . salvation of one modern woman" through the force of the male phallus in heterosexual sex. To Millet, *Lady Chatterley's Lover* thus provided seemingly "irrefutable evidence that male supremacy is founded upon the most real and incontrovertible grounds."[33]

Lessing admits that as a young woman, she was, like Millet, absorbed by the treatment of sexuality. In reading the novel now and recognizing it as "one of the most powerful anti-war novels ever written," she asks: "How was it I had not seen that, when I first read it? (xxi)"

The aptness of *Tenderness* as a potential title is apparent as the word *tender* recurs insistently to describe both Mellors and the love between him and Lady Chatterley. It is this tenderness that awakens them both to life. Lawrence has set his novel in the aftermath of the First World War, and the wounds it has inflicted on English manhood resemble the wounds that have been inflicted on the English landscape. What once was beautiful has been rendered desolate. Lord Chatterley is literally impotent as the result of injuries sustained in the war. But like the other novelists we consider here, Lawrence offers a way of understanding both what made such violence possible and the role of sexual love in making possible forms of resistance. In both respects, he is more radical than Hemingway, yet in their focus on the natural world, both suggest that something has gone radically amiss in human nature. For Lawrence, the psychology that resists the violence of patriarchal manhood is also a psychology that resists social injustice. And his novel, which does not end in death, reflects a guarded optimism very much in the spirit of Apuleius's *Metamorphoses* in tying pleasure in sexual love to religious celebration.

There is, perhaps, no more devastating portrayal of the wounded psyche of patriarchal manhood than in Lawrence's Lord Clifford Chatterley. As we see him through the eyes of his wife, we follow her dawning realization that this English lord, this privileged man, was numbed by fear and paralyzed by shock:

> But now, as the years went by, slowly, slowly Connie felt the bruise of fear and horror coming up and spreading in him. For a time it had been so deep as to be numb, as it were, non-existent. Now slowly it began to assert itself, in a spread of fear, almost paralysis. Mentally, he still was alert. But the paralysis, the bruise of the too-great shock was gradually spreading in his affective self.
>     And as it spread in him, Connie felt it spread in her. An inward dread, an emptiness, an indifference to everything gradually spread in her soul. (p. 49)

The psychic wounds of the war were as devastating as its physical destruction of his potency: "it was the bruise of the war, that had been in abeyance, slowly rising to the surface and creating the great ache of unrest, the stupor of discontent. The bruise was deep, deep, deep – the bruise of the false and inhuman war" (p. 50).

Constance first observes the effects of such trauma in her husband's loss of the capacity for feeling, the grounds of relational life: "[S]ome of his feelings were gone. There was a blank of insentience" (p. 6). She soon becomes a close student of the comparable effects on other men, including the Irish playwright Michaelis, with whom she has a brief affair.

Michaelis was stuck in a rigidly defined social role: "Aeons of acquiescence in a race destiny, instead of our individual resistance" (p. 23). She silently listens as several male friends of her husband discuss their cold, unfeeling conception of sexual relationships with women – "immensely important speculations of these highly-mental gentlemen" (p. 35). What Constance registers is the dissociation from personal voice and memory. The insentience that makes tenderness or loving relationship impossible leads her husband to a growing absorption in the technical improvement of his coal business and also to his defense of the British class system and his elevated place in it. The irony here is that this patriarchal man has been rendered literally unable to become a father.

The capacity of Constance, as a woman, to recognize the sources and consequences of the massive dissociation of the men around her is counterpointed by another woman in the novel, Mrs. Bolton, a nurse who has come professionally to care for Lord Chatterley. Mrs. Bolton had been passionately in love with her coal-miner husband, who had been killed in an accident, a loss from which, she confesses to Constance, she has never recovered. What Mrs. Bolton senses is what Constance is coming to understand: that the very existence of such a loving sexual relationship between a man and woman constitutes a threat to the social system:

> "You feel folks *wanted* him killed. You feel the pit fair *wanted* to kill him ... But they all *want* to separate a woman and a man, if they're together – "
> "If they're physically together," said Connie." (pp. 163–4)

Constance has come to such an understanding through the experience of sexual love with Mellors, the gamekeeper on the estate of Lord Chatterley. Mellors, like Clifford Chatterley, had been a soldier. He served, however, not in World War I but in India and under an officer whom, he admits to Constance, he loved. He had been unhappily married to a woman who left him and with whom he had a child, a son who lives with his mother. Mellors is now quite alone, and his tender sexual responsiveness to Constance arises when this beautiful, intelligent woman breaks into heart-rending tears on watching young chicks with their mothers. The several scenes of sexual love are sensually frank and intimately responsive, tender and playful in a way Constance had not experienced before. This experience of tenderness and pleasure makes psychologically possible a new understanding of human relationship, and on this basis, she comes to see the patriarchal lies that had previously engulfed and silenced her. Sex with Mellors becomes for her an awakening to the felt beauties of nature and life; with him she experiences "the resurrection of the body! the democracy of touch!" (pp. 75–6). Her experience is cast in the religiously pagan terms of spring awakening, "the breath of Persephone" (p. 85) and the philosophically pagan terms of Plato's myth of love in the *Phaedrus* (p. 179); Mellors's experience is expressed in the religiously Christian terms of Pentecost, "my little pentecost flame" (p. 301).

There are two remarkable scenes that show what the love of Constance and Mellors now makes psychologically possible – resistance to social injustice and a cooperative sharing of life on terms of equality. Both take place after a sexual scene in which she initially experienced "her own double consciousness" of Mellors's pleasure but not her own (p. 172), and then is moved to loving pleasure herself with him when she realizes that he knows and wants to give her what she wants.

The first scene takes place in the woods, Clifford Chatterley in his motored chair, Constance escorting. Clifford speaks at length about his role as a member of the British upper class, a role he justifies by dehumanizing the lower classes, regarding them as more animal than human. For Clifford, British mass democracy must be managed as the Roman people were: "Panem et circenses!" (p. 182). Constance, who throughout most of the novel has listened silently to men's views, is empowered now to express her own, and what we hear is an active resistance to and criticism of her husband's position in her assertion of a democratic conception of humanity and social justice. To take the point further, Lawrence's emphasis in this novel on the physical realities and psychic costs of social injustice as well as of war leads to questions germane to our present inquiry: Why is this social analysis embedded in a sexual love story? Why does tenderness become the emotional bedrock of resistance to injustice and war?

The second scene follows on the first. Clifford insists, over Constance's objections, on motoring his chair down into a ravine. The chair's motor breaks down, as she had warned, and Mellors is summoned to assist the couple. Mellors offers to push, but Clifford obstinately refuses help, continuing to jab at the controls, "pale with anger" (p. 188). Finally, he accepts that he must be pushed by Mellors, who realizes that to extricate the chair, he must lift it with Clifford in it. Constance fears that this may be beyond his strength, and when over her objections he lifts Clifford in the chair, she sees Mellors's exhaustion and moves to help push the chair up the hill.

> "I'm going to push too!" she said.
> And she began to shove with a woman's turbulent energy of anger.
> The chair went faster. Clifford looked round.
> "Is that necessary?" he said.

"Very! Do you want to kill the man! If you'd let the motor work while it would – "

But she did not finish. She was already panting. She slackened off a little, for it was surprisingly hard work.

"Ay, slower!" said the man at her side, with a faint smile of the eyes.

"Are you sure you've not hurt yourself?" she said fiercely.

He shook his head. She looked at his smallish short, alive hand, browned by the weather. It was the hand that caressed her. She had never even looked at it before. It seemed so still, like him, with a curious inward stillness that made her want to clutch it, as if she could not reach it. All her soul suddenly swept towards him: he was so silent, and out of reach! And he felt his limbs revive. Shoving with his left hand, he laid his right on her round white wrist, softly enfolding her wrist, with caress. And the flamy sort of strength went down his back and his loins, reviving him. And she, panting, bent suddenly and kissed his hand. Meanwhile the back of Clifford's head was held sleek and motionless, just in front of them. (pp. 191–2)

In this moment, Constance realizes she hates Clifford and cannot live without Mellors, whose vulnerability she takes in: "[T]his bit of work together had brought them much closer than they had been before" (p. 192).

Lawrence has a clear intention for his novel; it could show "a spirit of respect for the struggling, battered thing which any human soul is, and in a spirit of fine, discriminative sympathy.... It can inform and lead into new places the flow of our sympathetic consciousness, and it can lead our sympathy away in recoil from things gone dead" (p. 101). More specifically, it shows the human soul awakening through sexual love to the ravages of the social system that Lord Clifford embodies and defends: a patriarchy at once lifeless and enraged in its sense of insult. Its manhood has been insulted, but lacking feeling and the capacity for tender, sexual love, its men lack the capacity for resistance, the means to extricate themselves. The scene of Clifford driving himself into a ravine over Connie's objections symbolizes this larger predicament. As she and Mellors help each other push Lord Chatterley up the hill, we see, in the invocation of their sexual love, a recognition of human vulnerability, a knowing and a love free of idealization or denigration. As with Psyche, it is when Connie sees Mellor's humanness that she falls in love with him, and he in turn, like Cupid, no longer hides his love of her.

The sexual love between Lady Chatterley and Mellors is clearly anti-patriarchal in its reversal of gender hierarchy and crossing of class boundaries. The lovers act on their experience and their desire, and it is Constance who proposes marriage and a life together to Mellors. In doing so, she has the financial independence to make this feasible. She recognizes in him a manhood not contingent on hierarchy but manifest in his having "the courage of [his] own tenderness" (p. 277). We have left the world of Roman militarism, and in case we should miss the gender implications of this new understanding of courage, Mellors observes, "They used to say I had too much of the woman in me." As their lovemaking is unapologetic in its celebration of his tenderness and her pleasure, we can imagine, when Constance becomes pregnant, that like Cupid and Psyche, they will become parents of a daughter named Pleasure.

We can understand how absorption in the novel's frank treatment of women's sexual pleasure may well have distracted the young Doris Lessing from its rather blatant antiwar message. We are more puzzled by the interpretive lapse in the otherwise perceptive feminist Kate Millett, who offers careful textual interpretations of Lawrence's other novels but dismisses *Lady Chatterley's Lover* on grounds of its sexual politics. In doing so, she overlooks the opening passage where Lawrence diagnoses the traumatized patriarchal psychology that made World War I possible:

> Ours is essentially a tragic age, so we refuse to take it tragically. The cataclysm has happened, we are among the ruins, we start to build up new little habitats, to have new little hopes. It is rather hard work: there is now no smooth road into the future: but we go round, or scramble over the obstacles. We've got to live, no matter how many skies have fallen. (p. 5)

This is Constance's vision, and the novel is largely from her point of view as she comes through the experience of erotic pleasure and tenderness to question and resist the patriarchal forms that had imprisoned both her and Mellors. It is Mellors who gives expression to what we and Millet today find to be not only a sexist conception of female sexuality (favoring vaginal over clitoral orgasm and preferring anal intercourse to both) but also a homophobic rejection of lesbian sexuality.[34] We appreciate Millet's sensitivity to this issue and also understand her response in light of the fact that she and other lesbians were marginalized in the early period of second-wave feminism as "the lavender menace."[35] But the lapses in Lawrence's treatment of sex, which reflect conventional beliefs held at the time he wrote, can to our contemporary eyes become further evidence of the kinds of dissociation he otherwise criticizes.

Constance's love for Mellors and her decision to marry him, when they are both legally free from their current spouses, break the British Love Laws, precisely because Constance has come to see through her love for Mellors (a lower-class man) that what sustains the British class system is the "utter death of the human intuitive faculty" (p. 152). Men like her husband are so deadened in the essential moral faculties of humane connection that they live on lies: "Ravished by dead words become obscene, and dead ideas become obsessions" (p. 94).

We note, finally, the role of religious resurrection in Lawrence's understanding of what sexual love makes possible, as Constance, like Isis in Apuleius's *Metamorphoses*, rescues Mellors from his deathlike existence, and he in turn rescues her. Correspondingly, when Lawrence explores Clifford's descent into "male hysteria" after Constance leaves him (p. 289), he explains its psychology in terms of "his very passivity and prostitution to the Magna Mater" (p. 291), the celibate cult of Cybele that opposed the Isis religion in the ancient world.[36] Lawrence grounds his antiwar novel in a sexually driven resistance to the patriarchal psychology and politics that in his eyes had made his age "essentially tragic." From the very outset, he underscores the denial and dissociation that explain our "refus[al] to take it tragically."

*Lady Chatterley's Lover* thus brilliantly anatomizes as the root of the problem the traumatic disruption of intimate sexual life through patriarchal gender stereotypes, which crush any voice that might reasonably challenge such disruption. Consequently, the trauma feeds on itself in an endless circle of violence in both personal and political life. What makes Lawrence's novel so remarkable in our eyes is the recognition that he, like Hawthorne, comes to: The realization of democracy depends on challenging what has come to be taken as natural manhood and womanhood.

Our reliance on the voices of artists to deepen and expand our argument reflects our view that through their use of associative methods, artists can undo or free themselves from the dissociations of patriarchy. Their access to the body, a body no longer divided from the mind, and to feelings that are joined with, rather than severed from, thought allows them to explore both the costs of dissociation and the wellsprings of resistance. In literature, we find depicted most starkly the dissociations on which patriarchy depends. If the consequences of trauma include loss of memory and of voice, and with it the loss of the ability to tell one's story accurately, then the very act of novel writing may in itself be healing, in part because in doing so, the artist, under the protection of fiction, is challenged to confront and potentially to overcome his or her own dissociation: to say what could not be spoken, to find a voice for the unspeakable.

Trauma existed long before we had a good psychological understanding of its mechanisms and consequences. Even in the earliest periods of civilization, great art – *Gilgamesh* in Babylonia, the *Iliad* and the *Odyssey* in Greece – moving associatively under the radar of patriarchy, has taken as its theme the impact of patriarchy on men and women and the linkages between tragic love and political violence.

The ancient Athenians, who invented democratic institutions, innovated as well a theater in which great artists confronted the minds and hearts of its citizenry with tragedies that revealed issues and tensions that its philosophers could not even acknowledge.[37] The devastating consequences of these tensions – both to our loves and our very lives – as they continue into the present is the subject to which we now turn.

# 9  Resistance: Politics

## 1. BETWEEN PATRIARCHY AND DEMOCRACY: CONTRADICTIONS IN AMERICAN CONSTITUTIONALISM

When Amish school girls were raped and killed in 2006, Bob Herbert asked in the *New York Times* why seemingly no one had questioned whether this was a hate crime against women. His point was that had the target been African-Americans or Jews, the charge of hate crime would surely have followed.[1] Our intention is not to pit one irrational prejudice against another but rather to observe how much we still live between democracy and patriarchy. The founding of American constitutional democracy was informed by a consciousness of the many experiments both in republican government and in forms of a federal state, including republican Rome with its balanced constitution and its growing empire.[2] Vergil's *Aeneid* was read by the Founders in their studies at university,[3] and the founding of Rome was one of the historical precedents they had in mind in establishing the American republic in the Constitution of 1787, amended by the Bill of Rights of 1791.

The Great Seal of the United States, adopted in 1782, consists of an American bald eagle holding an olive branch in his right talon and a bundle of thirteen arrows in his left. His beak carries a scroll inscribed *E Pluribus Unum*. The reverse shows an unfinished pyramid and an eye in a shining triangle. Over the eye, the words *Annuit coeptis* ("he approves of the beginnings") appear; at the base of the pyramid the letters MDCCLXXVI and the motto *novus ordo seclorum* ("a new order of the ages"). The words *Annuit Coeptis* are usually thought to come from Vergil's *Georgics*: enjoining Augustus *audacibus adnue coeptis*,[4] which Vergil echoes in Book 9 of the *Aeneid: Juppiter omnipotens, audacibus annue coeptis.*[5] *Novus ordo seclorum* evokes Vergil's fourth *Eclogue*.[6] Whereas Romans conceived their founding as a refounding of Troy, the Americans saw themselves as beginning anew. As Hannah Arendt observes in *The Life of the Mind*, "[t]his was the moment when those who had started as men of action and had been transformed into men of revolution changed Vergil's great line *Magnus ab integro saeclorum nascitur ordo* ('the great order of the ages is [re]born as it was in the beginning')[7] to the *Novus Ordo Seclorum* (the 'new order'), which we still find on our dollar bills."[8]

For the Founders, this sense of themselves as establishing a new Rome carried with it a vision of heroic man that they inherited from Rome and its founding narrative.[9] Benjamin Rush confessed that "[n]othing struck me more than the moving story of [Aeneas's] leaving Dido at Carthage," which illustrated "that manly heroism which the prospect of establishing a kingdom and being the author of an illustrious race of heroes in a distant country naturally fired his soul."[10] American constitutional law has come a long way since 1787–91, its development marked crucially by the second refounding of the Constitution in the Reconstruction Amendments of 1865–70, following the Civil War[11] and by the impact on the interpretation of the Constitution of the resistance movements starting in the 1960s.[12] But persistent American problems with patriarchy can be seen to date from the uncritical incorporation of Aeneas as founder among the sources of our "new order." The tension between patriarchy and democracy thus has long existed in America.

There were, of course, important differences between Roman and American slavery. Roman slavery was not racially or ethnically defined, and manumission to freedom was much more easily available in Rome than in antebellum America. Furthermore, freedom in Rome could lead to a kind of mobility and opportunity not available in racist America.[13] However, Roman patriarchy played a central role in legitimizing the treatment of Roman slaves as lacking basic human dignity[14] in the same way that the patriarchal family in the antebellum South rationalized the dehumanization of people of color held in slavery. Because slaves were seen as so lacking in human feeling as to be incapable of family relations, they allegedly bore easily the separations (through sale of relatives) common under American slavery.[15] We see the stark force of such patriarchally rooted racism in the infamous 3/5 Clause of the United States Constitution that accorded the southern states disproportionate political power (each slave being accorded three-fifths the representative weight of a citizen) until the Civil War.[16]

Such power made possible the growing importance, under the leadership of John Calhoun, of proslavery constitutionalism, a view that entrenched slavery not only in the states that allowed it but in the territories as well, a constitutional interpretation accepted by the Supreme Court of the United States in *Dred Scott v. Sanford*.[17] No historical precedent was more important to Calhoun than the central place of slavery both in the Athenian democracy and in the Roman Republic, which makes clear how influential these precedents were in both the design and interpretation of the U.S. Constitution.[18] In contrast, abolitionists in the antebellum period rejected the historical precedents of Greece and Rome on grounds that the fundamental American constitutional value of universal human rights rendered slavery illegitimate in principle.[19] No war in American history was more rooted in the defense of patriarchal honor than the Civil War, and no war, as our argument would suggest, was more violent and costly in American lives. It is when patriarchy most uncritically consumes us that our putative constitutional piety (to which all sides in the Civil War appealed) turns us, like Aeneas, into savages.

The view of patriarchy as at the root of slavery and racism is hardly novel, as the abolitionist feminists make clear. Yet patriarchal assumptions proved so powerful that the anti-patriarchal core of the abolitionist feminist movement was marginalized with the Reconstruction Amendments that emancipated black men and women from slavery but emancipated black women into patriarchy. Elizabeth Stanton, who had been a crucial figure in securing ratification of the Thirteenth Amendment, opposed both the Fourteenth and Fifteenth Amendments for this reason. As the Fifteenth Amendment gave the vote only to black men,[20] black women were no longer black but women. The force of patriarchy explains the continuing acceptance of prejudices inconsistent with democratic values.[21]

Consider, for example, the Supreme Court's decision in 1896[22] that held state-imposed racial segregation consistent with the Equal Protection Clause of the Fourteenth Amendment (a decision unanimously reversed in 1954).[23] What had rendered such segregation acceptable was in part, as Charles Lofgren has shown,[24] the dominant racist social science of the late 19th century. This "science" of natural race differences in moral capacity (American ethnology) measured them in alleged physical differences (brain capacity or cephalic indices),[25] providing a putatively scientific basis for the judgment that the separation of the races was justified. Segregation in transportation (the issue in *Plessy*) thus discouraged forms of social intercourse that might result in degenerative forms of miscegenation, and segregation in education reflected race-linked differences in capacity best dealt with in separate schools, as well as preventing social intercourse.

The antebellum abolitionists, however, had offered plausible objections to the scientific status of American ethnology, and similarly forceful objections were available at the time *Plessy* was decided in 1896. In 1894, Franz Boas, a German Jewish immigrant, had published his anthropological study debunking the weight accorded race in the social sciences.[26] Yet the ostensible scientific basis for *Plessy* was not, in fact, critically stated or discussed in the opinion but, rather, conclusorily assumed. Even given the state of the human sciences at the time of *Plessy*, the interpretive argument in the decision did not meet impartial standards of reason. Rather, our highest court accepted controversial scientific judgments hostage to a political ideology that protected the increasingly racist character of the American South. John Marshall Harlan, a southern justice, made precisely this point in his dissent in *Plessy*.

The South's defeat in the Civil War, like Germany's defeat in World War I, was experienced as a blow to its honor; black men and women freed from slavery by the Thirteenth Amendment were turned on in the same way that a defeated Germany turned on the Jews. During Reconstruction, "the South was united on racism as it had not been on slavery."[27] The constitutional abolition of slavery and guarantee of equal rights of citizenship to black (male) Americans were dead letters without some effective constitutional protection of their rights against the populist racism that now flourished as the terms of southern unity.

If the abolitionists with their historical mission of persuasion by conscience were unprepared for the task before them, the nation at large had even less understanding of what was required to achieve its publicly avowed constitutional aims of rectifying the American heritage of slavery and the cultural construction of racism. The principles of the Reconstruction Amendments could only have been effectively realized by a continuing national commitment to the ongoing federal enforcement of constitutional rights in the South; such federal programs would have included land distribution and integrated education for the freedmen (of the sort suggested by Thaddeus Stevens in the House[28] and Charles Sumner in the Senate[29]) as well as active and ongoing federal protection of black voting rights. The dominant view in the Reconstruction Congress itself was that the guarantee of equal protection would not condemn state-sponsored racial segregation or anti-miscegenation laws.[30] The failure adequately to protect the freedmen exposed them to the hostile environment of a South now committed with redoubled fury to a politically aggressive racism that the victory of the Union had, if anything, worsened. By 1877, the congressional and presidential commitment to black rights – protecting voting rights and prosecuting the Ku Klux Klan – effectively ceased.[31]

The patriarchal assumptions that compromised the Reconstruction Amendments further explain the complicity of the Supreme Court in *Plessy* with the racism it should have questioned. What led the Court to its decision was in part its tacit acceptance of the racialized pedestal that elevated and idealized white women as pure and asexual and denigrated blacks as sexual. On these grounds, the state might segregate whites from blacks to protect white women from the sexual advances of black men. The racism of this proposition was invisible to the Court.

This blindness becomes more shocking when we consider that a remarkable black woman, Ida Wells-Barnett, had in this period exposed the irrationalism underlying the racialized pedestal. We need to be clear about Wells-Barnett's background and critique in order to comprehend both the force that patriarchy played in supporting American racism at this time and the courage of her resistance. Wells had been born in 1862 in Mississippi, the child of slave parents. Upon the death of her parents in a yellow fever epidemic in 1878, she assumed responsibility for her siblings. After attending Shaw University, she taught school to support her family and moved to Memphis to improve her career opportunities. As early as 1887, she found her life work as a journalist and became editor of a Memphis newspaper, *Free Speech*.[32]

In 1892, when Wells was in Natchez in connection with her work, three young black businessmen were lynched in Memphis. Wells knew one of them, considering him and his family her best friends in Memphis. She initially used her newspaper to urge blacks to leave Memphis and, in response, many did. Because of the subsequent loss of labor and business income, members of the white community pleaded with Wells to halt the exodus; she refused. Shortly thereafter, further lynchings occurred. Wells had believed the conventional wisdom, as she put it, "that although lynching was irregular and contrary to law and order, unreasoning anger over the terrible crime of rape led to the lynching; that perhaps the brute deserved death anyhow and the mob was justified in taking his life."[33] But upon investigation, she discovered that the Memphis lynchings were of men who had committed no crime against white women; rather, lynching was "[a]n excuse to get rid of negroes who were acquiring wealth and property." She therefore investigated each lynching she heard about and "stumbled on the amazing record that every case of rape reported in the three months became such only when it became public" (Duster, pp. 64–5). In fact, the sexual relationship had been consensual. In May 1892, she published an editorial in her newspaper to set out her findings:

> Eight Negroes lynched since last issue of the *Free Speech*. Three were charged with killing white men and five with raping white women. Nobody in this section believes the old thread-bare lie that Negro men assault white women. If Southern white men are not careful they will over-reach themselves, and a conclusion will be reached which will be very damaging to the moral reputation of their women. (pp. 65–6)

A few days later, her editorial was republished in another newspaper along with an editorial that "called on the chivalrous white men of Memphis to do something to avenge this insult to the honor of their women" (p. 66). A committee of citizens met, after which a group went to the *Free Speech* office and destroyed its type and furnishings. Her life threatened, Wells, who had left the day before the editorial was published for a vacation in New York, never returned, becoming an exile from a South too intolerant to respect the right of free speech. She became a journalist for the *New York Age*, initially publishing a seven-column article on the front page of this newspaper "giving names, dates, and places of many lynchings for alleged rape" (p. 69) and later expanding the article into her 1892 work, *Southern Horrors: Lynch Law in All Its Phases*.[34]

Wells had stumbled across "facts of illicit [consensual] association between black men and white women" and had concluded that "what the white man of the South practiced as all right for himself, he assumed to be unthinkable in white women." Her discoveries put lynching in an entirely new light as an irrational expression of the white Southerner's "resentment that the Negro was no longer his plaything, his servant, and his source of income" (p. 70). This resentment reflected a political epistemology of race and gender that dehumanized African-Americans as sexually rapacious animals (nonbearers of human rights) and distorted reality to comply with its terms, repressing by "the cold-blooded savagery of white devils under lynch law" the exercise of basic human rights that would challenge this orthodoxy. Lynching was the terroristic mechanism of enforcing this dehumanization; it denied the right of intimate association between black men and white women, "striking terror into the hearts of other Negroes who might be thinking of consorting with willing white women"; it abridged the basic rights of conscience and speech by which such atrocities might be reasonably understood and protested by branding African-Americans "as moral monsters and despoilers of white womanhood and childhood," robbing them of "the friends we had and silencing any protest" (p. 71). Like anti-Semitism, the irrationalist power of the ideology denied reality and imposed crude stereotypes of sexuality, in this case negating the will of white women and turning black men into rapists.

At the root of such racist ideology, as Wells came to see, lay fear and hypocrisy. The anti-miscegenation laws, she observed,

> only operate against the legitimate union of the races; they leave the white man free to seduce all the colored girls he can, but it is death to the colored man who yields to the force and advances of a similar attraction in white women. White men lynch the offending

Afro-American, not because he is a despoiler of virtue, but because he
succumbs to the smiles of white women. (p. 19)

Lydia Maria Child had made a related point when she condemned
northern anti-miscegenation laws for the role they played not only in the
denial of a basic human right but also in constructing African-Americans
as nonbearers of rights.[35] Wells deepened Child's condemnation by offering a cogent analysis of the double standard that governed interracial sex.
White men could acceptably have sexual relations with black women, but
white women could not even imaginably desire sexual relations with black
men. Wells thus laid bare the role that the idealization of white women
played in American racism. White women were ascribed by law and convention a sexual virtue they often lacked; black women, similarly, a sexual
vice. Writing from within the experience of a southern black woman, as
Harriet Jacobs had earlier,[36] Wells gave voice to the profound injury this
racist mythology inflicted: "many a slave woman had fought and died
rather than yield to the pressure and temptations to which she was subjected," suffering "as no white women has ever been called upon to suffer
or to understand." She would not keep silent if white women's alleged
feminism failed to take seriously the experience of black women, and
she argued powerfully against Frances Willard, founder of the Women's
Christian Temperance Union, whom she saw as such a feminist.[37]
    Wells thus probed the common roots of American racism and sex-
ism. Many, including apologists for lynching, had observed before her
"that the Southern people are now and always have been most sensitive
concerning the honor of their women – their mothers, wives, sisters, and
daughters."[38] But Wells gave this fact a new interpretation in terms of its
place in a code of chivalry that dehumanized white women by idealizing
them, as it denigrated black women by casting them in mirror-image.
She insisted that her defense of black women had no purpose "to say one
word against the white women of the South. . . . [I]t is their misfortune"
to be treated not as persons but as tropes in a mythology of chivalry that
in fact rationalized "barbarism."
    Wells's analysis was directed against the patriarchal assumptions
underlying both the South's racism and the mainstream racism underlying the opinion of the Supreme Court in *Plessy*. She was addressing
all Americans, black and white, women and men, who had accommodated themselves to the patriarchal terms of American racism, including
suffrage feminists, and her argument explains why the ratification of
the Nineteenth Amendment in 1920 in the end disappointed them. Suffrage feminists had expected the vote to lead to political reform and had
made compromises of principle to secure it, but the very compromises

undermined their aspirations.[39] Only second-wave feminism, emerging in the 1960s, would expose for public discussion the issues of abolitionist feminism that had united black and white women.[40]

It is surely striking that the leading critics of American racism in the 1890s are a German Jewish immigrant (Boas) and a black woman of the South (Wells-Barnett). Both were outsiders to American patriarchy, but while Boas was ignored, Wells-Barnett became a target of patriarchal violence. The culturally induced deafness of Americans in this period shows the power of patriarchy. Most Americans could not hear or attend to the voices of a Jewish man (not, for anti-Semites, a true man) or a black woman (for racists and sexists, a bad woman, all the worse for speaking about sexuality). The only voices that carried authority were those of white men, speaking in a hermetically sealed echo chamber.

It was an important feature of the struggle of the NAACP to secure the overruling of *Plessy* that the American conception of free speech be expanded to include protest of American racism,[41] and such protest undoubtedly had a profound impact both on the overruling of *Plessy* by *Brown v. Board of Education* in 1954[42] and on the Supreme Court's striking down of anti-miscegenation laws in 1967.[43] Constitutional and legal developments after *Brown* were also facilitated by the further expansion of the American doctrine of free speech under the impact of the Civil Rights movement led by Martin Luther King.[44] King certainly worked within the patriarchal assumptions dominant in the black churches, assumptions that the black gay novelist James Baldwin exposed and criticized in his novel, *Go Tell It on the Mountain*.[45] But even Baldwin found something in King he never found in other black ministers[46]: a loving voice that spoke to him as well as to black women, who played important roles in the Civil Rights movement. Later on, many black women would more deeply question the patriarchal assumptions in black culture and discover their relationship to white women and gay men on common anti-patriarchal grounds.[47]

## 2. THE PSYCHOLOGICAL ROOTS OF FASCISM AND THE REBIRTH OF DEMOCRATIC CONSTITUTIONALISM

No one has illuminated the political anti-Semitism of 20th-century totalitarianism more profoundly than Hannah Arendt. In *The Origins of Totalitarianism*[48] Arendt describes the role in totalitarianism of state-enforced terror, directed in both public and private life toward the end of crushing the faculties of the human mind – thinking, willing, and judging.[49] Yet while seeing so much, including the roots of totalitarianism in European racism, she overlooked its roots in patriarchy.

We find this surprising in light of her early, pathbreaking study of the Berlin Jewess Rahel Varnhagen, where Arendt showed remarkable sensitivity to Varnhagen's assimilationist struggles as a woman and a Jew in the late 18th–early 19th century.[50] Arendt herself was a brilliant woman attracted to brilliant men: Martin Heidegger, her professor, with whom she had a love affair, and Heinrich Blucher, whom she married, spending the rest of her life with him in what appears to have been an egalitarian relationship.[51] She was, however, hostile to the women's movements she encountered[52] and never explored the connections between her work and a feminist analysis – perhaps because such analysis did not in this period embrace sexual love, a value for Arendt of fundamental human importance. Her treatment of Augustine is illustrative. Arendt engaged with Augustine both early and late in her career, but only in terms of the prominent role played by love in his thought[53] and his tripartite division in the soul as the model for the Trinity.[54] She did not engage with his reading misogyny into the Christian tradition or his role in Christian anti-Semitism.

The modernist political techniques of state-imposed terror that Arendt identifies and describes arose in Nazi Germany and Stalinist Russia, both deeply hostile to conventional religions, not only Judaism but Christianity as well. Their ideologies were supposedly scientific (not religious), but the science was the pseudo-science of Hitler's racism and Stalin's iron laws of history. On such grounds, the ethical constraints and sensitivities that had held earlier forms of Christian anti-Semitism under at least some measure of control were removed. And without any such controls, totalitarianism, as Arendt saw, sanctioned a use of terror aimed at crushing mental faculties and thus laying the psychological grounds for the often romantic, abject devotion to the patriarchal leader, no matter how vicious his aims.[55] In *Where Do We Fall When We Fall in Love?* Elisabeth Young-Bruehl observes that the mechanism lay in substituting "antinatural technologization" by the state for the intimate relationality of family life. Heinrich Himmler thus spoke of the heroism required to execute the Holocaust, and his adjutant, addressing recent recruits, enjoined them not to be "soft": "[Y]ou are disciplined, but stand together hard as Krupp steel. Don't be soft, be merciless, and clear out everything that is not German and could hinder us in the work of construction."[56]

The power and appeal of patriarchy in modern times drew on Nietzsche's influential attack not only on feminism and liberal values of equality and human rights but also on Judaism and Christianity[57] – all in the name of a kind of ethical perfectionism that takes as ultimate such values as courage and artistic creativity that, in his view, only a few people possess.[58] Nietzsche's appeal to a superman reveals the fundamentalist roots of this conception, calling for a return to a Greek form of radical patriarchy, ruled by the "superman" who displays this human excellence, all else being in service of him.[59] What we find striking is that Nietzsche should have been taken so seriously. It was the power and appeal of patriarchy, we suggest, that struck such a resonant chord, leading Nietzsche's nihilistic attack on liberal equality to be taken up by such shrewd politicians as Mussolini and Hitler.[60]

Benito Mussolini forged in Italy a politically successful fascist ideology and practice on which Hitler was later to model German fascism. In contrast to liberalism or Marxism (both of which he opposed), Mussolini's political movement was empty of any coherent political theory.[61] Instead fascism was marked by its "legitimation of violence against a demonized internal enemy."[62] Because the appeal was never its ideas, its force lay in a political psychology – the Roman patriarchal psychology that we have studied at length in this book. Our point is not merely the cosmetic one that fascism first arose and flourished in modern Italy on the ruins of the Roman Empire, but that the roots of the political psychology of fascism lay in similar experiences of traumatic loss and idealization. The experience of soldiers in World War I, in which both Mussolini and Hitler served, left feelings of shame that Mussolini understood and exploited in mobilizing violence against internal and external enemies, a violence modeled on that of ancient Rome. A few weeks after Mussolini took power, his triumph was celebrated by the creation of a new national symbol – not "the fasces of the Risorgimento" but "the Roman version, presumably to cleanse its emblem of a past that included a symbol of liberty, the Phrigian cap."[63]

This would not have been psychologically possible if Italian culture in the early 20th century were not still remarkably patriarchal. Certainly, it was the home of the most patriarchal form of the Christian religion, the Catholic Church, which still prided itself on its Augustinian rejection of religious toleration.[64] And while the Italian constitutional monarchy after 1870 had appealed to liberal principles that were quite anti-clerical, these principles were circumscribed to the small elite of leaders and voters (universal suffrage came late to Italy) and did not penetrate deeply into Italian cultural life.[65] The forms of Italian family life, for example, remained rooted in codes of honor in a nation still largely illiterate and thus largely ignorant of the liberalizing views on women being articulated in Britain, France, and the United States.[66]

During the Risorgimento that led to unification in 1870, Italians had recalled memories of Roman greatness that could now be revived. This explains in part why, long before Mussolini took power, Italy engaged in imperialistic wars in Africa. In its imperialism, the Italian state during this period was following the example of other European imperial powers, all of whom drew, to greater or lesser extents, on the example of the Roman Empire.

Mussolini had renounced socialism in his nationalistic fervor that Italy enter World War I, a war most Italians did not want to enter and that left 680,000 dead, half a million disabled, and more than a million wounded, most of them peasants.[67] Italy was on the side of the victors in this war, but both its earlier defeat at Caporetto and the peace terms, which did not give Italy the territories in Dalmatia it claimed as its own, were interpreted by Mussolini and others as humiliating defeats.[68] The roots of fascism lay largely in small groups of ex-soldiers to whom Mussolini appealed to organize themselves into "fasci di combattimento," bringing the redemptive military discipline and solidarity they experienced in World War I into political life in the form of "squadrismo . . . the armed terrorist reaction against the Socialist Party and the unions." Strikingly, he referred to such murders in the classical Roman terms of "his 'list' of proscriptions,"[69] the Roman practice in the civil wars of listing enemies of the triumvirate who might be killed by anyone and whose property might be taken.

Mussolini's driving ambition for power now led him pragmatically to improvise a movement that was, he insisted, not a political party but a kind of cultural and political revolution.[70] At the psychological heart of the movement was a sense of humiliated manhood that expressed itself in the rhetoric of fascist virility that Mussolini had absorbed from artists like Filippo Marinetti and Gabriele D'Annunzio.[71] Mussolini gave political expression to this psychology by calling for repressive violence against any person who or viewpoint that might challenge its legitimacy, in particular, liberalism and socialism, both of which appeal to the principle of treating persons as equals. As quoted by Robert O. Paxton: "'The fist,' asserted a Fascist militant in 1920, 'is the synthesis of our theory.'"[72] While Mussolini was personally quite anti-clerical, he accommodated his regime to the Catholic Church (the Lateran pacts)[73] for pragmatic reasons (the Catholic piety of many Italians) and because his own repression of dissent was, in fact, in line with and even modeled on the church's endorsement of Augustinian intolerance and anti-liberal government.[74] What Mussolini admired in and took from the church was precisely its more theocratically Roman features.

Among the sources of Mussolini's invention of fascism was the syndicalism of Georges Sorel that called for violent action in service of left-wing aims and sought to forge a new conception of manhood:

"a producer and a warrior, nurtured on heroic values, like the early Christians, the Roman legionnaires, the soldiers of the revolutionary wars, and the disciples of Mazzini. He was a combatant avid for glory, full of abnegation, and ever ready for sacrifice, like the soldiers of Napoleon."[75]

Sorel was calling for the savage heroism of Aeneas in modern garb.

Mussolini had absorbed from the Italian writer D'Annunzio (sometimes called his John the Baptist), a blending of Darwin and Nietzsche, the role in the ruthless survival of the fittest of a hypermasculine hero (rejecting "the laughable and wretched feminization of the ancient European soul, the monstrous reflorescence of Christianity among the decrepit races").[76] In contrast to Nietzsche, D'Annunzio specifically called for a return to Roman militarism, self-consciously inverted both the Beatitudes and the Lord's Prayer of Jesus into war manifestos, and "seems genuinely to have been excited by the mere accoutrements of a soldier, regarding himself almost as a member of a religious order."[77] He thus unites, in his conception of manhood, the Roman patriarchal soldier and priest: It was also D'Annunzio who, in his leadership of the short-lived invasion of Fiume after the end of World War I, innovated new forms of political liturgies, including speeches, celebrations of and identifications with dead heroes, and even the use in war of the "Graeco-Roman 'battle-cry', 'Eia, eia, eia, alala'" which was to be used by Italian fighting men for the next twenty-four years.[78]

In contrast to Mussolini, D'Annunzio was a genuine war hero and a longtime monarchist, whose Cornaro Charter for Fiume was genuinely liberal.[79] His idealism was no match for Mussolini's cynical pragmatism, and Mussolini easily triumphed in the competition for power. D'Annunzio's affairs with women were legendary, almost always ending badly for the women, repeating the pattern of Aeneas with Dido.[80] Mussolini's affairs tell a similar psychological story, one frankly confided by him to a colleague: "[M]an in general...always kills what he most loves."[81]

Mussolini thus found in the traumatic war experience of Italian soldiers the basis for a political psychology he was to rationalize, mobilize, and extend into what Emilio Gentile has properly called the modern political religion of fascism, a religion very much modeled on Roman patriarchal religion.[82] It included mass parades and rituals centering on honoring the dead war heroes or heroes of the fascist revolution, the audience identifying themselves with the dead hero by responding collectively, when his name was called, "present,"[83] an heroic idealization covering desolating loss in the familiar pattern of Roman patriarchal psychology. Mussolini's political religion, like that of Augustus earlier, also included massive building programs that were self-consciously designed to connect modern Rome with its past,[84] as well as new forms of historic representation and education: Augustan Rome culminating in Mussolini, the modern imperial autocrat, the patriarchal Caesar.[85] Although Mussolini thought of his improvisatory politics as more that of Julius Caesar than Augustus,[86] he publicly identified himself not only with Augustus but with "a Constantine or a Justinian,"[87] a secular and religious autocrat.

The success of Mussolini shows us the power of Roman patriarchal psychology in the modern world. It flourishes specifically when warfare is rationalized and justified as an antidote to humiliated manhood. Hitler's experience as a soldier in World War I was more traumatic than Mussolini's,[88] and his fascism was correspondingly more fanatical, more lethal, and probably more sincere. His politics appealed to the defeated Germans by holding out a way to regain honor and pride.

Anti-Semitism was much more central to Hitler than it was for Mussolini. Both drew upon Nietzsche, but Nietzsche hated all forms of irrationalism and nationalism.[89] Yet his highly patriarchal views were all too easily assimilated by Hitler as a rationale for debunking liberal values and legitimating a political anti-Semitism that invoked a pseudo-science of race in support of its genocidal aims. What we see so starkly in the modern period is how powerful patriarchy is, not only distorting politics and religion but also undermining science and ethics.

The great historical lesson of the 20th century is the terrifying price we pay when our technology is so much in advance of our ethics and politics. We know that the political violence of fascism was motivated by an aggressively political anti-Semitism and that it fed upon and cultivated a sense of manhood based on codes of honor at least as old as the *Iliad*. Gender stereotypes were central to a Nazi manhood hardened to the murder of six million Jews.[90] And the bloody totalitarianism of Stalin's communism, including the starvation of at least five million peasants,[91] was crucially actuated by an indoctrination into an ideal of the soldier constantly on duty[92] that, as with Hitler's fascism, bizarrely justified state-imposed mass killing as self-defense.[93] It is no accident that there are close links between fascism and Soviet communism, based, as they are, on conceptions of a hardened manhood committed to violence against any dissent against or doubt about the terms of state-enforced injustice.[94] Using modern technologies, both forms of totalitarianism inflicted appalling levels of violence.

The victory of the Allies in World War II then set the stage, in both America and Europe, for a rebirth of democratic constitutionalism. Having triumphed over an aggressively racist power hostile to the very idea of universal human rights, the United States in particular was compelled to question the degree to which its constitutional law, grounded in the protection of such rights, had failed to protect the rights of people of color and many others as well. A growing American sensitivity to anti-patriarchal voices arose from revulsion at the violence of political fascism, itself grounded in Roman patriarchal manhood. Thus the astonishing developments in American constitutional law after World War II can both be explained and normatively defended in terms of the theory of resistance to patriarchy we offer and defend in this book.

Beginning in the 1960s, American constitutional law came to recognize anti-Semitism, racism, sexism, and homophobia as constitutional injustices. The common features of these otherwise disparate injustices arise from their investment in the patriarchal Love Laws. The 1960s become so pivotally important in American constitutional law and development because a series of resistance movements found a strong resonance in the values and institutions of American democracy. The very success of their appeal and the notable achievements of the Civil Rights and feminist movements, the war on poverty, the move to stop atmospheric testing of nuclear weapons, and the protest that arose within the military to stop the Vietnam War render shocking current depictions of this decade as an era of "sex, drugs, and rock and roll." This linking of sex with drugs and rock and roll rather than with the political movements of the '60s became the rationale for a reassertion of patriarchal institutions and values, notably its Love Laws.

## 3. IRRATIONAL PREJUDICE: ANTI-SEMITISM AS THE MODEL FOR RACISM, SEXISM, AND HOMOPHOBIA

A man who has suffered traumatic loss and renounced tenderness suppresses his own voice in aligning himself with patriarchal authority. Taking on its idealized image of women, he denigrates sexuality. By then regarding people of color as sexual, he denigrates them and thus can rationalize their sexual exploitation and his own racism. Sexism more baldly reflects the division of women into madonnas and whores. a division that justifies male dominance in the name of protecting women's purity and also alienates women from one another and from vital parts of themselves. Dividing love from sexuality and virtue from pleasure, sexism similarly introduces a psychic rent within men, requiring their repression of vital parts of themselves and encouraging violence against women who resist patriarchal demands. Finally, homophobia reflects the underlying gender binary and hierarchy, which require a man not to be a woman and also to be on top. Male homoeroticism flourished in Augustan Rome, but its homophobic character is evident in the stigma attached to the bottom or passive role. Thus only slave boys could serve as men's sexual objects.

Anti-Semitism is central to our analysis because its historical development so clearly exemplifies the pivotal role of patriarchal norms and values in giving rise to and sustaining such a prejudice. Not only is it the historically most ancient and enduring of such prejudices, but its structure also gives us a model for how patriarchal authorities enlist such prejudices in rationalizing their demands. As the traumatic loss imposed on intimate life leads through the repression of personal voice to identification with the voice of the father, a fissure develops within the psyche. Anti-Semitism particularly exploits this division, rationalizing the gender binary and hierarchy by placing Jews in subordinate status as sexualized and effeminate in contrast to ascetic, Christian men – a status that by definition they are not able to contest.

What Christians did to the Jews could, of course, be done to any group, placing them a position of moral slavery to serve political or economic or ideological ends. On this model, patriarchal societies have sustained a dominant group over a subordinate sexualized group, whether people of color, women, or homosexuals. The Love Laws of patriarchy, establishing who should be loved and how and how much, enforce this hierarchy.

The Love Laws lie at the heart of patriarchy, enforcing demands that divide us and obscure our common humanity. Their form is historically familiar: prohibitions on sexual relations between Jews and non-Jews, between people of color and not of color, between women and men not their husbands, nonprocreative sex between married couples (laws criminalizing sodomy, or use of contraceptives, or access to abortion), between gay men or between lesbians, between the touchable and the untouchable. What is not so clear is why such laws play the role they do.

In *The Anatomy of Prejudices*, Elisabeth Young-Bruehl's analyzes prejudices as social mechanisms of defense, exemplifying features of hysterical, obsessional, and narcissistic disorders and rooted in repression that expresses itself in forms of violence.[95] Bringing the lens of gender to her analysis, we add the pivotal role of patriarchy in both the repression of voice and its expression in violence.[96] The relational sensitivity and responsiveness of one person as an individual to another person as an individual are in tension with its hierarchical demands. And the very irrationality of prejudice reflects the lapse of intelligence that accompanies the suppression of sexual voice and experience. All forms of prejudice war on loving connection across the barriers they artificially impose, precisely because such loving connection exposes the lies such prejudices enforce. The stability of the practices underwritten by patriarchy is supported by the repression of a free and loving sexual voice and the relationships to which such a voice would otherwise lead. The Love Laws direct patriarchal violence against this very real threat to its authority.

Our analysis thus clarifies how important the lens of gender is for both understanding and resisting such prejudices. It is through such a lens that we discern how the discrediting of one such prejudice has a way of leading to the expression of another. We argued, by way of illustration, that the discrediting of the Catholic Church's role in Christian anti-Semitism has now led to the displacement of this prejudice to homophobia.

## 4. THE RESISTANCE MOVEMENTS OF THE 1960S AND LATER

The impact of the resistance movements starting in the 1960s – the Civil Rights and antiwar movements, second-wave feminism, gay rights – was both to expand the constitutional conception of American free speech to include the voices of people of color, women, gays, and lesbians and to move the contemporary constitutional interpretation of the Reconstruction Amendments, most notably, the Fourteenth Amendment, much closer to the views of the abolitionist feminists.[97] At the heart of these transformative developments were the morally empowered voices of people who challenged the repressive force of patriarchy, very much in the spirit of Ida Wells-Barnett. What made this challenge so fundamental and so compelling was that it broke the repression and dissociation of sexual voice imposed by the Love Laws.

The demonizing of pleasure and the acceptance of violence are hallmarks of patriarchy. The joining of the antiwar protest with a call for the freeing of love thus struck at its core. Even today we see the disproportionate moral outrage at violations of the Love Laws in comparison, say, with violation of the Geneva accords. It is shocking when sex becomes more taboo than waterboarding.

Constitutional democracy has at its core a normative conception of respect for equal human rights that include, prominently, respect for voices speaking from personal conviction, a right protected in the United States by the guarantees of the First Amendment (including the protection of conscience from improper exercises of state power as well as the protection of speech expressing conscience). Such guarantees of free and equal voice are in tension with a patriarchal conception of authority. Indeed, the stability of patriarchy rests on the denial and abridgement of such voices, in particular, the voices of those who would resist its demands. Such resistance rests on a normative conception of rights and freedom fundamentally at odds with the traditional place of patriarchy in our lives. Indeed, we would generalize the point in terms of a contradiction, both normative and psychological, between democracy and patriarchy.

Given this tension, indeed contradiction, between democracy and patriarchy, resistance to the continuing role of patriarchy in our lives is both democratic and democratizing. The liberation movements of the 1960s asserted the basic right to equal voice and respect. What makes such resistance psychologically possible and appealing – in the face of the traditional power of patriarchy – is the way it breaks a silence imposed by the taboo on seeing, knowing, and speaking about love. We must love one another or die, Auden wrote, in a poem that now seems prophetic.[98] The Love Laws that would keep us from loving certain others thus may stand in the way of survival.

The Civil Rights movement resisted American racism, entrenched through laws requiring racial segregation and condemning miscegenation that had only recently been struck down as unconstitutional by the Supreme Court.[99] Women in second-wave feminism challenged the patriarchal ideal of selflessness by claiming their voices and their moral agency.[100] In "Professions of Women," Virginia Woolf, reflecting on the psychological blocks she had encountered, captured the phantom that had silenced her: "the Angel in the House."

> I will describe her as shortly as I can. She was intensely sympathetic. She was immensely charming. She was utterly unselfish. She excelled in the difficult arts of family life. She sacrificed herself daily . . . in short she was so constituted that she never had a mind or a wish of her own, but preferred to sympathize always with the minds and wishes of others. Above all – I need not say it – she was pure. Her purity was supposed to be her chief beauty – her blushes, her great grace. . . . And when I came to write I encountered her with the very first words. The shadow of her wings fell on my page; I heard the rustling of her skirts in the room. Directly, that is to say, I took my pen in hand to review that novel by a famous man, she slipped behind me and whispered: "My dear, you are a young woman. You are writing about a book that has been written by a man. Be sympathetic; be tender; flatter; deceive; use all the arts and wiles of our sex. Never let anybody guess that you have a mind of your own. Above all, be pure." And she made as if to guide my pen. I now record the one act for which I take some credit to myself, though the credit rightly belongs to some excellent ancestors of mine who left me a certain sum of money . . . so that it was not necessary for me to depend solely on charm for my living. I turned upon her and caught her by the throat. I did my best to kill her. My excuse, if I were to be had up on a court of law, would be that I acted in self-defense. Had I not killed her she would have killed me.[101]

In the 1960s, women more generally and also men came to see the destructive power of such images.

In the antiwar movement, men who had served with distinction in Vietnam protested a war they had come to regard as unjust. Others refused as conscientious objectors to serve, taking on the construction of manhood that would deem them unmanly.[102] As a priest, James Carroll, found a voice not only to object to the war himself but also to question the role of fathers in supporting it.[103] Behind all these forms of resistance lay the question: What does it mean to be a man and a father?

Men and women in the gay rights movement similarly took on constructions of manhood and womanhood that impeded their capacity to love. For gay men, resistance to homophobic lies was a necessary condition for experiencing love, for coming to trust themselves and others to live in the truth of a loving relationship.[104] In so doing, such men come fundamentally to question patriarchy, which, imposing hierarchy not only between men and women but also between men and men, undermines the free and equal voice in relationship that makes love possible and sustaining.

At the heart of these resistance movements is speaking in a different voice,[105] one that resists patriarchal norms and values, a voice grounded in experience, in the body and in relationship. The prominent role of women in these resistance movements is not surprising, or that of men who come to resist patriarchy through relationships with such women. It is what the Cupid and Psyche story would lead us to expect: a woman's resistance to blinding and silencing herself impels a man to stop hiding his love.

Such resistance inevitably raises the complex questions about identity and assimilation framed by W. E. B. Du Bois. In *The Souls of Black Folks* (1903) he writes about "double consciousness," the psychic splitting that Breuer and Freud described in *Studies on Hysteria*. Reflecting on black men's struggle for identity under conditions of racial oppression, Du Bois observes,

> a world which yields him no true self-consciousness, but...this double-consciousness, this sense of always looking at one's self through the eyes of others, of measuring one's soul by the tape of a world that looks on in amused contempt and pity. One ever feels his two-ness, – an American, a Negro; two souls, two thoughts, two unreconciled strivings; two warring ideals in one dark body.

The struggle for justice was thus inseparable from a struggle for integrity and self-respect.

> The history of the American Negro is the history of this strife, – this longing to attain self-conscious manhood, to merge his double self into a better and truer self. In this merging he wishes neither of the older selves to be lost. He would not Africanize America, for America has too much to teach the world and Africa. He would not bleach his Negro soul in a flood of white Americanism, for he knows that

Negro blood has a message for the world. He simply wishes to make it possible for a man to be both a Negro and an American, without being cursed and spit upon by his fellows, without having the door of Opportunity closed roughly in his face.[106]

It is illusory to think that one can resist one form of moral or political injustice without resisting the others; that one can oppose racism, for example, without taking on economic inequalities. As Martin Luther King observed, injustice anywhere is injustice everywhere; a single garment of destiny ties us. King, like Tolstoy and Gandhi, took on the problem of violence, but without seeing the violence of their own attitudes and behavior toward women. The patriarchal core of intolerance has remained invisible in part because to challenge patriarchy is to expose oneself to shame by putting one's manhood or womanhood on the line.

## 5. RESISTANCE TO FUNDAMENTALISM IN AMERICAN CONSTITUTIONAL LAW

John Rawls has observed that "fundamentalist religious doctrines and autocratic and dictatorial rulers will reject the ideas of public reason and deliberative democracy."[107] Instead, they appeal to the certainty of a specific understanding of authority rooted in the past, a certainty that is to guide thought and conduct today irrespective of reasonable contemporary argument and experience to the contrary. A source-based fundamentalism is rooted in certain texts or in interpretations of such texts to which are ascribed an apodictic meaning and truth value not available or accessible to nonbelievers. Protestant fundamentalism is usually of this form, placing an interpretive weight on certain texts that are not open to other, often more reasonable interpretations, let alone to nonbelievers who do not regard such texts as authoritative.[108]

In America, historical originalism in constitutional interpretation is another form of source-based fundamentalism, not specifically religious but still objectionable. The only consistent originalist in the United States has been Raoul Berger, who argued that no interpretation of a constitutional text can be correct that does not track the things in the world to which the text was or would have been applied by the founding generation who enacted the provision in question (whether the Constitutional Convention of 1787 and ratifying states, or the Congress and ratifying states for the Bill of Rights of 1791, or the Reconstruction Congress and ratifying states for the Reconstruction Amendments, including the Fourteenth Amendment of 1868).[109] Berger thus argued that most of the modern judiciary's interpretation of the Fourteenth Amendment, including striking down state-sponsored racial segregation as unconstitutional in *Brown v. Board of Education*,[110] was wrong because the Reconstruction Congress regarded racial segregation as not violative of equal protection. A somewhat less consistent originalist was Judge Robert Bork, abortively proposed by President Reagan for appointment to the U.S. Supreme Court. Bork accepted the current judicial understanding that racial classifications, including those underlying racial segregation, were forbidden, but thought it was wrong to extend constitutional interpretation any further. In particular, Judge Bork sharply objected to the principle of constitutional privacy in general, because, he argued, it did not correspond to any reasonably specific originalist understanding.[111] Judge Bork's appointment was resisted by many constitutional lawyers because his defense of originalism was clearly directed at the advances made in American constitutional interpretation under the impact of the resistance movements of the 1960s and later.

We consider originalism as a source-based fundamentalism because it ascribes decisive normative weight not to the text of the Constitution or to its interpretation over time but solely to a certain view of the authority of Founders, in particular, the ways in which they applied or would have applied the constitutional text in their enactment circumstances, what may be called Founders' denotations. What makes this approach so unreasonable is not only that it fails to fit with the text and interpretive traditions over time of authoritative institutions like the Supreme Court, but also that it corresponds to no defensible political theory of the values of constitutionalism and certainly not to the view of their authority taken by leading Founders such as James Madison.[112] For all these reasons, originalism is an objectionable source-based fundamentalism, as objectionable as Protestant fundamentalism because it appeals, as a decisive source in constitutional interpretation, to a form of historical understanding that is not sensitive to reason and deliberation in contemporary circumstances – that indeed expressly refuses to accept such reasonable argument as relevant in legitimate constitutional interpretation.

We can bring this objectionable source-based fundamentalism closer to the argument of this book by considering the form recently advocated by Hadley Arkes, who has supported many of the reactionary constitutional positions on matters of gender and sexuality of fundamentalist religious conservatives.[113] Arkes claims to ground his position not in religion at all but, rather, in an argument of historical originalism that appeals to the place of natural rights in the constitutional thought of the Founders, as well as in the constitutionally influential thought of Abraham Lincoln. Arkes is particularly exercised by what he argues is the illegitimacy of *Roe v. Wade* because, in his view, the case appeals to a right that is inconsistent with an originalist understanding of natural rights.

The only plausible interpretation of Arkes's position is Bork's original-ist objection to the principle of constitutional privacy, namely, that the Founders both of the Bill of Rights and of the Reconstruction Amend-ments would not have accepted in their circumstances a right to con-stitutional privacy that encompassed contraception, abortion, and con-sensual gay/lesbian sex. Nor would they have accepted, we hasten to add, the Supreme Court's contemporary understanding of race and gen-der as highly suspect classifications. Arkes is, like Bork, not a consistent originalist; his critical attention is similarly riveted not by the whole of contemporary constitutional interpretation but only by selective bits of it – in particular, those parts that also absorb the other contemporary fundamentalists, especially the cases that challenge patriarchal views of sexuality and gender.

But historical originalism ascribes to the Founders an authority that leaders such as Madison believed they lacked. A political liberal in the tradition of the revolutionary constitutionalism of John Locke, Madison rejected any conception of his having as a Founder the kind of patriar-chal authority defended by Robert Filmer, against whom Locke wrote his *Two Treatises of Government*.[114] Locke had claimed "that *a Child is born a Subject of no Country or Government* . . . nor is he bound up, by a Compact of his Ancestors."[115] Locke had made the argument against Filmer's patriarchal historicism, that is, the claim that political legitimacy today had to be traced lineally to the authority of the original father of the human race. In contrast, Locke argued that no such past figure could have a legitimate claim on his or her descendants, because the normative basis of political legitimacy was not history but respect for the inalienable human rights that protected the spheres of reasonable self-government of free people. What made originalism so unacceptable to Madison is that it would have ascribed to him a patriarchal authority that it was the aim of liberal constitutionalism forever to repudiate. The better way to square the authority of a written constitution with this view of the Founders' authority is to allow later interpretive generations, including the Supreme Court, reasonably to recontextualize the abstract conno-tations of constitutional guarantees of human rights in contemporary circumstances.[116] It is from this perspective that the constitutional right to privacy is a legitimate principle of constitutional law in the United States, judged in the light of a contemporary constitutional culture that respects the voices of women, gays, and lesbians.[117]

Source-based fundamentalism specifically targeted many of the con-stitutional advances in the United States that took place under the impact of the resistance movements of the mid-20th century, in particular, those advances dealing with matters of sexuality and gender (abortion and gay rights, including gay marriage). To us, this suggests that precisely because these constitutional advances recognized the legitimacy of claims made in resistance to the patriarchal Love Laws, they have elicited the kind of repressive violence that fundamentalism incites. The tenacity of the resistance to originalism by those Americans who successfully opposed the appointment of Judge Bork may be understood in these terms: as based on the recognition of a fundamental antagonism between the Love Laws and democratic freedoms.

# Part Three

Democracy's Future

# 10  *The Contemporary Scene*

In contemplating democracy's future, we turn to the contemporary scene and enlarge the scope of our analysis to include other cultures. At home, our politics has become increasingly polarized under the influence of a fundamentalism that wars precisely on what made possible the most important and effective resistance movements in American history: namely, any love that resists the Love Laws of patriarchy. Internationally, Christian, Islamic, Hindu, and Jewish fundamentalists are united in their patriarchal assumptions, repressing resisting voices in themselves and going to war on the resisting voices of others.

In our concluding discussion, we take up three questions: Is our analysis relevant in Asian and Middle-Eastern contexts? Why are we again at war? and How is the freeing of sexual voice in the '60s being framed? In considering these questions, we turn to three writers, Martha Nussbaum, Stephen Holmes, and Tom Brokaw, whose recent books on the subjects of fascist violence in India, the war on terror, and the legacy of the 1960s speak directly to our concerns.

## 1. THE IMPACT OF WESTERN COLONIALISM IN ASIA AND THE MIDDLE EAST

We have told a largely Western story about the tension between democracy and patriarchy and the forms of resistance in religion, psychology, the arts, and politics. Our story is rooted in Western culture because the Athenians invented democracy and lived with it in tension with their patriarchal practices in public and private life. The Roman republic offers a variation on this theme, one that culminated in imperialism. In tracing the legacy of Roman patriarchy as it continues to compromise democratic institutions and values, we asked ourselves: How relevant is this argument outside the West? India as the world's largest democracy lives in tension with forms of patriarchy both indigenous and imported, and their underlying dynamic is the same.

We see the central importance of shame and a sense of humiliated manhood as the psychological basis for violence not only in James Gilligan's analysis of the contemporary American scene but also in Martha Nussbaum's recent study of Hindu violence against Muslims in India. In *The Clash Within: Democracy, Religious Violence, and India's Future*, Nussbaum traces this movement to the construction of patriarchal manhood that Hindu nationalists absorbed from the imperial models of British and German masculinity, including European fascist ideology. But the Hindu sense of humiliated manhood was also based on historical memories of Mughal rule over Hindus.

At the heart of the problem, Nussbaum argues, lie uncritical gender stereotypes, reflecting long-standing patterns of patriarchal family life in India, including the role of arranged marriages in sustaining the caste system.[1] Such marriages perpetuate the patriarchal Love Laws, ensuring, for example, that couples remain largely within their caste and advance patriarchal ends. These institutions rest, as we have argued, on a psychology of traumatic breaks in intimate relationships. For example, Indian women, when married, historically lived within the husband's family, subject to the authority of a mother-in-law: "Marriage began with a forced parting from everything she [the wife] loved. The event was synonymous with great grief, with copious weeping . . . a traumatic experience."[2] The very rhetoric of Hindu nationalism – protecting the purity of Mother India – expresses an idealization and denigration, keyed to gender stereotypes, that cover traumatic loss and feed the psychology that sustains such stereotypes, a psychology elucidated by the Indian novelist Arundhati Roy in *The God of Small Things*.[3] What Roy shows us so clearly is how incendiary a love that transgresses the Love Laws remains in contemporary India. The violence enforcing the Love Laws wars not only on sexuality but also on moral intelligence, as we see in the "orthodox critics [in India] of women's education," who "were convinced of an equation between the woman's intellectual desires and her sexual immorality."[4] It is not surprising, from this perspective, that in contrast to China, only half of Indian women are today literate.[5]

What makes India especially interesting from our perspective is the significant role that British imperialism also played in sustaining patriarchal practices in Indian religious and family life that were very much under question by feminists in Britain. As Tanika Sarkar cogently observes in *Hindu Wife, Hindu Nation*:

These decades had in England seen profound changes in women's rights *vis-à-vis* property holding, marriage, divorce, and the rights of prostitutes to physical privacy. Englishmen in India were divided about the direction of these changes and a significant section felt disturbed by the limited, though real, gains made by contemporary English feminists. They turned with relief to the so-called relative stability and strictness of Hindu rules. The Hindu joint-family system, whose collective aspects supposedly fully submerged and subordinated individual rights and interests, was generally described with warm appreciation. Found here was a system of relatively unquestioned patriarchal absolutism which promised a more comfortable state of affairs than what emerged after bitter struggles with Victorian feminism at home.[6]

While the British ended some practices like sati (the compulsory suicide of wives on the death of the husband) and modified others (raising the age of child marriage), its dominant approach was to respect patriarchal practices in religiously based family life.

In his classic *The Discovery of India*, Jawaharlal Nehru analyzed British rule in India as grounded in a racism akin to that of Hitler, a racism in which the British were superimposed on the existing caste system as a racialized highest caste, irrespective of their class position in Britain.[7] Indian men in their public lives were thus subject to rules of subordination imposed by the colonizers, but "[t]he forced surrender and real dispossession of the former was counterposed to the allegedly loving, willed surrender and ultimate self-fulfillment of [the subordinated Hindu wife at home]." In effect, the patriarchal assumptions of the Western imperial power both shaped and hardened the forms of patriarchal family life in India, supporting a "[c]onjugality ... based on the apparent absolutism of one partner and the total subordination of the other." Hindu nationalism "begins its career by defining itself as the realm of unfreedom ... [its] defence of community custom ... represses the pain of women whose protest was drowned to make way for a putative consensus"; its terms are "close to being intellectually Fascist in its authoritarian insistence on the purity of indigenous epistemological and autarkic conditions," expressing itself in "a fundamentalist millenarianism." "Community leaders demand a human sacrifice in the name of the threatened community."[8]

A patriarchally founded British imperialism thus enforced on Indian life a conception that led colonized Indian men, in their own abject status, to require and rationalize the more radically abject subordination of Indian women, whose goodness, identified as sexual purity, was idealized as self-sacrifice. Even suspicion of impurity justified rejection and even suicide, as the Indian epic *The Ramayana* makes quite clear[9]; and the humiliation of a patriarchal woman could justify illimitable violence in revenge, as in the disrobing of Draupadi in the Kaurava court in *The Mahabharata*. We recognize that Indian feminist scholars have found in Draupadi resistance to her plight, but it is a resistance crushed by pariarchy.[10] This highly gendered conception of the honor codes of family life, not subject to state power but regulated by religious authorities, was a patriarchal legacy of the British to the Indians, underlying the contemporary problem of plural systems of religious personal life that exist in tension with Indian constitutional guarantees of both a secular state and nondiscrimination on grounds of gender. Both Nussbaum and Indian scholar Ratna Kapur (on erotic justice) identify this tension as a contradiction within India's democratic constitutionalism. From our perspective, patriarchy, here as elsewhere, darkens ethical intelligence.[11]

Western imperialism (itself modeled on Roman patriarchy) thus contributes to the tensions between democracy and patriarchy in India in two ways. First, its model of patriarchal manhood is itself appealed to in the development of a Hindu fascism that expresses itself in violence. Second, the British colonial experience heightened and enforced a patriarchal conception of family life resting on the sacrifice of women's interests. In both, traumatic loss makes psychologically possible the forms of violence from which India continues to suffer: Hindu-Muslim violence, violence against minority religions, and intercaste violence when caste barriers are challenged.[12]

Both the British Empire and other Western colonial powers stood in a similar relationship to other nations, including the many contemporary nations of the Middle East that were carved out of the British and Ottoman Empires. We can see in these nations a legacy resembling that which we have already analyzed in the case of India: absorbing from the West a conception of patriarchal manhood and a colonial experience that reinforced indigenous forms of patriarchy. In the postcolonial period, the United States has played the role of an American Empire, a kind of latter-day Roman Empire – like Rome more patriarchal than democratic – that has supported nondemocratic allies, notably Egypt and Saudi Arabia, and, in the case of Saudi Arabia and the Afghan resistance to the Soviet Union, highly patriarchal forms of Islam. The patriarchal legacy of the former colonial powers has thus been strengthened by the United States in these nations. It is not surprising that hostility to our role including our support of Israel has taken the form of an extreme Islamic fundamentalism, fueled by a sense of manhood humiliated by the United States and asserting itself in the terroristic violence of 9/11. The perpetrators of this terror were, unsurprisingly, dominantly from Egypt and Saudi Arabia.[13] From the perspective of their ideology, the United States and its allies are the embodiment of all the sins of the colonialist imperial West against Islam, including the Crusades: "This is one reason that Qutb [the founder of Al-Qaeda], Osama bin Ladin, and other jihadis call their current enemies 'Zionist-Crusaders.'"[14]

## 2. THE WAR ON TERROR

The power of the gender lens that we bring to our analysis appears in the very terms of our current war on terror. In *Terror in the Mind of God: The Global Rise of Religious Violence*, Mark Juergensmeyer interprets the global rise of fundamentalist violence as a response to perceived insults to manhood:

> Nothing is more intimate than sexuality, and no greater humiliation can be experienced than failure over what one perceives to be one's sexual role. Such failures are often the basis of domestic violence; and when these failures are linked with the social roles of masculinity and femininity, they can lead to public violence. Terrorist acts, then, can be forms of symbolic empowerment for men whose traditional sexual roles – their very manhood – is perceived to be at stake.[15]

The terrorism of Islamic fundamentalism exemplifies the toxic combination of technological know-how with extreme religious intolerance, most obviously anti-Semitism. Most believers in Islam condemn such terrorism, but there is a larger problem that makes such fundamentalism possible. In terms of democratic values, the political culture of most Islamic nations is problematic on two scores: its lack of separation of church and state and its sexism.[16] These are interdependent problems, as it is the elaboration of the argument for toleration underlying separation of church and state that makes possible the protest of forms of structural injustice, including sexism. Any religion can be corrupted to unjust ends when used by political leaders to entrench and legitimate their own power. Islam is only the most notable contemporary example of a phenomenon that has, at earlier historical points, afflicted other religions, notably, the various forms of Christianity before constitutional developments within dominantly Christian nations called for a separation of church and state. It would be a great mistake to suppose that these nations are still not afflicted by sectarian religious, ethnic, and gender intolerance or to overlook the fact that such intolerance sometimes drives ethnocentric forms of imperialism. And there is no reason to think that believers in Islam cannot reasonably free themselves of the corrupt politicians who afflict them. One place to start would be by taking seriously the feminist voices of Islamic women.[17]

Conversely, we can see what motivated the violence of Islamic fundamentalism in one of its founding martyrs, Sayyid Qutb, who warred both on the separation of church and state and on the sexual freedom of women. Qutb had turned his back on marriage in Egypt because "he had been unable to find a suitable bride from the 'dishonorable' women who allowed themselves to be seen in public." If the problem in Egypt was that women were not traditionally patriarchal enough, what threatened Qutb in his 1948 visit to the United States was, above all, the freer sexuality of American women and, more generally, an American sexual permissiveness that he took to be established by the Kinsey Report, including the reported high incidence of homosexual relations among American men.[18] Qutb advocated Islamic fundamentalism as a response to the freer sexual lives of women in Egypt and the United States, and out of this swamp emerged the ideology and terror of Al-Qaeda.

When Ian Buruma writes about the murder of the Dutch movie maker Theo van Gogh by an Islamic fundamentalist, Mohammed Bouyeri, a Dutch citizen and son of Moroccan immigrants, he traces the violence to patriarchal rage at the freer sexuality of Moroccan women immigrants, including Bouyeri's own sister,[19] as well as to the resisting voice of the Dutch politician Ayaan Hirsi Ali, who with van Gogh made a movie objecting to the way Islam treated women. Ali had come fundamentally to question her own Islamic heritage as a Somali immigrant to Holland and as a woman. "What," Buruma asks, "turned Mohammed into a character from Conrad [or Dostoevski]?"[20] To a patriarchal man like Bouyeri, nothing was more incendiary that the voice of the women from his tradition who questioned its patriarchal Love Laws. Such violence is as ancient as Rome and as contemporary as van Gogh's murder. Our argument, while rooted in history, could not be more urgently contemporary.

We agree with Elisabeth Young-Bruehl that aspects of Hannah Arendt's analysis of totalitarianism illuminate our contemporary situation in which violence is directed at the very exercise of voice that Arendt regarded as central to democratic politics.[21] What Arendt painfully learned from her analysis of the roots of totalitarianism in a German high culture she loved was that it expressed strands of a nihilist romanticism that, having no ethical core, could be enlisted in support of genocidal murder. Such political romanticism, a kind of narcissistic idealism,[22] is made psychologically possible by the crushing of human faculties that are at the heart of democratic politics. What distinguishes such politics is the priority accorded to the constitutional protection of free and equal voice, a voice preserved from any threat of violence or intimidation, as the necessary condition for resolving political disagreements through dialogue and debate and by means of elections shaped by such debate.

It is a profound misunderstanding of the role of free conscience and speech in constitutional democracies to limit the scope of constitutional protection only to convictions that offend no one. This effectively censors convictions worthy of reasonable discussion and debate among free people, including religious convictions. Such censorship, now quite widespread even in constitutional democracies in Europe including Britain, compromises the value of free and equal voice that legitimates democracy and cannot be justified on the ground that it lessens the popularity of anti-Semitism, racism, sexism, and homophobia when it immunizes them from the reasonable challenge they deserve.[23]

What made totalitarianism so distinctive in the modern period was its techniques of terror and a violence directed at quashing democratic voice, making possible not only Hitler's Germany and Stalin's Russia, but also Mao's China and Pol Pot's Cambodia. This problem is still very much with us as forms of terror now mobilize networks of fundamentalists operating largely outside the state system. The root of the problem is the degree to which patriarchal patterns persist not only abroad but also at home, where they are expressed in violence directed at women and men only recently emancipated by the resistance movements we have discussed. We need more than ever to understand why free and equal sexual voice is so incendiary, sparking forms of violence, including terror, that seek, as Arendt clearly saw, to crush human faculties. We cannot be the democrats we believe we are until the persistence of patriarchy becomes a focus of resistance.

Specifically, our analysis of the tension between patriarchy and democracy in American law and politics is all too explanatory of how we have come to respond to the challenge of the war on terror. As Stephen Holmes explains in *The Matador Cape: America's Reckless Response to Terror*, the conduct of this war has been deeply unreasonable, revealing the depths of the American psychological problem. Holmes cites Robert Kagan, a leading conservative defender of the war on terror and the invasion of Iraq, who characterized the American as opposed to the European attitude to the invasion as a contrast between "masculine Americans and effeminate Europeans."[24] The fact that America was humiliated by 9/11 required and justified a level of military violence that rendered any opposition "effeminate" or treasonous. The degree to which a patriarchal psychology still shapes our uses of military force explains both our mistakes and the ways in which we rationalize such mistakes. In Kagan's starkly gendered terms, *"Americans are from Mars and Europeans are from Venus."*[25]

The terroristic violence against us thus challenges our manhood, a manhood now self-consciously in transition between patriarchal and democratic values. Yet our response has been inconsistent with these values, ignoring traditions of nonviolent dissent that we honor. In *War Talk*, Arundhati Roy observes:

> Any government's condemnation of terrorism is only credible if it shows itself to be responsive to persistent, reasonable, closely argued, nonviolent dissent. And yet, what's happening is just the opposite. The world over, nonviolent resistance movements are being crushed and broken. If we do not respect and honor them, by default we privilege those who turn to violent means.[26]

We need then to remind ourselves of the traditions Roy worries we have forgotten. The American Civil Rights movement of the 1960s achieved success at a cost in human life that was small compared with "a single day of battle in the Civil War or World War II."[27] She points acidly to the rise of religious fascism in Gandhi's democratic India, as politicians manipulatively encourage and fail to punish pogroms that use political violence to sustain religious and ethnic intolerance.[28] But she also finds in democratic America a comparable betrayal of the politics of Martin Luther King in its response to terrorism, both the war in Afghanistan and in Iraq.

The Roman example – a republic that collapses under the impact of its imperial successes into an autocracy – may well worry us. Our response to the terroristic threat has fostered an acquiescence in the increasingly imperial presidency of George W. Bush in much the same way that supposed external threats made it easier for Romans to abandon their republican institutions.[29] When Augustus rationalized the autocracy he appealed to patriarchy, not republican institutions, as what made Rome great. In the United States following 9/11, we have witnessed a similar appeal to patriarchal ("family") values as the grounds for justifying an analogous concentration of power.

Finally, why is so much of the world still violently aggressive against the State of Israel? We certainly do not defend everything Israel has done, but we agree with Alan Dershowitz that much that is said against Israel ignores the fact that the Jews have forged one of the very few working constitutional democracies in the Middle East.[30] How, at the beginning of the 21st century, is anti-Semitism psychologically, let alone ethically, thinkable? How can President Mahmoud Ahmadinejad of Iran appeal to political anti-Semitism to advance the aims of Iran?[31]

Anti-Semitism has been so central to our analysis because it arose when Augustine read into Christianity the patriarchal conceptions that he had absorbed as a late Roman man. He repudiated sexuality entirely, a traumatic loss that expressed itself in his idealization of ascetic women like his mother and his denigration of sexual women as well as the Jews, carnal Israel. Many Christians have now repudiated Augustine's views,[32] and even the contemporary Catholic Church has tried to distance itself from its past anti-Semitism.[33] But the conception of patriarchal manhood, transmitted through Roman patriarchy and Augustinian Christianity to the modern world, continues to structure the sense of manhood not only in the Christian West but also in the Islamic world where Islam builds upon the Christian tradition. Fundamentalist Islamic states are particularly affronted by the life and politics of a democratic, liberal Israel, which stands as a rebuke to their own lack of democracy and respect for civil liberties.

That Israel should have survived at all against the violence directed against it may be as much a humiliation to patriarchal manhood as Germany's defeat in World War I. In fact, the humiliation of Jewish manhood in World War II may have contributed to the readiness of the State of Israel to respond with violence to any perceived threat. Yet the longstanding and continuing tradition of Jewish resistance accords the Jews a starring role in the understanding of ethically based resistance movements in human history.[34] It is a mark of how powerful patriarchal ideas and institutions still are that such resistance should still be so necessary, so just, and so important to democratic peoples everywhere.

## 3. SEXUAL VOICE AND THE INTERPRETATION OF THE 1960S

The resistance movements of the 1960s transformed American constitutional law by protesting institutions and practices inconsistent with democratic principles and values. Woven through these movements was a freeing of sexual voice from the patriarchal Love Laws. Thus the Winter Soldiers' movement was joined by the Summer of Love. How do we remember the 1960s? What troubles us is the extent to which it has come to be seen as an era of "sex, drugs, and rock 'n' roll," evoking scenes of sexual license and sordid, drug-infested Bacchanalian festivals where the music was deafening and naïve youth sought to "make love, not war." Through this haze, it becomes difficult to recall the remarkable accomplishments and hopes of the time.

In *Boom! Voices of the Sixties*, Tom Brokaw sets out to record this historical period. Yet while he heralds the achievements of the Civil Rights and feminist movements, his study centers on Vietnam and its ambivalent legacy. He observes that the generation of the 1960s were the children of "the greatest American generation," but in focusing on the dishonor of Vietnam, he doesn't consider that the ethical struggles of the '60s generation may reflect lessons they learned about war and manhood and the costs of combat, if not directly from then by observing their parents.

With the end of World War II, Rosie the Riveter became the suburban housewife of the 1950s, suffering from what Betty Friedan called "the problem without a name." In a time when patriarchy was tied to patriotism, to name it as a problem was tantamount to treason. Not so for the children who came of age in the '60s, the time, Brokaw notes, when everything changed. The experience of sudden, radical transformation captured by his title "*Boom!*" reflects the hand on the master-switch, patriarchy. Emboldened by the success of their parents' generation in taking on fascism, the generation of the 1960s took on patriarchy by questioning the legitimacy of its authority. And as with Martin Luther King when he moved from contesting segregation to opposing war, the response was swift and unequivocal: The nonviolent man was struck down by violence, and the make-love-not-war generation was deemed too sexual.

The distortions in recalling the 1960s are singularly instructive from our perspective in that the questioning of the Love Laws has come to the fore. Not the stopping of war or of atmospheric testing, or the moves to end poverty and segregation, or the claims to equal rights under the law, but the separation of sex from procreation, the legalizing of abortion, and the acceptance of sex outside of marriage and marriage outside heterosexuality. A resistance to patriarchy that is historically unprecedented, given the scale and broad front of interconnected movements opposing anti-Semitism, racist and sexist intolerance, and homophobia, has yet to be fully honored and understood – in part because a reactionary move to downgrade these achievements and reinstate patriarchy has succeeded in naming the '60s a time of sex, drugs, and rock 'n' roll.[35]

Brokaw brings too many patriarchal assumptions to his telling of this history to even raise these questions. Yet among the many voices he brings forward, two say what he cannot bring himself to say: Jacqueline Kennedy reportedly observed that, "The problem with Vietnam is that we had three consecutive presidents who all believed their manhood had to be proven in the terrible excesses of military power"[36] and former President William Clinton identified the problem of Vietnam as "much more the result of culture and psychology than it was of economics."[37] The ubiquitous peace symbols, the strollers with banners proclaiming "another mother for peace," the mass demonstrations and the exodus of young men to Canada attest to the groundswell of opposition to the culture and psychology of militarism. The hypocrisy of patriotism, the lies and distortions of democratic values, was matched by the hypocrisy of Puritanism, and the call for peace was joined by a call to free love from deceptions and double standards. Such were the culture wars of that time.

Brokaw records his deep ambivalence about the sexual emancipation of the '60s, which he links with the abuse of drugs. The subsequent "war on drugs"[38] in its embrace of toughness reflects the same excesses and misguided strategy, the same psychology and culture of manhood that led to the quagmire of Vietnam. Patriarchy was resurgent, and Brokaw, in celebrating his marriage, laments the erosion of the nuclear family. It is notable that not one gay or lesbian voice is heard in his book, and the only gay person mentioned is Mary Cheney, who as the vice president's daughter has patriarchal sanction.[39]

Tom Stoppard's play *Rock 'n' Roll* takes us into the third term of '60s dismissal in a way that illuminates the contribution of artists in piercing the defenses that would keep us from seeing or saying what we know. Stoppard writes not of America but of events in his native Czechoslovakia, notably resistance to communist political repression that was epitomized, in the view of the resistance leader Vaclav Havel, by a Czech band, the Plastic People of the Universe, inspired by American rock 'n' roll. What struck Havel about the Plastic People was that "truth was on their side . . . in their music was an experience of metaphysical sorrow and a longing for salvation."[40] The savage repression, including imprisonment of the Plastic People, by the communist regime crystallized for Havel the grounds for resistance.

Jan, the play's hero (modeled on Havel), explains that it was the emotional force of the repression and the fear that incited it, that made the state's attack on the Plastic People so important. It was not that the Plastic had insulted a secret policeman. Rather,

> " . . . the policemen insulted *him*. About his hair. Jirous doesn't cut his hair. It makes the policeman angry, so he starts something and it ends with Jirous in jail. But what is the policeman angry about? The policeman is angry about his fear. The policeman's fear is what makes him angry. He's frightened by indifference. Jirous doesn't *care*. He doesn't care enough even to cut his hair."[41]

Hair length is, of course, highly gendered, and the state's response is a form of patriarchal rage. In Stoppard's play, the rigid communism of the Czech authorities, as well as of Max, the Cambridge academic who was once Jan's teacher, is expressed in ideological terms. In the most dramatic scene, Max's dying wife Eleanor attacks Max's materialism as a mode of dissociation that keeps him from feeling his love and his grief at her imminent death. And it is Max who dismisses the liberation of the

'60s as "sex, drugs, and rock 'n' roll": "It was like opening the wrong door in a highly specialized brothel" (p. 96).

Max's new love Lenka, an intelligent and sexual woman like Eleanor, repudiates Max's view: "Don't try to put me on your side, Max. 'Make love, not war' was more important than 'Workers of the world unite'" (p. 99). The end of the play finds Jan in a loving, sexual relationship with Esme, the daughter of Eleanor and Max, who has sought his attentions throughout her young life.

Brokaw discusses at some length the music of the 1960s, but he makes little or no sense of how and why the music was connected to the resistance. Yet music, whether the tragic operas of Giuseppe Verdi or contemporary rock 'n' roll, gives expression to emotions that cannot otherwise be spoken.[42] In doing so, it works under the radar of patriarchy, as Jan observes in the play: "[T]he Plastics [are] unbribable. They're coming from somewhere else, from where the Muses come. They're not heretics. They're pagans" (p. 36). The appeal of the Plastics is not a rejection of orthodoxy but rather a celebration of nature, a freeing of sexuality, a choice of love over violence, and Stoppard sees in American rock 'n' roll precisely this appeal. Much of rock 'n' roll gives expression to our sexual rhythms, the beat of erotic desire and response. Eleanor, Max's resisting wife, makes this point about sexual love early in the play in discussing the meaning of Sappho's poetry:

> "So, *a-machanon* – *un*-machine, *non*-machine. Eros is *amachanon*, he's spirit as opposed to machinery, Sappho is making the distinction. He's not naughty, he's – what? Uncontrollable. Uncageable." (p. 9)

At the dramatic high point of the play, Eleanor tells the dissociated Max,

> "I don't want your 'mind' which you can make out of beer cans [Max's way of putting his materialism about mind]. Don't bring it to the funeral. I want your grieving soul or nothing. I do not want your amazing biological machine – I want what you love me with." (p. 51)

Stoppard's play captures how through music we can retrieve the losses and uncover the lies that patriarchy imposes. "We have," Jan argues, "to begin again with the ordinary meaning of words. Giving new meanings to words is how systems lie to themselves, beginning with the word for themselves – socialism, democracy" (p. 101). Rock 'n' roll exposed to Jan, as to Havel, a truth that was covered over, denied, repressed, indeed lied about. And it is linked in the play to a release from violence, as Eleanor rejects Max's communist slogan for the '60s' motto "make love, not war."

The play reminds us that we are as if in the hold of a patriarchally induced repetition compulsion. We are once again unjustly at war abroad, ostensibly against Islamic fundamentalism, and paradoxically once again at home too much in thrall to a fundamentalism at war with the resistance movements of the '60s. Seen through the prism of gender, these reactions reveal the continuing power of Roman patriarchy over our public and private lives. Those who have engineered the mistakes of the American Empire abroad have, like Augustus, rationalized their betrayal of democratic values by defending at home a return to the patriarchal family.

There is no clearer example of this problem than the war of American Christian fundamentalists, supported and fomented by politicians, on constitutionally recognized rights. The freeing of women's moral voices includes their right (rather than their father's or husband's or judge's) to decide whether to bear a child. In the view of fundamentalists, the right of gays and lesbians to love becomes inflammatory, lawless passions that defy patriarchal control. Such loss of control, as Stoppard's play dramatizes, arouses fear and then the anger that leads to violence. Thus, abortion and gay marriage in their challenge to the Love Laws become lightning-rod issues in American politics.

When the Supreme Court in *Lawrence v. Texas*,[43] overruling *Bowers v. Hardwick*,[44] struck down statutes criminalizing sodomy, it recognized a right accepted constitutionally in the many nations subject to the European Court of Human Rights.[45] An elaboration of this basic right was then extended by the Supreme Judicial Court of Massachusetts under its state constitution to protect the right to marriage of homosexuals and heterosexuals in accordance with the principle of equality underlying *Lawrence v. Texas*.[46]

American religious fundamentalists, already enraged by judicial recognition of a constitutional right to reproductive autonomy, warred on same-sex marriage, going so far as to enlist President Bush in support of a constitutional amendment that would ban it. There is no reason to believe that the availability of marriage to gays and lesbians any more harms marriage than its availability to couples of different ethnicities or religions. What strikes us as indicative of the continuing power of patriarchal norms and values is not only the ferocity of the fundamentalist reaction but the support it has enjoyed mainly from Republicans, but also from Democrats. As in our analysis of the roots of fascism, when a political movement is so empty of ideas but appeals nonetheless, we must turn for an explanation to psychology.

A still-powerful American patriarchy thus explains both the attacks of the American empire abroad and the defense of the patriarchal family at home. The political dynamic is that of another wily, shrewd,

opportunistic, religiously moralistic politician, who, like Augustus, rationalizes the end of the republic. We are hopefully not even close to witnessing this end, but we are compromising and betraying our democratic constitutionalism when our politics rests on a psychology that dims
the lights of our ideals and intelligence, creating the darkness we see as
deepening.

There is no example of this problem that is more important, or more
threatening to our constitutional democracy, than the politics of judicial
appointments, including appointments to the Supreme Court. We have
argued that the fundamentalist approach to constitutional interpretation
(originalism) is an indefensible view. Closely examined for its inconsis-
tencies, it can be seen for what it is: an attempt to reverse the advances
of the 1960s and to realign American constitutional law with patriarchy.
What originalism does is to remove from constitutional interpretation
any sense of the tension between historical injustices and the democratic
values of constitutional law.

Chief Justice Roger Taney in *Dred Scott v. Sanford* led a majority of
the Supreme Court on such originalist grounds, not only to entrench slavery both in the states and territories but to exclude people of color from
the protections of the United States Constitution.[47] Better lawyers than
Taney, notably Abraham Lincoln, condemned his originalism because it
indulged America's most debased impulses, its racism, at the expense of
the text and history that appealed to universal human rights as a powerful constitutional counterweight to such impulses. The condemnation by
Lincoln and others of Taney's originalism, as betraying democratic constitutionalism, precipitated the constitutional crisis that led to the Civil
War.[48]

Our contemporary experience with the revival of originalism is not
dissimilar. Even its leading advocates do not consistently apply it, for
such consistency would undermine the legitimacy of cases – like those
repudiating state-imposed racial segregation – that such advocates are
now eager to endorse. We are thus left with a deeply unreasonable interpretive attitude that is only aggressively applied to those developments in
constitutional interpretation that question traditional patriarchal views
of sexuality and gender, thus perhaps inadvertently revealing the root of
the problem. Lincoln's criticism of Stephen Douglas for indulging racism
applies to politicians who indulge sexism and homophobia today: "[H]e
is blowing out the moral lights around us . . . he is, in my judgment, penetrating the human soul and eradicating the light of reason and the love
of liberty in this American people."[49]

Nonetheless, politicians, including presidents and presidential can-
didates from the party of Lincoln, continue to align themselves with

appointments of originalist judges in order to draw support from the religious fundamentalists and the political constituencies they mobilize. Given the age of current Supreme Court justices and the threat of such appointments to reverse advances in American constitutional interpretation, the Court, and with it the country, are now at a tipping point. The stakes could not be higher.

"What is it you would see"? we asked in the Introduction. With our return to war and the appeal to "family values," the elephant in the room, so to speak, is patriarchy. When violence is acceptable and pleasure is demonized, when newspapers print photographs of dead bodies and ruined houses while censoring bare breasts and the word "fucking," when Love Laws are enforced with righteousness and fervor while torture is condoned and Geneva conventions violated, the shadow of patriarchy is unmistakable. Like the Angel in the House, it falls between us and our creativity, our democracy, our humanity.

# Conclusion

Toward the end of *Macbeth*, when Macduff learns that his wife and children have been slain, Malcolm enjoins him to "give sorrow words," explaining that "The grief that does not speak/ Whispers the o'erfraught heart and bids it break." Malcolm, the son of the king whom Macbeth murdered, has experienced such grief himself. As this extraordinary conversation continues, he urges Macduff to make "med'cines of our great revenge/ To cure this deadly grief" and "Dispute it like a man." At which point, Macduff replies, "I shall do so,/ But I must also feel it as a man" (IV, iii).[1]

In this most terrifying of Shakespeare's tragedies where "man" and "blood" are repeated words, the psychology of patriarchy is laid bare. Macbeth's "vaulting ambition" to be king is spurred by his wife's taunts to his manhood: "Art thou afeared," she asks him, "wouldst thou . . . live a coward?" And when Macbeth responds, "I dare do all that may become a man./ Who dares do more is none," she ups the ante, telling him, "When you durst do it, then you were a man;/ And to be more than what you were, you would/ Be so much more the man" (I, vii).

From the beginning, two constructions of manhood thus vie with each other in Shakespeare's tragedy: one that admits "the milk of human kindness" and one that rejects it as unmanly. "Bring forth men children only," Macbeth tells his wife, "for thy undaunted mettle should compose/ Nothing but males." Yet nature, a third player along with time, links the untrammeled ambition of the Macbeths with illness, meaning with evil. "Thou wouldst be great," Lady Macbeth tells her husband, "but without/ The illness should attend it." As Macbeth would kill the king, so Lady Macbeth would kill "the babe that milks me" in a similar show of "manly readiness." Like the horses that have turned unnatural ("'Tis said they eat each other"), this manhood "makes war with mankind."

The corruption of manhood has been our theme. Beginning with Aeneas, whose "divinely ordained duty" turns him from pious to savage,

264

we have observed a systematic distortion of men's and women's nature in the service of maintaining a patriarchal order. But we have also observed a resistance to that order grounded, as Shakespeare suggests, in our human nature, in a grief that does not "convert to anger" and a heart not "blunt(ed)" by rage. In rendering a darkness visible, we have sought to give sorrow words. "What's done cannot be undone," as Lady Macbeth observes. The history we have traced stands behind us as a lesson from which we can learn both the sources of human violence and the roots of human goodness.[2] Lennox, one of the lords in *Macbeth*, notes that there are "many unrough youths that even now/ Protest their first of manhood," and this tension between voice and violence becomes explicit when Macduff prepares to exact his revenge on Macbeth: "I have no words;/ My voice is in my sword" (V, viii).

This tension lies at the heart of the struggle between democracy and patriarchy, one relying on voice, the other on violence. In plumbing the wellsprings of voice, we have been led repeatedly to our desire for love and to the foundations of deliberative democracy. The toxin of shame injected by patriarchy infects the hearts of men and women alike, dividing us from those parts of ourselves that would resist its gendered hierarchy. And the link between shame and violence that extends from Homer's *Iliad* to James Gilligan's analysis of our current epidemic has been forged on the anvil of patriarchy, bending manhood into a shape where the human capacity to feel love and sorrow is undermined by what is celebrated as "manly readiness."

What has surprised us most, taking us back to what seems a lost insight of psychoanalysis, is the central role sexuality plays in this drama. As we have noted, it was in the late Roman empire that for the first time a model of equality and reciprocity in sexual relations developed, against which Christianity marked a major break in its demonizing of pleasure per se. Constraints, fears, anger, and dominance need ideological support and justification when they are challenged. These ideologies are by definition reactionary because they react to a change. Such was the case with racism. Such is the case today with fundamentalism, be it Islamic, Hindu, Jewish, or Christian. We have suggested that rather than warring ideologies, we struggle today with a single ideology that wars on our human nature, and because sexuality is part of our nature, it plays a part in this struggle.

Pleasure is written on the body. And since, as Damasio has shown, body and emotion are involved in the making of consciousness, the demonizing of pleasure requires a split in consciousness, a split deepened and enforced by the Love Laws of patriarchy. But to continue with Damasio's argument that we register our experience – the music or "feeling of what happens" – in our bodies and in our emotions, this core consciousness or core sense of self must be silenced in order to still our awareness of desire or pleasure. The danger here lies in the realization that in dissociating ourselves from pleasure, we lose the voice of experience that can counter unjust or false authority. Thus, our capacity to function as citizens in a democratic society becomes compromised, opening the way to various forms of tyranny.

As we have found the roots of intolerance – whether racist, sexist, or homophobic – in the traumatic rupture of intimate relationships that marks the initiation into patriarchy, so the splits between mind and body, thought and emotion, self and relationships signal a dissociation that keeps us from knowing what we otherwise would know. It impedes the voice of experience, grounded in the body and in emotion and fostered by relationships, that would speak to the voices of authority, thus posing a threat to democracy in much the same ways that totalitarianism targets the functions of the human mind. We see children, boys around five and girls at adolescence, resisting an initiation that would confuse their ability to read the human world and impede them from saying what they feel and think and know. In recent advances in the human sciences, most notably in developmental psychology and neurobiology, we see evidence of a paradigm shift, reframing what once was seen as a resistance to development as a resistance to losing the grounds of our ethical and emotional intelligence.

In contrast to patriarchal manhood, democratic manhood protects the exercise of free and equal voice from violence and intimidation and gives expression to a sense of honor and even heroism more like Leopold Bloom's than Ulysses's. When Jesus questioned the violence of patriarchal manhood, he espoused the deeper values of democracy in religion. It was Augustine who read patriarchy into this tradition, a tradition that T. S. Eliot understood only too well when he cited Vergil's Aeneas as the model in the Christian tradition for Jesus – the heroic, suffering Roman soldier becoming the heroic, suffering son of God.[3]

The dark story of Roman patriarchy and its enduring legacy do not lead us to despair. We recall how resistance arose in the very heart of this darkness, in the protest of Roman women against the indignities heaped on their search for loving relationship. We have listened to Apuleius telling us in the story of Cupid and Psyche how such resistance leads to the birth of pleasure. There were alternatives to the road that Christianity took under the impact of Augustine, alternatives probably much closer to the historical Jesus, very much a Jew, more like Bloom than Augustine. We want to open yet again this awareness of alternatives to patriarchal fragmentation and dissociation. And in this spirit, we return to where we began: between Semitic Carthage, where a queen opened her heart and rule to a man on equal terms, and patriarchal Rome, where the repudiation of the love of equals was honored as manly.

We end with a question: Why is the love of equals unmanly?

# Notes

## 1. Why Rome? Why Now?

1. Jean Baker Miller, *Toward a New Psychology of Women*, second edition (Boston: Beacon Press, 1986), p. 1.
2. David Ferry, *Gilgamesh: A New Rendering in English Verse* (New York: Farrar, Straus and Giroux, 1993), pp. 4, 5, 15, 16.
3. Ferry, pp. 10, 26.

## 2. Roman Patriarchy and Violence

1. For an illuminating overview and summary of this literature, see F. W. Walbank, A. E. Astin, M.W. Frederiksen, R. M. Ogilvie, *The Cambridge Ancient History, Second Edition, Volume VII, The Rise of Rome to 220 B.C.E.* (Cambridge: Cambridge University Press, 1989); A. E. Astin, F. W. Walbank, M. W. Frederiksen, R. M. Ogilvie, *The Cambridge Ancient History, Second Edition, Volume VIII, Rome and the Mediterranean to 133 B.C.E.* (Cambridge: Cambridge University Press, 1989); J. A. Crook, Andrew Lintott, Elizabeth Rawson, *The Cambridge Ancient History, Second Edition, Volume IX, The Last Age of the Roman Republic, 146–43 B.C.E.* (Cambridge: Cambridge University Press, 1994); Alan K. Bowman, Edward Champlin, Andrew Lintott, *The Cambridge Ancient History, Second Edition, Volume X, The Augustan Empire, 43 B.C.E.–A.D. 69* (Cambridge: Cambridge University Press, 1996); Alan K. Bowman, Peter Garnsey, Dominic Rathbone, *The Cambridge Ancient History, Volume XI, The High Empire, A.D. 70–192* (Cambridge: Cambridge University Press, 2000); Alan K. Bowman, Peter Garnsey, Averil Cameron, *The Cambridge Ancient History, Second Edition, Volume XII, The Crisis of Empire, A.D. 193–337* (Cambridge: Cambridge University Press, 2005); Averil Cameron, Peter Garnsey, *The Cambridge Ancient History, Volume XIII, The Late Empire, A.D. 337–425* (Cambridge: Cambridge University Press, 1998)
2. See Edward Gibbon, *The Decline and Fall of the Roman Empire*, volumes I, II, and IIII (New York: The Modern Library, n.d.) (originally published in six volumes between 1776 and 1788).
3. See, for example, Judith P. Hallett, *Fathers and Daughters in Roman Society: Women and the Elite Family* (Princeton: Princeton University Press, 1984); Susan Treggiari, *Roman Marriage* (Oxford: Clarendon Press, 1991); Richard P. Saller, *Patriarchy, Property and Death in the Roman Family* (Cambridge: Cambridge University Press, 1994); Suzanne Dixon, *The Roman Mother* (Norman: Oklahoma University Press, 1988); Suzanne Dixon, *The Roman Family* (Baltimore: The Johns Hopkins University Press, 1992); Beryl Rawson, ed., *Marriage, Divorce, and Children in Ancient Rome* (Oxford: Clarendon Press, 2004); Suzanne Dixon, *Reading Roman Women* (London: Duckworth, 2001); Jane F. Gardner, *Women in Roman Law and Society* (Bloomington: Indiana University Press,

1995); Sarah B. Pomeroy, *Goddesses, Whores, Wives, and Slaves: Women in Classical Antiquity* (New York: Schocken Books, 1995); Eva Cantarella, *Pandora's Daughters: The Role and Status of Women in Greek and Roman Antiquity*, translated by Maureen B. Fant, (Baltimore: The Johns Hopkins University Press, 1987); Rebecca Langlands, *Sexual Morality in Ancient Rome* (Cambridge: Cambridge University Press, 2006); Richard A. Bauman, *Women and Politics in Ancient Rome* (London: Routledge, 1992); John K. Evans, *War, Women and Children in Ancient Rome* (London: Routledge, 1991); and Miles McDonnell, *Roman Manliness: Virtues and the Roman Republic* (Cambridge: Cambridge University Press, 2006).

4. See Judith P. Hallett, *Fathers and Daughters in Roman Society;* John K. Evans, *War, Women, and Children in Ancient Rome.*

5. Carol Gilligan, *The Birth of Pleasure* (Alfred A. Knopf: New York, 2002), pp. 4–5.

6. See Polybius, *The Rise of the Roman Empire*, translated by Ian Scott-Kilvert (London: Penguin, 1979), at p. 349.

7. See Niccolo Machiavelli, *The Discourses*, in Niccolo Machiavelli, *The Prince and Discourses* (New York: The Modern Library, 1950), pp. 101–540, at pp. 145–58.

8. See Christian Meier, *Caesar: A Biography*, translated by David McLintock (New York: Basic Books, 1982), at pp. 160–2, 164, 169. See also Adrian Goldsworthy, *Caesar: Life of a Colossus* (New Haven, Conn.: Yale University Press, 2006).

9. See, on this point, Andrew Lintott, *The Constitution of the Roman Republic* (Oxford: Oxford University Press, 2004), pp. 65–88.

10. See, on this point, Mary Beard, "Priesthood in the Roman Republic," in Mary Beard and John North, eds., *Pagan Priests: Religion and Power in the Ancient World* (Ithaca, N.Y.: Cornell University Press, 1990), at pp. 19–48.

11. See R. E. A. Palmer, *The Archaic Community of the Romans* (Cambridge: Cambridge University Press, 1970, pp. 220 ff.

12. See, on this point, R. M. Ogilvie, *A Commentary on Livy Books 1–5* (Oxford: Oxford at the Clarendon Press, 1965), at pp. 234, 283–9, 302, 307–9, 314–21, 353–66, 390–411, 521–5, 567–74, 584–9, 597–606, 620–32.

13. F. W. Walbank, et al., *The Cambridge Ancient History, Volume VII, The Rise of Rome to 220 B.C.E.*, at p. 383.

14. See F. W. Walbank, et al., *id.*, p. 384.

15. For a powerful questioning of the Roman view, shared by some historians, see William V. Harris, *War and Imperialism in Republic Rome 327–70 B.C.E.* (Oxford: Clarendon Press, 1985).

16. See, on this point, Adrian Goldsworthy, *Caesar: Life of a Colossus* (New Haven; Yale University Press, 2006), *circa* and at p. 303.

17. See, in general, Anthony Everitt, *Cicero: The Life and Times of Rome's Greatest Politician* (New York: Random House, 2003). On Cicero's limited role in Roman politics, see Anthony Everitt, *Augustus: The Life of Rome's First Emperor* (New York: Random House, 2006), p. 67.

18. See Andrew Lintott, *Violence in Republican Rome* (Oxford: Oxford University Press, 1999).

19. Emiel Eyben, "Fathers and Sons," in Beryl Rawson, ed., *Marriage, Divorce, and Children in Ancient Rome*, pp. 114–143, at p. 115. Eyben notes that these powers were significantly limited by the time of the Empire.

20. Josephus, *The Jewish Wars Books III–IV*, translated by H. St. J. Thackeray (Cambridge, Mass.: Harvard University Press, 1997), p. 27.

21. See, for example, Bessel A. van der Kolk Alexander C. McFarlane, and Lars Weisaeth, editors., *Traumatic Stress: The Effects of Overwhelming Experience on Mind, Body, and Society* (New York: The Guilford Press, 1996); Judith Herman, *Trauma and Recovery.* (New York: Basic Books, 1997).

22. See J. Laplanche and J.-B. Pontalis, *The Language of Psycho-Analysis*, translated by Donald Nicholson-Smith (New York: W. W. Norton, 1973), at pp. 208–9.

23. Sandor Ferenczi, "The Confusion of Tongues between Adult and Child," English translation in *International Journal of Psychoanalysis* 30 (1949), 225, German original in *Int. Z. F. Psa.* 19 (1933), 5. Paper read at the Twelfth International Psycho-Analytical Congress, Wiesbaden, September, 1932.

24. See, for a good general treatment, Susan Treggiari, *Roman Marriage: Iusti Coniuges from the Time of Cicero to the Time of Ulpian* (Oxford: Oxford University Press, 2002). See also Richard P. Saller, *Patriarchy, Property and Death in the Roman Family* (Cambridge: Cambridge University Press, 1994).

25. Polybius, *The Rise of the Roman Empire*, at p. 348.

26. Polybius, *The Rise of the Roman Empire*, at pp. 346–7.

27. See, in general, Judith P. Hallett, *Fathers and Daughters in Roman Society*.

28. See, on this point, Adrian Goldsworthy, *Caesar: Life of a Colossus* (New Haven: Yale University Press, 2006), at p. 294.

29. See, on this point, Judith P. Hallett, *Fathers and Daughters in Roman Society*, at pp. 69, 211–48, 235 ff.

30. Suetonius, *The Twelve Caesars*, at pp. 112–13.

31. See, for fuller discussion, Anthony A. Barrett, *Livia: First Lady of Imperial Rome* (New Haven: Yale University Press, 2002); Susan E. Wood, *Imperial Women: A Study in Public Images 40 B.C.E.–AD 69* (Leiden: Brill, n.d.).

32. Herod's wife, Mariamne (as told in Josephus), is a good contrast. Herod killed her brother and grandfather, but loves her, so he gives her too much license, and she insults and betrays him, leading to her own execution – a patriarchal horror story. See Josephus, *The Jewish War Books I–II*, translated by H. St. J. Thackeray (Cambridge, Mass.: Harvard University Press, 1997), at pp. 205–211.

33. Livy, *The Early History of Rome* Aubrey De Selincourt trans. (London: Penguin, 2002), at p. 101, p. 102.

34. *Ibid.*, pp. 246–66.

35. On the long history of the role of Lucretia in patriarchal fantasy (including Renaissance story that she kills herself because of shame because she enjoyed the rape), see Ian Donaldson, *The Rapes of Lucretia: A Myth and its Transformations* (Oxford: Clarendon Press, 1982).

36. On Julius Caesar's relationship to this mother, see Adrian Goldsworthy, *Caesar*, at pp. 33, 35, 36, 49–50, 52, 59, 87, 100, 125–6, 146, 148, 293–4; on Octavian's relationship, see Anthony Everitt, *Augustus: The Life of Rome's First Emperor* (New York: Random House, 2006), at pp. 32, 45.

37. Tacitus, *A Dialogue on Oratory*, in Tacitus, *Agricola, Germania, Dialogus*, translated by W. Peterson (Cambridge, Mass.: Harvard University Press, 1970), pp. 231–347, at p. 307.

38. See, Suzanne Dixon, *The Roman Mother*, at pp. 146–9.

39. Agrippina was exiled by Caligula, her brother, to the Pontian isles, during which time Nero was brought up by his aunt Domitia. See Anthony A. Barrett, *Agrippina: Sex, Power and Politics in the Early Empire* (New Haven: Yale University Press, 1996), pp. 69–70.

40. Suzanne Dixon, *The Roman Mother*, at p. 145.

41. Livy, *The Early History of Rome*, at pp. 156–7.

42. Tacitus, *The Annals of Imperial Rome*, p. 34.

43. See, on this point, Tacitus, *The Annals of Imperial Rome*, at p. 41.

44. See, in general, Anthony A. Barrett, *Agrippina*; Edward Champlin, *Nero* (Cambridge: Mass.: Belknap Press of Harvard University Press, 2003).

45. On the forms and extent of Roman violence, see Keith Hopkins, *Conquerors and Slaves* (Cambridge: Cambridge University Press, 1978); Keith Hopkins, *Death and Renewal* (Cambridge: Cambridge University Press, 1983). On the competitive codes of Roman honor, see J. E. Lendon, *Empire of Honour* (Oxford: Oxford University Press, 2005); Carlin A. Barton, *Rome Honor: The Fire in the Bones* (Berkeley: University of California Press, 2001). See also Carlin A. Barton, *The Sorrows of the Ancient Romans: The Gladiator and the Monster* (Princeton, N. J.: Princeton University Press, 1993).

46. For a contemporary exploration of this psychology of violent manhood, see James Gilligan, *Violence: Reflections on a National Epidemic* (New York: Vintage Books, 1996).

47. See Livy, *The Early History of Rome*, at pp. 365–435.

48. See Livy, *The War with Hannibal*, translated by Aubrey De Selincourt (London: Penguin, 1965), pp. 144–9.

49. Montesquieu, *Considerations on the Causes of the Greatness of the Romans and Their Decline*, David Lowenthal trans. (Indianapolis: Hackett Publishing Company, Inc., 1965), pp. 45, 93, 136.

50. See, on this point, Adrian Goldsworthy, *Caesar*, pp. 57–9, 91.

51. See *ibid.*, pp. 303, 355.

52. Anthony Everitt, *Augustus: The Life of Rome's First Emperor* (New York: Random House, 2006), p. 35.

53. For Caesar's political resistance to the Senate's execution of Catiline, see Adrian Goldsworthy, *Caesar*, p. 135.

54. Julius Caesar, *The Civil War*, translated by John Carter (Oxford: Oxford University Press, 1998), at p. 5.

55. See, for example, Julius Caesar, *The Conquest of Gaul*, translated by S. A. Handford (London: Penguin, 1982), in which Caesar always speaks of himself in the third person.

56. Julius Caesar, *The Civil War*, at p. 8.

57. For illuminating comparisons, see Sarah B. Pomeroy, *Goddesses, Whores, Wives, and Slaves*.

58. Andrew Lintott, *Violence in Republican* Rome (Oxford: Oxford University Press, 2004), p. 40. See also Keith Hopkins, *Death and Renewal* (Cambridge: Cambridge University Press, 1983), at pp. 1–30.

59. See Catharine Edwards, *The Politics of Immorality in Ancient Rome* (Cambridge: Cambridge University Press, 2002), pp. 118–19.

60. See Donald Earl, *The Moral and Political Tradition of Rome* (Ithaca, N.Y.: Cornell University Press, 1967), pp. 40–1. See Tim Whitmarsh, *Greek Literature and the Roman Empire: The Politics of Imitation* (Oxford: Oxford University Press, 2001), p. 10.

61. See Donald Earl, op.cit., pp. 61, 91.

62. See, in general, Tim Whitmarsh, *Greek Literature and the Roman Empire*.

63. Tacitus, *The Annals of Ancient Rome*, translated by Michael Grant (London: Penguin, 1996), at p. 383.

64. See, on these points, Andrew Lintott, *The Constitution of the Roman Republic*, at pp. 191–213.

65. See, in general, Lintott, *The Constitution*; on the increasing openness of Roman citizenship, as a distinctive mark of Roman politics and identity, see Emma Dench, *Romulus' Asylum: Roman Identities from the Age of Alexander to the Age of Hadrian* (Oxford: Oxford University Press, 2005).

66. See, on the new woman, Elaine Fantham, Helene Peet Foley, Natalie Boymel Kampen, Sarah B. Pomeroy, and H. Alan Shapiro, *Women in the Classical World* (New York: Oxford University Press, 1994), pp. 280–93.

67. See, in general, Paul Veyne, *Roman Erotic Elegy: Love, Poetry, and the West*, translated by David Pellauer (Chicago: University of Chicago Press, 1988); Maria Wyke, *The Roman Mistress* (Oxford: Oxford University Press, 2002). Regarding Sulpicia, see John Heath-Stubbs, translator, *The Poems of Sulpicia* (London: Hearing Eye, 2000); Stephen Hinds, "The Poetess and the Reader: Further Steps towards Sulpicia," *Hermathena* 143 (1987). 29–46; Mathile Skoe, "Sublime Poetry or Feminine Fiddling? Gender and Reception: Sulpicia Through the Eyes of Two 19th Century Scholars," Nordic Symposium on Women's Lives in Antiquity, *Aspects of Women in Antiquity: Proceedings of the First Nordic Symposium on Women's Lives in Antiquity, Goteborg 12–15 June 1997* (Jonsered: P. Astroms Forlag, 1998), pp. 169–80l; Alison Keith, "*Tandem Venit Amor*: A Roman Woman Speaks of Love," in Judith P. Hallett and Marilyn B. Skinner, eds., *Roman Sexualities* (Princeton: Princeton University Press, 1997), pp. 295–310.

68. Appian, *The Civil Wars*, translated by John Carter (London: Penguin, 1996), at p. 225.
69. See also Richard A. Bauman, *Women and Politics in Ancient Rome*, at pp. 81–3.
70. *Ibid.*, pp. 86–7.
71. *Ibid.*, p. 88.
72. *Ibid.*, p. 88.
73. See, on this point, Suetonius, *The Twelve Caesars*, at pp. 50–1.
74. See, for a good general treatment, Mary Beard, John North, and Simon Price, *Religions of Rome, Volume 1 – A History* and *Religions of Rome, Volume 2 – A Sourcebook* (Cambridge: Cambridge University Press, 1998).
75. See, on the Roman response, Harriet I. Flower, *The Cambridge Companion to the Roman Republic* (Cambridge: Cambridge University Press, 2004), at pp. 148–9, 207.
76. Livy, *Rome and the Mediterranean*, translated by Henry Bettenson (London: Penguin, 1976), at p. 410.
77. Sallust, *The Conspiracy of Catiline*, in *The Jugurthine War/The Conspiracy of Catiline*, translated by S. A. Handford (London: Penguin, 1963), pp. 175–233, at p. 192.
78. *Ibid.*, at p. 193.
79. See Anthony Everitt, *Augustus: The Life of Rome's First Emperor* (New York: Random House, 2006).
80. See Adrian Goldsworthy, *Caesar*, p. 445.
81. Suetonius, *The Twelve Caesars*, at p. 58.
82. See, on this point, Ronald Syme, *The Roman Revolution* (Oxford: Oxford University Press, 1985), at pp. 98–9.
83. Anthony Everitt, *Cicero: The Life and Times of Rome's Greatest Politician* (New York: Random House Trade Paperbacks, 2003), at p. 319.
84. Edward Champlin, *Nero* (Cambridge, Mass.: Belknap Press of Harvard University Press, 2003), at p. 172.
85. Cicero, *Philippics*, translated by Walter C. A. Ker (Cambridge, Mass.: Harvard University Press, 2001), at pp. 109, 141, 149. On Curio, see Anthony Everitt, *Cicero*, at pp. 119–20; and on his marriage to Fulvia, see Richard A. Bauman, *Women and Politics in Ancient Rome*, p. 84.
86. Ronald Syme, *The Roman Revolution*, p. 150. See, on this point, Cicero, *Philippics*, at p. 141.
87. See Hans Volkmann, *Cleopatra: A Study in Politics and Propaganda*, translated by T. J. Cadoux (London: Elek Books, Ltd., 1958), at pp. 125–6.
88. Christian Meier, *Caesar*, at p. 409.
89. For a more skeptical view, see Anthony Everitt, *Augustus*, at pp. 147–8, 156–7.
90. Plutarch, *Antony*, in Plutarch, *The Lives of Noble Grecians and Romans*, translated by John Dryden (New York: Modern Library, n.d.), pp. 1105–1153, at p. 1142.
91. See Hans Volkmann, *Cleopatra*, pp. 155–62; Josiah Osgood, *Caesar's Legacy: Civil War and the Emergence of the Roman Empire* (Cambridge: Cambridge University Press, 2006), at pp. 344–7.
92. See, for illuminating history of these events, Robert Alan Gurval, *Actium and Augustus: The Politics and Emotions of Civil War* (Ann Arbor: The University of Michigan Press, 1995); Josiah Osgood, *Caesar's Legacy*; Ronald Syme, *The Roman Revolution*.
93. See Mary Beard, John North, and Simon Price, *Religions of Rome, Volume I – A History* (Cambridge: Cambridge University Press, 1998), pp. 230–1.
94. Suetonius, *The Twelve Caesars*, at p. 86.
95. See, on these points, Paul Zanker, *The Power of Images in the Age of Augustus*, translated by Alan Shapiro (Ann Arbor: The University of Michigan Press, 1990); Karl Galinsky, *Augustan Culture* (Princeton, N. J.: Princeton University Press, 1996).
96. Anthony A. Barrett, *Livia*, at p. 205.
97. See Thomas A. J. McGinn, *Prostitution, Sexuality, and the Law in Ancient Rome* (New York: Oxford University Press, 1998), at pp. 70–104.
98. *Ibid.*, at pp. 140–215.

99. See David Cohen, "The Augustan Law on Adultery: The Social and Cultural Context," in David I. Kertzer and Richard P. Saller, *The Family in Italy from Antiquity to the Present* (New Haven, Conn.: Yale University Press, 1991), pp. 109–126, at p. 125.

100. See Thomas A. J. McGinn, *Prostitution, Sexuality, and the Law in Ancient Rome*, at pp. 216–19.

101. Suetonius, *The Twelve Caesars*, at p. 82.

102. Tacitus, *The Annals of Imperial Rome*, p. 63.

103. Suetonius, *The Twelve Caesars*, at pp. 112–13.

104. *Ibid.*, at p. 85.

105. See Pat Southern, *Augustus* (London: Routledge, 2001), at p. 154. See also Anthony Everitt, *Augustus: The Life of Rome's First Emperor* (New York: Random House, 2006).

106. Macrobius, *Saturnalia*, translated by Percival Vaughan Davies (New York: Columbia University Press, 1969), at p. 177.

107. See Beth Severy, *Augustus and the Family at the Birth of the Roman Empire* (London: Routledge, 2003), at pp. 158–61.

108. Cassius Dio, *The Roman History: The Reign of Augustus*, Ian Scott-Kilvert trans. (London: Penguin, 1987), p. 199.

109. Quoted in Thomas A. J. McGinn, *Prostitution, Sexuality, and the Law in Ancient Rome*, at pp. 168–9.

110. Seneca, *On the Shortness of Life*, translated by C. D. N. Costa (London: Penguin, 1997), at p. 7.

111. Velleius Paterculus, *Res Gestae Divi Augusti* (Cambridge, Mass.: Harvard University Press, 2002), at p. 259.

112. Cassius Dio, *The Roman History: The Reign of Augustus*, at p. 199.

113. Suetonius, *The Twelve Caesar*, at pp. 82–3.

114. Velleius Paterculus, *Rest Gestae Divi Augusti*, at p. 259.

115. Suetonius, *The Twelve Caesars*, at p. 83.

116. Lucius Annaeus Seneca, *On Benefits* (Objective Systems Pty Ltd., 2006), at p. 415.

117. Tacitus, *The Annals of Imperial Rome*, at p. 131.

118. Pliny the Elder, *Natural History: A Selection*, translated by John F. Healy (London: Penguin, 2004), at p. 98.

119. See, on this point, Arthur Ferrill, "Augustus and his Daughter: A Modern Myth," in Carl Deroux, ed., *Studies in Latin Literature and Roman History II* (Bruxelles: Latomus, 1980), pp. 332–46.

120. Macrobius, *The Saturnalia*, p. 176.

121. On Julia's wit, see Amy Richlin, "Julia's Jokes, Galla Placidia, and the Roman Use of Women as Political Icons," in Barbara Garlick, Suzanne Dixon, and Pauline Allen, *Stereotypes of Women in Power: Historical Perspectives and Revisionist Views* (New York: Greenwood Press, 1992), at pp. 65–91.

122. Macrobius, *Saturnalia*, p. 177.

123. *Ibid.*, p. 177.

124. *Ibid.*, p. 176.

125. See, for such defenses, Matthew B. Roller, *Constructing Autocracy: Aristocrats and Emperors in Juliu-Claudian Rome* (Princeton, N. J.: Princeton University Press, 2001).

126. Tacitus, *The Annals of Imperial Rome*, at p. 133.

127. *Ibid.*, p. 132.

128. *Ibid.*, p. 133.

129. Leo Ferrero Raditsa, "Augustus' Legislation Concerning Marriage, Procreation, Love Affairs, and Adultery," *Aufstieg und Niedergang der Romischen Welt* (Berlin: Walter De Gruyter, 1980), pp. 278–339, at p. 329.

130. On the role of disassociation as the basis for political tyranny, see *ibid.*, pp. 329, 335.

131. Velleius Paterculus, *op. cit.*, at p. 259.

132. See Tacitus, *The Annals of Imperial Rome*, at pp. 192–3; Ronald Syme, *The Roman Revolution*, p. 432.

133. Ronald Syme, *The Roman Revolution*, at p. 468.

134. Suetonius, *The Twelve Caesars*, p. 104, 105.

135. Tacitus, *Annals of Imperial Rome*, at pp. 33, 35.

136. See, in general, Anthony A. Barrett, *Livia: First Lady of Imperial Rome* (New Haven, Conn.: Yale University Press, 2002).

137. Tacitus, *The Annals of Imperial Rome*, at p. 225.

138. See, on these points, Lawrence Keppie, *The Making of the Roman Army From Republic to Empire* (Norman: University of Oklahoma Press, 1984), at pp. 147–55.

139. See Suetonius, *The Twelve Caesars*, at p. 94.

140. *Ibid.*, at p. 162.

141. See, on these points, Anthony A. Barrett, *Agrippina: Sex, Power, and Politics in the Early Empire* (New Haven, Conn.: Yale University Press, 1996), at pp. 26–27.

142. See, for an illuminating study, Anthony A. Barrett, *Agrippina*.

### 3. Vergil on the Darkness Visible

1. For a contemporary retelling of this story, told from Dido's perspective, see Carol Gilligan's novel *Kyra* (New York: Random House, 2008).

2. On the poet Ovid's subversive reading of this patriarchal Augustan view, see Alessandro Barchiesi, *The Poet and the Prince: Ovid and Augustan Discourse* (Berkeley: University of California Press, 1997).

3. Ronald Syme, *The Roman Revolution*, at p. 225.

4. See, for illuminating studies of the relationship of the poets to these political events, Peter White, *Promised Verse: Poets in the Society of Augustan Rome* (Cambridge, Mass.: Harvard University Press, 1993); Anton Powell, ed., *Roman Poetry and Propaganda in the Age of Augustus* (London: Bristol Classical Press, 1997); Jasper Griffin, *Latin Poets and Roman Life* (London: Bristol Classical Press, 2004).

5. See Vergil, *The Eclogues of Vergil*, translated by David Ferry (New York: Farrar, Straus, and Giroux, 1999).

6. Suetonius, *Vergil*, in *Suetonius, Volume II*, translated by J. C. Rolfe (Cambridge, Mass.: Harvard University Press, 2001), pp. 443–59, at p. 449.

7. See, on Vergil's first *Eclogue*, Peter White, *Promised Verse*, at pp. 159–61, 171–3.

8. See Vergil, *The Georgics of Vergil*, translated by David Ferry (New York: Farrar, Straus, and Giroux, 2005).

9. Suetonius, *Vergil, op. cit.*, at pp. 451, 445.

10. See Vergil, *Georgics*, at pp. 141–65.

11. See, for example, C. Nicolet, "Economy and Society, 133–43 B.C.E.," in J. A. Crook, et al., *The Cambridge Ancient History, Second Edition, Volume IX, The Last Age of the Roman Republic, 146–43 B.C.E.*, at pp. 599–643; also Alan K. Bowman, et al., *The Cambridge Ancient History, Second Edition, Volume XI, The High Empire, A.D. 70–192*, at pp. 679–816.

12. See Vergil, *Georgics*, at p. 5.

13. Suetonius, *Vergil*, in *Suetonius Volume II*, pp. 443–59, at p. 451.

14. See Homer, *Iliad*, translated by Richard Lattimore (Chicago: University of Chicago Press, 1951), at p. 331.

15. On the poetics of loss in the *Iliad*, see Michael Lynn-George, *Epos: Word, Narrative, and the Iliad* (London: Macmillan, 1988).

16. We are indebted to this point to Elisabeth Young-Bruehl, *Where Do We Fall When We Fall in Love?* (New York: Other Press, 2003), at pp. 327–8.

17. W. R. Johnson, *Darkness Visible: A Study of Vergil's Aeneid* (Berkeley: University of California Press, 1976).

18. See also Marilyn B. Skinner, "The Last Encounter of Dido and Aeneas," *Vergilius* 29 (1983), 12–18.

19. See Skinner, "The Last Encounter of Dido and Aeneas."

20. The encounter here of Aeneas with his father echoes the comparable scene in the underworld in the *Odyssey* where Odysseus tries to grasp his mother three times. See Homer, *The Odyssey*, translated by Robert Fagles (New York: Penguin, 1996), at p. 256.
21. See Vergil, *Aeneid 7–12 Appendix Vergiliiana*, translated by H. R. Fairclough, revised by G. P. Goold (Cambridge, Mass.: Harvard University Press, 2002); cf. p. 226 and p. 298.
22. Suetonius, *Vergil*, *op. cit.*, p. 445.
23. See, for example, Jasper Griffin, *Vergil* (Oxford: Oxford University Press, 1986), pp. 26, 94. For the contrary view, see Richard Jenkyns, *Vergil's Experience*, at pp. 6–13.
24. See, on this point, David A. J. Richards, *Disarming Manhood: Roots of Ethical Resistance* (Athens, Ohio: Swallow Press, 2005), at pp. 51–75.
25. See Jasper Griffin, *Vergil*, p. 11.
26. Suetonius, *Vergil*, *op. cit.*, p. 453.
27. See Donald Levy, *Freud Among the Philosophers* (New Haven, Conn.: Yale University Press, 1996).
28. Quoted by Jonathan Barnes, *The Presocratic Philosophers* (London: Routledge, 2006), at p. 459.
29. See Jonathan Barnes, *id.*, pp. 459–61.
30. Lucretius, *On the Nature of the Universe*, p. 158.
31. Judith P. Hallet, "*Feminae Furentes*: The Frenzy of Noble Women in Vergil's *Aeneid* and the Letter of Cornelia, Mother of the Gracchi," in William S. Anderson and Lorina N. Quartarone, eds., *Approaches to Teaching Vergil's Aeneid* (New York: The Modern Language Association of America, 2002), at pp. 159–67.
32. See, on this point, Ronald Syme, *The Roman Revolution*, at pp. 202–7.
33. On Livia and Augustus's relationship to her, see Ronald Syme, *The Roman Revolution*, at pp. 229, 340 f., 345, 385, 414, 425, 427.
34. See, on Tolstoy's crisis of vocation and its consequences, David A. J. Richards, *Disarming Manhood: Roots of Ethical Resistance, op. cit.*, pp. 75–87.
35. See, on this point, Hermione Lee, *Virginia Woolf* (New York: Alfred A. Knopf, 1998), pp. 491–504.
36. See, on this point, Frederick R. Carol, *Joseph Conrad: The Three Lives* (New York: Farrar, Straus, and Giroux, 1979), pp. 680–4.
37. Suetonius, *Vergil*, *op. cit.*, p. 455.

## 4. Apuleius on Conversion

1. Gibbon, *The Decline and Fall of the Roman Empire*, Volume 1, at p. 70.
2. Elaine Pagels, *Adam, Eve, and the Serpent* (New York: Random House, 1988), at p. 53.
3. See Marcus Aurelius, *Meditations*, translated by Gregory Hays (New York: The Modern Library, 2003).
4. New York: Farrar, Straus and Giroux, 1990; originally published 1954.
5. London: Macmillan and Co., 1914.
6. Yourcenar, *Memoirs of Hadrian*, p. 134.
7. *Ibid.*, pp. 111, 133.
8. See Joan Acocella, "Marguerite Yourcenar and the Emperor," *The New Yorker*, February 14 & 21, 2005, at p. 242.
9. See St. Justin Martyr, *Dialogue with Trypho*, translated by Thomas B. Falls (Washington, D.C.: The Catholic University of America Press, 2003); St. Justin Martyr, *The First and Second Apologies*, translated by Leslie William Barnard (New York: Paulist Press, 1997).
10. *The Decline and Fall*, Volume 1, p. 454.
11. See Peter Brown, "Christianization and Religious Conflict," in Averil Camerson and Peter Garnsey, eds., *The Cambridge Ancient History, Volume XIII, The Late Empire, A.D. 337–425* (Cambridge: Cambridge University Press, 1998), at pp. 632–64.
12. *Marius the Epicurean*, Part III, p. 186; for Peter's express distinction of the Christianity of Marius from the Christianity of Constantine, see *Marius the Epicurean*, Part III, pp. 117–18.

13. See Apuleius, *The Golden Ass*, translated by E. J. Kenney (London: Penguin, 1998).

14. Edited with translation by J. Gwyn Griffiths (University of Wales Press, 1970).

15. Apuleius marks this influence in *Metamorphoses* when Byrrhena, his foster mother, claims that both she and Lucius's natural mother "are descended from Plutarch." Apuleius, *The Golden Ass*, at p. 23. See also *id.*, p. 7, where Lucius himself claims such ancestry.

16. See, for a collection of these works, Apuleius, *Rhetorical Works.*

17. See Apuleius, *Apology*, translated by Vincent Hunink, in *Rhetorical Works*, at pp. 11–121.

18. See Harald Hagendahl, *Augustine and the Latin Classics* (Goteborg: Elanders Boktryckeri Aktiebolag, 1967), at p. 681.

19. See Apuleius, *Apology, op. cit.*, at p. 103. On Pudentilla, see Elaine Fantham, "Aemilia Pudentilla: or the Wealthy Widow's Choice," in Richard Hawley and Barbara Levick, eds., *Women in Antiquity: New Assessments* (London: Routledge, 1995), at pp. 220–32.

20. Augustine, *The City of God*, translated by Henry Bettenson (Harmondsworth, Middlesex, England: Penguin, 1972), p. 782.

21. Apuleius, *The Golden Ass*, at p. 212.

22. See Ovid, *Metamorphoses*, translated by A. D. Melville (Oxford: Oxford University Press, 1986).

23. See Pseudo-Lucian, *The Ass*, translated by J. P. Sullivan, in B. P. Reardon, ed., *Collected Ancient Greek Novels* (Berkeley: University of California Press, 1989), at pp. 589–618.

24. Berkeley: University of California Press, 1989. For novels that have come down to us in fragments, see Susan A. Stephens and John J. Winkler, *Ancient Greek Novels The Fragments* (Princeton, N.J.: Princeton University Press, 1995).

25. Translated by John J. Winkler, in B. P. Reardon, ed., *Collected Ancient Greek Novels*, at pp. 170–284.

26. Translated by Christopher Gill, in B. P. Reardon, ed., *id.*, pp. 285–348.

27. *Leucippe and Clitophon*, B .P. Reardon, *op. cit.*, at p. 240.

28. See, on this point, Margaret Anne Doody, *The True Story of the Novel* (New Brunswick, N.J.: Rutgers University Press, 1997), pp. 160–70.

29. See, for example, Apuleius, *The Golden Ass*, pp. 10–17, 47–9, 83 ff.

30. Apuleius, *The Golden Ass*, at p. 145.

31. See Fergus Millar, "The World of the Golden Ass," *The Journal of Roman Studies* 71 (1981), 63–75.

32. All quotations in the text are to page numbers in the E. J. Kenney translation of Apuleius, *The Golden Ass* (London: Penguin, 1998). On the transmission of the novel, see Julia Haig Gaisser, *The Fortunes of Apuleius and The Golden Ass: A Study in Transmission and Reception* (Princeton, N.J.: Princeton University Press, 2008).

33. See, on this point, Keith Bradley, "Animalizing the Slave: The Truth of Fiction," *The Journal of Roman Studies* 90 (2000), 110–25.

34. Carol Gilligan, *The Birth of Pleasure: A New Way to Love* (New York: Vintage, 2003), at p. 28.

35. *Ibid.*

36. *Ibid.*, p. 29.

37. *Ibid.*, p. 29.

38. *Ibid.*, p. 30.

39. Ian D. Suttie, *The Origins of Love and Hate*, at pp. 80–96.

40. See, on this point, Gilligan, *The Birth of Pleasure*, at pp. 30–2.

41. We are grateful to Eva Cantarella for this information.

42. See Apuleius, *The Golden Ass*, at pp. 71–108.

43. See Erich Neumann, *Amor and Psyche: The Psychic Development of the Feminine; A Commentary on the Tale by Apuleius*, translated by Ralph Manheim (Princeton, N.J.: Princeton University Press, 1956); Mary-Louise von Franz, *Apuleius' Golden Ass* (New York; Analytical Psychology Club, 1970); For a feminist literary analysis, see Lee Ewards, *Psyche as Hero: Female Heroism and Fictional Form* (Dartmouth, NH: University Press of New England, 1984).

44. Ross Shepard Kraemer, ed., *Women's Religions in the Greco-Roman World: A Sourcebook* (New York: Oxford University Press, 2004), at p. 456.

45. See, on these points, Sarah B. Pomeroy, *Goddesses, Whores, Wives, and Slaves: Women in Classical Antiquity* (New York: Schocken Books, 1995); Sarah B. Pomeroy, *Women in Hellenistic Egypt: From Alexander to Cleopatra* (Detroit: Wayne State University Press, 1990); Roger S. Bagnall, *Egypt in Late Antiquity* (Princeton, N.J.: Princeton University Press, 1993); Ross Shepard Kraemer, *Her Share of the Blessings: Women's Religions Among Pagans, Jews, and Christians in the Greco-Roman World* (New York: Oxford University Press, 1992); John Ferguson, *The Religions of the Roman Empire* (Ithaca, N.Y.: Cornell University Press, 1970); Walter Burkert, *Ancient Mystery Cults* (Cambridge, Mass.: Harvard University Press, 1987); Robert Turcan, *The Cults of the Roman Empire* (Malden, Mass.: Blackwell Publishing, 2005); Mary Beard, John North, and Simon Price, *Religions of Rome, Volume 1 – A History* (Cambridge: Cambridge University Press, 2004). For specialized studies of the Isis religion itself, see R. E. Witt, *Isis in the Ancient World* (Baltimore: The Johns Hopkins University Press, 1971); Sharon Kelly Heyob, *The Cult of Isis Among Women in the Graeco-Roman World* (Ann Arbor, Mich.: UMI Dissertation Services, 2003); John B. Stambaugh, *Sarapis Under the Early Ptolemies* (Leiden: E. J. Brill, 1972); Petra Pakkanen, *Interpreting Early Hellenistic Religion* (Athens: E. Souvatzidakis, 1996); Malcolm Drew Donalson, *The Cult of Isis in the Roman Empire* (Lewiston, N.Y.: The Edwin Mellen Press, 2003); Friedrich Solmsen, *Isis among the Greeks and Romans* (Cambridge, Mass.: Harvard University Press, 1979).

46. See, for example, Mary Beard, John North, and Simon Price, *Religions of Rome, Volume 2 – A Sourcebook* (Cambridge: Cambridge University Press, 2005), at pp. 298–300.

47. Apuleius, *The Golden Ass*, p. 71.

48. See, on this point, *ibid.*, at pp. 197–8.

49. *Ibid.*, p. 103.

50. Friedrich Nietzche. *The Birth of Tragedy and The Genealogy of Morals*, translated by Francis Golffing (New York: Doubleday & Company, 1956), pp. 3–146. See also, for a discussion of the role patriarchy plays as the framework for Greek tragedy, David A. J. Richards, *Tragic Manhood and Democracy: Verdi's Voice and the Powers of Musical Art* (Brighton, U.K.: Sussex Academic Press, 2004).

51. See Plutarch, "Of Curiosity, or an Over-Busy Inquisitiveness into Things Impertinent," in William W. Goodwin, translator, *Plutarch's Morals*, Volume II (Boston: Little, Brown, and Company, 1878), pp. 424–45.

## 5. Augustine on Conversion

1. See, on these points, Peter Heather, *The Fall of the Roman Empire: A New History of Rome and the Barbarians* (Oxford: Oxford University Press, 2006).

2. See Rodney Stark, *The Rise of Christianity: A Sociologist Reconsiders History* (Princeton, N.J.: Princeton University Press, 1996).

3. See Ramsay MacMullen, *Christianizing the Roman Empire A.D. 100–400* (New Haven: Yale University Press, 1984).

4. See Neil B. McLynn, *Ambrose of Milan: Church and Court in a Christian Capital* (Berkeley: University of California Press, 1994).

5. See, on all these points, Peter Brown, *Augustine of Hippo: A Biography* (Berkeley: University of California Press, 2000) (first published 1967).

6. See, on this history, Richard Regan, S.J., *Conflict and Consensus: Religious Freedom and the Second Vatican Council* (New York: The Macmillan Company, 1967).

7. See, on this point, David A. J. Richards, *Toleration and the Constitution* (New York: Oxford University Press, 1986).

8. Karol Jackowski, *The Silence We Keep: A Nun's View of the Catholic Priest Scandal* (New York: Harmony Books, 2004), at p. 43.

9. *Ibid.*, p. 43. See, for an important scholarly study confirming Jackowski's analysis, Uta Ranke-Heinemann, *Eunuchs for Heaven: The Catholic Church and Sexuality*, translated by John Brownjohn (London: Andre Deutsch, 1988).

10. See Augustine, *The City of God*, translated by Henry Bettenson (Harmondsworth, Middlesex, England: Penguin, 1972).

11. See Saint Augustine, *Confessions*, translated by Henry Chadwick (Oxford: Oxford University Press, 1991).

12. Augustine, *The City of God*, pp. 570, 588, 577.

13. *Ibid.*, p. 586.

14. A leading anthropological study of cross-cultural sexual practices reports that, universally, sexual intercourse occurs in private. See Clellan S. Ford and Frank A. Beach, *Patterns of Sexual Behavior* (New York: Harper & Row, 1959), pp. 68–72. This is not a characteristic of animal sexual behavior. "A desire for privacy during sexual intercourse seems confined to human beings. Male-female pairs of other animal species appear to be unaffected by the presence of other individuals and mate quite as readily in a crowd as when they are alone." *Id.*, at p. 71.

15. See, on this point, David A. J. Richards, *A Theory of Reasons for Action* (Oxford: Clarendon Press, 1971), at p. 254.

16. See Elaine Pagels, *Adam, Eve, and the Serpent* (New York: Random House, 1988), at pp. 98–126.

17. See John H. Hick, "An Irenaean Theodicy," reprinted at pp. 222–7, Eleanor Stump and Michael J. Murray, eds., *Philosophy of Religion: The Big Questions* (Oxford: Blackwell Publishers, 1999). We are grateful to Donald Levy for this reference.

18. Quoted in Henry Chadwick, "Introduction," *Confessions*, pp. ix–xxvi, at pp. xviii–xix.

19. See, on these points, Garry Wills, *Saint Augustine* (New York: A Lipper/Viking Book, 1999), at pp. 58–63.

20. *The Bible*, authorized King James Version (Oxford: Oxford University Press, 1998).

21. Albright and Mann, *The Anchor Bible: Matthew*, at p. 83.

22. See, on these points, David A. J. Richards, *Disarming Manhood: Roots of Ethical Resistance* (Athens: Ohio University/Swallow Press, 2005), at pp. 27–40.

23. For an express identification of his mother with Eve, see Augustine, *Confessions*, p. 82.

24. See, on this point, Augustine, *Confessions*, pp. 81–2.

25. Peter Brown, *Augustine of Hippo* (London: Faber & Faber, 1967), at p. 175. See also, in general, Peter Brown, *The Body and Society: Men, Women, and Sexual Renunciation in Early Christianity* (New York: Columbia University Press, 1988).

26. Augustine, *Confessions*, p. 82.

27. *Ibid.*, at p. 26; see also p. 14.

28. *Ibid.*, p. 39.

29. See Anna Freud, *The Ego and the Mechanisms of Defense* (Madison, Wisc.: International Universities Press, rev. ed. 2000), at p. 153.

30. See Erik Erikson, *Gandhi's Truth: On the Origins of Militant Nonviolence* (New York: W.W. Norton, 1993), pp. 110–11.

31. See, for example, Augustine, *Confessions*, pp. 56–60.

32. See, on this point, *ibid.*, pp. 111–32. The central text would have been Plotinus, *The Enneads*, translated by Stephen MacKenna (London: Penguin, 1991), parts of which Augustine read in Latin translation (Plotinus wrote in Greek). On the parts of Plotinus he read, see Eugene TeSelle, *Augustine the Theologian* (Eugene, Ore.: Wipf and Stock, 2002), at pp. 43–5, 53, 68; John M. Rist, *Augustine: Ancient Thought Baptized* (Cambridge: Cambridge University Press, 1997), p. 188.

33. Porphyry, *The Life of Plotinus*, translated by Stephen McKenna (Edmonds, Wash.: Holmes Publishing Group, 2001), at p. 5.

34. See, on this point, Gareth B. Matthews, *Thought's Ego in Augustine and Descartes* (Ithaca, N.Y.: Cornell University Press, 1992). See also Gareth B. Matthews, *Augustine*

(Malden, Mass.: Blackwell, 2005); Stephen Menn, *Descartes and Augustine* (Cambridge: Cambridge University Press, 2002).

35. See Neil B. McLynn, *Ambrose of Milan: Church and Court in a Christian Capital* (Berkeley: University of California Press, 1994).

36. See Augustine, *Confessions*, pp. 131, 134, 141, 153. See also, for illuminating commentary, Stephen Menn, *Descartes and Augustine*, at pp. 192–206.

37. See, on these points, Elaine Pagels, *Adam, Eve, and the Serpent*.

38. See, on this point, Augustine, *The Confessions*, at pp. 127, 134, 141, 145.

39. *Ibid.*, p. 180; see also p. 202.

40. See, on this point, Augustine, *The City of God*, at pp. 97–9, 104, 139, 142, 154–5, 205–7, 207–12, 401.

41. See, for study of this point, David A. J. Richards, *Disarming Manhood: Roots of Ethical Resistance in Jesus, Garrison, Tolstoy, Gandhi, King, and Churchill* (Athens, Ohio:Ohio University Press, 2005).

42. Harald Hagendahl, *Augustine and the Latin Classics*, at pp. 680–1.

43. Apuleius, *The Golden Ass*, p. 88.

44. See Augustine, Confessions, ibid., pp. 210–12, 215, 291.

45. *Ibid.*, p. 278.

46. See, on this point, Michael P. Carroll, *The Cult of the Virgin Mary: Psychological Origins* (Princeton, N.J.: Princeton University Press, 1986).

47. See, for support of this essential critical point, Kathy L. Gaca, *The Making of Fornication: Eros, Ethics, and Political Reform in Greek Philosophy and Early Christianity* (Berkeley: University of California Press, 2003); Simon Goldhill, *Foucault's Virginity: Ancient Erotic Fiction and the History of Sexuality* (Cambridge: Cambridge University Press, 1995).

48. For a useful study of the early Christian period, see John A. Gager, *The Origins of Anti-Semitism: Attitudes Toward Judaism in Pagan and Christian Antiquity* (New York: Oxford University Press, 1983). The classic general study is Leon Poliakov, *The History of Anti-Semitism*, Volume 1, translated by Richard Howard (New York: Vanguard Press, 1965); Volume 2, translated by Natalie Gerardi (New York: Vanguard Press, 1973); Volume 3, translated by Miriam Kochan (New York: Vanguard Press, 1975); Volume 4, translated by George Klin (Oxford: Oxford University Press, 1985).

49. See Peter Schafer, *Judeophobia: Attitudes toward the Jews in the Ancient World* (Cambridge, Mass: Harvard University Press, 1997).

50. See Martin Goodman, *Rome and Jerusalem: The Clash of Ancient Civilizations* (New York: Alfred A. Knopf, 2007), p. 471.

51. See, on these points, *ibid.*, pp. 488–557.

52. See, on this point, Kathy L. Gaca, *The Making of Fornication*.

53. See Augustine, *The City of God*, at pp. 136–7, 318–26, 344–5, 351–3, 357–9, 410.

54. *Ibid.*, p. 51.

55. See E. R. Dodds, *Pagan and Christian in an Age of Anxiety* (Cambridge: Cambridge University Press, 1965).

56. Augustine, *The Confessions*, at p. 140.

57. See, on this point, *ibid.*, pp. 140, 160, 206, 254.

58. See, on this point, David A. J. Richards, *Toleration and the Constitution* (New York: Oxford University Press, 1986), at pp. 85–95. See also James Carroll, *Constantine's Sword: The Church and the Jews* (Boston: Houghton Mifflin Company, 2001).

59. See Eugene TeSelle, *Augustine the Theologian*, pp. 272–3.

60. See James J. O'Donnell, *Augustine: A New Biography* (New York: HarperCollins, 2005), at p. 225.

61. Quoted in David Richards, *Women, Gays, and the Constitution*, at p. 403.

62. See David Cohen, "The Augustan Law on Adultery: The Social and Cultural Context," in David I. Kertzer and Richard P. Saller, *The Family in Italy from Antiquity to the Present* (New Haven, Conn.: Yale University Press, 1991), pp. 109–26, at p. 125.

63. See, in general, on the close relationship of psychology and theology in Luther's life and thought, Erik H. Erikson, *Young Man Luther: A Study in Psychoanalysis and History* (New York: W. W. Norton, 1962).

64. See Martin Luther, *The Judgment of Martin Luther on Monastic Vows, 1521*, in Martin Luther, *Luther's Works, Volume 44, The Christian in Society I*, edited and translated by Martin Atkinson (Philadelphia: Fortress Press, 1966), at pp. 245–400.

65. See Martin Luther, *To Hans Luther Wartburg, November 21, 1521*, in Martin Luther, *Luther's Works, Volume 48, Letters I*, edited and translated by Gottfried G. Krodel (Philadelphia: Fortress Press, 1963), at pp. 329–36.

66. See *ibid.*, p. 332.

67. See, on this point, Eugene Kennedy, *The Unhealed Wound: The Church and Human Sexuality* (New York: St. Martin's Press, 2001), at pp. 60–2, 128–32.

68. Thomas Aquinas, *On the Truth of the Catholic Faith, Book Three: Providence, Part 2*, translated by Vernon J. Bourke (Garden City, N.Y. Image, 1956), at p. 194.

## 6. Resistance: Religion

1. See, for example, Karen L. King, *The Gospel of Mary of Magdala: Jesus and the First Woman Apostle* (Santa Rosa, Calif.: Polebridge Press, 2003), and Elaine Pagels, *Beyond Belief: The Secret Gospel of Thomas* (New York: Random House, 2003).

2. See, in general, Elaine Pagels, *The Gnostic Gospels* (New York: Vintage, 1981), at pp. 74–5.

3. Among important studies along these lines are Geza Vermes, *Jesus the Jew: A Historian's Reading of the Gospels* (Philadelphia: Fortress Press, 1981) (originally published 1973); Geza Vermes, *Jesus and the World of Judaism* (London: SCM Press, 1983); Geza Vermes, *The Religion of Jesus the Jew* (Minneapolis: Fortress Press, 1993); Geza Vermes, *The Changing Faces of Jesus* (New York: Viking Compass, 2001); David Flusser, *Jesus* (Jerusalem: The Hebrew University Magnes Press, 2001); David Flusser, *Judaism and the Origins of Christianity* (Jerusalem: The Magnes Press, The Hebrew University, 1988); Paula Fredriksen, *From Jesus to Christ* (New Haven, Conn.: Yale University Press, 2nd edition, 2000); Paula Fredriksen, *Jesus of Nazareth, King of the Jews: A Jewish Life and the Emergence of Christianity* (New York: Alfred A. Knopf, 2000); E. P. Sanders, *Jesus and Judaism* (Philadelphia: Fortress Press, 1985); E. P. Sanders, *The Historical Figure of Jesus* (London: Allen Lane, 1993); John P. Meier, *A Marginal Jew: Rethinking the Historical Jesus: Volume I: The Roots of the Problem and the Person* (New York: Doubleday, 1991); John P. Meier, *A Marginal Jew: Rethinking the Historical Jesus: Volume II: Mentor, Message, and Miracles* (Doubleday: New York, 1993); John P. Meier, *A Marginal Jew: Rethinking the Historical Jesus: Volume III: Companions and Competitors* (New York: Doubleday, 2001); David Daube, *The New Testament and Rabbinic Judaism* (Peabody, Mass.: Hendrickson, 1998); A. N. Wilson, *Jesus: A Life* (New York: Fawcett Columbine, 1992).

4. See, on this point, David Flusser, *Judaism and the Origins of Christianity*, at pp. 509–14; Geza Vermes, *The Religion of Jesus the Jew*, at p. 40–1.

5. See, for a good examination of this contrast, Walter Kaufmann, *Critique of Religion and Philosophy* (Princeton, N.J.: Princeton University Press, 1958), at pp. 278–85.

6. Geza Vermes, *The Changing Faces of Jesus*, p. 174.

7. *Ibid.*, p. 220.

8. Martin Buber, *I and Thou*, translated by Walter Kaufmann (New York: Charles Scribner's Sons, 1970), at pp. 66–7.

9. *Ibid.*, at p. 117.

10. For a good discussion, see John P. Meier, *A Marginal Jew: Volume I*, pp. 332–42 (for comment on Matt. 19–12, see pp. 342–3).

11. See, on this point, John Meier, *A Marginal View: Volume III*, pp. 73–80.

12. See *ibid.*, at p. 75.

13. For a good discussion, see Ben Witherington III, *Women and the Genesis of Christianity* (Cambridge: Cambridge University Press, 1990), at pp. 52–64.

14. See, for illuminating discussion of these forms of the ministry of Jesus, *ibid.*, at pp. 74–77.

15. See, for good discussion of both these events, *ibid.*, at pp. 65–74.

16. A. N. Wilson, *Jesus: A Life* (New York: Fawcett Columbine, 1992), at p. 5; see also pp. 67–8. The author astutely connects such remarkable insight and sympathy with the ways in which women, as feminists, have read the Gospels as calling for forms of political liberation, beginning in the 19th century.

17. See Ben Witherington III, *Women and the Genesis of Christianity*, at p. xiv; see also p. 15.

18. See for plausible arguments along these lines, Rosemary Radford Ruether, *Sexism and God-Talk: Toward a Feminist Theology* (Boston: Beacon Press, 1993); Elisabeth Schussler Fiorenza, *Jesus: Miriam's Child, Sophia's Prophet* (New York: Continuum, 1994); Elisabeth Schussler Fiorenza, *In Memory of Her: A Feminist Theological Reconstruction of Christian Origins* (New York: Crossroad, 2002); Elisabeth Schussler Fiorenza, ed., *Searching Scriptures: Volume One: A Feminist Introduction* (New York: Crossroad Publishing Company, 1993); Elisabeth Schussler Fiorenza, ed., *Searching the Scriptures: Volume Two: A Feminist Commentary* (New York: Crossroad Publishing Company, 1994).

19. See *The New Oxford Annotated Bible* (New York: Oxford University Press, 1991), at p. 181. For relevant commentary, see Aaron Wildavsky, *The Nursing Father: Moses as a Political Leader* (University: University of Alabama Press, 1984).

20. See *The New Oxford Annotated Bible*, at p. 923. (See also Isaiah 40:11: "He will feed his flock like a shepherd;/he will gather the lambs in his arms,/and carry them in his bosom, and gently lead the mother sheep" at p. 918.)

21. Cited in Geza Vermes, *The Religion of Jesus the Jew*, at p. 177.

22. Sara Ruddick, *Maternal Thinking: Toward a Politics of Peace* (Boston: Beacon Press, 1989).

23. See, for example, David Flusser, *Jesus*, p. 28.

24. Erik H. Erikson, "The Galilean Sayings and the Sense of 'I'," *The Yale Review* 70 (1981), 321 at 349

25. See, on this point, David Daube, *The New Testament and Rabbinic Judaism* (Peabody, Mass.: Hendrickson, 1998), at p. 69, n. 39.

26. Joachim Jeremias, *The Sermon on the Mount* (London: The Athlone Press, 1961), at p. 27.

27. David Daube, *The New Testament and Rabbinic Judaism*, at pp. 258–9.

28. See, on this point, W. D. Davies, *The Setting of the Sermon on the Mount* (Cambridge: Cambridge University Press, 1964), at p. 427.

29. See, on these points, David Flusser, *Judaism and the Origins of Christianity*, at pp. 193–201.

30. See Geza Vermes, *The Changing Faces of Jesus*, at p. 275.

31. John P. Meier, *A Marginal Jew: Volume Two*, p. 149.

32. Cited at *ibid.*, pp. 148–9.

33. Later on, such patriarchal conceptions (rooted on Roman patriarchy) were, in largely illiterate Mediterranean societies, understood in terms of how matters publicly appeared, so that men were vulnerable to dishonor because women (often in fact quite innocent of sexual relations) merely appeared less strictly modest and reticent in relations to men. Such masculine dishonor, sometimes arising only from gossip, required violence, killing wives or daughters. See J. G. Peristiany, ed., *Honour and Shame: The Values of Mediterranean Society* (Chicago: University of Chicago Press), at pp. 66–7, 253–4, 256–7.

    We can see the continuing force of these conceptions, rooted in Roman patriarchy, in the patriarchal culture of 19th-century Italy, where the sacrifice of children born out of wedlock imposed the kind of tragic losses and repressed voices that such objectifying gender stereotypes, as a general matter, both inflicted and covered over. The honor code condemned both sexual relations out of wedlock and the illegitimate children often born of such relations as intrinsically shameful. The honor code, enforced by local Catholic priests and the police, rationalized bullying unwed mothers to abandon children to public institutions and sometimes effectively imprisoning them in such institutions as compulsory wet nurses. The consequence for the babies was usually death. (On the continuity of these patriarchal conceptions over time, see Eva Cantarella, "Homicides of Honor: The Development of Italian Adultery Law over Two Millennia," in David I. Kertzer and Richard P. Saller, eds. *The Family in Italy from Antiquity to the Present*, at pp. 229–46. See also David I. Kertzer, *Sacrifices for Honor: Italian Infant Abandonment and the Politics of Reproductive Control* [Boston: Beacon Press, 1993], p. 125; David D. Gilmore, ed., *Honour and Shame and the Unity of the Mediterranean* [Washington, D.C.: American Anthropological Association, 1987], at p. 110,)

Families sometimes protested such separations in terms of their "infinite grief," robbing a mother "of the dearest object of her heart," suggesting traumatizing emotional losses that must have been widespread. But such losses, consistent with the political psychology of patriarchy, were often not acknowledged but covered over with gender-stereotypical idealizations, as of the foundlings in Naples as "children of the Madonna," most of whom in fact died. Meanwhile, their real mothers, if they were wet nurses in the foundling homes, were "treated as livestock." (See Kertzer, *Sacrifices for Honor*, pp. 56, 107, 122, 148.)

The high rates of both illegitimacy and abandonment of infants during this period were common knowledge (*ibid.*, p. 55), yet the underlying emotional trauma and loss could be given no voice and weight. The tragic music dramas of Verdi so absorbed Italians and others because they gave powerful expression to widespread feelings that could not otherwise be acknowledged. (See David A. J. Richards, *Tragic Manhood and Democracy: Verdi's Voice and the Powers of Musical Art* [Brighton, UK: Sussex Academic Press, 2004].)

34. See Raymond E. Brown, *The Anchor Bible: The Gospel According to John I–XII* (New York: Doubleday, 1966), at p. 332.
35. See, on this point, *ibid.*, p. 335.
36. On this tradition, see Abraham Heschel, *The Prophets* (New York: Perennial Classics, 2001).
37. *The Bible*, Authorized King James Version, at p. 45.
38. See, on this point, John P. Meier, *A Marginal Jew: Volume Three*, at pp. 495, 623.
39. *The Bible*, Authorized King James Version, at p. 40.
40. Cited at p. 166, David Flusser, *Jesus*, p. 16.
41. See, on these points, Richard Alston, "Arms and the Man: Soldiers, Masculinity, and Power in Republican and Imperial Rome," in Lin Foxhall and John Salmon, eds., *When Men Were Men: Masculinity, Power and Identity in Classical Antiquity* (London: Routledge, 1998), at pp. 205–23; Aldo Schiavone, *The End of the Past: Ancient Rome and the Modern West*, Margery J. Schneider trans. (Cambridge, Mass.: Harvard University Press, 2000).
42. For an illuminating discussion, see David Flusser, *Jesus*, at pp. 155–73.
43. On the Zealots and Jesus's relation to them, see John P. Meier, *A Marginal Jew: Volume III: Companions and Competitors*, pp. 205–8, 565–9.
44. See, in general, John Hope Franklin, *The Militant South, 1800–1861* (Cambridge, Mass.: Harvard University Press, Belknap Press, 1956); Bertram Wyatt-Brown, *Honor and Violence in the Old South* (New York: Oxford University Press, 1986); cf. W. J. Cash, *The Mind of the South* (New York: Vintage Books, 1941).
45. See Richards, *Women, Gays, and the Constitution*, pp. 42–4.
46. See Gavin I. Langmuir, *Toward a Definition of Antisemitism* (Berkeley: University of California Press, 1990); *History, Religion, and Antisemitism* (Berkeley: University of California Press, 1990).
47. See pp. 57–62, Langmuir, *Toward a Definition of Antisemitism*.
48. *Ibid.*, p. 302.

49. See Langmuir, *Toward a Definition of Antisemitism*, at p. 334.

50. See R. I. Moore, *The Formation of a Persecuting Society: Power and Deviance in Western Europe, 950–1250* (Oxford: Basil Blackwell, 1987).

51. Langmuir, *Toward a Definition of Antisemitism*, p. 45.

52. See, on these and related points, Daniel Boyarin, *Carnal Israel: Reading Sex in Talmudic Culture* (Berkeley: University of California Press, 1993).

53. But, see, for a recent study of resurrection beliefs in classical Judaism, Jon D. Levenson, *Resurrection and the Restoration of Israel: The Ultimate Victory of the God of Life* (New Haven, Conn.: Yale University Press, 2006).

54. See, on these points, Daniel Boyarin, *Unheroic Conduct: The Rise of Heterosexuality and the Invention of the Jewish Man* (Berkeley: University of California Press, 1997).

55. See, on this point, Herbert N. Schneidau, *Sacred Discontent: The Bible and Western Tradition* (Baton Rouge: Louisiana State University Press, 1976); Moshe Halbertal and Avishai Margalit, *Idolatry*, translated by Naomi Goldblum (Cambridge, Mass.: Harvard University Press, 1992). See also Dan Jacobson, *The Story of Stories: The Chosen People and Its God* (New York: Harper & Row, 1982). On these mythological religions, see Henri Frankfort, *Kingship and the Gods: A Study of Ancient Near Eastern Religion as the Integration of Society and Nature* (Chicago: University of Chicago Press, 1948); Henri Frankfort, H. A. Frankfort, John A. Wilson, and Thorkild Jacobsen, *Before Philosophy: The Intellectual Adventure of Ancient Man* (Baltimore: Penguin, 1961).

56. See, on this point, Robert Alter, *The Art of Biblical Narrative* (New York: Basic Books 1981). See also Moshe Halbertal, *People of the Book: Canon, Meaning, and Authority* (Cambridge, Mass.: Harvard University Press, 1997).

57. Robert Alter, *The Art of Biblical Narrative*, p. 22.

58. See 1 Samuel; 2 Samuel; and 1 Kings 1–2.

59. See Genesis 18:23–33 (Abraham persuades God to moderate what Abraham regards as His excessive anger against Sodom: "Will thou also destroy the righteous with the wicked?", Genesis 18:23, *The Bible: Authorized King James Version*, Robert Carroll and Stephen Prickett, eds. (Oxford: Oxford University Press, 1998), at p. 197).

60. See Genesis 22.

61. Quoted in Daniel Boyarin, *Carnal Israel: Reading Sex in Talmudic Culture* (Berkeley: University of California Press, 1993), at p. 171.

62. "You shall not lie with a male as one lies with a woman: it is an abomination," Leviticus 18:22, in Jacob Milgrom, *Leviticus 17–22: The Anchor Bible* (New York: Doubleday, 2000), at p. 1515.

63. "If a man lies with a male as one lies with a woman, the two of them have done an abhorrent thing; they must be put to death – the bloodguilt is upon them," Leviticus 20:13, in Jacob Milgrom, *id.*, at p. 1727.

64. For such an interpretation by a leading Jewish scholar, see Jacob Milgrom, *Leviticus 17:22*, at pp. 1515, 1565–70, 1727, 1749–50, 1785–88 (prohibitions applicable only in Israel, and only in circumstances where necessary to increase population, thus not applicable when population control is urgent and when gay/lesbian Jewish couples can adopt children, an option not historically available); see also Rabbi Steven Greenberg, *Wrestling with God and Men: Homosexuality in the Jewish Tradition* (Madison: University of Wisconsin Press, 2004). For Mary Douglas's pathbreaking arguments about the limited and differing application of the Biblical prohibitions (the most demanding ones, like Leviticus 20:13, only applicable to the sacred space of the priesthood of the Temple), see Mary Douglas, *Leviticus as Literature* (Oxford: Oxford University Press, 1999). See also Mary Douglas, *In the Wilderness: The Doctrine of Defilement in the Book of Numbers* (Sheffield: Sheffield Academic Press, 1993).

65. For an illuminating historical study of Jewish views of sexuality, see David Biale, *Eros and the Jews: From Biblical Israel to Contemporary America* (New York: Basic Books, 1992). On the problematic stance of the contemporary hierarchy of the Catholic Church, see Nicholas Bamforth and David A. J. Richards, *Patriarchal Religion, Sexuality, and*

*Gender: Critique of New Natural Law* (Cambridge University Press, 2008). On the psychological space for liberal views within traditional religions, see Tova Hartman Halbertal, *Appropriately Subversive: Modern Mothers in Traditional Religions* (Cambridge, Mass.: Harvard University Press, 2002).

66. On Paul's life and thought, see Samuel Sandmel, *The Genius of Paul: A Study in History* (Philadelphia: Fortress Press, 1979); Daniel Boyarin, *A Radical Jew: Paul and the Politics of Identity* (Berkeley: University of California Press, 1994); Alan F. Segal, *Paul the Convert: The Apostolate and Apostasy of Saul the Pharisee* (New Haven: Yale University Press, 1990); Jacob Taubes, *The Political Theology of Paul*, translated by Dana Hollander (Stanford, Calif.: Stanford University Press, 2004).

67. Cited in Daniel Boyarin, *Carnal Israel: Reading Sex in Talmudic Culture* (Berkeley: University of California Press, 1993), at p. 1.

68. See, on this point, James Carroll, *Constantine's Sword: The Church and the Jews: A History* (Boston: Houghton Mifflin Company, 2001), at pp. 208–19.

69. Cited in Langmuir, *History, Religion, and Antisemitism*, p. 294.

70. See, on the hatred underlying asceticism, especially Christian asceticism, Friedrich Nietzsche, *On the Genealogy of Morals*, translated by Douglas Smith (Oxford: Oxford University Press, 1996), pp. 77–136. Nietzsche criticizes the Jews largely because they prepare the way for Christianity. See *id.*, pp. 35–36. To the extent the Jews are less ascetic than Christians, they are, for Nietzsche, in fact less objectionable than Christians.

71. See James Gilligan, *Violence*, on this point.

72. On the powerful role of patriarchal conceptions of gender in Hitler's fascism, see Claudia Koonz, *Mothers in the Fatherland: Women, the Family, and Nazi Politics* (New York: St. Martin's Press, 1987); Claudia Koonz, *The Nazi Conscience* (Cambridge Mass.: Belknap Press at Harvard University Press, 2003).

73. See, in general, Amos Elon, *The Pity of It All: A Portrait of the German-Jewish Epoch 1743–1933* (New York: Picador, 2002).

74. On this point, see Sigmund Freud, *Civilization and Its Discontents*, in *Standard Edition of the Complete Psychological Works of Sigmund Freud*, edited and translated by James Strachey (London: Hogarth Press, 1961), 21:114; see also *Moses and Monotheism* (1964), 23:91.

75. See, on this point, Michael Marissen, "Unsettling History of That Joyous 'Hallelujah'," *The New York Times*, Sunday, April 8, 2007, pp. 24 and 30. For recent debate over Marissen's claims, see James R. Oestreich, "Hallelujay Indeed: Debating Handel's Anti-Semitism," *The New York Times*, Monday April 23, 2007, at p. E3.

76. See Leon Poliakov, *The Aryan Myth: A History of Racist and Nationalist Ideas in Europe*, translated by Edmund Howard (London: Sussex University Press, 1971), pp. 380–457. For good general studies of Wagner and Wagnerism (including their political uses by Hitler), see L. J. Rather, *Reading Wagner: A Study in the History of Ideas* (Baton Rouge: Louisiana State University Press, 1990); David C. Large and William Weber, eds., *Wagnerism in European Culture and Politics* (Ithaca, N.Y.: Cornell University Press, 1984).

77. See Amos Elon, *Herzl* (New York: Holt, Rinehart and Winston, 1975); Geoffrey Wheatcroft, *The Controversy of Zion: Jewish Nationalism, the Jewish State, and the Unresolved Jewish Dilemma* (Reading, Mass.: Addison-Wesley Publishing Company, 1996).

78. See Hannah Arendt, *The Origins of Totalitarianism* (New York: Harcourt Brace Jovanovich, 1973). On Arendt's early life, education (including her affair with the philosopher Heidegger), and flight from Germany to the United States, see Elisabeth Young-Bruehl, *Hannah Arendt: For Love of the World* (New Haven, Conn.: Yale University Press, 1982), pp. 5–163.

79. See Hannah Arendt, *Eichmann in Jerusalem: A Report on the Banality of Evil* (New York: Penguin, 1992).

80. See, on this point, John W. deGruchy, ed., *The Cambridge Companion to Dietrich Bonhoeffer* (Cambridge: Cambridge University Press, 2002), at p. 158.

81. Dietrich Bonhoeffer, *Letters and Papers from Prison*, edited by Eberhard Bethge (Touch-stone Book: New York, 1971), at p. 17.

82. See, on these points, Renate Bethge, "Bonhoeffer's Family and Its Significance for His Theology," in Larry Rasmussen, *Dietrich Bonhoeffer – His Significance for North Americans* (Minneapolis: Fortress Press, 1990), pp. 1–30.

83. See, on these points, Philip P. Hallie, *Let Innocent Blood Be Shed: The Story of the Village of Le Chambon and How Goodness Happened There* (New York: Harper & Row, 1979).

84. For fuller examination of the argument in Locke and Bayle and its American elabo-ration notably by Jefferson and Madison, see David A. J. Richards, *Toleration and the Constitution* (New York: Oxford University Press, 1986), at pp. 89–128.

85. See, on this point, Perez Zagorin, *How the Idea of Religious Toleration Came to the West* (Princeton, N.J.: Princeton University Press, 2003).

86. Elisabeth Labrousse, *Bayle*, translated by Denys Potts (Oxford: Oxford University Press, 1983), p. 31.

87. See, on this point, Jeremy Waldron, *God, Locke, and Equality: Christian Foundations in Locke's Political Thought* (Cambridge: Cambridge University Press, 2002), pp. 21–43.

88. On Locke's "very pious . . . and affectionate mother," and a relationship to a father with whom "he lived perfectly . . . as a friend," see H. R. Fox Bourne, *The Life of John Locke*, Volume I (New York: Harper & Brothers, 1876), at p. 13.

89. See, on this point, Roger Woolhouse, *Locke: A Biography* (Cambridge: Cambridge Uni-versity Press, 2007), at pp. 139, 148–9; on his relationships to women, see pp. 222–3.

90. Both do not extend the principle of toleration to Catholics or atheists. For commentary and critique, see Richards, *Toleration and the Constitution*, pp. 95–8.

91. See, in general, Arthur O. Lovejoy, *The Great Chain of Being* (Cambridge, Mass.: Harvard University Press, 1964).

92. For the following discussion of their argument, see Richards, *Toleration*, pp. 25–7, 84–98, 105, 125–6.

93. See, for a recent review of the question, I. Bernard Cohen, ed., *Puritanism and the Rise of Modern Science: The Merton Thesis* (New Brunswick, N.J.: Rutgers University Press, 1990).

94. See Richards, *Toleration*, pp. 119–20.

95. See Spinoza, *Theological-Political Treatise*, second edition, translated by Samuel Shirley (Indianapolis: Hackett Publishing Company, 2001), at pp. 103, 222–30.

96. See Steven Nadler, *Spinoza: A Life* (Cambridge: Cambridge University Press, 1999).

97. Spinoza's own views on women were conventionally sexist. See Benedict de Spinoza, *A Political Treatise*, in Benedict de Spinoza, *A Theological-Political Treatise and A Polit-ical Treatise*, translated by R. H. M. Elwes (Mineola, N.Y.: Dover Publication, 2004), pp. 281–387, at pp. 386–7.

98. See, on all these points, Jonathan I. Israel, *Radical Enlightenment: Philosophy and the Making of Modernity 1650–1750* (Oxford: Oxford University Press, 2001).

99. For one view of his heresy, see Steven Nadler, *Spinoza's Heresy: Immortality and the Jewish Mind* (Oxford: Oxford University Press, 2001).

100. See Benedict de Spinoza, *Ethics*, translated by Edwin Curley translation (London: Pen-guin, 1996).

101. On the relationship between Descartes and Spinoza, see Edwin Curley, *Behind the Geometrical Method: A Reading of Spinoza's Ethics* (Princeton, N.J.: Princeton University Press, 1988).

102. See, for example, Antonio Damasio, *Looking for Spinoza: Joy, Sorrow, and the Feeling Brain* (Orlando, Fla.: Harcourt, Inc., 2003); Rebecca Goldstein, *Betraying Spinoza: The Renegade Jew Who Gave Us Modernity* (New York: Nextbook-Schocken, 2006).

103. There is only one report of Spinoza's romantic involvement with a woman, probably apocryphal. See Steven Nadler, *Spinoza: A Life*, at pp. 108–9. One of his closest male friends, Simon Joosten de Vries, expresses in a latter to Spinoza "perceptibly phys-ical yearning" for the presence of his friend that Spinoza deflects, which leads one

biographer to speculate about homosexual feeling between the friends. See Margaret Gullan-Whur, *Within Reason: A Life of Spinoza* (New York: St. Martin's Press, 1998), pp. 141–3.

104. See William Lloyd Garrison, *Thoughts on African Colonization* (1832; reprint, New York: Arno Press and the New York Times, 1968).
105. Henry Mayer, *All on Fire: William Lloyd Garrison and the Abolition of Slavery* (New York: St. Martin's Griffin, 1998), p. 69.
106. *Ibid.*, p. 134.
107. For Garrison's identification with Jesus, see *id.*, at pp. 125, 204–5, 210, 224, 449.
108. See *ibid.*, pp. 203–20.
109. See *ibid.*, pp. 207, 202.
110. See Richards, *Women, Gays, and the Constitution*, at pp. 102–14; Henry Mayer, *All on Fire*, at pp. 285–99.
111. See, for example, Joanne B. Freeman, *Affairs of Honor: National Politics in the New Republic* (New Haven, Conn.: Yale University Press, 2001); Bertram Wyatt-Brown, *Southern Honor: Ethics and Behavior in the Old South* (New York: Oxford University Press, 1982); Kenneth S. Greenberg, *Honor and Slavery* (Princeton, N.J.: Princeton University Press, 1996).
112. See Henry Mayer, *All on Fire*, at pp. 350–1.
113. On Child's pacifism, see Carolyn L. Karcher, *The First Woman in the Republic: A Cultural Biography of Lydia Maria Child* (Durham, N.C.: Duke University Press, 1994), at pp. 281, 416; on the non-resistance of the Grimke sisters during the period of their activism and their later doubts, see Richards, *Women, Gays, and the Constitution*, at p. 107, n. 187.
114. See L. Maria Child, *An Appeal in Favor of Americans Called Africans* (New York: Arno Press and New York Times, 1968) (originally published 1833). For discussion, see Richards, *Women, Gays, and the Constitution*, pp. 55–62; Karcher, *The First Woman in the Republic*, at pp. 182–3.
115. On Child's support for Jacobs, see *id.*, pp. 435–7.
116. See Mayer, *All on Fire*, pp. 230–7.
117. See Karcher, *The First Woman in the Republic*, p. 215.
118. The best general study is Gerda Lerner, *The Grimke Sisters from South Carolina: Pioneers for Woman's Rights and Abolition* (New York: Schocken Books, 1971). See also Jean Fagan Yellin, *Women and Sisters: The Antislavery Feminists in American Culture* (New Haven, Conn.: Yale University Press, 1989); Blanche Glassman Hersh, *The Slavery of Sex: Feminist-Abolitionists in America* (Urbana: University of Illinois Press, 1978); Keith E. Melder, *Beginnings of Sisterhood: The American Woman's Rights Movement, 1800–1850* (New York: Schocken, 1977); Katharine Du Pre Lumpkin, *The Emancipation of Angelina Grimke* (Chapel Hill: University of North Carolina Press, 1974).
119. See, on these points, Richards, *Women Gays, and the Constitution*, pp. 102–24.
120. See Angelina Grimke, *Letters to Catherine E. Beecher*, reprinted in Larry Ceplair, *The Public Years of Sarah and Angelina Grimke: Selected Writings 1835–1839* (New York: Columbia University Press, 1989), at p. 167.
121. See Angelina Grimke, *Appeal to the Women of the Nominally Free States* (New York: William S. Dorr, 1837), at p. 43.
122. See, for example, *ibid.*, at pp. 21–3.
123. *Ibid.*, at p. 22.
124. [Louisa McCord], "Enfranchisement of Woman," Southern Quarterly Review 21 (April 1852), 233–341, at p. 340.
125. See George Fitzhugh, *Cannibals All!: or, Slaves without Masters*, edited by C. Vann Woodward (Cambridge, Mass.: Harvard University Press, Belknap Press, 1960), at pp. 190–8.
126. See, for fuller discussion of these points, David Richards, *Women, Gays, and the Constitution*, pp. 81–102.
127. See Eve LaPlante, *American Jezebel* (San Francisco: HarperSanFrancisco, 2004).

128. See Taylor Branch, *Parting the Waters: Martin Luther King and the Civil Rights Movement 1954–63* (London: Papermac, 1988); see also Taylor Branch, *Pillar of Fire: America in the King Years 1963–65* (New York: Simon & Schuster, 1998).

129. See, on this point, Taylor Branch, *Parting the Waters*, pp. 56, 389, 390–1, 571, 589–9.

130. See, for fuller study and defense of these points, David A. J. Richards, *Disarming Manhood*, Chapter 4.

131. See Taylor Branch, *Parting the Waters*, pp. 128–34, 139, 655.

132. See, on these points, Mary Fair Burks, "Trailblazers: Women in the Montgomery Bus Boycott," in Vicki L. Crawford, Jacqueline Anne Rouse, and Barbara Woods, eds., *Women in the Civil Rights Movement* (Bloomington: Indiana University Press, 1993), pp. 71–84; Belinda Robnett, *How Long? How Long?: African-American Women in the Struggle for Civil Rights* (New York: Oxford University Press, 1997), pp. 53–70; Lynne Olston, *Freedom's Daughters: The Unsung Heroines of the Civil Rights Movement from 1830 to 1970* (New York: Scribner, 2001), pp. 87–131; Taylor Branch, *Parting the Waters*, p. 149.

133. Branch, *Parting the Waters*, p. 136.

134. Constance Baker Mottley, *Equal Justice Under Law* (New York: Farrar, Straus and Giroux, 1998), p. 157.

135. Branch, *Parting the Waters*, pp. 136–7.

136. Quoted in *ibid.*, pp. 138–9.

137. *Ibid.*, pp. 139–40.

138. Quoted at *id.*, p. 140.

139. See Andrew Young, *An Easy Burden: The Civil Rights Movement and the Transformation of America* (New York: HarperCollins, 1996), p. 295.

140. See, on this important constitutional development, Harry Kalven, Jr., *The Negro and the First Amendment* (Chicago: University of Chicago Press, 1965).

141. See, on this point, James M. Washington, ed., *A Testament of Hope*, at pp. 50, 71, 88, 265, 266, 290, 294, 300, 328, 347, 349.

142. See, for a discussion of these free speech principles, David A. J. Richards, *Free Speech and the Politics of Identity* (Oxford: Oxford University Press, 1999); Harry Kalven, Jr., *The Negro and the First Amendment*.

143. See, on the role of this text in King's statements, James Melvin Washington, ed., *A Testament of Hope: The Essential Writings of Martin Luther King, Jr.* (San Francisco: Harper and Row, 1986) , at pp. 38, 47, 90, 140, 216, 256, 297, 436, 447.

144. See Martin Luther King, Jr., "Loving Your Enemies," in Clayborne Carson and Peter Holloran eds., *A Knock at Midnight: Inspiration from the Great Sermons of Reverend Martin Luther King, Jr.* (New York: Warner Books, 2000), pp. 41–64, at p. 59.

145. See, for example, Joseph R. Washington, Jr., *Black Religion: The Negro and Christianity in the United States* (Boston: Beacon Press, 1964).

146. See, for an autobiography of one such woman who participated, as a student, in the civil rights movement, Charlayne Hunter-Gault, *In My Place* (New York: Vintage Books, 1993). For a rather different perspective by an activist woman who was not part of the nonviolent civil rights movement, see Angela Davis, *An Autobiography* (New York: International Publishers, 1988) (originally published 1974).

147. See, for important studies, Peter J. Ling and Sharon Monteith, *Gender in the Civil Rights Movement* (New York: Garland Publishing 1999); Lynne Olson, *Freedom's Daughters*; Belinda Robnett, *How Long? How Long?*; Vicki Crawford, Jacqueline Anne Rouse, and Barbara Woods, *Women in the Civil Rights Movement;* Bettye Collier-Thomas and V. P. Franklin, eds., *Sisters in the Struggle: African American Women in the Civil Rights–Black Power Movement* (New York: New York University Press, 2001); Paula Giddings, *When and Where I Enter, The Impact of Black Woman on Race and Sex in America* (New York: William Morrow and Company, 1984).

148. See Branch, *Parting the Waters*, at pp. 231–3, 258, 264, 273–6, 292–3, 317, 392, 466–7, 487, 518; Branch, *Pillar of Fire*, pp. 192–3, 439, 457.

149. See Branch, *Parting the Waters*, pp. 263–4, 290, 381–2, 573, 576–7, 899; Branch, *Pillar of Fire*, pp. 124, 191.

150. See Branch, *Parting the Waters*, pp. 279–80, 295, 392, 424, 428–9, 437, 439, 449, 455, 466–7, 487, 559, 588, 712, 754, 892–3; Branch, *Pillar of Fire*, pp. 54–5, 68, 139–41, 165, 285, 524, 553, 559, 579, 587, 599.

151. See Branch, *Parting the Waters* , pp. 636, 819; Branch, *Pillar of Fire*, pp. 57, 71, 74, 109, 179, 219, 240, 329, 458–9, 461, 465, 474, 481, 547–8.

152. See, on this development, Sara Evans, *Personal Politics: The Roots of Women's Liberation in the Civil Rights Movement and the New Left* (New York: Vintage Books, 1980)

153. See, on this point, David L. Chappell, *A Stone of Hope: Prophetic Religion and the Death of Jim Crow* (Chapel Hill: University of North Carolina Press, 2004).

154. See, on this point in King's statements, James M. Washington, ed., *A Testament of Hope*, pp. 210, 254, 269, 290, 474, 588, 594, 626.

155. See, on this point, Martin Luther King, Jr., "Letter from Birmingham Jail," in James M. Washington, Jr., *A Testament of Hope*, at pp. 289, 292.

156. See, on the new natural lawyers, Nicholas C. Bamforth and David A. J. Richards, *Patriarchal Religion, Sexuality, and Gender: A Critique of New Natural Law* (Cambridge: Cambridge University Press, 2008).

157. See, for an excellent discussion of these and related points, John Boswell, *The Kindness of Strangers: The Abandonment of Children in Western Europe from Late Antiquity to the Renaissance* (Chicago: University of Chicago Press, 1988).

158. See Martin Luther, *The Judgment of Martin Luther on Monastic Vows, 1521*, in Martin Luther, *Luther's Works Volume 44 The Christian in Society* J. Martin Atkinson ed. and translator (Philadelphia: Fortress Press, 1966), pp. 245–400, at pp. 339–40, 343, 369–70.

159. See *ibid.*, at pp. 370–2; see also his references to Paris as "Sodom" and "Gomorrah," pp. 259, 300, 328.

160. See, for fuller discussion of both issues, A. W. Richard Sipe, *Celibacy in Crisis: A Secret World Revisited* (New York: Brunner-Routledge, 2003).

161. See, in general, Kennedy, *The Unhealed Wound*.

162. In the Synoptics, Jesus is pictured as showing reserve, verging on hostility, to his family, including his mother, Mary. Mark (3:21) bluntly reports that his family held him to be mad, to the point that they wanted forcibly to remove him from his public ministry.

163. See, for example, Garry Wills, *Papal Sin: Structures of Deceit* (New York: Doubleday, 2000); Gary Wills, *Why I Am a Catholic* (Boston: Houghton Mifflin Company, 2002); Peter Steinfels, *A People Adrift: The Crisis of the Roman Catholic Church in America* (New York: Simon & Schuster, 2003).

164. For research bearing on this point, see David France, *Our Fathers: The Secret Life of the Catholic Church in an Age of Scandal* (Broadway Books: New York, 2004), at p. 158; Andrew M. Greeley, *Priests: A Calling in Crisis* (Chicago: University of Chicago Press, 2004), pp. 36–47.

165. See, for other important studies, Jason Berry, *Lead Us Not into Temptation: Catholic Priests and the Sexual Abuse of Children* (Urbana: University of Illinois Press, 2000); Jason Berry and Gerald Renner, *Vows of Silence: The Abuse of Power in the Papacy of John Paul II* (New York: The Free Press, 2004); Thomas G. Plante, *Sin Against the Innocents: Sexual Abuse by Priests and the Role of the Catholic Church* (Westport, Conn.: Praeger, 2004); A. W. Richard Sipe, *Celibacy in Crisis*.

166. David France, *Our Fathers: The Secret Life of the Catholic Church in an Age of Scandal* (New York: Broadway Books, 2004), pp. 156, 158.

167. *Ibid.*, pp. 157, 555.

168. *Ibid.*, p. 351.

169. *Ibid.*, p. 372.

170. France, *Our Fathers*, pp. 203–4, 230.

171. France, *Our Fathers*, pp. 423–5.

172. *Ibid.*, p. 516.

173. See, on this point, Kennedy, *The Unhealed Wound*, pp. 6–62, 128–32.

174. Mark D. Jordan, *Telling Truths in Church: Scandal, Flesh, and Christian Speech* (Boston: Beacon Press, 2003), p. 13.

175. On "the narcissism of small differences," see Sigmund Freud, *Civilization and Its Discontents*, in *Standard Edition of the Complete Psychological Works of Sigmund Freud*, edited and translated by James Strachey (Hogarth Press: London, 1961), 21:114; see also *Moses and Monotheism* in *Standard Edition of the Complete Psychological Works of Sigmund Freud*, edited and translated by James Strachey (Hogarth Press: London, 1964), 23:91.

176. For fuller discussion, see Bamforth and Richards, *Patriarchal Religion, Sexuality, and Gender*.

177. See Carroll, *Constantine's Sword*, at pp. 155–236.

178. See also James Carroll, *House of War: The Pentagon and the Disastrous Rise of American Power* (Boston: Houghton Mifflin Company, 2006).

179. *Ibid.*, p. 241.

### 7. Resistance: Psychology

1. See Sandor Ferenczi, "The Confusion of Tongues between Adult and Child: The Mixing of Tenderness and Passion," and Ian Suttie, *The Origins of Love and Hate*.

2. Josef Breuer and Sigmund Freud, *Studies on Hysteria*, in *The Standard Edition of the Complete Psychological Works of Sigmund Freud* [hereinafter, Freud, *Standard Edition*], *Volume II (1893–1895)*, translated by James Strachey (London: Hogarth Press, 1955), at pp. 1–305.

3. Freud, *Standard Edition, Volume II*, at p. 157.

4. Carol Gilligan, *The Birth of Pleasure* (2003), p. 217.

5. *Ibid.*, p. 135.

6. See for example his statement to this effect in the case of Lucy von R., *Studies on Hysteria*, in Freud, *Standard Edition*, Volume II, at p. 110.

7. *Ibid.*, p. 153.

8. *Ibid.*, p. 154.

9. Freud, *Standard Edition, Volume II*, p. 140.

10. Freud, *Standard Edition, Volume II*, p. 181.

11. Judith Herman, *Trauma and Recovery* (New York: Basic Books, 1997).

12. Bessel A. van der Kolk, Alexander C. McFarlane, and Lars Weisaeth, editors, *Traumatic Stress: The Effects of Overwhelming Experience on Mind, Body, and Society* (New York: The Guilford Press, 1996).

13. Freud, *Standard Edition, Volume II*, p. 160.

14. *The Freud/Jung Letters: The Correspondence Between Sigmund Freud and C. G. Jung*, edited by William McGuire, translated by Ralph Manheim and R. F. C. Hull (Cambridge, Mass.: Harvard University Press, 1988), at pp. 12–13.

15. Freud, *Standard Edition, Volume II*, p. 144.

16. *Ibid.*, p. 136.

17. For this phrase, we are indebted to the writings of Jean Baker Miller. See for example, Jean Baker Miller and Irene Pierce Stiver, *The Healing Connection*.

18. Freud, *Three Essays on Sexuality*, in *Standard Edition, Volume VII (1901–1905)*, pp. 125–243, at p. 151.

19. Freud, *On Narcissism: An Introduction*, in *Standard Edition, Volume XIV (1914–1916)*, pp. 73–102, at p. 89.

20. Freud, *The Question of Lay Analysis*, in *Standard Edition, Volume XX (1925–1926)*, pp. 179–258, at p. 212.

21. Freud, *Some Psychical Consequences of the Anatomical Distinction Between the Sexes*, in Freud, *Standard Edition, Volume XIX* (1923–1925), pp. 243–58, at pp. 257–8.

22. Freud, *New Introductory Lectures on Psycho-Analysis*, in Freud, *Standard Edition, Volume XXII (1932–36)*, pp. 3–182, at p. 134.

23. Freud, *Civilization and Its Discontents*, in Freud, *Standard Edition, Volume XXI* (1927–1931), pp. 59–145, at p. 104.

24. Freud, *Female Sexuality*, in Freud, *Standard Edition, Volume XXI (1927–1931)*, pp. 223–43.

25. Freud, *'Civilized' Sexual Morality and Modern Nervous Illness*, in Freud, *Standard Edition, Volume IX (1906–1908)*, pp. 179–204, at p. 199.

26. See Freud, *A Special Type of Choice of Object Made by Men (Contributions to the Psychology of Love I*, in Freud, *Standard Edition, Volume XI (1910)*, pp. 163–176; *On the Universal Tendency to Debasement in the Sphere of Love (Contributions to the Psychology of Law II)*, id., pp. 177–90; *The Taboo of Virginity (Contributions to the Psychology of Love III)*, pp. 191–208.

27. Karen Horney, "The Flight from Womanhood," in Jean Baker Miller, ed., *Psychoanalysis and Women* (Harmondsworth, Middlesex, England: Penguin, 1973), pp. 5–20, at p. 8.

28. Gilligan, *The Birth of Pleasure*, p. 226.

29. Freud, *The Interpretation of Dreams (First Part)*, in Freud, *Standard Edition, Volume IV (1900)*, pp. 1–338, at p. 106n.

30. See *ibid.*, p. 107.

31. See, on these and following points, Peter Gay, *Freud: A Life for Our Time* (Norton: W. W. Norton, 2006), pp. 80–7.

32. Erik Erikson, "The Dream Specimen of Psychoanalysis (1954)," in Erik H. Erikson, *A Way of Looking at Things: Selected Papers*, edited by Stephen Schlein (New York: W. W. Norton, 1987), pp. 237–79.

33. See Peter Gay, *Freud*, pp. 83–7.

34. See also Tova Hartman, *Feminism Encounters Traditional Judaism: Resistance and Accommodation* (Waltham, Mass.: Brandeis University Press, 2007), for an insightful reading of the Irma Dream.

35. Quoted in Gilligan, *The Birth of Pleasure*, p. 227 (from Sigmund Freud, *The Complete Letters of Sigmund Freud and Wilhelm Fliess 1887–1907*. Edited by Jeffrey Moussaieff Mason (Cambridge, Mass.: Harvard University Press, 1986)).

36. For a powerful study of this period along these lines, see Carl E. Schorske, *Fin-de-Siecle Vienna: Politics and Culture* (New York: Vintage Books, 1981).

37. See *ibid.*, p. 183.

38. Freud, *The Interpretation of Dreams (First Part)*, p. 208, n2.

39. Freud, *The Interpretation of Dreams (Second Part)*, in Freud, *Standard Edition, Volume V (1900–1901)*, pp. 339–625, at p. 428.

40. Freud, *The Interpretation of Dreams (First Part)*, p. 257.

41. See Freud, *The Interpretation of Dreams (First Part)*, pp. 298–302.

42. Peter Gay, *Freud*, p. 504.

43. See Plate VIII, between pages 211–12, Schorske, *Fin-de-Siecle Vienna*.

44. Sophocles, *Oedipus Tyrannus* translated and edited by Luci Berkowitz and Theodore F. Brunner (New York: W. W. Norton, 1970), at p. 28.

45. *Ibid.*, pp. 28–9.

46. See Freud, *Why War?*, Freud, *Standard Edition Volume XXII (1932–1936)*, pp. 199–215. *op. cit.*

47. Freud, *Civilization and Its Discontents*, p. 111.

48. See Freud, *A Special Type of Choice of Object Made by Men (Contributions to the Psychology of Love I*, in Freud, *Standard Edition, Volume XI (1910)*, pp. 163–76; *On the Universal Tendency to Debasement in the Sphere of Love (Contributions to the Psychology of Law II)*, id., pp. 177–90; *The Taboo of Virginity (Contributions to the Psychology of Love III)*, pp. 191–208.

49. See Janine Burke, *The Sphinx on the Table: Sigmund Freud's Art Collection and the Development of Psychoanalysis* (New York: Walker & Company, 2006), at pp. 53, 72, 92, 229, 248, 299, 310, 340.

50. See Freud, *Totem and Taboo*, Freud, *Standard Edition Volume XIII (1913–1914)*, pp. 1–162, at p. 144.

51. See Janine Burke, *op. cit.*, p. 53.

52. See *id.*, p. 310. For a forceful critique of the view that Isis is the model for the Virgin Mary, see Michael P. Carroll, *The Cult of the Virgin Mary: Psychological Origins* (Princeton, N.J.: Princeton University Press, 1986).

53. See, on this point, Peter Gay, *Freud*, pp. 162–4.

54. *Sigmund Freud and Lou Andreas-Salome Letters*, edited by Ernst Pfeiffer, translated by William and Elaine Robson-Scott (New York: W. W. Norton & Co. 1972), p. 45.

55. *Letters of Sigmund Freud*, edited by Ernst Freud (New York: Basic Books, 1960), pp. 312, 454–5.

56. See, for an illuminating study of Horney's dissenting role, Susan Quinn, *A Mind of Her Own: The Life of Karen Horney* (New York: Summit Books, 1987).

57. *Letters of Sigmund Freud*, p. 312.

58. For an example of a range of such early critical views, see Jean Baker Miller, *Psychoanalysis and Women* (Harmondsworth, Middlesex, England: Penguin, 1973), and subsequently works of Elisabeth Young-Bruehl, for example, Elisabeth Young-Bruehl, "The 'Taboo on Tenderness' in the History of Psychoanalysis," in Martin S. Bergmann, ed., *Understanding Dissidence and Controversy in the History of Psychoanalysis* (New York: Other Press, 2004), at pp. 229–47.

59. See, on this point, Benedict Carey, "An Analyst Questions the Self-Perpetuating Side of Therapy," *The New York Times*, October 10, 2006, p. F2; see also Owen Renik, *Practical Psychoanalysis for Therapists and Parents* (New York: Other Press, 2006).

60. Renik, *Ibid.*, at pp. 2, 153–5.

61. T. S. Eliot, *On Poets and Poetry* (New York: Farrar, Straus and Cudahy, 1957), at p. 63.

62. Vergil, the *Aeneid*, p. 176.

63. *Ibid.*, pp. 207–8.

64. See Freud, *Screen Memories*, in Freud, *Standard Edition, Volume III (1893–1899)*, pp. 303–22, at p. 317.

65. *Ibid.*, p. 311.

66. See Freud, *The Theme of the Three Caskets*, in Freud, *Standard Edition, Volume XII (1911–1913)*, pp. 291–301, at p. 300, n1.

67. See Freud, *Screen Memories*, pp. 312–13.

68. See Freud, *Screen Memories,*, p. 311.

69. Freud, *The Psychopathology of Everyday Life*, in Freud, *Standard Edition, Volume VI (1901)*, pp. 1–279, at pp. 8–14.

70. See, on this point, Paul Zanker, *The Power of Images in the Age of Augustus*, at pp. 72, 98, 105–6, 108, 110–11, 114–15, 148, 155, 194–6, 201, 213–15.

71. See Freud, *A Special Type of Choice of Object Made by Men (Contributions to the Psychology of Love I)*, in Freud, *Standard Edition, Volume XI (1910)*, pp. 163–76; *On the Universal Tendency to Debasement in the Sphere of Love (Contributions to the Psychology of Love II)*, *id.*, pp. 177–90; *The Taboo of Virginity (Contributions to the Psychology of Love III)*, pp. 191–208.

72. See, for a good general study, Lisa Appignanesi and John Forrester, *Freud's Women* (New York: Other Press, 2000).

73. See, for historical background, Judith Hallett, "*Feminae Furentes*: The Frenzy of Noble Women in Vergil's *Aeneid* and the Letter of Cornelia, Mother of the Gracchi," in William S. Anderson and Lorina N. Quartarone, eds., *Approaches to Teaching Vergil's Aeneid* (New York: The Modern Language Association of America, 2002), at pp. 159–67.

74. Ian D. Suttie, *The Origins of Love and Hate* (London: Free Association Books, 1999) (first published 1935).

75. See Sandor Ferenczi, "The Confusion of Tongues between Adult and Child: The Mixing of Tenderness and Passion."

76. See Elisabeth Young-Bruehl, "The 'Taboo on Tenderness' in the History of Psychoanalysis," at pp. 229–47.

77. See, on the importance of Suttie in the history of psychoanalysis, Elisabeth Young-Bruehl,: The 'Taboo on Tenderness' in the History of Psychoanalysis," at pp. 229–47. For further illuminating background on resistance within psychoanalysis to Freud's views and cogent argument for an alternative view along the lines we endorse, see Elisabeth Young-Bruehl, *Where Do We Fall When We Fall in Love?* (New York: Other Press, 2003).

78. For Freud's statement of this view, see Freud, *Beyond the Pleasure Principle*, in Freud, *Standard Edition, Volume XVIII (1920–1922)*, pp. 7–64.

79. See Freud, *Why War?*, in Freud, *Standard Edition, Volume XXII (1932–1936)*, pp. 203–15.

80. Suttie, *The Origins of Love and Hate*, at p. 86.

81. See *ibid.*, pp. 80–96.

82. See, on this point, *ibid.*, pp. 82–3.

83. See, on this point, *ibid.*, pp. 82–3.

84. There are other rather speculative anthropological arguments about anti-patriarchal forms of religion, including J. J. Bachofen, *Myth, Religion, and Mother Right*, and Robert Graves, *The White Goddess*, which we regard as not sufficiently well grounded for consideration here.

85. Suttie, *The Origins of Love and Hate*, pp. 3, 146.

86. *Ibid.*, pp. 141–2, 217.

87. See, *ibid.*, pp. 137, 223, 227.

88. See, for example, Carol Gilligan, *In a Different Voice: Psychological Theory and Women's Development* (Cambridge, Mass.: Harvard University Press, 1982); Jean Baker Miller, *Toward a New Psychology of Women*, second edition (Boston: Beacon Press, 1986); Jean Baker Miller and Irene Pierce Stiver, *The Healing Connection: How Women Form Relationships in Therapy and in Life* (Boston: Beacon Press, 1997); Carol Gilligan, *The Birth of Pleasure* (2002), Christina Robb, *This Changes Everything: The Relational Revolution in Psychology* (New York: Farrar, Straus and Giroux, 2006); Elisabeth Young-Bruehl, *Where Do We Fall When We Fall in Love?*

89. See, for example, L. Murray and C. Trevarthen, "Emotional Regulation of Interactions Between Two-Month-Olds and Their Mothers," in *Social Perception in Infants*, T. M. Fields and N. A. Fox, eds. (Norwood, N.J.: Ablex Publishing, 1985); L. Murray and C. Trevarthen, "The Infant's Role in Mother-Infant Communication," *Journal of Child Language* 13 (1986), 15–29; Edward Z. Tronick, "Emotions and Emotional Communication in Infants," *American Psychologist* 44(2) (1989), 112–19; E. Z. Tronick and M. K. Weinberg, "Depressed Mothers and Infants: Failure to Form Dyadic States of Consciousness," in *Postpartum Depression and Child Development*, L. Murray and P. J. Cooper, eds. (New York: Guilford Press, 1997); E. Z. Tronick and A. Gianino, "Interactive Mismatch and Repair Challenges in the Coping Infant," *Zero to Three* 6, 1–6; 1999 Beatrice Beebe and Frank Lachmann, *Infant Research and Adult Treatment: Co-Constructing Interactions* (Hillsdale, N.J.: The Analytic Press, 2002); Daniel N. Stern, *The Interpersonal World of the Infant* (New York: Basic Books, 1998). Carol Gilligan, "The Centrality of Relationship in Human Development: A Puzzle, Some Evidence, and a Theory" in K. Fischer and G. Noam, eds. *Development and Vulnerability in Close Relationships* (New York: Erlbaum, 1996); see also Daniel Goleman, "Friends for Life: An Emerging Biology of Emotional Healing," *The New York Times*, October 10, 2006, p. F5.

90. See Lyn Mikel Brown and Carol Gilligan, *Meeting at the Crossroads: Women's Psychology and Girls' Development* (Cambridge, Mass.: Harvard University Press, 1992), at pp. 136–40.

91. For further discussion of the research on girls' development, see Carol Gilligan, "Joining the Resistance: Psychology, Politics, Girls and Women," *Michigan Quarterly Review*, 29(4) (1990), 505–36; Carol Gilligan, Janie Victoria Ward, and Jill McLean Taylor, *Mapping the Moral Domain: A Contribution of Women's Thinking to Psychological Theory and Education* (Cambridge, Mass.: Harvard University Press, 1988); Lyn Mikel Brown and

Carol Gilligan, *Meeting at the Crossroads: Women's Psychology and Girls' Development* (Cambridge, Mass.: Harvard University Press, 1992); Carol Gilligan, Annie G. Rogers, and Deborah Tolman, *Women, Girls, and Psychotherapy: Reframing Resistance* (Binghamton, N.Y.: Haworth Press, 1991); Carol Gilligan, Nona Lyons, and Trudy Hanmer, eds., *Making Connections: The Relational Worlds of Adolescent Girls at Emma Willard School* (Cambridge, Mass.: Harvard University Press, 1990); Jill McLean Taylor, Carol Gilligan, and Amy M. Sullivan, *Between Voice and Silence: Women and Girls, Race and Relationship* (Cambridge, Mass.: Harvard University Press, 1995); Gilligan, *The Birth of Pleasure*.

92. See on this research, Carol Gilligan, *The Birth of Pleasure*, and Carol Gilligan, "The Centrality of Relationship in Human Development: A puzzle, some evidence, and a theory."

93. Elisabeth Young-Bruehl. "The 'Taboo on Tenderness' in the History of Psychoanalysis," in Martin S. Bergmann, ed., *Understanding Dissidence and Controversy in the History of Psychoanalysis* (New York: Other Press, 2004), pp. 229–47.

## 8. Resistance: The Artists

1. Paul Fussell, *The Great War and Modern Memory* (New York: Oxford University Press, 2000) (originally published 1975). For a related study, see Samuel Hynes, *The Auden Generation: Literature and Politics in England in the 1930s* (New York: The Viking Press, 1977).

2. Ernest Hemingway, *A Farewell to Arms* (New York: Scribner Classics, 1997) (first published 1929), at p. 169, quoted in Fussell, *The Great War and Modern Memory*, at p. 21.

3. See J. J. M. Tobin, *Shakespeare's Favorite Novel: A Study of the Golden Ass as Prime Source* (Lanham, Md.: University of America, 1984).

4. See, on this point, Richards, *Tragic Manhood and Democracy*, at pp.124–9.

5. See Miguel de Cervantes, *Don Quixote*, translated by Edith Grossman (New York: HarperCollins, 2003); Miguel de Cervantes, *Exemplary Stories*, translated by Lesley Lipson (Oxford; Oxford University Press, 1998). See, for a reference to "the genre of Milesian tales," of which Apuleius's *Metamorphoses* is a leading example, Cervantes, *Don Quixote*, p. 411; and, for an explicit reference to Apuleius, see Cervantes, *Exemplary Stories*, pp. 283, 285. For references to Ovid's *Metamorphoses*, see *id*., pp. 199, 234. See Ludovico Ariosto, *Orlando Furioso*, Part One, translated by Barbara Reynolds (London: Penguin 1975); *Orlando Furioso*, Part Two, translated by Barbara Reynolds (London: Penguin, 1977). Torquato Tasso, *Jerusalem Delivered*, translated by Anthony M. Esolen (Baltimore: The Johns Hopkins University Press, 2000). See, on Cervantes's disillusionment, Jean Canavaggio, *Cervantes*, translated from the French by J. R. Jones (New York: W. W. Norton, 1990), at p. 180.

6. On the Apuleian influence, see Jacques Chailley, *The Magic Flute, Masonic Opera: An Interpretation of the Libretto and Music*, translated by Herbert Weinstock (New York: Alfred A. Knopf, 1971), p. 37.

7. See, on this point, Richards, *Tragic Manhood and Democracy*.

8. Nathaniel Hawthorne, *The Scarlet Letter* (New York: Penguin, 1983) (originally published, 1850), p. 227.

9. Hawthorne, *The Scarlet Letter*, p. 143.

10. See, on these points, *The Dangerous Lives of Printers: The Evolution of Freedom of the Press*, at http://www.assumption.edu/ahc/1770s/ppressfree.html, at p. 4; Mukhtar Ali Isani, "Hawthorne and the Branding of William Prynne," *New England Quarterly*, 45 (June, 1972), 182–95; Jeffery A. Smith, *Printers and Press Freedom: The Ideology of Early American Journalism* (New York: Oxford University Press, 1988), pp. 20–2; Akhil Reed Amar, *The Bill of Rights: Creation and Reconstruction* (New Haven: Yale University Press, 1998), pp. 82, 87. We are indebted for this reference to Mr. Prynne to James Gilligan.

11. James Joyce, *Ulysses* (New York: Vintage International, 1990) (originally published 1934).
12. Monteverdi, *Il Ritorno D'Ulisse in Patria*, libretto by Diacomo Badoaro, at p. 117 (English translation from Italian), musical realization by Rene Jacobs in three CDs (Germany: Harmonia Mundi, 1992).
13. Sue Blundell, *Women in Ancient Greece* (Cambridge, Mass.: Harvard University Press, 1995), at p. 56.
14. Of the emission of semen apart from procreation in marriage, Thomas Aquinas wrote: "[A]fter the sin of homicide whereby a human nature already in existence is destroyed, this type of sin appears to take next place, for by it the generation of human nature is precluded." Thomas Aquinas, *On the Truth of the Catholic Faith: Summa Contra Gentiles*, translated by Vernon Bourke (New York: Image, 1956), Part 2, Chapter 122(9), p. 146.
15. For a full discussion, see Thomas W. Laqueur, *Solitary Sex: A Cultural History of Masturbation* (New York: Zone Books, 2004).
16. Joyce, *Ulysses*, p. 464. See also *Id.*, pp. 692, 696, 724.
17. See, for Joyce's autobiographical treatment of these issues, James Joyce, *A Portrait of the Artist as a Young Man* (New York; Penguin, 2003) (originally published 1916).
18. On Joyce's early relationship to Nora, see Richard Ellmann, *James Joyce* New and Revised Edition (Oxford: Oxford University Press, 1983), pp. 159–79. See also Brenda Maddox, *Nora: The Real Life of Molly Bloom* (Boston: Houghton Mifflin Company, 1988). On the fraught relationship of Joyce and Nora to their daughter, Lucia, see Carol Loeb Schloss, *Lucia Joyce: To Dance in the Wake* (New York: Farrar, Straus, and Giroux, 2005).
19. See, on these points, Richards, *Disarming Manhood*, at pp. 51–87.
20. For the ruling, see Joyce, *Ulysses*, pp. ix–xiv.
21. See, on this point, Richards, *Women, Gays, and the Constitution*, pp. 297–8.
22. Edith Wharton, *Summer* (New York: Penguin, 1993) (originally published 1917).
23. Edith Wharton, *The Age of Innocence* (New York: Oxford University Press, 2006) (originally published 1920).
24. Virginia Woolf, *Three Guineas*, Jane Marcus edition (Orlando: Harvest, 2006), p. 121.
25. Virginia Woolf, *Mrs. Dalloway* (San Diego: Harvest, 1997) (first published 1925).
26. Virginia Woolf, *To the Lighthouse* (San Diego: Harvest, 1981) (originally published 1927).
27. See Judith Herman, *Trauma and Recovery* (New York, Basic Books, 1997).
28. See, on this point, Woolf, *Three Guineas*, p. 122.
29. Virginia Woolf, *A Room of One's Own* (San Diego: Harvest, 1981) (originally published 1929), p. 35.
30. See, on this point, Woolf, *Three Guineas*, pp. 132, 135.
31. D. H. Lawrence, *Lady Chatterley's Lover*, introduction by Doris Lessing (New York: Penguin, 2006) (originally published 1928), at p. xxvi.
32. See Kate Millett, *Sexual Politics* (Urbana: University of Illinois Press, 2000) (originally published 1969), at pp. 237–93.
33. Lessing, *op. cit.*, p. xxi.
34. See Lawrence, *Lady Chatterley's Lover*, at pp. 200–3.
35. See Richards, *Women, Gays, and the Constitution*, at p. 340.
36. See, on this point, Michael P. Carroll, *The Cult of the Virgin Mary*.
37. See on this point, Walter Kaufman, *Tragedy and Philosophy* (Garden City, N.Y.: Doubleday, 1968).

## 9. Resistance: Politics

1. See, on this point, Bob Herbert, "Why Aren't We Shocked?" *The New York Times*, October 16, 2006, at A19.

2. See, for an overview of these historical sources, David A. J. Richards, *Foundations of American Constitutionalism* (New York: Oxford University Press, 1989). See also M. N. S. Sellers, *American Republicanism: Roman Ideology in the United States Constitution* (New York: New York University Press, 1994); Carl J. Richard, *The Founders and the Classics: Greece, Rome, and the American Enlightenment* (Cambridge, Mass.: Harvard University Press, 1994).

3. See, on the classical education of the Founders, Carl J. Richard, *The Founders and the Classics*, pp. 13, 17–25, 33–5, 221.

4. Vergil, *Georgics of Vergil*, 1. 40, at pp. 4–5 ("Grant me the right to enter upon this bold/Adventure of mine").

5. Vergil, *Aeneid*, IX:625: "All-powerful Jupiter, favor my daring undertakings."

6. See, on these points, M. N. S. Sellers, *American Republicanism*, pp. 17–18.

7. Vergil, *Eclogue IV*, l. 5, in Vergil, *Eclogues, Georgics, Aeneid 1–6*, at p. 48.

8. Arendt, *The Life of the Mind*, Two/Willing, p. 207.

9. See, on this point, Arendt, *The Life of the Mind*, Two/Willing, pp. 195–217; Carl J. Richard, *The Founders and the Classics*, pp. 23, 55, 182, 207, 224.

10. Quoted in Richard, *ibid.*, p. 207.

11. See David A. J. Richards, *Conscience and the Constitution: History, Theory, and Law of the Reconstruction Amendments* (Princeton, N.J.: Princeton University Press, 1993).

12. See, on this point, David A. J. Richards, *Women, Gays, and the Constitution: The Grounds for Feminism and Gay Rights in Culture and Law* (Chicago: University of Chicago Press, 1998).

13. See, on these points, William D. Phillips, Jr., "Continuity and change in Western slavery: ancient to modern times," in M. L. Bush, ed., *Serfdom and Slavery: Studies in Legal Bondage* (London: Longman, 1999), at pp. 71–88.

14. See, on this point, Richard Saller, "The hierarchical household in Roman society: a study of domestic slavery," *id.*, pp. 112–29.

15. On this point, see Richards, *Conscience and the Constitution*, at pp. 226-8.

16. See, on this point, Richards, *Conscience and the Constitution*, at pp. 24, 92, 120.

17. *Dred Scott v. Sanford*, 19 Howard 393 (1857). For commentary, see Richards, *Conscience and the Constitution*, at pp. 41, 54–5, 78, 81, 106, 113, 120, 125, 129, 137, 200, 217, 258.

18. See, for an extended treatment of proslavery constitutionalism, Richards, *Conscience and the Constitution*, pp. 28–42. Abolitionist constitutional thought, in contrast, argued that Roman and Greek slavery were inconsistent with the fundamental American constitutional commitment to universal human rights. See *id.*, pp. 61–2, 91, 130, 132.

19. See Richards, *Conscience and the Constitution*, 61–2, 91, 130, 132.

20. See, on this point, Richards, *Women, Gays, and the Constitution*, pp. 138–9.

21. See, for a general critique of and commentary on constitutional interpretation of the Reconstruction Amendments along these lines, Richards, *Conscience and the Constitution*; Richards, *Women, Gays, and the Constitution*.

22. See *Plessy v. Ferguson*, 163 U.S. 537 (1896).

23. *Brown v. Board of Education*, 347 U.S. 483 (1954) (state-imposed racial segregation violation of equal protection).

24. Charles A. Lofgren, *The Plessy Case: A Legal Historical Interpretation* (New York: Oxford University Press, 1987).

25. See, for good general treatments, Stephen Jay Gould, *The Mismeasure of Man* (New York: W. W. Norton, 1981); Thomas F. Gossett, *Race: The History of an Idea in America* (New York: Schocken Books, 1965); George M. Fredrickson, *The Black Image in the White Mind: The Debate on Afro-American Character and Destiny, 1817–1914* (Middletown, Conn.: Wesleyan University Press, 1981); John S. Haller, Jr., *Outcasts from Evolution: Scientific Attitudes of Racial Inferiority, 1859–1900* (New York: McGraw-Hill, 1971); Reginald Horsman, *Race and Manifest Destiny: The Origins of American Racial Anglo-Saxonism* (Cambridge, Mass.: Harvard University Press, 1981).

26. See Franz Boas, "Human Faculty as Determined by Race" (1894), in George W. Stocking, Jr., ed., *A Franz Boas Reader: The Shaping of American Anthropology, 1833–1911* (Chicago: University of Chicago Press, 1974), pp. 221–42.

27. C. Van Woodward, "Emancipations and Reconstructions: A Comparative Study," in C. Van Woodward, *The Future of the Past* (New York: Oxford University Press, 1989), at p. 166.

28. On Stevens's abortive proposals for confiscation and distribution of Southern plantations to the freedmen, see Eric Foner, *Reconstruction: America's Unfinished Revolution 1863–1877* (New York: Harper & Row, 1988), 222, 235–7, 245–6, 308–10.

29. On Sumner's proposals for federally sponsored land distribution and integrated education for the freedmen, see Foner, *Reconstruction*, pp. 236, 308.

30. See, on these points, William E. Nelson, *The Fourteenth Amendment: From Political Principle to Judicial Doctrine* (Cambridge, Mass.: Harvard University Press, 1988).

31. See C. Vann Woodward, *Reunion and Reaction: The Compromise of 1877 and the End of Reconstruction* (New York: Oxford University Press, 1966).

32. See, on these points, Trudier Harris, "Introduction," in *Selected Works of Ida B. Wells-Barnett*, Trudier Harris, ed. (New York: Oxford University Press, 1991), pp. 3–13; see also Alfred M. Duster, ed., *Crusade for Justice: The Autobiography of Ida B. Wells* (Chicago: University of Chicago Press, 1970); Gail Bederman, *Manliness and Civilization: A Cultural History of Gender and Race in the United States, 1880–1917* (Chicago: University of Chicago Press, 1995), at pp. 45–76.

33. Duster, *Crusade for Justice*, p. 64.

34. See *Southern Horrors: Lynch Law in All Its Phases*, in *Selected Works of Ida B. Wells-Barnett*, pp. 14–45.

35. See, on this point, Richards, *Women, Gays, and the Constitution*, at pp. 55–6.

36. See, on this point, *ibid.*, 115–24.

37. See, on this point, *ibid.*, pp. 188–90.

38. See Ida Wells-Barnett, *A Red Record: Tabulated Statistics and Alleged Causes of Lynchings in the United States, 1892–1893–1894* (1895), in *Selected Works of Ida B. Wells-Barnett*, 138–252, at pp. 146–7.

39. See, for fuller exploration of this point, Richards, *Women, Gays, and the Constitution*, at pp. 190–8.

40. See, on this point, *ibid.*, pp. 199–287.

41. *See ibid.*, pp. 208–24.

42. See *Brown v. Board of Education*, 347 U.S. 483 (1954).

43. See *Loving v. Virginia*, 388 U.S. 1 (1967).

44. See Harry Kalven, Jr., *The Negro and the First Amendment* (Chicago: University of Chicago Press, 1965).

45. See James Baldwin, *Go Tell It on the Mountain*, in Baldwin, *Early Novels and Stories*, Toni Morrison, ed. (New York: Library of America, 1998), pp. 1–215. For commentary, see David A. J. Richards, *Disarming Manhood: Roots of Ethical Resistance* (Athens, Ohio: Swallow Press, 2005), pp. 138–42.

46. See Richards, *Disarming Manhood*, p. 140.

47. See Paula Giddings, *When and Where I Enter: The Impact of Black Women on Race and Sex in America* (New York: William Morrow, 1984).

48. See Hannah Arendt, *The Origins of Totalitarianism* (New York; Harcourt Brace Jovanovich, 1973). See also Hannah Arendt, *Eichmann in Jerusalem: A Report on the Banality of Evil* (New York: Penguin, 1994).

49. See Hannah Arendt, *The Life of the Mind*, one-volume Edition (New York: Harcourt Brace Jovanovich, 1978).

50. See Hannah Arendt, *Rahel Varnhagen: The Life of a Jewess*, translated by Richard and Clara Winston (Baltimore: The Johns Hopkins University Press, 1997) (first published 1958).

51. See, on these points, Elisabeth Young-Bruehl, *Hannah Arendt: For Love of the World* (New Haven, Conn.: Yale University Press, 1982).

52. On this point, see *ibid*., at pp. 95–7, 238, 272–3. See also David Laskin, *Partisans: Marriage, Politics, and Betrayal Among the New York Intellectuals* (New York: Simon & Schuster, 2000), at pp. 146–62, 216–23. 238–44, 248–57.

53. See Hannah Arendt, *Love and Saint Augustine*, edited with an interpretive essay by Joanna Vecchiarelli Scott and Judith Chelius Stark (Chicago: University of Chicago Press, 1996) (first published 1929).

54. See Arendt, *The Life of the Mind*, Two/Willing, at pp. 84–110.

55. See Arendt, *The Origins of Totalitarianism*.

56. See Elisabeth Young-Bruehl, *Where Do We Fall When We Fall in Love?* (New York: Other Press, 2003), p. 36. For Himmler on heroism, see Ian Kershaw, *Hitler: 1936–1945: Nemesis*, at pp. 604–5. for Himmler's adjutant, see *id*., pp. 242–3.

57. See Nietzsche, *On the Genealogy of Morals*, at pp. 134–5.

58. On Nietzsche's ethical perfectionism and its normative consequences, see David A. J. Richards, *A Theory of Reasons for Action* (Oxford: Clarendon Press, 1971), pp. 116–7.

59. On the personal psychological roots of Nietzsche's rage in repressed homosexuality, see Joachim Kohler, *Zarathustra's Secret: The Interior Life of Friedrich Nietzsche*, translated by Ronald Taylor (New Haven, Conn.: Yale University Press, 2002).

60. On Hitler's reading of Nietzsche and, at one point, giving Mussolini a complete copy of his works, see Ian Kershaw, *Hitler: 1889–1936: Hubris* (New York: W. W. Norton, 1998), p. 240; Ian Kershaw, *Hitler: 1936–1945: Nemesis* (New York: W. W. Norton, 2000), p. 597. See also Joachim Kohler, *Zarathustra's Secret*, p. xix.

61. See, on this point, Robert O. Paxton, *The Anatomy of Fascism* (New York: Vintage Books, 2004), pp. 3–23.

62. See *ibid*., at p. 84. Mussolini himself defined fascism not positively, but solely in terms of its enemies. See, on this point, Benito Mussolini, "The Political and Social Doctrine of Fascism," in Benito Mussolini, *My Autobiography with "The Political and Social Doctrine of Fascism,"* translated by Jane Soames (Mineola, N.Y.: Dover Publications, 2006), at pp. 227–40.

63. Emilio Gentile, *The Sacralization of Politics in Fascist Italy*, translated by Keith Botsford (Cambridge, Mass.; Harvard University Press, 1996), p. 44.

64. See, on this point, Nicholas Bamforth and David A. J. Richards, *Patriarchal Religion, Sexuality, and Gender: a Critique of New Natural Law* (Cambridge: Cambridge University Press, 2007).

65. See, in general, A. Rossi, *The Rise of Italian Fascism 1918–1922*, translated by Peter and Dorothy Wait (New York: Gordon Press, 1976; Stanley G. Payne, *A History of Fascism 1914–1945* (Madison: University of Wisconsin Press, 1995); Adrian Lyttelton, *The Seizure of Power Revised Edition Fascism in Italy 1919–1929* (London: Routledge, 2004).

66. See, on this point, David I. Kertzer, *Sacrifices of Honor: Italian Infant Abandonment and the Politics of Reproductive Control* (Boston: Beacon Press, 1993).

67. Rossi, *The Rise of Italian Fascism*, p. 9.

68. See Lyttelton, *The Seizure of Power*, pp. 25–76.

69. R. J. B. Bosworth, *Mussolini* (London: Hodder Arnold, 2002), p. 88.

70. See, for the most penetrating biography of Mussolini, Bosworth, *Mussolini*. See also Denis Mack Smith, *Mussolini: A Biography* (New York: Vintage, 1983).

71. See Barbara Spackman, *Fascist Virilities: Rhetoric, Ideology, and Social Fantasy in Italy* (Minneapolis: University of Minnesota Press, 1996).

72. Paxton, *The Anatomy of Fascism*, p. 17.

73. See Bosworth, *Mussolini*, pp. 237–9.

74. See, on this point, Emilio Gentile, *The Sacralization of Politics in Fascist Italy*, pp. 55–6, 62–4, 64–6.

75. Zeev Sternhell with Mario Sjnajder and Maia Asheri, *The Birth of Fascist Ideology*, translated by David Maisel (Princeton, N.J.: Princeton University Press, 1994), p. 61.

76. John Woodhouse, *Gabriele D'Annunzio: Defiant Archangel* (New York: Oxford University Press, 1998), p. 120.

77. *Ibid.*, p. 296; see also pp. 386–93, 312.

78. *Ibid.*, p. 307

79. *Ibid.*, pp. 345–6.

80. See, in general, Woodhouse, *Gabriele D'Annunzio*.

81. Bosworth, *Mussolini*, p. 278.

82. See, in general, Emilio Gentile, *The Sacralization of Politics in Fascist Italy*. See, for a good general study, Michael Burleigh, *Sacred Causes: The Clash of Religion and Politics, from the Great War to the War on Terror* (New York: HarperCollins, 2007).

83. See Gentile, *The Sacralization of Politics in Fascist Italy*, at p. 27.

84. See Borden W. Painter, Jr., *Mussolini's Rome: Rebuilding the Eternal City* (New York; Palgrave Macmillan, 2005).

85. Claudio Fogu, *The Historic Imaginary: Politics of History in Fascist Italy* (Toronto: University of Toronto Press, 2003).

86. See Jan Nelis, "Constructing Fascist Identity: Benito Mussolini and the Myth of *Romanita*," *Classical World* 100.4 (2007), 391–415, at pp. 405–7.

87. Bosworth, *Mussolini*, at p. 243.

88. See Kershaw, *Hitler: 1889–1936, Hubris*, at pp. 101–5. On Mussolini, see Bosworth, *Mussolini*, pp. 114–20.

89. See, for a defense of Nietzsche along these lines, Walter Kaufman, *Nietzsche*, fourth edition (Princeton, N.J.: Princeton University Press, 1974).

90. See, for a general study of this gender issue in German fascism, Claudia Koonz, *The Nazi Conscience* (Cambridge Mass.: Belknap Press at Harvard University Press, 2003); see also Claudia Koonz, *Mothers in the Fatherland: Women, the Family, and Nazi Politics* (New York: St. Martin's Press, 1987).

91. See Robert Conquest, *Stalin: Breaker of Nations* (New York: Penguin, 1991), at pp. 163–5.

92. See Walter Laqueur, *The Dream That Failed: Reflections on the Soviet Union* (New York: Oxford University Press, 1994), p. 13.

93. See, on all these and other points in this paragraph, Francois Furet, *The Passing of an Illusion: The Idea of Communism in the Twentieth Century*, translated by Deborah Furet (Chicago: University of Chicago Press, 1999).

94. See, on these points, Arthur Koestler, *Darkness at Noon*, translated by Daphne Hardy (New York: Bantam Books, 1968) (first published 1941), at pp. 124–9, 134–7, 153, 182–5, 189–90, 205.

95. See Elisabeth Young-Bruehl, *The Anatomy of Prejudices* (Cambridge, Mass.: Harvard University Press, 1996). See also Young-Bruehl, *Where Do We Fall When We Fall in Love?*

96. See, for a psychoanalytically informed study of this phenomenon, James Gilligan, *Violence: Reflections on a National Epidemic* (New York: Vintage Books, 1996).

97. See, for defense of this view, Richards, *Women, Gays, and the Constitution*.

98. See W. H. Auden, "September 1, 1939," at: http://www.poets.org?viewmedia.php/prinID/15545, from *Another Time* by W. H. Auden, published by Random House, 1940.

99. See *Brown v. Board of Education*, 347 U.S. 483 (1954) (laws requiring racial segregation held unconstitutional); *Loving v. Virginia*, 386 U.S. 1 (1967) (anti-miscegenation laws held unconstitutional).

100. See, on this point, Carol Gilligan, *In a Different Voice: Psychological Theory and Women's Development* (Cambridge, Mass.: Harvard University Press, 1982).

101. Virginia Woolf, "Professions of Women," in Virginia Woolf, *Women and Writing*, Michele Barrett, ed. (Orlando, Fla.: Harvest Book, 1980), pp. 57–63, at p. 59.

102. See, for example, Tim O'Brien, *The Things They Carried* (New York: Broadway Books, 1990), pp. 39–61.

103. See James Carroll, *An American Requiem: God, My Father, and the War that Came Between Us* (Boston: Houghton Mifflin Company, 1996).

104. See, on these points, David A. J. Richards, *The Case for Gay Rights: From Bowers to Lawrence and Beyond* (Lawrence: University Press of Kansas, 2005).

105. See, on this point, Gilligan, *In a Different Voice*.

106. W. E. B. Du Bois, *The Souls of Black Folk*, in *W. E. B. Du Bois*, Nathan Higgins, ed. (1903; New York, Library of America, 1986), pp. 364–5.

107. John Rawls, *Collected Papers*, Samuel Freeman, ed. (Cambridge, Mass.: Harvard University Press, 1999), at p. 613.

108. See George M. Marsden, *Fundamentalism and American Culture: The Shaping of Twentieth Century Evangelicalism, 1870–1925* (New York: Oxford University Press, 1980).

109. See Raoul Berger, *Government by Judiciary* (Cambridge, Mass.: Harvard University Press, 1977); *Death Penalties* (Cambridge, Mass.: Harvard University Press, 1982).

110. 347 U.S. 483 (1954).

111. See Robert H. Bork, *Tradition and Morality in Constitutional Law* (Washington, D.C.: American Enterprise Institute, 1984); "Neutral Principles and Some First Amendment Problems," 47 *Ind. L.J.* 9 (1971).

112. See, on this point, Richards, *Foundations of American Constitutionalism*, pp. 102–5, 131–71.

113. See Hadley Arkes, *Natural Rights and the Right to Choose* (Cambridge: Cambridge University Press, 2002).

114. See Richards, *Foundations of American Constitutionalism*, at pp. 134–6.

115. John Locke, *The Second Treatise of Government*, in John Locke, *Two Treatises of Government*, Peter Laslett, ed. (Cambridge: Cambridge University Press, 1960), p. 365 (sec. 118). See, for illuminating commentary on Locke's opposition to Filmer's historicism, Richard Ashcraft, *Locke's Two Treatises of Government* (London: Allen & Unwin, 1987), pp. 60–79.

116. See, on this point, Richards, *Foundations of American Constitutionalism*, pp. 131–71.

117. See, on this point, *ibid.*, pp. 202–47.

### 10. The Contemporary Scene

1. See, on these points, Martha C. Nussbaum, *The Clash Within: Democracy, Religious Violence, and India's* Future (Cambridge, Mass.: Belknap Press of Harvard University Press, 2007).

2. Tanika Sarkar, *Hindu Wife, Hindu Nation: Community, Religion, and Cultural Nationalism* (Bloomington: Indiana University Press, 2001), pp. 118–9.

3. For an early statement of this critique, controversially suggesting that on this ground the British should not give India its political freedom, see Katherine Mayo, *Mother India* Mrinalini Sinha, ed. (Ann Arbor: The University of Michigan Press, 2000). In fact, British colonialism may have reinforced patriarchal practices in India. On this point, see Sarkar, *Hindu Wife, Hindu Nation*.

4. Sarkar, *Hindu Wife, Hindu Nation*, p. 128.

5. Amartya Sen, *The Argumentative Indian: Writings on Indian History, Culture and Identity* (New York: Picador, Farrar, Straus and Giroux, 2005), p. 195.

6. Sarkar, *Hindu Wife, Hindu Nation*, p. 201

7. See on this point Jawaharlal Nehru, *The Discovery of India* (New Delhi: Penguin, 2004) (first published 1946), pp. 556–7.

8. Sarkar, *Hindu Wife, Hindu Nation*, pp. 39, 198, 224, 193, 225, 235.

9. Valmiki, *The Ramayana*, translated by Arshia Sattar (New Delhi: Penguin, 1996), at pp. 633–8; see also pp. 661–70, 677–9.

10. See Romesh C. Dutt, translator, *The Mahabharata* (Delhia: Vijay Goel, 2005), at pp. 56–60. See, on use of the story for political purposes, Sarkar, *Hindu Wife, Hindu Nation*, p. 255. See for a plausible feminist reading of this episode, Rajeswari, Sunder Rajan,

"The Story of Draupadi's disrobing meanings for Our Times, in Rajeswari, Sunder Rajan, ed., *Signposts: Gender Issues in Post-Independence India* (New Brunswick, N.J.: Rutgers University Press, 2001), pp. 332–359.

11. See, on this point, Nussbaum, *The Clash Within*, pp. 141–51. See also Ratna Kapur, *Erotic Justice: Law and the New Politics of Postcolonialism* (London: Glasshouse Press, 2005); Brenda Cossman and Ratna Kapur, *Secularism's Last Sign: Hindutva and the (Mis)Rule of Law* (Oxford: Oxford University Press, 2001).

12. See Yaroslav Trofimov, "Brutal Attack in India Shows How Caste System Lives On," *The Wall Street Journal*, Thursday, December 27, 2007, Vol. CCL, No. 150, at pp. A1 and A9.

13. See, in general, Lawrence Wright, *The Looming Tower: Al-Qaeda's Road to 9/11* (New York: Alfred A. Knopf, 2006).

14. Mary R. Habeck, *Knowing the Enemy: Jihadist Ideology and the War on Terror* (New Haven, Conn.: Yale University Press, 2006), at p. 91.

15. Mark Juergensmeyer, *Terror in the Mind of God: The Global Rise of Religious Violence* (Berkeley: University of California Press, 2000), at p. 195.

16. See, on these points, Bernard Lewis, *What Went Wrong? Western Impact and Middle Eastern Response* (Oxford: Oxford University Press, 2002).

17. See, for example, Leila Ahmed, *A Border Passage: From Cairo to America – A Woman's Journey* (New York: Farrar, Straus and Giroux, 1999); Fatema Mernissi, *Islam and Democracy: Fear of the Modern World*, translated by Mary Jo Lakeland (Cambridge, Mass.: Perseus, 1992); *The Veil and the Male Elite: A Feminist Interpretation of Women's Rights in Islam* (Cambridge, Mass.: Perseus, 1991).

18. Wright, *The Looming Tower*, pp. 9, 12

19. See, on this point, Ian Buruma, *Murder in Amsterdam: The Death of Theo van Gogh and the Limits of Tolerance* (New York: Penguin, 2006).

20. See *ibid.*, p. 195.

21. See Elisabeth Young-Bruehl, *Why Arendt Matters* (New Haven, Conn.: Yale University Press, 2006).

22. See, on this point, Buruma, *Murder in Amsterdam*, p. 220.

23. See, for an elaboration of this argument, David A. J. Richards, *Free Speech and the Politics of Identity* (Oxford: Oxford University Press, 1999).

24. Stephen Holmes, *The Matador's Cape: America's Reckless Response to Terror* (Cambridge: Cambridge University Press, 2007), at p. 74.

25. *Ibid.*

26. Arundhati Roy, *War Talk* (Cambridge, Mass.: South End Press, 2003).

27. See David L. Chappell, *A Stone of Hope: Prophetic Religion and the Death of Jim Crow* (Chapel Hill: University of North Carolina Press, 2004), at p. 153.

28. See Roy, *War Talk*, at pp. 18–19, 34, 50, 105.

29. See, on this point, Robert Harris, "Pirates of the Mediterranean," *The New York Times*, September 30, 2006, p. A15.

30. See Alan Dershowitz, *The Case for Israel* (New York: John Wiley & Sons, 2003). See also David Mamet, *The Wicked Son: Anti-Semitism, Self-Hatred and the Jews* (New York: Schocken, 2006).

31. See, on this point, Mark Bowden, "The Six-Million Question," *The Wall Street Journal*, October 4, 2006, p. A14.

32. See, for example, Elaine Pagels, *Adam, Eve, and the Serpent* (New York: Random House, 1988).

33. On this traditional role, see David I. Kertzer, *The Popes Against the Jews: The Vatican's Role in the Rise of Modern Anti-Semitism* (New York: Alfred A. Knopf, 2001).

34. See, on this point, Mamet, *The Wicked Son*.

35. For a striking example of this ideological distortion, see the book review of David A. J. Richards' *Sex, Drugs, Death and the Law: An Essay on Human Rights and Overcriminalization* (Totowa, N.J.: Rowman & Littlefield, 1982) by Mark V. Tushnet, "Sex, Drugs

and Rock 'n' Roll: Some Conservative Reflections on Liberal Jurisprudence," *Columbia Law Review* 82 (November, 1982), 1531–43.

36. Tom Brokaw, *Boom! Voices of the Sixties* (New York: Random House, 2007), at p. 480.
37. Brokaw, *Boom!*, at pp. 352–3.
38. For critique, see Richards, *Sex, Drugs, Death, and the Law*, pp. 157–212.
39. Brokaw, *Boom!*, pp. 389–90.
40. See Tom Stoppard, *Rock 'n' Roll* (New York: Grove Press, 2006), p. xvii. See, for an illuminating collection of Havel's writings during the period of his active resistance to the repressive communist Czech regime, Vaclav Havel, *Open Letters: Selected Writings 1965–1990* (New York: Vintage Books, 1992).
41. Stoppard, *Rock 'n' Roll*, p. 36.
42. For fuller argument for and defense of this position, see David A. J. Richards, *Tragic Manhood and Democracy: Verdi's Voice and the Powers of Musical Art* (Brighton, U.K.: Sussex Academic Press, 2004).
43. *Lawrence v. Texas*, 539 U.S. 558 (2003).
44. *Bowers v. Hardwick*, 478 U.S. 186 (1986).
45. See *Dudgeon v. United Kingdom*, 45 Eur. Ct. H.R. (1981) P 52.
46. See *Goodridge v. Department of Public Health*, 440 Mass. 309 (2003).
47. See *Dred Scott v. Sanford*, 60 U.S. (19 How.) 393 (1857). For a penetrating critique of the opinion, see Don E. Fehrenbacher, *The Dred Scott Cases: Its Significance in American Law and Politics* (New York: Oxford University Press, 1978).
48. On Lincoln's critique of *Dred Scott* and its role in precipitating the Civil War, see David A. J. Richards, *Conscience and the Constitution: History, Theory, and Law of the Reconstruction Amendments* (Princeton: Princeton University Press, 1993), pp. 41, 54–7, 81.
49. Quoted at p. 55, Richards, *Conscience and the Constitution*.

## Conclusion

1. William Shakespeare, *Macbeth*, Folger Shakespeare Library (New York: Washington Square Press, 1992).
2. Martha C. Nussbaum, *The Fragility of Goodness: Luck and Ethics in Greek Tragedy and Philosophy*, updated ed. (Cambridge: Cambridge University Press, 2001, originally published 1986).
3. See, on this point, T. S. Eliot, "Vergil and the Christian Tradition," in T. S. Eliot, *On Poetry and Poets* (New York: Farrar, Straus and Cudahy, 1957), pp. 135–48.

# Bibliography

Acocella, Joan. "Marguerite Yourcenar and the Emperor," *The New Yorker*, February 14 & 21, 2005.

Ahmed, Leila. *A Border Passage: From Cairo to America – A Woman's Journey* (New York: Farrar, Straus and Giroux, 1999).

Albright, W.E. and C. S. Mann, *The Anchor Bible: Matthew* (New York: Doubleday, 1971).

Alter, Robert. *The Art of Biblical Narrative* (New York: Basic Books 1981).

Amar, Akhil Reed. *The Bill of Rights: Creation and Reconstruction* (New Haven: Yale University Press, 1998).

Anonymous, *The Story of Apollonius King of Tyre*, translated by Gerlad N. Sandy, in B. P. Reardon, ed., *Collected Greek Novels* (Berkeley: University of California Press, 1989) .

Anthony Everitt, *Augustus: The Life of Rome's First Emperor* (New York: Randon House, 2006).

Appian, *The Civil Wars* John Carter trans. (London: Penguin, 1996).

Appignanesi, Lisa and John Forrester, *Freud's Women* (New York: Other Press, 2000).

Apuleius, *Rhetorical Works* translated by Stephen Harrison, John Hilton, and Vincent Hunink, edited by Stephen Harrison (Oxford: Oxford University Press, 2001).

Apuleius, *The Golden Ass*, translated by E. J. Kenney (London: Penguin, 1998).

Aquinas, Thomas, *On the Truth of the Catholic Faith, Book Three: Providence Part 2*, Vernon J. Bourke trans. (Garden City, N.Y. Image, 1956),

Aquinas, Thomas. *On the Truth of the Catholic Faith: Summa Contra Gentiles* trans. Vernon Bourke (New York: Image, 1956).

Arendt, Hannah, *Eichmann in Jerusalem: A Report on the Banality of Evil* (New York: Penguin, 1992).

Arendt, Hannah. *Love and Saint Augustine* edited with an interpretive essay by Joanna Vecchiarelli Scott and Judith Chelius Stark (Chicago: University of Chicago Press, 1996) (first published, 1929).

Arendt, Hannah, *Rahel Varnhagen: The Life of a Jewess* translated by Richard and Clara Winston (Baltimore, Maryland: The Johns Hopkins University Press, 1997) (first published, 1958).

Arendt, Hannah. *The Life of the Mind*, one-volume edition (New York: Harcourt Brace Jovanovich, 1978).

Arendt, Hannah. *The Origins of Totalitarianism* (New York: Harcourt Brace Jovanovich, 1973) (first publishlished, 1951).

Ariosto, Ludovico. *Orlando Furioso*, Part One, Barbara Reynolds, trans. (London: Penguin 1975).

Ariosto, Ludovico. *Orlando Furioso*, Part Two, Barbara Reynolds, trans. (London: Penguin, 1977).

Arkes, Hadley. *Natural Rights and the Right to Choose* (Cambridge: Cambridge University Press, 2002).

Ashcraft, Richard. *Locke's Two Treatises of Government* (London: Allen & Unwin, 1987).

Astin A.E., F.W. Walbank, M.W. Frederiksen, R.M. Ogilvie, *The Cambridge Ancient History Second Edition Volume VIII Rome and the Mediterranean to 133 B.C.E.* (Cambridge: Cambridge University Press, 1989).

Auden, W.H., "September 1, 1939," at: *http://www.poets.org?viewmedia.php/prinID/15545*, from *Another Time* by W.H. Auden, published by Random House, 1940.

Augustine, *Confessions* Henry Chadwick trans. (Oxford: Oxford University Press, 1991).

Augustine, *The City of God* Henry Bettenson trans. (Harmondsworth, Middlesex, England: Penguin, 1972).

Aurelius, Marcus. *Meditations* Gregory Hays trans. (New York: The Modern Library, 2003).

Bachofen, J.J., *Myth, Religion, and Mother Right*, translated by Ralph Manheim (Princeton, N.J.: Princeton University Press, 1967).

Bagnall, Roger S. *Egypt in Late Antiquity* (Princeton: Princeton University Press, 1993).

Baldwin, James. *Go Tell It on the Mountain*, in Baldwin, *Early Novels and Stories,* ed. Toni Morrison (New York: Library of America, 1998).

Bamforth, Nicholas C. and David A.J. Richards, *Patriarchal Religion, Sexuality, and Gender: A Critique of New Natural Law* (Cambridge: Cambridge University Press, 2008).

Barnres, Jonathan. *The Presocratic Philosophers* (London: Routledgtge, 2006).

Barrett, Anthony A. *Agrippina: Sex, Power and Politics in the Early Empire* (New Haven: Yale University Press,1996).

Barrett, Anthony A. *Livia: First Lady of Imperial Rome* (New Haven: Yale University Press, 2002).

Barton, Carlin A. *Rome Honor: The Fire in the Bones* (Berkeley: University of California Press, 2001).

Barton, Carlin A. *The Sorrows of the Ancient Romans: The Gladiator and the Monster* (Princeton: Princeton University Press, 1993).

Bauman, Richard A. *Women and Politics in Ancient Rome* (London: Routledge, 1992).

Beard, Mary and John North, eds., *Pagan Priests: Religion and Power in the Ancient World* (Ithaca, N.Y.: Cornell University Press, 1990).

Beard, Mary, John North, and Simon Price. *Religions of Rome Volume 1-A History* (Cambridge: Cambridge University Press, 2004).

Beard, Mary, John North and Sim Price. *Religions of Rome Volume 2 – A Sourcebook* (Cambridge: Cambridge University Press, 2005).

Bederman, Gail. *Manliness and Civilization: A Cultural History of Gender and Race in the United States*, *1880–1917* (Chicago: University of Chicago Press, 1995).

Beebe, Beatrice and Frank Lachmann, *Infant Research and Adult Treatment: Co-Constructing Interactions*, (Hillsdale, N.J.: The Analytic Press, 2002).

Benedict, Michael Les, *A Compromise of Principle: Congressional Republicans and Reconstruction, 1863–1869* (New York: W.W. Norton, 1974).

Berger, Raoul. *Death Penalties* (Cambridge, Mass.: Harvard University Press, 1982).

Berger, Raoul. *Government by Judiciary* (Cambridge, Mass.: Harvard University Press, 1977).

Berry, Jason. *Lead Us Not into Temptation: Catholic Priests and the Sexual Abuse of Children* (Urbana, Ill.: University of Illinois Press, 2000).

Berry, Jason and Gerald Renner, *Vows of Silence: The Abuse of Power in the Papacy of John Paul II* (New York: The Free Press, 2004).

Bessel A. Van Der Kolk, Alexander C. McFarlane, and Lars Weisaeth, eds., *Traumatic Stress: The Effects of Overwhelming Experience on Mind, Body, and Society* (New York: Guilford Press, 1993).

Biale, David. *Eros and the Jews: From Biblical Israel to Contemporary America* (New York: BasicBooks, 1992).

Blumstein, Philip, and Pepper Schwartz, *American Couples* (New York: William Morrow, 1983).

Blundell, Sue, *Women in Ancient Greece* (Cambridge, Mass.: Harvard University Press, 1995).

Bonhoeffer, Dietrich. *Letters and Papers from Prison* edited by Eberhard Bethge (Touchstone Book: New York, 1971).

Bork, Robert H. "Neutral Principles and Some First Amendment Problems," 47 Ind. L.J. 9 (1971).

Bork, Robert H. *Tradition and Morality in Constitutional Law* (Washington, D.C.: American Enterprise Institute, 1984).

Boswell, John. *The Kindness of Strangers: The Abandonment of Children in Western Europe from Late Antiquity to the Renaissance* (Chicago: University of Chicago Press, 1988).

Bosworth, R. J. B., *Mussolini* (London: Hodder Arnold, 2002).

Bowden, Mark. "The Six-Million Question," *The Wall Street Journal*, October 4, 2006.

*Bowers v. Hardwick*, 478 U.S. 186 (1986).

Bowman, Alan K., *Life and Letters of the Roman Empire: Vindolanda and its People* (New York: Routledge, 1994).

Bowman, Alan K., Edward Champlin, Andrew Lintott, *The Cambridge Ancient History Second Edition Volume X The Augustan Empire, 43 B.C.E.–A.D. 69* (Cambridge: Cambridge University Press, 1996).

Bowman, Alan K., et al., *The Cambridge Ancient History Second Edition Volume XI The High Empire, A.D. 70–192*.

Bowman, Alan K., Peter Garnsey, Averil Cameron, *The Cambridge Ancient History Second Edition Volume XII The Crisis of Empire, A.D. 193–337* (Cambridge: Cambridge University Press, 2005).

Bowman, Alan K., Peter Garnsey, Dominic Rathbone, *The Cambridge Ancient History Volume XI The High Empire, A.D. 70–192* (Cambridge: Cambridge University Press, 2000).

Bowman, Alan K. and J. David Thomas, *The Vindolanda Writing Tablets* (*Tabulae Vindolandenses II*) (London: The British Museum Press, 1994).

Boyarin, Daniel. *A Radical Jew: Paul and the Politics of Identity* (Berkeley: University of California Press, 1994).

Boyarin, Daniel. *Carnal Israel: Reading Sex in Talmudic Culture* (Berkeley: University of California Press, 1993).

Boyarin, Daniel. *Unheroic Conduct: The Rise of Heterosexuality and the Invention of the Jewish Man* (Berkeley: University of California Press, 1997).

Bradley, Keith. "Animalizing the Slave: The Truth of Fiction," *The Journal of Roman Studies*, Vol. 90 (2000).

Bradshaw, Timothy, ed., *The Way Forward? Christian Voices on Homosexuality and the Church* (London: SCM Press, 2003).

Branch, Taylor. *Parting the Waters: Martin Luther King and the Civil Rights Movement 1954–63* (London: Papermac, 1988).

Branch, Taylor. *Pillar of Fire: America in the King Years 1963–65* (New York: Simon & Schuster, 1998).

Braudy, Leo, *From Chivalry to Terrorism: War and the Changing Nature of Masculinity* (New York: Alfred A. Knopf, 2003).

Breidenthal, Thomas E., *Christian Households: The Sanctification of Nearness* (Cambridge: Cowley Publications, 1997).

Breuer, Josef and Sigmund Freud, *Studies on Hysteria, in The Standard Edition of the Complete Psychological Works of Sigmund Freud Volume II (1893–1895)* James Strachey trans. (London: Hogarth Press, 1955), at pp. 1–305.

Brokaw, Tom, *Boom! Voices of the Sixties* (New York: Random House, 2007).

Brown, Lyn Mikel and Gilligan, Carol Gilligan, *Meeting at the Crossroads: Women's Psychology and Girls' Development* (New York: Ballantine Books, 1993; first published 1992, Harvard University Press).

Brown, Peter. *Augustine of Hippo: A Biography* (Berkeley: University of California Press, 2000) (first published, 1967).

Brown, Peter. *Augustine of Hippo* (London: Faber & Faber, 1967).

Brown, Peter, *The Body and Society: Men, Women, and Sexual Renunciation in Early Chris-tianity* (New York: Columbia University Press, 1988).

Brown, Raymond E. *The Anchor Bible: The Gospel According to John I-XII* (New York: Doubleday, 1966).

Buber, Martin. *I and Thou*, Walter Kaufmann trans. (New York: Charles Scribner's Sons, 1970).

Burke, Janine. *The Sphinx on the Table: Sigmund Freud's Art Collection and the Development of Psychoanalysis* (New York: Walker & Company, 2006).

Burkert, Walter. *Ancient Mystery Cults* (Cambridge, Mass.; Harvard University Press, 1987).

Burleigh, Michael, *Sacred Causes: The Clash of Religion and Politics, from the Great War to the War on Terror* (New York: HarperCollins, 2007).

Buruma, Ian. *Murder in Amsterdam: The Death of Theo van Gogh and the Limits of Tolerance* (New York: Penguin, 2006).

Bush, M.L. ed., *Serfdom and Slavery: Studies in Legal Bondage* (London: Longman, 1999).

Caesar, Julius. *The Civil War* translation by John Carter (Oxford: Oxford University Press, 1998).

Caesar, Julius. *The Conquest of Gaul* S.A. Handford trans. ((London: Penguin, 1982).

Camerson, Averil and Peter Garnsey, eds., *The Cambridge Ancient History Volume XIII The Late Empire, A.D. 337–425* (Cambridge: Cambridge University Press, 1998).

Canavaggio, Jean. *Cervantes* translated from the French by J.R. Jones (New York: W.W. Norton, 1990).

Cantarella, Eva. *Pandora's Daughters: The Role and Status of Women in Greek and Roman Antiquity* translated by Maureen B. Fant, (Baltimore: The Johns Hopkins University Press, 1987).

Carey, Benedict. "An Analyst Questions the Self-Perpetuating Side of Therapy," *The New York Times*, October 10, 2006.

Carroll, James. *An American Requiem: God, My Father, and the War that Came Between Us* (Boston: Houghton Mifflin Company, 1996).

Carroll, James. *Constantine's Sword: The Church and the Jews: A History* (Boston: Houghton Mifflin Company, 2001).

Carroll, James. *House of War: The Pentagon and the Disastrous Rise of American Power* (Boston: Houghton Mifflin Company, 2006).

Carroll, Michael P. *The Cult of the Virgin Mary: Psychological Origins* (Princeton: Princeton University Press, 1986).

Carson, Clayborne and Peter Holloran, eds., *A Knock at Midnight: Inspiration from the Great Sermons of Reverend Martin Luther King, Jr.* (New York: Warner Books, 2000).

Cash, W.J. *The Mind of the South* (New York: Vintage Books, 1941).

Ceplair, Larry, *The Public Years of Sarah and Angelina Grimke: Selected Writings 1835–1839* (New York: Columbia University Press, 1989).

Cervantes, Miguel De. *Don Quixote* Edith Grossman translation (New York; HarperCollins, 2003).

Cervantes, Miguel De. *Exemplary Stories* Lesley Lipson translation (Oxford; Oxford University Press, 1998).

Chailley, Jacques. *The Magic Flute, Masonic Opera: An Interpretation of the Libretto and Music* Herbert Weinstock trans. (New York: Alfred A. Knopf, 1971).

Champlin, Edward. *Nero* (Cambridge, Mass.: Belknp Press of Harvard University Press, 2003).

Chappell, David L. *A Stone of Hope: Prophetic Religion and the Death of Jim Crow* (University of North Carolina Press: Chapel Hill, 2004).

Child, L. Maria. *An Appeal in Favor of Americans Called Africans* (New York: Arno Press and New York Times, 1968) (originally published, 1833).

Cicero, *Philippics* Walter C.A. Ker trans. (Cambridge, Mass.: Harvard University Press, 2001).

Cohen, I. Bernard ed., *Puritanism and the Rise of Modern Science: The Merton Thesis* (New Brunswick: Rutgers University Press, 1990).

Cohen, David, and Richard Saller, "Foucault on Sexuality in Graeco-Roman Antiquity," in Jan Goldstein, ed., *Foucault and the Writing of History* (Oxford: Blackwell, 1994), at pp. 35–59.

Collier-Thomas, Bettye and V.P. Franklin (eds.), *Sisters in the Struggle: African American Women in the Civil Rights-Black Power Movement* (New York: New York University Press, 2001).

Conquest, Robert. *Stalin: Breaker of Nations* (New York: Penguin, 1991).

Cossman, Brenda and Ratna Kapur, *Secularism's Last Sigh?: Hindutva and the (Mis)Rule of Law* (Oxford: Oxford University Press, 2001).

Crawford, Vicki L., Jacqueline Anne Rouse, and Barbara Woods (eds.). *Women in the Civil Rights Movement* (Bloomington: Indiana University Press, 1993).

Crook, J.A. Andrew Lintott, Elizabeth Rawson, *The Cambridge Ancient History Second Edition Volume IX The Last Age of the Roman Republic, 146–43 B.C.E.* (Cambridge: Cambridge University Press, 1994).

Curley, Edwin, *Behind the Geometrical Method: A Reading of Spinoza's Ehics* (Princeton: Princeton University Press, 1988).

Damasio, Antonio R., *Descartes' Error: Emotion, Reason, and the Human Brain* (New York: Avon Books, 1994).

Damasio, Antonio, *Looking for Spinoza: Joy, Sorrow, and the Feeling Brain* (Orlando: Harcourt, Inc. 2003).

Damasio, Antonio R., *The Feeling of What Happens: Body and Emotion in the Making of Consciousness* (New York: Harcourt Brace & Company, 1999).

David Daube, *The New Testament and Rabbinic Judaism* (Peabody, Mass.: Hendrickson, 1998).

Davies, W.D., *The Setting of the Sermon on the Mount* (Cambridge: Cambridge University Press, 1964).

Davis, Angela. *An Autobiography* (New York: International Publishers, 1988) (originally published, 1974).

de Gruchy, John W. ed., *The Cambridge Companion to Dietrich Bonhoeffer* (Cambridge: Cambridge University Press, 2002).

Degler, Carl N., *At Odds: Women and the Family in America from the Revolution to the Present* (New York: Oxford University Press, 1980).

D'Emilio, John, and Estelle B. Freedman, *Intimate Matters: A History of Sexuality in America* (New York: Harper & Row, 1988).

Dench, Emma. *Romulus' Asylum: Roman Identities from the Age of Alexander to the Age of Hadrian* (Oxford: Oxford University Press, 2005).

Deroux, Carl ed., *Studies in Latin Literature and Roman History II* (Bruxelles: Latomus, 1980).

Dershowitz, Alan. *The Case for Israel* (New York: John Wiley & Sons, 2003).

Dio, Cassius. *The Roman History: The Reign of Augustus*, Ian Scott-Kilvert trans. (London: Penguin, 1987).

Dixon, Suzanne. *Reading Roman Women* (London: Duckworth, 2001).

Dixon, Suzanne. *The Roman Family* (Baltimore: The Johns Hopkins University Press, 1992).

Dixon, Suzanne. *The Roman Mother* (Norman, Oklahoma: Oklahoma University Press, 1988).

Dodds, E.R. *Pagan and Christian in an Age of Anxiety* (Cambridge: Cambridge University Press, 1965).

Donalson, Malcolm Drew. *The Cult of Isis in the Roman Empire* (Lewiston, New York: The Edwin Mellen Press, 2003).

Donaldson, Ian, *The Rapes of Lucretia: A Myth and its Transformations* (Oxford: Clarendon Press, 1982).

Doody, Margaret Anne. *The True Story of the Novel* (New Brunswick, N.J.: Rutgers University Press, 1997).

Douglas, Mary. *In the Wilderness: The Doctrine of Defilement in the Book of Numbers* (Sheffield: Sheffield Academic Press, 1993).

Douglas, Mary. *Leviticus as* Liteature (Oxford: Oxford University Press, 1999).

Du Bois, W.E.B. *Black Reconstruction in America, 1860–1880* (1935; New York: Atheneum, 1969).

Du Bois, W.E.B. *The Souls of Black Folk*, in *W.E.B. Du Bois,* ed. Nathan Higgins (1903; New York: Library of America, 1986).

Du Bois, W.E.B. *The Suppression of the African Slave-Trade*, in *W.E.B. Du Bois,* Nathan Higgins, ed. (1896; New York: Library of America, 1986).

Du Pre Lumpkin, Katharine. *The Emancipation of Angelina Grimke* (Chapel Hill: University of North Carolina Press, 1974).

Duster, Alfred M. ed., *Crusade for Justice: The Autobiography of Ida B. Wells* (Chicago: University of Chicago Press, 1970).

Dutt, Romesh C., translator, *The Mahabharata* (Delhi: Vijay Goel, 2005).

Earl, Donald. *The Moral and Political Tradition of Rome* (Ithaca, N.Y.: Cornell University Press, 1967).

Edwards, Catharine, *The Politics of Immorality in Ancient Rome* (Cambridge: Cambridge University Press, 2002).

Edwards, Lee R. *Psyche as Hero: Female Heroism and Fictional Form* (Darthnmouth, NH: University Press of New England, 1984).

Ehrenreich, Barbara, Elizabeth Hess, and Gloria Jacobs, *Remaking Love: The Feminization of Sex* (New York: Anchor, 1986).

Elaine Pagels, *The Gnostic Gospels* (New York: Vintage, 1981).

Eliot, T.S.. *On Poets and Poetry* (New York: Farrar, Straus and Cudahy, 1957).

Elliott, J.H., *Empires of the Atlantic World: Britain and Spain in America 1492–1830* (New Haven, Conn.: Yale University Press, 2006).

Ellmann, Richard. *James Joyce* New and Revised Edition (Oxford: Oxford University Press, 1983).

Elon, Amos. *Herzl* (New York: Hold, Rinehart and Winston, 1975).

Elon, Amos. *The Pity of It All: A Portrait of the German-Jewish Epoch 1743–1933* (New York: Picador, 2002).

Erikson, Erik H., *A Way of Looking at Things: Selected Papers* edited by Stephen Schlein (New York: W.W. Norton, 1987).

Erikson, Erik. "The Galilean Sayings and the Sense of 'I'", (1981) 70 The Yale Review 321.

Erikson, Erik. *Gandhi's Truth: On the Origins of Militant Nonviolence* (New York: W.W. Norton, 1993).

Erikson, Erik. *Young Man Luther: A Study in Psychoanalysis and History* (New York: W.W. Norton, 1962).

Evans, John K. *War, Women and Children in Ancient Rome* (London: Routledge, 1991).

Evans, Sara. *Personal Politics: The Roots of Women's Liberation in the Civil Rights Movement and the New Left* (New York: Vintage Books, 1980).

Everitt Anthony. *Augustus: The Life of Rome's First Emperor* (New York: Randon House, 2006).

Everitt, Anthony. *Cicero: The Life and Times of Rome's Greatest Politician* (New York: Random House, 2003).

Eyben, Emiel, "Fathers and Sons," in Beryl Rawson, ed., *Marriage, Divorce, and Children in Ancient Rome* (Oxford: Clarendon Press, 2004), at pp. 114–143.

Faludi, Susan, *The Terror Dream: Fear and Fantasy in Post-9/11 America* (New York: Henry Holt and Company, 2007).

Fantham, Elaine, Helene Peet Foley, Natalie Boymel Kampen, Sarah B. Pomeroy, and H. Alan Shapiro, *Women in the Classical World* (New York: Oxford University Press, 1994).

Fehrenbacher, Don E, *The Dred Scott Cases: Its Significance in American Law and Politics* (New York: Oxford University Press, 1978).

Ferenczi, Sandor, "The Confusion of Tongues between Adult and Child," English translation in *International Journal of Psychoanalysis* 30 (1949), 225, German original in *Int. Z. F. Psa.* 19 (1933), 5. Paper read at the Twelfth International Psycho-Analytical Congress, Wiesbaden, September 1932.

Ferguson, John *The Religions of the Roman Empire* (Ithaca, New York: Cornell University Press, 1970).

Ferry, David. *Gilgamesh: A New Rendering in English Verse* (New York: Farrar, Straus and Giroux, 1993).

Fields, T. M. and N. A. Fox, eds., *Social Perception in Infants* (Norwood, N.J.: Ablex Publishing, 1985).

Fiorenza, Elisabeth Schussler (ed.), *Searching Scriptures: Volume One: A Feminist Introduction* (New York: Crossroad Publishing Company, 1993).

Fiorenza, Elisabeth Schussler (ed.), *Searching the Scriptures: Volume Two: A Feminist Commentary* (New York: Crossroad Publishing Company, 1994).

Fiorenza, Elisabeth Schussler. *In Memory of Her: A Feminist Theological Reconstruction of Christian Origins* (New York: Crossroad, 2002).

Fiorenza, Elisabeth Schussler. *Jesus: Miriam's Child, Sophia's Prophet* (New York: Continuum, 1994).

Fitzhugh, George, *Cannibals All!: or, Slaves without Masters*. Edited by C. Vann Woodward (Cambridge, Mass.: Harvard University Press, Belknap Press, 1960),

Flower, Harriet I., *The Cambridge Companion to the Roman Republic* (Cambridge: Cambridge University Press, 2004).

Flusser, David. *Jesus* (Jerusalem: The Hebrew University Magnes Press, 2001).

Flusser, David. *Judaism and the Origins of Christianity* (Jerusalem: The Magnes Press, The Hebrew University, 1988).

Fogu, Claudio, *The Historic Imaginary: Politics of History in Fascist Italy* (Toronto: University of Toronto Press, 2003).

Foner, Eric. *Reconstruction: America's Unfinished Revolution 1863–1877* (New York: Harper & Row, 1988).

Ford, Clellan S. and Frank A. Beach, *Patterns of Sexual Behavior* (New York: Harper & Row, 1959).

Foucault, Michel, *The History of Sexuality, Volume 1, An Introduction*, translated by Robert Hurley (New York: Pantheon Books, 1978); *The Use of Pleasure: The History of Sexuality, Volume Two*, translated by Robert Hurley (New York: Pantheon Books, 1985); *The Care of Self: Volume 3 of The History of Sexuality*, translated by Robert Hurley (New York: Pantheon Books, 1986).

Fox Bourne, H.R. *The Life of John Locke* Volume I (New York: Harper & Brothers, 1876).

Fox, Robin Lane, *Pagans and Christians* (New York: Alfred A. Knopf, Inc., 1987).

Foxhall, Lin, "Pandora Unbound: A Feminist Critique of Foucault's *History of Sexuality*," in David H.J. Larmour, Paul Allen Miller, and Charles Platter, eds., *Rethinking Sexuality: Foucault and Classical Antiquity* (Princeton, N.J.: Princeton University Press, 1998), pp. 122–7.

Foxhall, Lin and John Salmon (eds.), *When Men Were Men: Masculinity, Power and Identity in Classical Antiquity* (London: Routledge, 1998).

France, David. *Our Fathers: The Secret Life of the Catholic Church in an Age of Scandal* (Broadway Books: New York, 2004).

Frankfort, Henri, H.A. Frankfort, John A. Wilson, and Thorkild Jacobsen. *Before Philosophy: The Intellectual Adventure of Ancient Man* (Baltimore: Penguin, 1961).

Frankfort, Henri. *Kingship and the Gods: A Study of Ancient Near Eastern Religion as the Integration of Society and Nature* (Chicago: University of Chicago Press, 1948).

Franklin, John Hope. *The Militant South, 1800–1861* (Cambridge, Mass.: Harvard University Press, Belknap Press, 1956).

Fredrickson, George M. *The Black Image in the White Mind: The Debate on Afro-American Character and Destiny, 1817–1914* (Middleton, Conn.: Wesleyan University Press, 1981).

Fredriksen, Paula. *From Jesus to Christ* (New Haven: Yale University Press, 2ne edition, 2000).

Fredriksen, Paula. *Jesus of Nazareth, King of the Jews: A Jewish Life and the Emergence of Christianity* (New York: Alfred A. Knopf, 2000).

Freeman, Joanne B. *Affairs of Honor: National Politics in the New Republic* (New Haven: Yale University Press, 2001).

Freud, Anna. *The Ego and the Mechanisms of Defense* (Madison: International Universities Press, rev.ed. 2000).

Freud, Ernest, ed., *Letters of Sigmund Freud* (New York: Basic Books, 1960).

Freud, Sigmund and Lou Andreas-Salome. Letters. Ernst Pfeiffer, ed.; William and Elaine Robson-Scott trans. *(New York: W.W. Norton & Company, 1972).*

Freud Sigmund. *The Complete Letters of Sigmund Freud to Wilhelm Fliess, 1887–1904.* Edited by Jeffrey Moussaieff Masson (Cambridge, Mass.: Harvard University Press, 1986).

*The Freud/Jung Letters: The Correspondence between Sigmund Freud and C.G. Jung.* Edited by William McGuire, Translated by Ralph Manheim and R.F.C. Hull (Cambridge, MA: Harvard University Press, 1988).

Freud, Sigmund. See Strachey, James.

Furet, Francois. *The Passing of an Illusion: The Idea of Communism in the Twentieth Century* Deborah Furet, trans. (Chicago: University of Chicago Press, 1999).

Fussell, Paul. *The Great War and Modern Memory* (New York: Oxford University Press, 2000) (originally published, 1975).

Gaca, Kathy L. *The Making of Fornication: Eros, Ethics, and Political Reform in Greek Philosophy and Early Christianity* (Berkeley: University of California Press, 2003).

Gager, John A. *The Origins of Anti-Semitism: Attitudes Toward Judaism in Pagan and Christian Antiquity* (New York: Oxford University Press, 1983).

Gaisser, Julia Haig, *The Fortunes of Apuleius and The Golden Ass: A Study in Transmission and Reception* (Princeton, N.J.: Princeton University Press, 2008).

Giddens, Anthony, *The Transformation of Intimacy: Sexuality, Love, and Eroticism in Modern Societies* (Cambridge: Polity, 1992).

Giddings, Paula. *When and Where I Enter: The Impact of Black Women on Race and Sex in America* (New York: William Morrow, 1984).

Gilligan, Carol. *In a Different Voice: Psychological Theory and Women's Development* (Cambridge, Mass.: Harvard University Press, 1982).

Gilligan, Carol. "Joining the Resistance: Psychology, Politics, Girls and Women." *Michigan Quarterly Review*, 29, 4:505–536 (1990); Also published in *The Female Body, L. Goldstein, ed. (Ann Arbor: University of Michigan Press, 1991).*

Gilligan, Carol, *Kyra: a Novel* (New York: Random House, 2008).

Gilligan, Carol, *The Birth of Pleasure* (Alfred A. Knopf: New York, 2002).

Gilligan, Carol, *The Birth of Pleasure: A New Map of Love* (Vintage Books: New York, 2003).

Gilligan, Carol. "The Centrality of Relationship in Human Development: A puzzle, some evidence, and a theory." In K. Fischer and G. Noam, eds. *Development and Vulnerability in Close Relationships. (New York: Erlbaum, 1996).*

Gilligan, Carol, Nona Plessner Lyons, and Trudy Hanmer, eds. *Making Connections: The Relational Worlds of Adolescent Girls at Emma Willard School (Cambridge, MA, Harvard University Press, 1990).*

Gilligan, Carol, Janie Victoria Ward, and Jill McLean Taylor, eds. *Mapping the Moral Domain: A Contribution of Women's Thinking to Psychological Theory and Education* (Cambridge, MA: Harvard University Press, 1988).

Gilligan, Carol, Annie G. Rogers, and Deborah Tolman, *Women, Girls, and Psychotherapy: Reframing Resistance* (Binghamton, N.Y., Haworth Press, 1991).

Gilligan, James, *Violence: Reflections on a National Epidemic* (New York: Vintage Books, 1997) (Original published as *Violence: Our Deadly Epidemic and Its Causes*, 1996, New York: Putnam Books).

Gilmore, David D ed., *Honour and Shame and the Unity of the Mediterranean* (Washington, D.C.: American Anthropological Association, 1987).

Goldhill, Simon. *Foucault's Virginity: Ancient Erotic Fiction and the History of Sexuality* (Cambridge: Cambridge University Press, 1995).

Goldhill, Simon, *Reading Greek Tragedy* (Cambridge: Cambridge University Press, 1986).

Goldin, Claudia, *Understanding the Gender Gap: An Economic History of American Women* (New York: Oxford University Press, 1990).

Goleman, Daniel. "Friends for Life: An Emerging Biology of Emotional Healing," *The New York Times*, October 10, 2006.

Goldstein, Joshua S., *War and Gender: How Gender Shapes the War System and Vice Versa* (Cambridge: Cambridge University Press, 2001).

Goldstein, Rebecca, *Betraying Spinoza: The Renegade Jew Who Gave Us Modernity* (New York: Nextbook-Schocken, 2006).

Goldsworthy, Adrian. *Caesar: Life of a Colossus* (New Haven; Yale University Press, 2006).

Goldsworthy, Adrian, *The Complete Roman Army* (London: Thames & Hudson, 2003).

Goodman, Martin, *Rome and Jerusalem: The Clash of Ancient Civilizations* (New York: Alfred A. Knopf, 2007).

Goodwin, William W. translator, *Plutarch's Morals* vol. II (Boston: Little, Brown, and Company, 1878).

Gossett, Thomas F. *Race: The History of an Idea in America* (New York: Schocken Books, 1965).

Gould, Stephen. Jay, *The Mismeasure of Man* (New York: W.W. Norton, 1981).

Graves, Robert, *The White Goddess: A Historical Grammer of Poetic Myth* (New York: Farrar, Straus and Giroux, 1975).

Greeley, Andrew M., *Priests: A Calling in Crisis* (Chicago: University of Chicago Press, 2004).

Greenberg, Kenneth S. *Honor and Slavery* (Princeton: Princeton University Press, 1996).

Greenberg, Rabbi Steven. *Wrestling with God and Men: Homosexuality in the Jewish Tradition* (Madison, Wisconsin: University of Wisconsin Press, 2004).

Griffin, Jasper. *Latin Poets and Roman Life* (London: Bristol Classical Press, 2004).

Griffin, Jasper. *Vergil* (Oxford: Oxford University Press, 1986).

Grimke, Angelina. *Appeal to the Women of the Nominally Free States* (New York: William S. Dorr, 1837).

Grimke, Angelina, *Letters to Catherine E. Beecher*, reprinted in Larry Ceplair, *The Public Years of Sarah and Angelina Grimke: Selected Writings 1835–1839* (New York: Columbia University Press, 1989).

Gullan-Whur, Margaret, *Within Reason: A Life of Spinoza* (New York: St. Martin's Press, 1998).

Gurval, Robert Alan, *Actium and Augustus: The Politics and Emotions of Civil War* (Ann Arbor: The University of Michigan Press, 1995).

Habeck, Mary R., *Knowing the Enemy: Jihadist Ideology and the War on Terror* (New Haven: Yale University Press, 2006).

Hagendahl, Harald, *Augustine and the Latin Classics* (Goteborg: Elanders Boktryckeri Aktiebolag, 1967).

Halbertal, Moshe and Avishai Margalit, *Idolatry* translated by Naomi Goldblum (Cambridge, Mass.: Harvard University Press, 1992).

Halbertal, Moshe. *People of the Book: Canon, Meaning, and Authority* (Cambridge, Mass.: Harvard University Press, 1997).

Halbertal, Tova Hartman. *Appropriately Subversive: Modern Mothers in Traditional Religions* (Cambridge, Mass.: Harvard University Press, 2002).

Haller, John S. Jr., *Outcasts from Evolution: Scientific Attitutdes of Racial Inferiority, 1859–1900* (New York: McGraw-Hill, 1971).

Hallett, Judith P. *Fathers and Daughters in Roman Society: Women and the Elite Family* (Princeton: Princeton University Press, 1984).

Hallett, Judith P., *"Feminae Furentes*: The Frenzy of Noble Women in Vergil's *Aeneid* and the Letter of Cornelia, Mother of the Gracchi," in William S. Anderson and Lorina N. Quartarone, eds., *Approaches to Teaching Vergil's Aeneid* (New York: The Modern Language Association of America, 2002), at pp. 159–167.

Hallett, Judith P., "Matriot Games? Cornelia, Mother of the Gracchi, and the Forging of Family-Oriented Political Values," in Fiona McHardy and Eireann Marshall, eds., *Women's Influence on Classical Civilization* (London: Routledge, 2004), pp. 26–39.

Hallett, Judith P. and Marilyn B. Skinner, eds., *Roman Sexualities* (Princeton: Princeton Univerrsity Press, 1997).

Hallie, Philip P. *Lest Innocent Blood Be Shed: The Story of the Village of Le Chambon and How Goodness Happened There* (Harper & Row: New York, 1979).

Harris, Robert. "Pirates of the Mediterranean," *The New York Times,* September 30, 2006.

Harris, Trudier ed. *Selected Works of Idea Wells-Barnett,* (New York: Oxford University Press, 1991).

Harris, William V. *War and Imperialism in Republic Rome 327–70 B.C.E.* (Oxford: Clarendon Press, 1985).

Harrison, S.J., *Apuleius: A Latin Sophist* (Oxford: Oxford University Press, 2004).

Hartman, Tova, *Feminism Encounters Traditional Judaism: Resistance and Accommodation* (Waltham, Mass.: Brandeis University Press, 2007).

Havel, Vaclav, *Open Letters: Selected Writings 1965–1990* (New York: Vintage Books, 1992).

Hawley, Richard and Barbara Levick, eds., *Women in Antiquity: New Assessments* (London: Routledge, 1995).

Hawthorne, Nathaniel, *The Scarlet Letter* (New York: Penguin, 1983) (originally published, 1850).

Heather, Peter. *The Fall of the Roman Empire: A New History of Rome and the Barbarians* (Oxford: Oxford University Press, 2006).

Heath-Stubbs, John, translator, *The Poems of Sulpicia* (London: Hearing Eye, 2000).

Hedges, Chris, *War Is a Force That Gives Us Meaning* (New York: Public Affairs, 2002).

Hemingway, Ernest. *A Farewell to Arms* (New York: Scribner, 2003 first published, 1929).

Herman, Judith, *Trauma and Recovery* (New York: Basic Books, 1997).

Hersh, Blanche Glassman. *The Slavery of Sex: Feminist-Abolitionists in America* (Urbana: University of Illinois Press, 1978).

Heschel, Abraham J. *The Prophets* (New York: Perennial Classics, 2001) (originally published, 1962).

Heyob, Sharon Kelly. *The Cult of Isis Among Women in the Graeco-Roman World* (Ann Arbor, Michigan: UMI Dissertation Services, 2003).

Hick, John H., "An Irenaean Theodicy," reprinted in Eleanor Stump and Michael J. Murray, eds., *Philosophy of Religion: The Big Questions* (Oxford: Blackwell Publishers, 1999).

Hinds, Stephen."The poetess and the reader: further steps towards Sulpicia," 143 *Hermathena* 29-46 (1987).

Holmes, Stephen, *The Matador's Cape: America's Reckless Response to Terror* (Cambridge: Cambridge University Press, 2007).

Homer, *Iliad* Richard Lattimore trans. (Chicago: University of Chicago Press, 1951).

Homer, *Odyssey* Robert Fagles translation (New York: Penguin, 1996).

Hopkins, Keith, *Conquerors and Slaves* (Cambridte: Cambridge University Press, 1978).

Hopkins, Keith, *Death and Renewal* (Cambridge: Cambridge University Press, 1983).

Horsman, Reginald. *Race and Manifest Destiny: The Origins of American Racial Anglo-Saxonism* (Cambridge: Harvard University Press, 1981).

Hunter-Gault, Charlayne. *In My Place* (New York: Vintage Books, 1993).

Hynes, Samuel, *The Auden Generation: Literature and Politics in England in the 1930s* (New York: The Viking Press, 1977).

Isani, Mukhtar Ali. "Hawthorne and the Branding of William Prynne," *New England Quarterly*, Vol. 45, No. 2 (June, 1972).

Ignatieff, Michael, *The Warrior's Honor: Ethnic War and the Modern Conscience* (New York: Henry Holt, 1997).

Israel, Jonathan I., *Radical Enlightenment: Philosophy and the Making of Modernity 1650–1750* (Oxford: Oxford University Press, 2001).

Jackowski, Karol. *The Silence We Keep: A Nun's View of the Catholic Priest Scandal* (New York: Harmony Books, 2004).

Jacobson, Dan. *The Story of Stories: The Chosen People and Its God* (New York: Harper & Row, 1982).

Jenkyns, Richard, ed., *The Legacy of Rome: A New Appraisal* (Oxford: Oxford University Press, 1992).

Jenkyns, Richard, *Vergil's Experience: Nature and History, Times, Names, and Places* (Oxford: Clarendon Press, 1998).

Jeremias, Joachim. *The Sermon on the Mount* (London: The Athlone Press, 1961).

John M. Rist, *Augustine: Ancient Thought Baptized* (Cambridge: Cambridge University Press, 1997).

Johnson, W.R. *Darkness Visible: A Study of Vergil's Aeneid* (Berkeley: University of California Press, 1976).

Jones, Howard, *The Epicurean Tradition* (London: Routledge, 1992).

Jordan, Mark D. Telling *Truths in Church: Scandal, Flesh, and Christian Speech* (Beacon Press: Boston, 2003).

Jordan, Mark D., *The Silence of Sodom: Homosexuality in Modern Catholicism* (Chicago: University of Chicago Press, 2000).

Josephus, *The Jewish War Books I–II* translated by H. St. J. Thackeray (Cambridge, Mass.: Harvard University Press, 1997).

Josephus, *The Jewish Wars Books III–IV* H. St. J. Thackeray trans. (Cambridge: Harvard University Press, 1997).

Joyce, James. *A Portrait of the Artist as a Young Man* (New York; Penguin, 2003) (originally published, 1916).

Joyce, James. *Ulysses* (New York: Vintage International, 1990) (originally published, 1934).

Juergensmeyer, Mark. *Terror in the Mind of God: The Global Rise of Religious Violence* (Berkelely: University of California Press, 2000).

Kalven, Harry. Jr., *The Negro and the First Amendment* (Chicago: University of Chicago Press, 1965).

Kapur, Ratna, *Erotic Justice: Law and the New Politics of Postcolonialism* (London: Glasshouse Press, 2005).

Karcher, Carolyn L. *The First Woman in the Republic: A Cultural Biography of Lydia Maria Child* (Durham: Duke University Press, 1994).

Karl, Frederick R., *Joseph Conrad: The Three Lives* (New York: Farrar, Straus and Giroux, 1979).

Kaufmann, Walter. *Critique of Religion and Philosophy* (Princeton: Princeton University Press, 1958).

Kaufman, Walter. *Nietzsche* 4th edition (Princeton, N.J.: Princeton University Press, 1974).

Kaufman, Walter. *Tragedy and Philosophy* (Garden City, N.Y.: Doubleday, 1968).

Keith, Alison, *"Tandem venit amor*: A Roman Woiman Speaks of Love," in Judith P. Hallett and Marilyn B. Skinner, *Roman Sexualities* (Princeton: Princeton University, 1997), at pp. 295–310.

Kennedy, Eugene. *The Unhealed Wound: The Church and Human Sexuality* (New York: St. Martin's Press, 2001).

Keppie, Lawrence. *The Making of the Roman Army From Republic to Empire* (Norman: University of Oklahoma Press, 1984).

Kershaw, Ian. *Hitler: 1889–1936: Hubris* (New York: W.W. Norton, 1998).

Kershaw, Ian. *Hitler: 1936–1945: Nemesis* (New York: W.W. Norton, 2000).

Kertzer, David I. and Richard P. Saller, *The Family in Italy from Antiquity to the Present* (New Haven: Yale University Press, 1991).

Kertzer, David I. *Sacrifices for Honor: Italian Infant Abandonment and the Politics of Reproductive Control* (Boston: Beacon Press, 1993).

Kertzer, David I. *The Popes Against the Jews: The Vatican's Role in the Rise of Modern Anti-Semitism* (New York: Alfred A. Knopf, 2001).

King, Karen L., *The Gospel of Mary of Magdala: Jesus and the First Woman Apostle* (Santa Rosa: Ca.: Polebridge Press, 2003).

Koestler, Arthur. *Darkness at Noon* Daphne Hardy trans. (New York: Bantam Books, 1968) (first published, 1941).

Kohler, Joachim. *Zarathustra's Secret: The Interior Life of Friedrich Nietzsche* translated by Ronald Taylor (New Haven: Yale University Press, 2002).

Koonz, Claudia. *Mothers in the Fatherland: Women, the Family, and Nazi Politics* (New York: St. Martin's Press, 1987).

Koonz, Claudia. *The Nazi Conscience* (Cambridge Mass.: Belknap Press at Harvard University Press, 2003).

Kraemer, Ross Shepard . *Her Share of the Blessings: Women's Religions Among Pagans, Jews, and Christians in the Greco-Roman World* (New York: Oxford University Press, 1992).

Kraemer, Ross Shepard, ed., *Women's Religions in the Greco-Roman World: A Source book* (New York: Oxford University Press, 2004).

Labrousse, Elisabeth. *Bayle* translated by Denys Potts (Oxford: Oxford University Press, 1983).

Langlands, Rebecca. *Sexual Morality in Ancient Rome* (Cambridge: Cambridge University Press, 2006).

Langmuir, Gavin I., *History, Religion, and Antisemitism* (Berkeley and Los Angeles: University of California Press, 1990).

Langmuir, Gavin I. *Toward a Definition of Antisemitism* (Berkeley: University of California Press, 1990).

Laplanche, J. and J.-B. Pontalis, *The Language of Psycho-Analysis* translated by Donald Nicholson-Smith (New York: W.W. Norton, 1973).

LaPlante, Eve, *American Jezebel: The Uncommon Life of Anne Hutchinson, the Woman Who Defied the Puritans* (New York: HarperCollins, 2004).

Laqueur, Thomas W. *Solitary Sex: A Cultural History of Masturbation* (New York: Zone Books, 2004).

Laqueur, Walter. *The Dream That Failed: Reflections on the Soviet Union* (New York: Oxford University Press, 1994).

Large, David C. and William Weber, eds., *Wagnerism in European Culture and Politics* (Ithaca: Cornell University Press, 1984).

Larmour, David H.J., Paul Allen Miller, and Charles Platter, eds., *Rethinking Sexuality: Foucault and Classical Antiquity* (Princeton, N.J.: Princeton University Press, 1998).

Laskin, David, *Partisans: Marriage, Politics, and Betrayal Among the New York Intellectuals* (New York: Simon & Schuster, 2000).

Lawrence, D.H., *Lady Chatterley's Lover* introduction by Doris Lessing (New York: Penguin, 2006).

Lee, Hermione. *Virginia Woolf* (New York: Alfred A. Knopf, 1998).

Lendon, J.E. *Empire of Honour*, (Oxford: Oxford University Press, 2005).

Levenson, Jon D. *Resurrection and the Restoration of Israel: The Ultimate Victory of the God of Life* (New Haven: Yale University Press, 2006).

Levy, Donald, *Freud Among the Philosophers* (New Haven, Conn.: Yale University Press, 1996).

Lewis, Bernard, *Semites and Anti-Semites: An Inquiry into Conflict and Prejudice* (New York: W.W. Norton, 1999).

Lewis, Bernard. *What Went Wrong?: Westerm Impact and Middle Eastern Response* (Oxford: Oxford University Press, 2002).

Ling, Peter J. and Sharon Monteith, *Gender in the Civil Rights Movement* (New York: Garland Publishing 1999).

Lintott, Andrew, *The Constitution of the Roman Republic* (Oxford: Oxford University Press, 2004).

Lintott, Andrew. *Violence in Republican Rome* (Oxford; Oxford University Press, 1999).

Livy, *Rome and the Mediterranean* Henry Bettenson trans. (London: Penguin, 1976).

Livy, *The Early History of Rome* Aubrey De Selincourt trans. (London: Penguin, 2002).

Livy, *The War with Hannibal*, translated by Aubrey De Selincourt (London: Penguin, 1965).

Lofgren, Charles A. *The Plessy Case: A Legal Historical Interpretation* (New York: Oxford University Press, 1987).

Lovejoy, Arthur O. *The Great Chain of Being* (Cambridge, Mass.: Harvard University Press, 1964).

Lucretius, *On the Nature of the Universe*, translated by R.E. Latham (London: Penguin, 1994).

Luther, Martin. *Luther's Works Volume 44 The Christian in Society I* Martin Atkinson ed. and translator (Philadelphia: Fortress Press, 1966).

Luther, Martin. *Luther's Works Volume 48 Letters I* edited and translated by Gottfried G. Krodel (Philadelphia: Fortress Press, 1963).

Lynn-George, Michael, *Epos: Word, Narrative, and the Iliad* (London: Macmillan, 1988).

Lyttelton, Adrian, *The Seizure of Power, Revised Edition, Fascism in Italy 1919–1929* (London: Routledge, 2004).

Maalouf, Amin, *In the Name of Identity: Violence and the Need to Belong*; Barbara Bray Trans. (New York: Penguin, 2003).

Machiavelli, Niccolo. *The Prince and Discourses* (New York: The Modern Library, 1950).

MacMullen, Ramsay. *Christianizing the Roman Empire A.D. 100–400* (New Haven: Yale University Press, 1984).

MacMullen, Ramsay, *Paganism in the Roman Empire* (New Haven, Conn.: Yale University Press, 1981).

Macrobius, *Saturnalia* Percival Vaughan Davies trans. (New York: Columbia University Press, 1969).

Maddox, Brenda. *Nora: The Real Life of Molly Bloom* (Boston: Houghton Mifflin Company, 1988).

Makiya, Kanan, *Cruelty and Silence: War, Tyranny, Uprising, and the Arab World* (New York: W. W. Norton, 1993).

Mamet, David. *The Wicked Son: Anti-Semitism, Self-Hatred and the Jews* (New York: Schocken, 2006).

Margalit, Avishai, "The Suicide Bombers," in *The New York Review of Books*, vol. L, No. 1, January 16, 2003.

Marissen, Michael. "Unsettling History of That Joyous 'Hallelujah'," *The New York Times*, Sunday, April 8, 2007.

Marsden, George M. *Fundamentalism and American Culture: The Shaping of Twentieth Century Evangelicalism, 1870–1925* (New York: Oxford University Press, 1980).

Marshall, Megan, *The Peabody Sisters: Three Women Who Ignited American Romanticism* (Boston: Houghton Mifflin Company, 2005).

Martyr, St. Justin, *Dialogue with Trypho* Thomas B. Falls trans. (Washington, D.C.: The Catholic University of America Press, 2003).

Martyr, St. Justin, *The First and Second Apologies* Leslie William Barnard translation (New York: Paulist Press, 1997).

Matthews, Gareth B., *Augustine* (Malden, Mass.: Blackwell, 2005).

Matthews, Gareth B. *Thought's Ego in Augustine and Descartes* (Ithaca: Cornell University Press, 1992).

Mayer, Henry. *All on Fire: William Lloyd Garrison and the Abolition of Slavery* (New York: St. Martin's Griffin, 1998).

Mayo, Katherine, *Mother India* edited by Mrinalini Sinha (Ann Arbor: The University of Michigan Press, 2000).

McCord, Louisa, 'Enfranchisement of Woman', (April 1852) 21 Southern Quarterly Review 233–341.

McDonnell, Miles, *Roman Manliness: Virtues and the Roman Republic* (Cambridge: Cambridge University Press, 2006).

McGinn, Thomas A.J. *Prostitution, Sexuality, and the Law in Ancient Rome* (New York: Oxford University Press, 1998).

McLynn, Neil B. *Ambrose of Milan: Church and Court in a Christian Capital* (Berkeley: University of California Press, 1994).

McPherson, James M., *The Struggle for Equality: Abolitionists and the Negro in the Civil War and Reconstruction* (Princeton, N.J.: Princeton University Press, 1964).

Mendelson, Edward, *The Things That Matter: What Seven Classic Novels Have to Say About the Stages of Life* (New York: Pantheon Books, 2006).

Menn, Stephen, *Descartes and Augustine* (Cambridge: Cambridge University Press, 2002).

Mernissi, Fatema. *Islam and Democracy: Fear of the Modern World* Mary Jo Lakeland trans. (Cambridge, Mass.: Perseus, 1992).

Mernissi, Fatema. *The Veil and the Male Elite: A Feminist Interpretation of Women's Rights in Islam* (Cambridge, Mass.: Perseus, 1991).

Merriam, Carol U., "The Other Sulpicia," *Classical World* 84(4) (1991), 303–305.

Mikel Brown, Lyn and Carol Gilligan, *Crossroads: Women's Psychology and Girls' Development* (Cambridge, Mass.: Harvard University Press, 1992).

Milgrom, Jacob. *Leviiticus 17–22: The Anchor Bible* (New York: Doubleday, 2000).

Millar, Fergus. "The World of the Golden Ass," *The Journal of Roman Studies*, Vol. 71 (1981).

Miller, Jean Baker and Irene Pierce Stiver, *The Healing Connection: How Women Form Relationships in Therapy and in Life* (Boston: Beacon Press, 1997).

Miller, Jean Baker, ed., *Psychoanalysis and Women* (Harmondsworth, Middlesex, England: Penguin, 1973).

Miller, Jean Baker. *Toward a New Psychology of Women* Second Edition (Boston: Beacon Press, 1986) (Originally published, 1976).

Millett, Kate, *Sexual Politics* (Urbana: University of Illinois Press, 2000).

Milnor, Kristina, *Gender, Domesticity, and the Age of Augustus: Inventing Private Life* (Oxford: Oxford University Press, 2005).

Montesquieu, *Considerations on the Causes of the Greatness of the Romans and Their Decline* David Lowenthal trans. (Indianapolis: Hackett Publishing Company, Inc., 1965).

Monteverdi, *Il Ritorno D'Ulisse in Patria* libretto by Giacomo Badoaro, musical realization by Rene Jacobs in three c.d.s (Germany: Harmonia Mundi, 1992).

Moore, Gareth, *A Question of Truth: Christianity and Homosexuality* (London: Continuum, 2003).

Moore, Gareth, *The Body in Context: Sex and Catholicism* (London: Continuum, 1992).

Murphy, Cullen, *Are We Rome? The Fall of an Empire and the Fate of America* (Boston: Houghton Mifflin Company, 2007).

Murphy, Cullen, *The World According to Eve: Woman and the Bible in Ancient Times and Our Own* (Boston: Mariner Books, 1999).

Murray, L and P.J. Cooper ed. *Postpartum Depression and Child Development* edited by (New York: Guilford Press, 1997).

Murray, L. and C. Trevarthen, "Emotional Regulation of Interactions Between two-month-olds and Their Mothers," in *Social Perception in Infants*, edited by T.M. Fields and N.A. Fox (Norwood, N.J.: Ablex Publishing, 1985).

Murray, L. and C. Trevarthen, "The Infant's Role in Mother-Infant Communication," *Journal of Child Language* 13 (1986).

Mussolini, Benito, *My Autobiography with "The Political and Social Doctrine of Fascism"* translated by Jane Soames (Mineola, N.Y.: Dover Publications, 2006).

Nadler, Steven, *Spinoza: A Life* (Cambridge: Cambridge University Press, 1999).

Nadler, Steven, *Spinoza's Heresy: Immortality and the Jewish Mind* (Oxford; Oxford University Press, 2001).

Nehru, Jawaharlal, *The Discovery of India* (New Delhi: Penguin, 2004) (first published, 1946).

Nelis, Jan, "Constructing Fascist Identity: Benito Mussolini and the Myth of *Romanita*," *Classical World* 100.4 (2007): 391–415.

Nelson, William E. *The Fourteenth Amendment: From Political Principle to Judicial Doctrine* (Cambridge: Harvard University Press, 1988).

Neumann, Erich. *Amor and Psyche: The Psychic Development of the Feminine; A Commentary on the Tale by Apuleius* translated by Ralph Manheim (Princeton: Princeton University Press, 1956).

Nietzsche, Friedrich. *The Birth of Tragedy and the Genealogy of Morals. Francis Golfing trans.* (New York: Doubleday & Company, 1956).

Nussbaum, Martha C., *The Clash Within: Democracy, Religious Violence, and India's Future* (Cambridge, Mass.: Belknap Press of Harvard University Press, 2007).

Nussbaum, Martha C., *The Fragility of Goodness: Luck and Ethics in Greek Tragedy and Philosophy*, updated edition (Cambridge: Cambridge University Press, 2001, originally published 1986).

Nussbaum, Martha C., and Juha Sihvola, *The Sleep of Reason: Erotic Experience and Sexual Ethics in Ancient Greece and Rome* (Chicago: University of Chicago Press, 2002).

O'Brien, Tim. *The Things They Carried* (New York: Broadway Books, 1990).

O'Donnell, James J. *Augustine: A New Biography* (New York: HarperCollins, 2005).

Oestreich, James R. "Hallelujay Indeed: Debating Handel's Anti-Semitism," *The New York Times*, Monday April 23, 2007.

Ogilvie, R.M. *A Commentary on Livy Books 1-5* (Oxford: Oxford at the Clarendon Press, 1965).

Olston, Lynne. *Freedom's Daughters: The Unsung Heroines of the Civil Rights Movement from 1830 to 1970* (New York: Scribner, 2001).

Osgood, Josiah, *Caesar's Legacy: Civil War and the Emergence of the Roman Empire* (Cambridge: Cambridge University Press, 2006).

Pagels, Elaine, *Adam, Eve, and the Serpent* (New York: Random House, 1988).

Painter, Jr., Borden W., *Mussolini's Rome: Rebuilding the Eternal City* (New York; Palgrave Macmillan, 2005).

Pakkanen, Petra. *Interpreting Early Hellenistic Religion* (Athen, Greece: E. Souvatzidakis, 1996).

Palmer, R.E.A. *The Archaic Community of the Romans* (Cambridge: Cambridge University Press, 1970).

Pater, Walter Horatio, *Greek Studies: a Series of Essays* (McKeab, Va.: IndyPublish.com, n.d., originally published 1894).

Pater, Walter. *Marius the Epicurean* (London: Macmillan and Co., 1914).

Paterculus, Velleius. *Res Gestae Divi Augusti*, (Cambridge, Mass.; Harvard University Press, 2002).

Payne, Stanley G., *A History of Fascism 1914–1945* (Madison: University of Wisconsin Press, 1995).

Paxton, Robert O., *The Anatomy of Fascism* (New York: Vintage Books, 2004).

Peristiany, J.G. ed., *Honour and Shame: The Values of Mediterranean Society* (Chicago: University of Chicago Press).

Pflugfelder, Gregory M., *Cartographies of Desire: Male-Male Sexuality in Japanese Discourse 1600–1950* (Berkeley: University of California Press, 1999).

Pipes, Daniel. *Militant Islam Reaches America* (New York: W. W. Norton, 2002).

Plante, Thomas G. *Sin Against the Innocents: Sexual Abuse by Priests and the Role of the Catholic Church* (Westport, Conn.: Praeger, 2004).

Pliny the Elder, *Natural History: A Selection*, John F. Healy trans. (London: Penguin, 2004).

Plotinus, *The Enneads* translated by Stephen MacKenna (London: Penguin, 1991).

Plutarch. *De Iside Et Osiride* edited with translation by J. Gwyn Griffiths, University of Wales Press, 1970.

Plutarch. *The Lives of Noble Grecians and Romans* John Dryden trans. (New York: Modern Library, n.d.).

Poliakov, Leon. *The Aryan Myth : A History of Racist and Nationalist Ideas in Europe* translated by Edmund Howard (London: Sussex Univesity Press, 1971).

Poliakov, Leon, *The History of Anti-Semitism* vol. 1 Richard Howard trans. (New York: Vanguard Press, 1965); vol. 2 Natalie Gerardi trans. (New York: Vanguard Press, 1973); vol. 3 Miriam Kochan trans. (New York: Vanguard Press, 1975); vol. 4 George Klin trans. (Oxford: Oxford University Press, 1985).

Polybius. *The Rise of the Roman Empire* Ian Scott-Kilvert trans. (London: Penguin, 1979).

Pomeroy, Sarah B. *Goddesses, Whores, Wives, and Slaves: Women in Classical Antiquity* (New York: Schocken Books, 1995).

Pomeroy, Sarah B. *Women in Hellenistic Egypt: From Alexander to Cleopatra* (Detroit: Wayne State University Press, 1990).

Porphyry. *The Life of Plotinus*, translated by Stephen McKenna (Edmonds, Wa.: Holmes Publishing Group, 2001).

Powell, Anton ed., *Roman Poetry and Propaganda in the Age of Augustus* (London: Bristol Classical Press, 1997).

Quinn, Susan, *A Mind of Her Own: The Life of Karen Horney* (New York: Summit Books, 1987).

Raditsa, Leo Ferrero, "Augustus' Legislation Concerning Marriage, Procreation, Love Affairs, and Adultery," *Aufstieg und Niedergang Der Romischen Welt* (Berlin: Walter De Gruyter, 1980).

Rajan, Rajeswari Sunder, *Signposts: Gender Issues in Post-Independence India* (New Brunswick, N.J.: Rutgers University Press, 2001).

Ranke-Heinemann, Uta. *Eunuchs for Heaven: The Catholic Church and Sexuality* translated by John Brownjohn (London, U.K.: Andre Deutsch, 1988).

Rasmussen, Larry. *Dietrich Bonhoeffer – His Significance for North Americans* (Fortress Press: Minnespolis, 1990).

Rather, L.J. *Reading Wagner: A Study in the History of Ideas* (Baton Rouge: Louisiana State University Press, 1990).

Rawls, John, *Collected Papers*, Samuel Freeman, ed. (Cambridge, Mass.; Harvard University Press, 1999).

Rawls, John, *A Theory of Justice* (Cambridge, Mass.: Harvard Univeersity Press, 1971).

Rawson, Beryl ed., *Marriage, Divorce, and Children in Ancient Rome* (Oxford: Clarendon Press, 2004).

Reardon, B.P. ed., *Collected Ancient Greek Novels* (Berkeley: University of California Press, 1989).

Regan, Richard S.J. *Conflict and Consensus: Religious Freedom and the Second Vatican Council* (New York: The Macmillan Company, 1967).

Renik, Owen, *Practical Psychoanalysis for Therapists and Parents* (New York: Other Press, 2006).

Richard, Carl J. *The Founders and the Classics: Greece, Rome, and the American Enlightenment* (Cambridge, Mass.: Harvard University Press, 1994).

Richards, David A.J. *Conscience and the Constitution: History, Theory, and Law of the Reconstruction Amendments* (Princeton: Princeton University Press, 1993).

Richards, David A.J. *A Theory of Reasons for Action* (Oxford: Clarendon Press, 1971).

Richards, David A.J., *Disarming Manhood: Roots of Ethical Resistance* (Athens, Ohio: Swallow Press, 2005).

Richards, David A.J. *Foundations of American Constitutionalism* (New York: Oxford University Press, 1989).

Richards, David A.J. *Free Speech and the Politics of Identity* (Oxford: Oxford University Press, 1999).

Richards, David A.J., *Identity and the Case for Gay Rights: Race, Gender, Religion as Analogies* (Chicago: University of Chicago Press, 1999).

Richards, David A.J., *Tragic Manhood and Democracy: Verdi's Voice and the Powers of Musical Art* (Brighton, U.K.: Sussex Academic Press, 2004).

Richards, David A.J. *Toleration and the Constitution* (New York: Oxford University Press, 1986).

Richards, David A.J., *Women, Gays, and the Constitution: The Grounds for Feminism and Gay Rights in Culture and Law* (Chicago: University of Chicago Press, 1998).

Richlin, Amy, "Foucault's *History of Sexuality*: A Useful Theory for Women?", in David H.J. Larmour, Paul Allen Miller, and Charles Platter, eds., *Rethinking Sexuality: Foucault and Classical Antiquity* (Princeton, N.J.: Princeton University Press, 1998, pp. 138–70.

Richlin, Amy, *The Garden of Priapus: Sexuality and Aggression in Roman Humor*, revised edition (New York: Oxford University Press, 1992).

Richlin, Amy, "Zeus and Metis: Foucault, Feminism, Classics," Helios, 18/1992, 160–80.

Robb, Christina. *This Changes Everything: The Relational Revolution in Psychology* (New York: Farrar, Straus and Giroux, 2006).

Robb, Graham, *Strangers: Homosexual Love in the Nineteenth Century* (New York: W.W. Norton, 2003).

Robnett, Belinda. *How Long? How Long?: African-American Women in the Struggle for Civil Rights* (New York: Oxford University Press, 1997).

Roller, Matthew B. *Constructing Autocracy: Aristocrats and Emperiors in Juliu-Claudian Rome* (Princeton: Princeton University Press, 2001).

Rossi, A., *The Rise of Italian Fascism 1918–1922* translated by Peter and Dorothy Wait (New York: Gordon Press, 1976).

Roy, Arundhati, *The God of Small Things* (New York: HarperPerennial, 1998).

Roy, Arundhati. *War Talk* (South End Press: Cambridge, Massachusetts, 2003).

Ruddick, Sara. *Maternal Thinking: Toward a Politics of Peace* (Boston: Beacon Press, 1989).

Ruether, Rosemary Radford. *Sexism and God-Talk: Toward a Feminist Theology* (Boston: Beacon Press, 1993).

Saller, Richard P., *Patriarchy, Property and Death in the Roman Family* (Cambridge: Cambridge University Press, 1994).

Sallust, *The Conspiracy of Catiline*, in *The Jugurthine War/The Conspiracy of Catiline* S.A. Handford trans. (London: Penguin, 1963).

Sanders, E.P. *Jesus and Judaism* (Philadelphia: Fortress Press, 1985).

Sanders, E.P. *The Historical Figure of Jesus* (London: Allen Lane, 1993).

Sandmel, Samuel. *The Genius of Paul: A Study in History* (Philadelphia: Fortress Press, 1979).

Sandy, Gerald, *The Greek World of Apuleius: Apuleius and the Second Sophistic* (Leiden: Brill, 1997).

Sarkar, Tanika, *Hindu Wife, Hindu Nation: Community, Religion, and Cultural Nationalism* (Bloomington: Indiana University Press, 2001).

Schafer, Peter, *Judeophobia: Attitudes toward the Jews in the Ancient World* (Cambridge, Mass: Harvard University Press, 1997).

Schiavone, Aldo. *The End of the Past: Ancient Rome and the Modern West* Margery J. Schneider trans. (Cambridge, Mass.: Harvard University Press, 2000).

Schloss, Carol Loeb. *Lucia Joyce: To Dance in the Wake* (New York: Farrar, Straua, and Giroux, 2005).

Schneidau, Herbert N. *Sacred Discontent: The Bible and Western Tradition* (Baton Rouge: Louisiana State University Press, 1976).

Schorske, Carl E. *Fin-de-Siecle Vienna: Politics and Culture* (New York: Vintage Books, 1981).

Segal, Alan F. *Paul the Convert: The Apostolate and Apostasy of Saul the Pharisee* (New Haven: Yale University Press, 1990).

Sellers, M.N.S. *American Republicanism: Roman Ideology in the United States Constitution* (New York: New York University Press, 1994).

Sen, Amartya, *The Argumentative Indian: Writings on Indian History, Culture and Identity* (New York: Picador, Farrar, Staus and Giroux, 2005).

Seneca, Lucius Annaeus. *On Benefits*, (Objective Systems Pty Ltd., 2006).

Seneca, *On the Shortness of Life*, C.D.N. Costa trans. (London: Penguin, 1997).

Severy, Beth. *Augustus and the Family at the Birth of the Roman Empire* (London: Routledge, 2003).

Shakespeare, William. *As You Like It* edited by Agnes Latham, The Arden Shakespeare (Walton-on-Thames Surrey: Thomas Nelson & Sons, 1997).

Shakespeare, William. *Macbeth*, Folger Shakespeare Library (New York: Washington Square Press, 1992).

Shakespeare, William. *Pericles* edited by E.D. Hoeniger The Arden Shakespeare (London: Routledge, 1990).

Shakespeare, William,*The Riverside Shakespeare Second Edition* G. Blakemore Evans at al., eds. (Boston: Houghton Mifflin Company, 1997).

Shakespeare, William. *Twelfth Night* in G. Blakemore Evans and J.J.M. Tobin, eds., *The Riverside Shakespeare Second Edition* (Boston: Houghton Mifflin Company, 1997).

Shumate, Nancy, *Crisis and Conversion in Apuleius' Metamorphoses* (Ann Arbor: The University of Michigan Press, 1996).

Sipe, A.W. Richard. *Celibacy in Crisis: A Secret World Revisited* (New York: Brunner-Routledge, 2003).

Skinner, Marilyn B. "The Last Encounter of Dido and Aeneas," 29 *Vergilius* 12–18 (1983).

Skoie, Mathilde, *Reading Sulpicia: Commentaries 1475–1990* (Oxford: Oxford University Press, 2002).

Skoie, Mathilde, "Sublime Poetry or Feminine Fiddling? Gender and Reception: Sulpicia Through the Eyes of Two 19th Century Scholars,' Nordic Symposium on Women's Lives in Antiquity, *Aspects of women in antiquity: proceedings of the first Nordic Symposium on Women's Lives in Antiquity, Goteborg 12–15 June 1997* (Jonsered: P. Astroms Forlag, 1998), pp. 169–80.

Slavitt, David R., editor and translator, *Aeschylus, 1: The Oresteia* (Philadelphia: University of Pennsylvania Press, 1998).

Smith, Denis Mack, *Mussolini: a Biography* (New York: Vintage, 1983).

Smith, Jeffery A. *Printers and Press Freedom: The Ideology of Early American Journalism* (New York: Oxford University Press, 1988).

Snitow, Ann, Christine Stansell, and Sharon Thompson, eds., *Powers of Desire* (New York: Monthly Review Press, 1983).

Solmsen, Friedrich. *Isis among the Greeks and Romans* (Cambridge, Mass.: Harvard University Press, 1979).

Sophocles, *Oedipus Tyrannus* translated and edited by Luci Berkowitz and Theodore F. Brunner (New York: W.W. Norton, 1970).

Southern, Pat, *Augustus* (London: Routledge, 2001).

Spackman, Barbara, *Fascist Virilities: Rhetoric, Ideology, and Social Fantasy in Italy* (Minneapolis: University of Minnesota Press, 1996).

Spinoza, Benedict de, *A Theological-Political Treatise and A Political Treatise* translated by R.H.M. Elwes (Mineola, N.Y.: Dover Publication, 2004).

Spinoza Benedict de, *Ethics* Edwin Curley translation (London: Penguin, 1996).

Spinoza, *Theological-Political Treatise* Second Edition translated by Samuel Shirley (Indianapolis: Hackett Publishing Company, 2001).

Stambaugh, John B. *Sarapis Under the Early Ptolemies* (Leiden: E.J. Brill, 10972).

Stark, Rodney. *The Rise of Christianity: A Sociologist Reconsiders History* (Princeton: Princeton University Press, 1996).

Steinfels, Peter, *A People Adrift: The Crisis of the Roman Catholic Church in America* (New York: Simon & Schuster, 2003).

Stephens, Susan A., and John J. Winkler, *Ancient Greek Novels The Fragments* (Princeton, N.J.: Princeton University Press, 1995).

Stern, Daniel N. *The Interpersonal World of the Infant* (New York: Basic Books, 1998).

Sternhell, Zeev with Mario Sjnajder and Maia Asheri, *The Birth of Fascist Ideology* translated by David Maisel (Princeton: Princeton University Press, 1994).

Stocking, George W. Jr., *A Franz Boas Reader: The Shaping of American Anthropology, 1833–1911* (Chicago: University of Chicago Press, 1974).

Stoppard, Tom, *Rock 'n' Roll* (New York: Grove Press, 2006).

Strachey, James, ed. and translator, *Standard Edition of the Complete Psychological Works of Sigmund Freud*, Vol. 2 (1893–1895) (London: Hogarth Press, 1955), Vol. 3 (1893–1899): 1962; Vol. 4 (1900): 1953; Vol. 5 (1900–1901): 1953; Vol. 6 (1901): 1960; Vol. 7 (1901–1905): 1953; Vol. 9 (1906–1908): 1959; Vol. 11 (1910): 1957; Vol. 12 (1911–1913): 1958; Vol. 13 (1913–1914): 1953; Vol. 18 (1920–1922): 1955; Vol. 14 (1914–1916): 1957; Vol. 19 (1923–1925): 1961; Vol. 20 (1925–1926): 1959; Vol. 21 (1927–1931): 1961; Vol. 22 (1932–1936): 1964; Vol. 23 (1937–1939): 1964.

Stuart, Elizabeth, *Gay and Lesbian Theologies: Repetitions with Critical Difference* (Hampshire, England: Ashgate, 2003).

Stump, Eleanor and Michael J. Murray, eds., *Philosophy of Religion: The Big Questions* (Oxford: Blackwell Publishers, 1999).

Styron, William, *Darkness Visible: A Memoir of Madness* (New York: Vintage, 1992).

Suetonius, *The Twelve Caesars*, translated by Robert Graves (London: Penguin, 1979).

*Suetonius, Volume II*, translated by J.C. Rolfe (Cambridge, Mass.: Harvard University Press, 2001).

Suttie, Ian D., *The Origins of Love and Hate* (London: Free Association Books, 1999) (first published 1935).

Syme, Ronald, *The Roman Revolution* (Oxford: Oxford University Press, 1985).

Tacitus, *A Dialogue on Oratory*, in Tacitus, *Agricola, Germania, Dialogus* translated by W. Peterson (Cambridge, Mass.: Harvard University Press, 1970).

Tacitus, *The Annals of Ancient Rome* Michael Grant trans. (London: Penguin, 1996).

Tasso, Torquato. *Jerusalem Delivered* Anthony M. Esolen, trans. (Baltimore: The Johns Hopkins University Press, 2000).

Taubes, Jacob. *The Political Theology of Paul* translated by Dana Hollander (Stanford: Stanford University Press, 2004).

Taylor, Jill McLean, Carol Gilligan, and Amy M. Sullivan, *Between Voice and Silence: Women and Girls, Race and Relationship* (Cambridge, Mass.: Harvard University Press, 1995).

TeSelle, Eugene. *Augustine the Theologian* (Eugene, Oreon: Wipf and Stock, 2002).

*The Bible* authorized King James Version (Oxford: Oxford University Press, 1998).

*The Bible: Authorized King James Version* Robert Carroll and Stephen Prickett, eds. (Oxford: Oxford University Press, 1998).

*The Dangerous Lives of Printers: The Evolution of Freedom of the Press*, at http://www.assumption.edu/ahc/1770s/ppressfree.html.

*The New Oxford Annotated Bible* (New York: Oxford University Press, 1991).

Theweleit, Klaus, *Male Fantasies*, 2 volumes (Minneapolis: University of Minnesota Press, 1987).

Tobin, J.J.M. *Shakespeare's Favorite Novel: A Study of the Golden Ass as Prime Source* (Lanham, Maryland: University of America, 1984).

Treggiari, Susan, *Roman Marriage: Iusti Coniuges From the Time of Cicero to the Time of Ulpian* (Oxford: Oxford University Press, 2002).

Trofimov, Yaroslav, "Brutal Attack in India Shows How Caste System Lives On," *The Wall Street Journal*, Thursday, December 27, 2007, Vol. CCL No. 150, at pp. A1 and A9.

Tronick, Z. and A. Gianino, "Interactive Mismatch and Repair Challenges in the Coping Infant," *Zero to Three*. 6:1–6. (1999).

Tronick, Edward Z. "Emotions and Emotional Communication in Infants," *American Psychologist* 44(2) 1989.

Turcan, Robert. *The Cults of the Roman Empire* (Malden, Mass.: Blackwell Publishing, 2005).

Tushnet, Mark V., "Sex, Drugs and Rock 'n' Roll: Some Conservative Reflections on Liberal Jurisprudence," *Columbia Law Review*, vol. 82, no. 7 (Nov. 1982), 1531–43.

Tyler May, Elaine, *Barren in the Promised Land: Childless Americans and the Pursuit of Happiness* (New York: Basic Books, 1995).

Valmiki, *The Ramayana* translated by Arshia Sattar (New Delhi: Penguin, 1996).

Vance, Carol S., ed., *Pleasure and Danger: Exploring Female Sexuality* (Boston: Routledge & Kegan Paul, 1984).

Van Der Kolk, Bessel A., Alexander C. McFarlane, and Lars Weisaeth, eds., *Traumatic Stress: The Effects of Overwhelming Experience on Mind, Body, and Society* (New York: The Guilford Press, 1996).

Vasey, Michael, *Strangers and Friends: A New Exploration of Homosexuality and the Bible* (London: Hodder & Stoughton, 1995).

Vermes, Geza. *Jesus and the World of Judaism* (London: SCM Press, 1983).

Vermes, Geza. *Jesus the Jew: A Historian's Reading of the Gospels* (Philadelphia: Fortress Press, 1981) (originally published, 1973).

Vermes, Geza. *The Changing Faces of Jesus* (New York: Viking Compass, 2001).

Vermes, Geza. *The Religion of Jesus the Jew* (Minneapolis: Fortress Press, 1993).

Veyne, Paul. *Roman Erotic Elegy: Love, Poetry, and the West* David Pellauer translation (Chicago: University of Chicago Press, 1988).

Vergil. *Aeneid 7–12 Appendix Vergiliana*, translated by H.R. Fairclough, revised by G.P. Goold (Cambridge, Mass.: Harvard University Press, 2002).

Vergil, *Eclogues, Georgics, Aeneid*, translated by H. R. Fairclough (Cambridge, Mass.: Harvard University Press, 2006).

Vergil, *First Eclogue*, Peter White, *Promised Verse*, at pp. 159–61, 171–3.

Vergil, *The Aeneid*, translated by Robert Fitzgerald (New York: Vintage Classics, 1990).

Vergil. *The Eclogues of Vergil* David Ferry trans. (New York: Farrar, Straus, and Giroux, 1999).

Vergil. *The Georgics of Vergil* David Ferry trans. (New York: Farrar, Straus, and Giroux, 2005).

Visser, Romke, "Fascist Doctrine and the Cult of the Romanita," *Journal of Contemporary History* 27 (1992), 5–22.

Volkmann, Hans. *Cleopatra: A Study in Politics and Propaganda* T.J. Cadoux trans. (London: Elek Books, Ltd., 1958).

von Franz, Mary-Louise. *Apuleius' Golden Ass* (New York; Analytical Psychology Club, 1970).

Walbank, F.W., A.E. Astin, M.W. Frederiksen, R.M. Ogilvie, *The Cambridge Ancient History Second Edition, volume VII, The Rise of Rome to 220 B.C.E.* (Cambridge: Cambridge University Press, 1989).

Waldron, Jeremy. *God, Locke, and Equality: Christian Foundations in Locke's Political Thought* (Cambiidge: Cambridge University Press, 2002).

Wallace-Hadrill, Andrew, *Houses and Society in Pompeii and Herculaneum* (Princeton, N.J.: Princeton University Press, 1994).

Washington, James Melvin, ed., *A Testament of Hope: The Essential Writings of Martin Luther King, Jr.* (San Francisco: Harper and Row, 1986).

Washington, Joseph R. Jr., *Black Religion: The Negro and Christianity in the United States* (Boston: Beacon Press, 1964).

Wells-Barnett, Ida, *Selected Works of Idea Wells-Barnett*, Trudier Harris, ed. (New York: Oxford University Press, 1991).

West, Rebecca, *St. Augustine* (Edinburgh: Peter Davies Limited, 1933).

Wharton, Edith. *Summer* (New York: Penguin, 1993) (originally published, 1917).

Wharton, Edith. *The Age of Innocence* (New York: Oxford University Press, 2006) (originally published 1920).

Wheatcroft, Geoffrey. *The Controversy of Zion: Jewish Nationalism, the Jewish State, and the Unresolved Jewish Dilemma* (Reading, Mass.: Addison-Wesley Publishing Company, 1996).

White, Peter. *Promised Verse: Poets in the Society of Augustan Rome* (Cambridge, Mass.: Harvard University Press, 1993).

Whitmarsh, Tim, *Greek Literature and the Roman Empire: The Politics of Imitation* (Oxford: Oxford University Press, 2001).

Wildavsky, Aaron, *The Nursing Father: Moses as a Political Leader* (University: University of Alabama Press, 1984).

Wills, Garry. *Saint Augustine* (New York: A Lipper/Viking Book, 1999).

Wills, Garry, *Papal Sin: Structures of Deceit* (New York: Doubleday, 2000).

Wills, Gary, *Why I Am a Catholic* (Boston: Houghton Mifflin Company, 2002).

Winkler, John J., *Auctor & Actor: A Narratological Reading of Apuleius's The Golden Ass* (Berkeley: University of California Press, 1985).

Wistrich, Robert W., *Anti-Semitism: The Longest Hatred* (London: Thames Methuen, 1991).

Witherington III, Ben. *Women and the Genesis of Christianity* (Cambridge: Cambridge University Press, 1990).

Witt, R.E. *Isis in the Ancient World* (Baltimore: The Johns Hopkins University Press, 1971).

Wood, Susan E. *Imperial Women: A Study in Public Images 40 B.C.E.–AD 69* (Leiden: Brill, n.d.).

Woodhouse, John, *Gabriele D'Annunzio: Defiant Archangel* (New York: Oxford University Press, 1998).

Woodward, C. Van. *The Future of the Past* (New York: Oxford University Press, 1989).

Woodward, Vann. *Reunion and Reaction: The Compromise of 1877 and the End of Reconstruction* (New York: Oxford University Press, 1966).

Woolf, Virginia. *Mrs. Dalloway* (San Diego: Harvest, 1997) (first published, 1925).

Woolf, Virginia. *To the Lighthouse* (San Diego: Harvest, 1981) (originally published, 1927).

Woolf, Virginia. *Three Guineas* Jane Marcus edition (Orlando: Harvest, 2006) (originally published, 1938).

Woolf, Virginia. *Women and Writing* edited by Michele Barrett (Orlando, Florida: Harvest Book, 1980).

Woolhouse, Roger, *Locke: A Biography* (Cambridge: Cambridge University Press, 2007).

Wright, Lawrence. *The Looming Tower: Al-Quaeda and the Road to 9/11* (New York: Alfred A. Knopf, 2006).

Wyatt-Brown, Bertram, *Honor and Violence in the Old South* (New York: Oxford University Press, 1986).

Wyatt-Brown, Bertram. *Southern Honor: Ethics and Behavior in the Old South* (New York: Oxford University Press, 1982).

Wyke, Maria. *The Roman Mistress* (Oxford: Oxford University Press, 2002).

Yellin, Jean Fagan, *Women and Sisters: The Antislavery Feminists in American Culture* (New Haven: Yale University Press, 1989).

Yoshino, Kenji, *Covering: The Hidden Assault on Our Civil Rights* (New York: Random House, 2006).

Young, Andrew. *An Easy Burden: The Civil Rights Movement and the Transformation of America* (New York: HarperCollins, 1996).

Young-Bruehl, Elisabeth. *Hannah Arendt: For Love of the World* (New Haven: Yale University Press, 1982).

Young-Bruehl, Elisabeth. *The Anatomy of Prejudices* (Cambridge, Mass.: Harvard University Press, 1996).

Young-Bruehl, Elisabeth, "The 'Taboo on Tenderness' in the History of Psychoanalysis," in Martin S. Bergmann, ed., *Understanding Dissidence and Controversy in the History of Psychoanalysis* (New York: Other Press, 2004), at pp. 229–47.

Young- Bruehl, Elisabeth, *Where Do We Fall When We Fall in Love?* (New York: Other Press, 2003).

Young-Bruehl, Elisabeth., *Why Arendt Matters* (New Haven; Yale University Press, 2006).

Yourcenar, Marguerite. *Memoirs of Hadrian* (New York: Farrar, Straus and Giroux, 1990, originally published, 1954).

Zagorin, Perez. *How the Idea of Religious Toleration Came to the West* (Princeton: Princeton University Press, 2003).

Zanker, Paul, *The Power of Images in the Age of Augustus*, translated by Alan Shapiro (Ann Arbor: The University of Michigan Press, 1990).

Zeitlin, Froma I., *Playing the Other: Gender and Society in Classical Greek Literature* (Chicago: University of Chicago Press, 1996).

**Cases**

*Bowers v. Hardwick,* 478 U.S. 186 (1986).
*Brown v. Board of Education,* 347 U.S. 483 (1954).
*Dred Scott v. Sanford,* 19 Howard 393 (1857).
*Dudgeon v. United Kingdom,* 45 Eur. Ct. H.R. (1981) P 52.
*Goodridge v. Department of Public Health,* 440 Mass. 309 (2003).
*Lawrence v. Texas,* 539 U.S. 558 (2003).
*Loving v. Virginia,* 386 U.S. 1 (1967).
*Plessy v. Ferguson,* 163 U.S. 537 (1896).

# *Index*